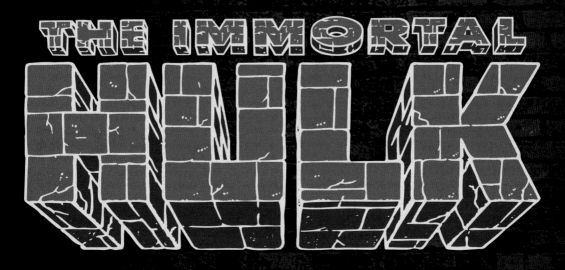

THE IMMORTAL HULK

OF HELL AND OF DEATH

AL EWING
WRITER

JOE BENNETT
PENCILER

RUY JOSÉ & BELARDINO BRABO
INKERS

PAUL MOUNTS
COLOR ARTIST

VC's CORY PETIT
LETTERERS

ALEX ROSS
COVER ART

WIL MOSS & SARAH BRUNSTAD
EDITORS

TOM BREVOORT
EXECUTIVE EDITORS

COLLECTION EDITOR: JENNIFER GRÜNWALD
ASSISTANT EDITOR: DANIEL KIRCHHOFFER
ASSISTANT MANAGING EDITOR: MAIA LOY
ASSISTANT MANAGING EDITOR: LISA MONTALBANO

VP PRODUCTION & SPECIAL PROJECTS: JEFF YOUNGQUIST
BOOK DESIGNER: ADAM DEL RE
SVP PRINT, SALES & MARKETING: DAVID GABRIEL
EDITOR IN CHIEF: C.B. CEBULSKI

HULK
CREATED BY
STAN LEE & JACK KIRBY

IMMORTAL HULK VOL. 10: OF HELL AND OF DEATH. Contains material originally published in magazine form as IMMORTAL HULK (2018) #46-50. First printing 2021. ISBN 978-1-302-92598-7. Published by MARVEL WORLDWIDE, INC., a subsidiary of MARVEL ENTERTAINMENT, LLC. OFFICE OF PUBLICATION: 1290 Avenue of the Americas, New York, NY 10104. © 2021 MARVEL No similarity between any of the names, characters, persons, and/or institutions in this magazine with those of any living or dead person or institution is intended, and any such similarity which may exist is purely coincidental. **Printed in the U.S.A.** KEVIN FEIGE, Chief Creative Officer; DAN BUCKLEY, President, Marvel Entertainment; JOE QUESADA, EVP & Creative Director; DAVID BOGART, Associate Publisher & SVP of Talent Affairs; TOM BREVOORT, VP, Executive Editor; NICK LOWE, Executive Editor, VP of Content, Digital Publishing; DAVID GABRIEL, VP of Print & Digital Publishing; JEFF YOUNGQUIST, VP of Production & Special Projects; ALEX MORALES, Director of Publishing Operations; DAN EDINGTON, Managing Editor; RICKEY PURDIN, Director of Talent Relations; JENNIFER GRÜNWALD, Senior Editor, Special Projects; SUSAN CRESPI, Production Manager; STAN LEE, Chairman Emeritus. For information regarding advertising in Marvel Comics or on Marvel.com, please contact Vit DeBellis, Custom Solutions & Integrated Advertising Manager, at vdebellis@marvel.com. For Marvel subscription inquiries, please call 888-511-5480. **Manufactured between 9/17/2021 and 10/19/2021 by FRY COMMUNICATIONS, MECHANICSBURG, PA, USA.**

10 9 8 7 6 5 4 3 2 1

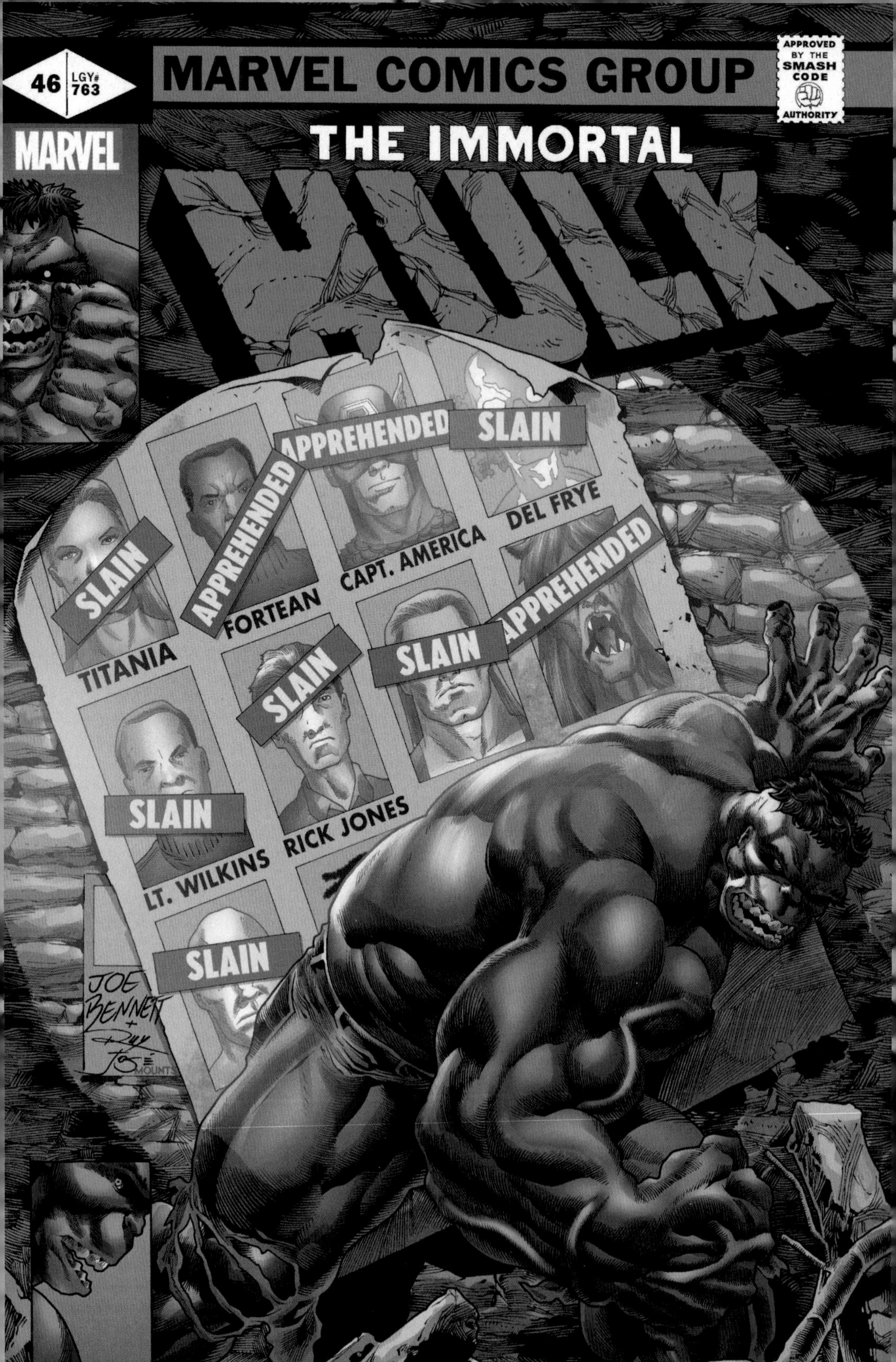
46 LGY# 763
MARVEL COMICS GROUP
APPROVED BY THE SMASH CODE AUTHORITY
MARVEL
THE IMMORTAL
HULK
APPREHENDED
SLAIN
DEL FRYE
CAPT. AMERICA
APPREHENDED
APPREHENDED
FORTEAN
SLAIN
TITANIA
SLAIN
SLAIN
APPREHENDED
SLAIN
LT. WILKINS
RICK JONES
SLAIN
JOE BENNETT + RUY JOSÉ

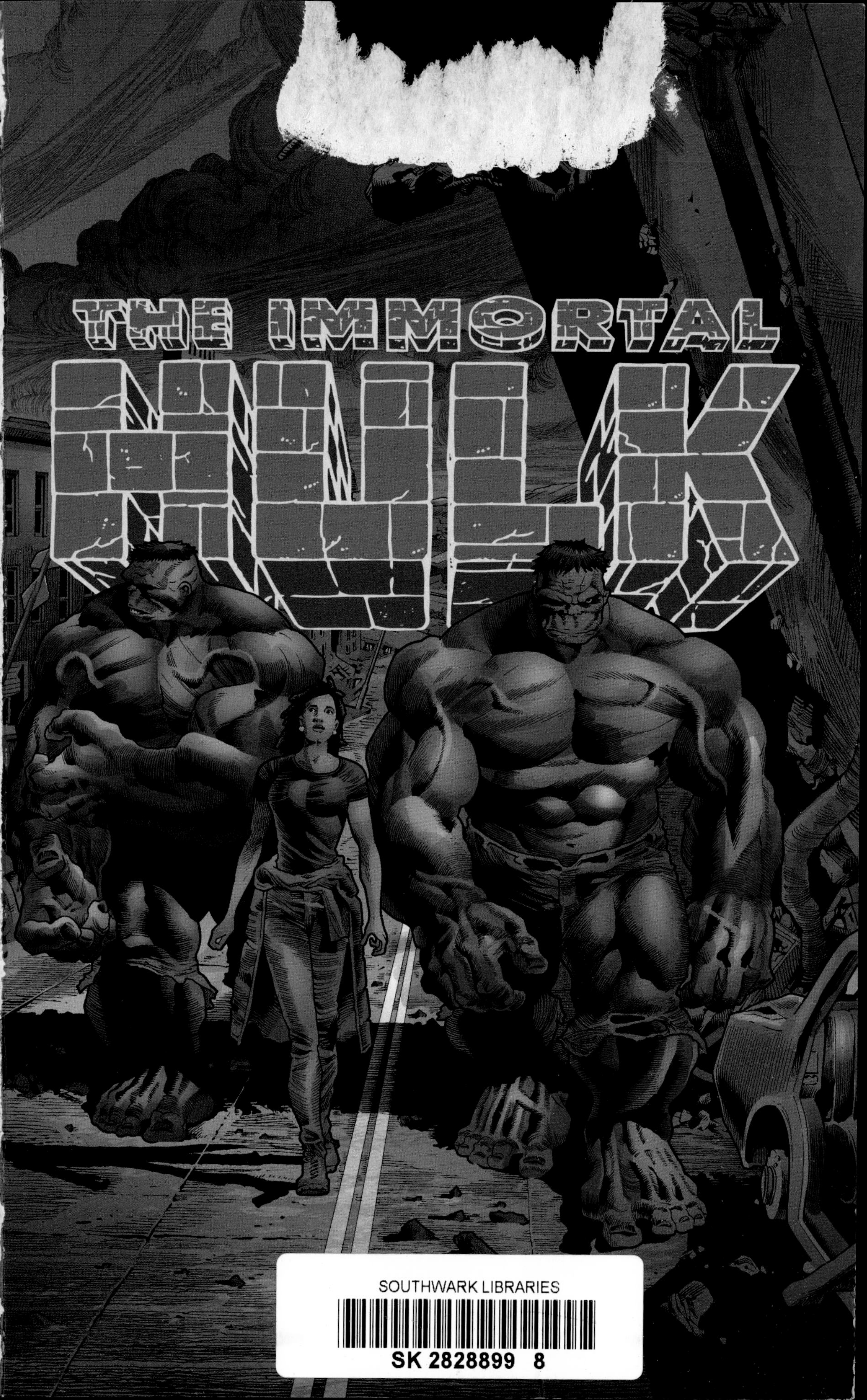
THE IMMORTAL
HULK

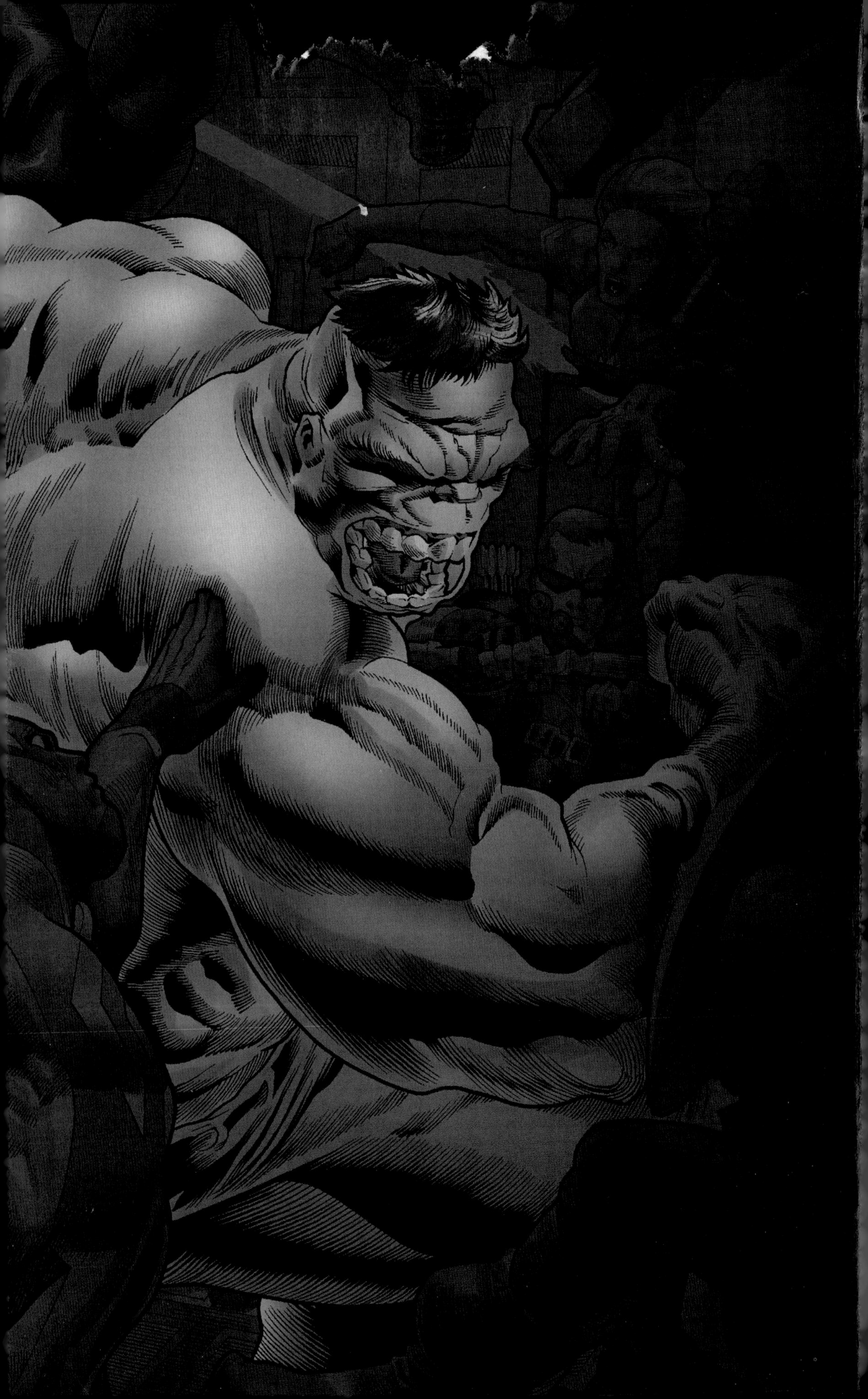

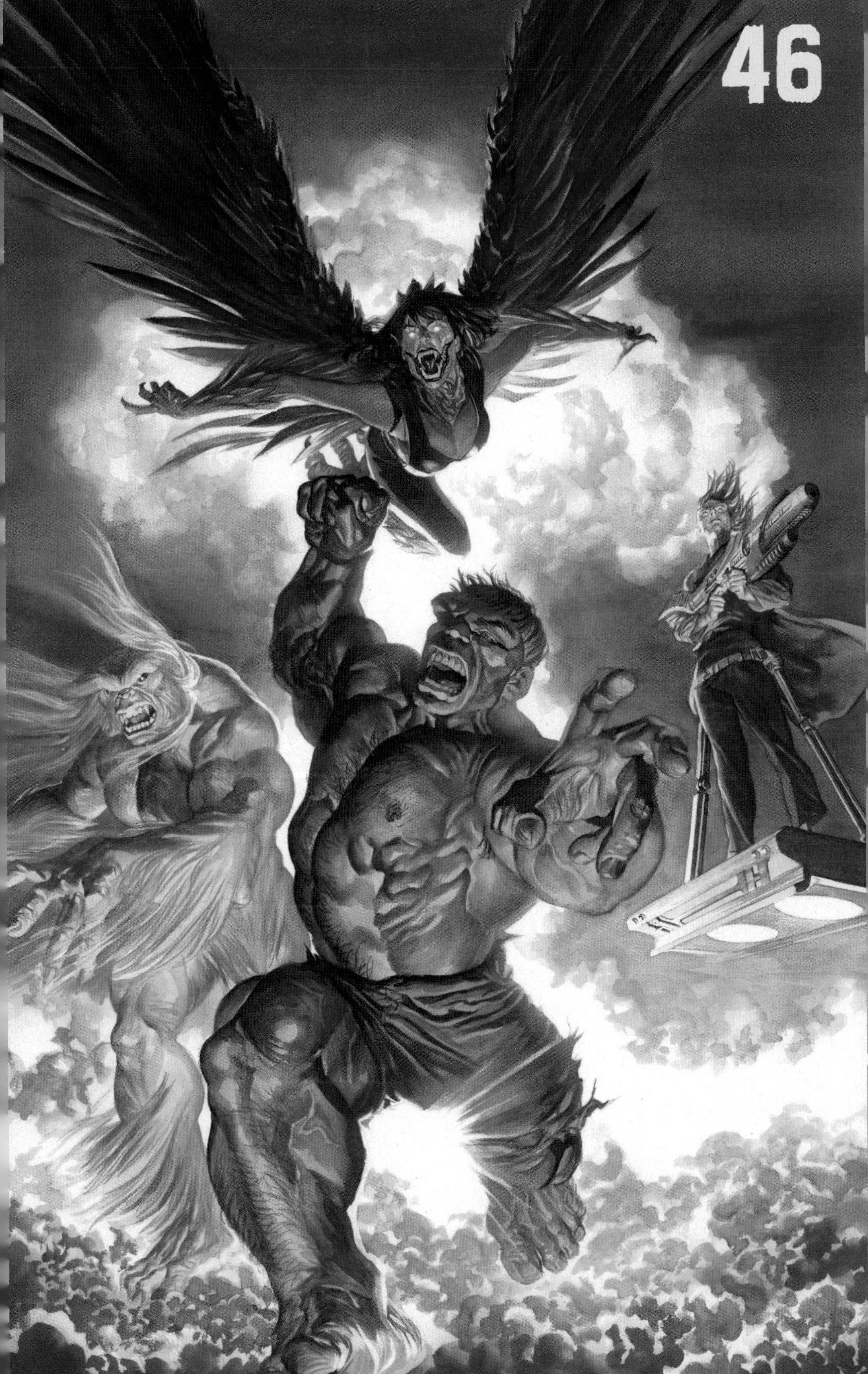
46

"REVENGE IS FROM THE INDIVIDUAL, PUNISHMENT IS FROM GOD."

– VICTOR HUGO,
THE LAST DAY OF A CONDEMNED MAN

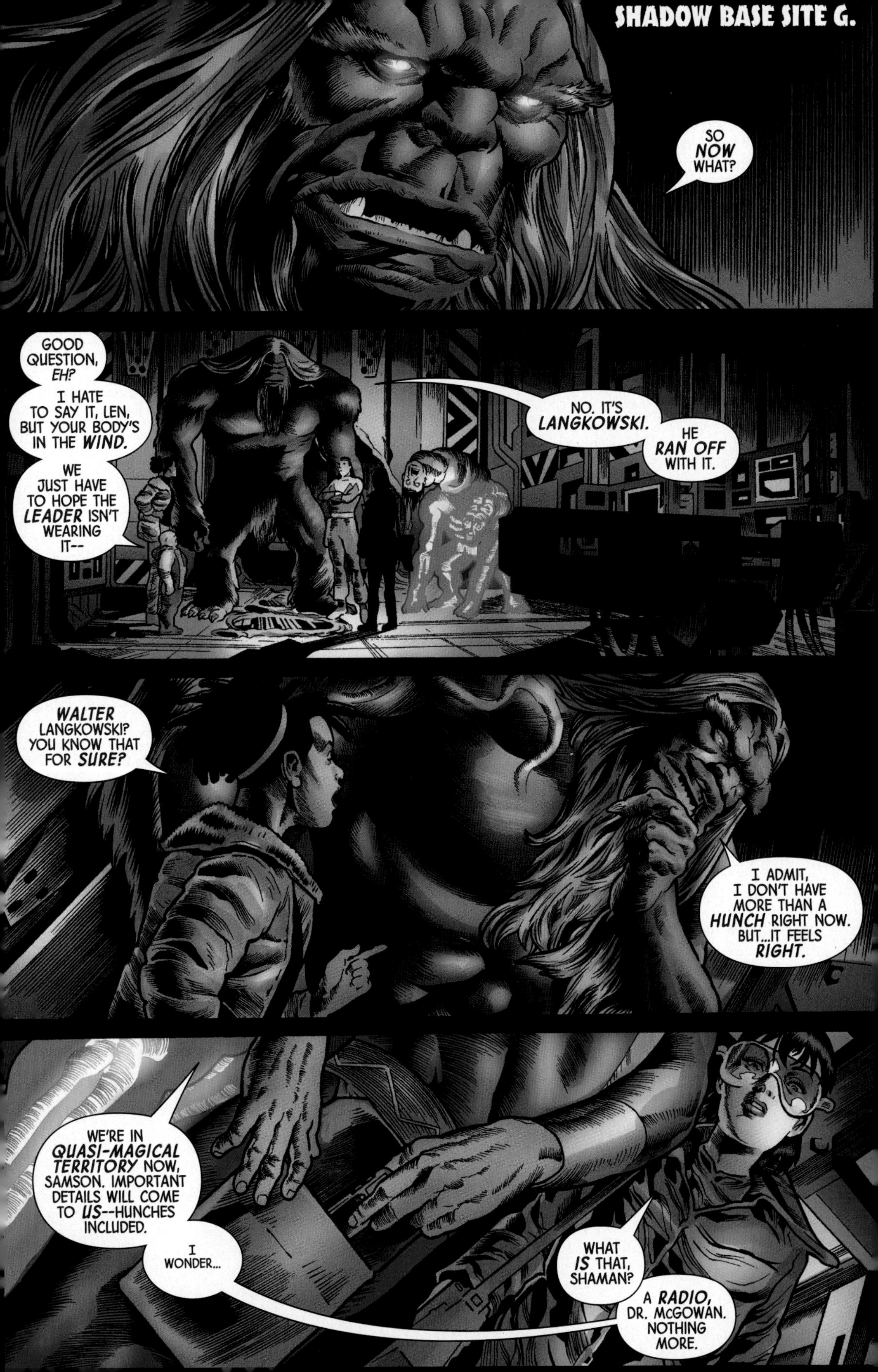
SHADOW BASE SITE G.
SO NOW WHAT?
GOOD QUESTION, EH?
I HATE TO SAY IT, LEN, BUT YOUR BODY'S IN THE WIND.
WE JUST HAVE TO HOPE THE LEADER ISN'T WEARING IT--
NO. IT'S LANGKOWSKI.
HE RAN OFF WITH IT.
WALTER LANGKOWSKI? YOU KNOW THAT FOR SURE?
I ADMIT, I DON'T HAVE MORE THAN A HUNCH RIGHT NOW. BUT...IT FEELS RIGHT.
WE'RE IN QUASI-MAGICAL TERRITORY NOW, SAMSON. IMPORTANT DETAILS WILL COME TO US--HUNCHES INCLUDED.
I WONDER...
WHAT IS THAT, SHAMAN?
A RADIO, DR. McGOWAN. NOTHING MORE.

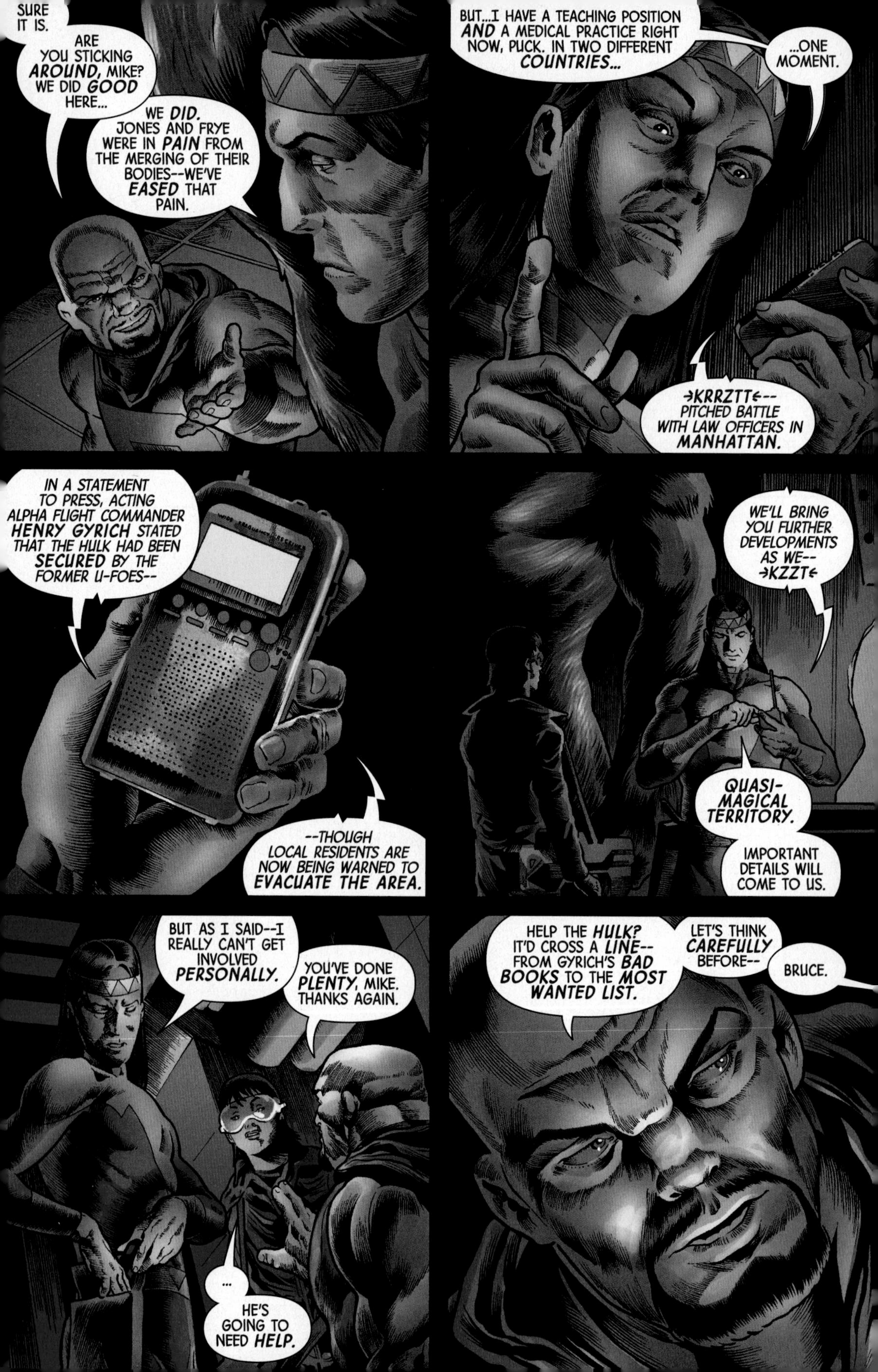
SURE IT IS.
ARE YOU STICKING AROUND, MIKE? WE DID GOOD HERE...
WE DID. JONES AND FRYE WERE IN PAIN FROM THE MERGING OF THEIR BODIES--WE'VE EASED THAT PAIN.
BUT...I HAVE A TEACHING POSITION AND A MEDICAL PRACTICE RIGHT NOW, PUCK. IN TWO DIFFERENT COUNTRIES...
...ONE MOMENT.
→KRRZTT←-- PITCHED BATTLE WITH LAW OFFICERS IN MANHATTAN.
IN A STATEMENT TO PRESS, ACTING ALPHA FLIGHT COMMANDER HENRY GYRICH STATED THAT THE HULK HAD BEEN SECURED BY THE FORMER U-FOES--
--THOUGH LOCAL RESIDENTS ARE NOW BEING WARNED TO EVACUATE THE AREA.
WE'LL BRING YOU FURTHER DEVELOPMENTS AS WE-- →KZZT←
QUASI-MAGICAL TERRITORY.
IMPORTANT DETAILS WILL COME TO US.
BUT AS I SAID--I REALLY CAN'T GET INVOLVED PERSONALLY.
YOU'VE DONE PLENTY, MIKE. THANKS AGAIN.
... HE'S GOING TO NEED HELP.
HELP THE HULK? IT'D CROSS A LINE--FROM GYRICH'S BAD BOOKS TO THE MOST WANTED LIST.
LET'S THINK CAREFULLY BEFORE--
BRUCE.

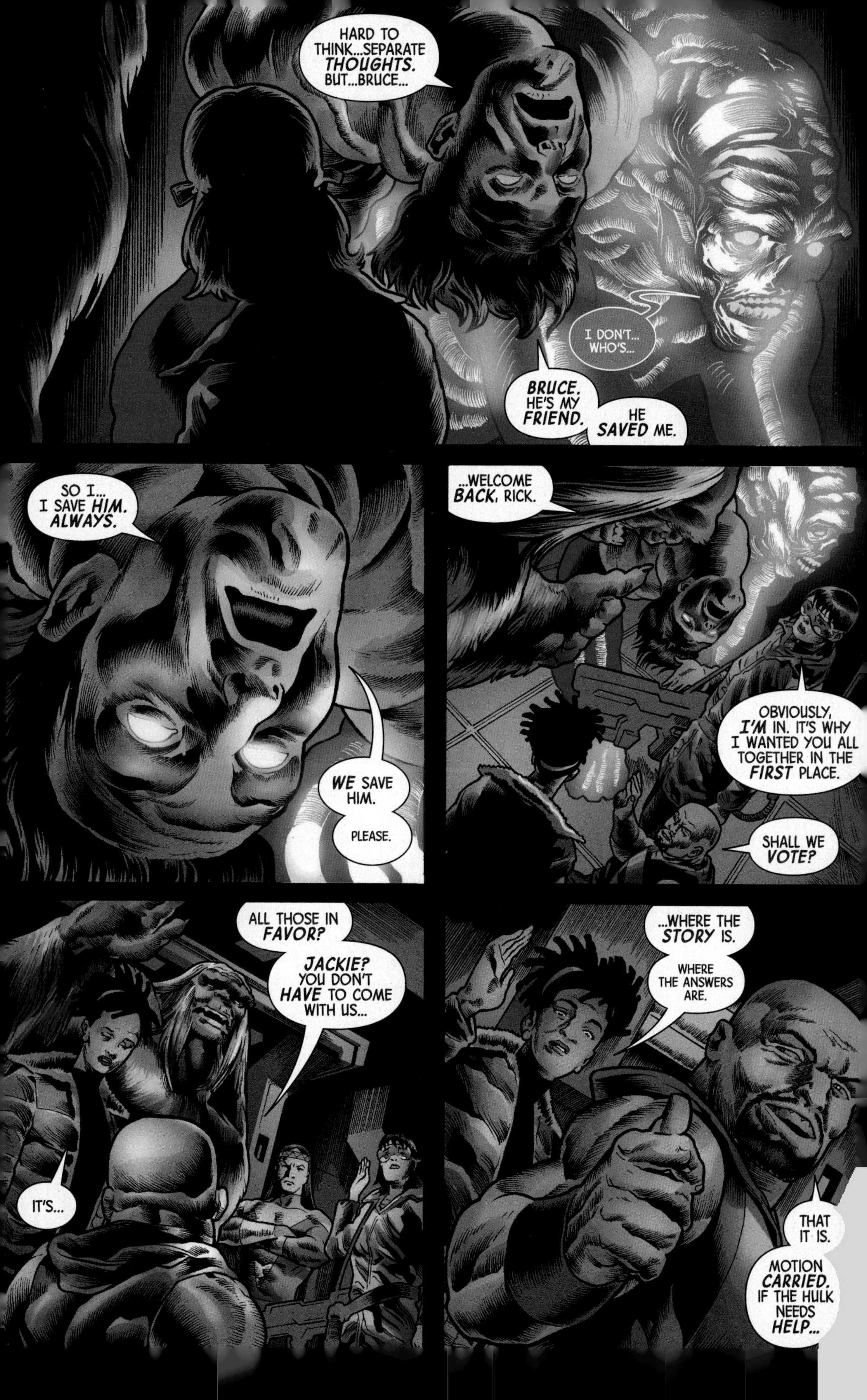
HARD TO THINK...SEPARATE THOUGHTS. BUT...BRUCE...
I DON'T... WHO'S...
BRUCE. HE'S MY FRIEND.
HE SAVED ME.
SO I... I SAVE HIM. ALWAYS.
WE SAVE HIM.
PLEASE.
...WELCOME BACK, RICK.
OBVIOUSLY, I'M IN. IT'S WHY I WANTED YOU ALL TOGETHER IN THE FIRST PLACE.
SHALL WE VOTE?
ALL THOSE IN FAVOR?
JACKIE? YOU DON'T HAVE TO COME WITH US...
IT'S...
...WHERE THE STORY IS.
WHERE THE ANSWERS ARE.
THAT IT IS.
MOTION CARRIED. IF THE HULK NEEDS HELP...

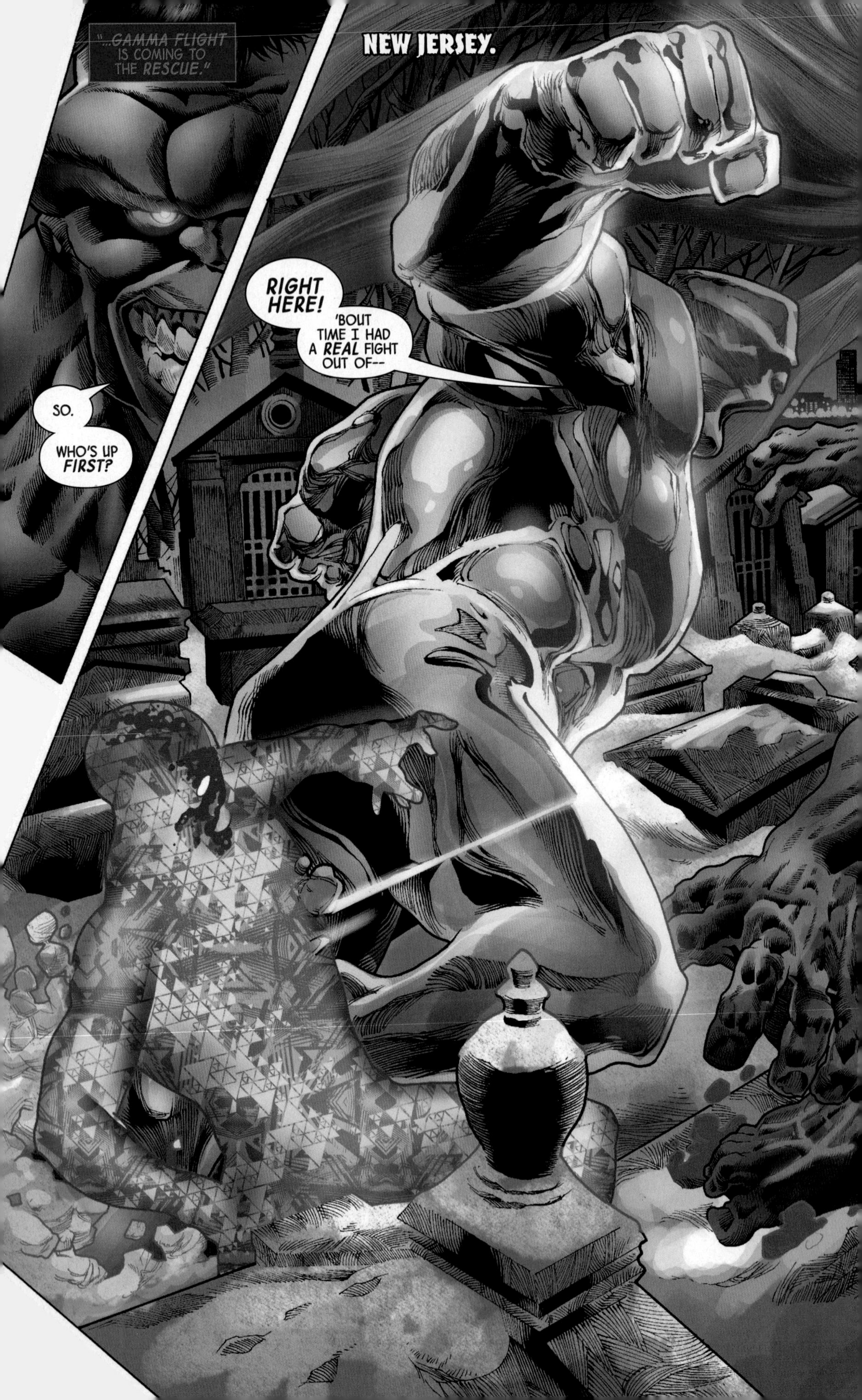
"...GAMMA FLIGHT IS COMING TO THE RESCUE."
NEW JERSEY.
SO.
WHO'S UP FIRST?
RIGHT HERE!
'BOUT TIME I HAD A REAL FIGHT OUT OF--

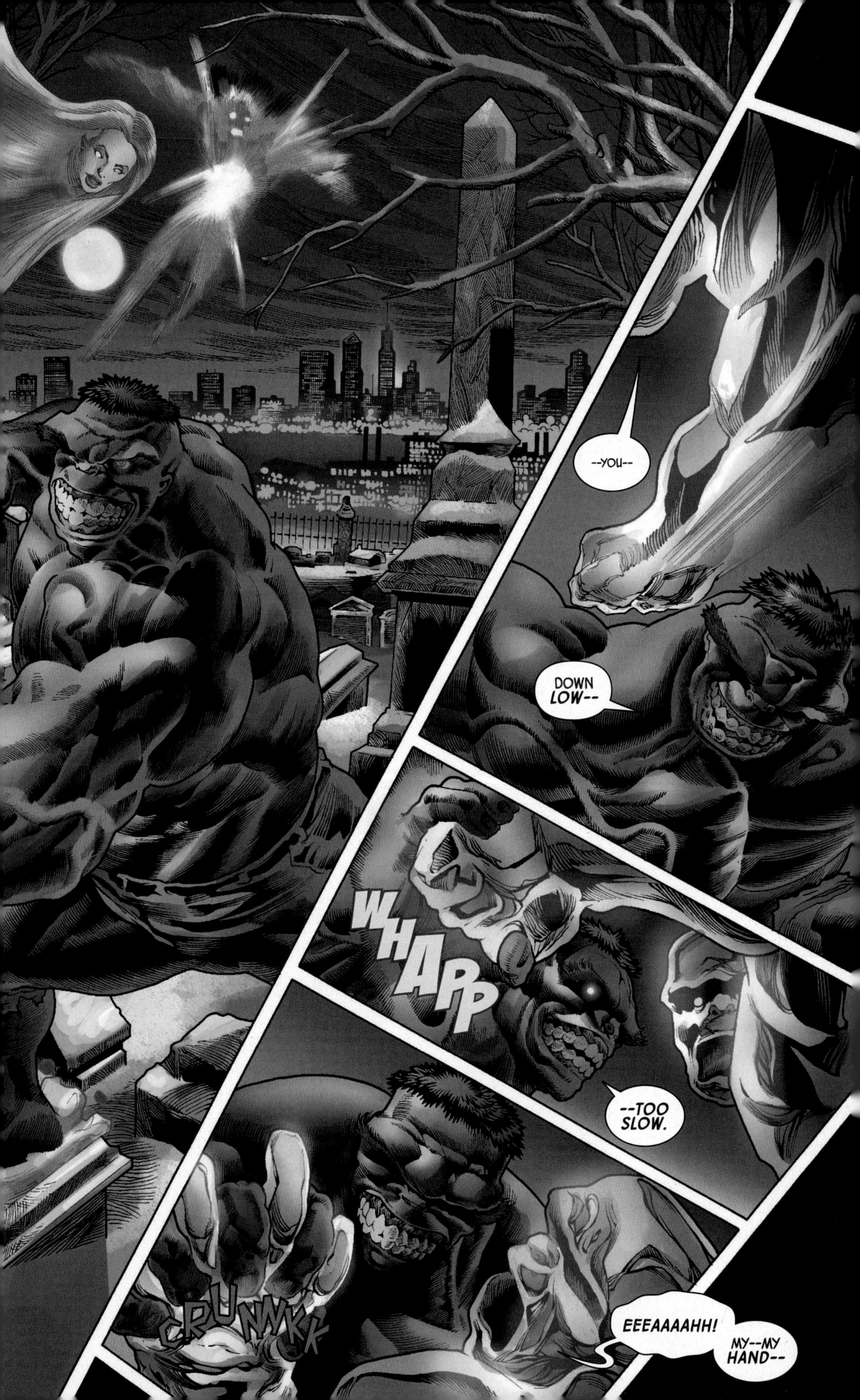
--YOU--
DOWN LOW--
WHAPP
--TOO SLOW.
CRUNNKK
EEEAAAAAHH!
MY--MY HAND--

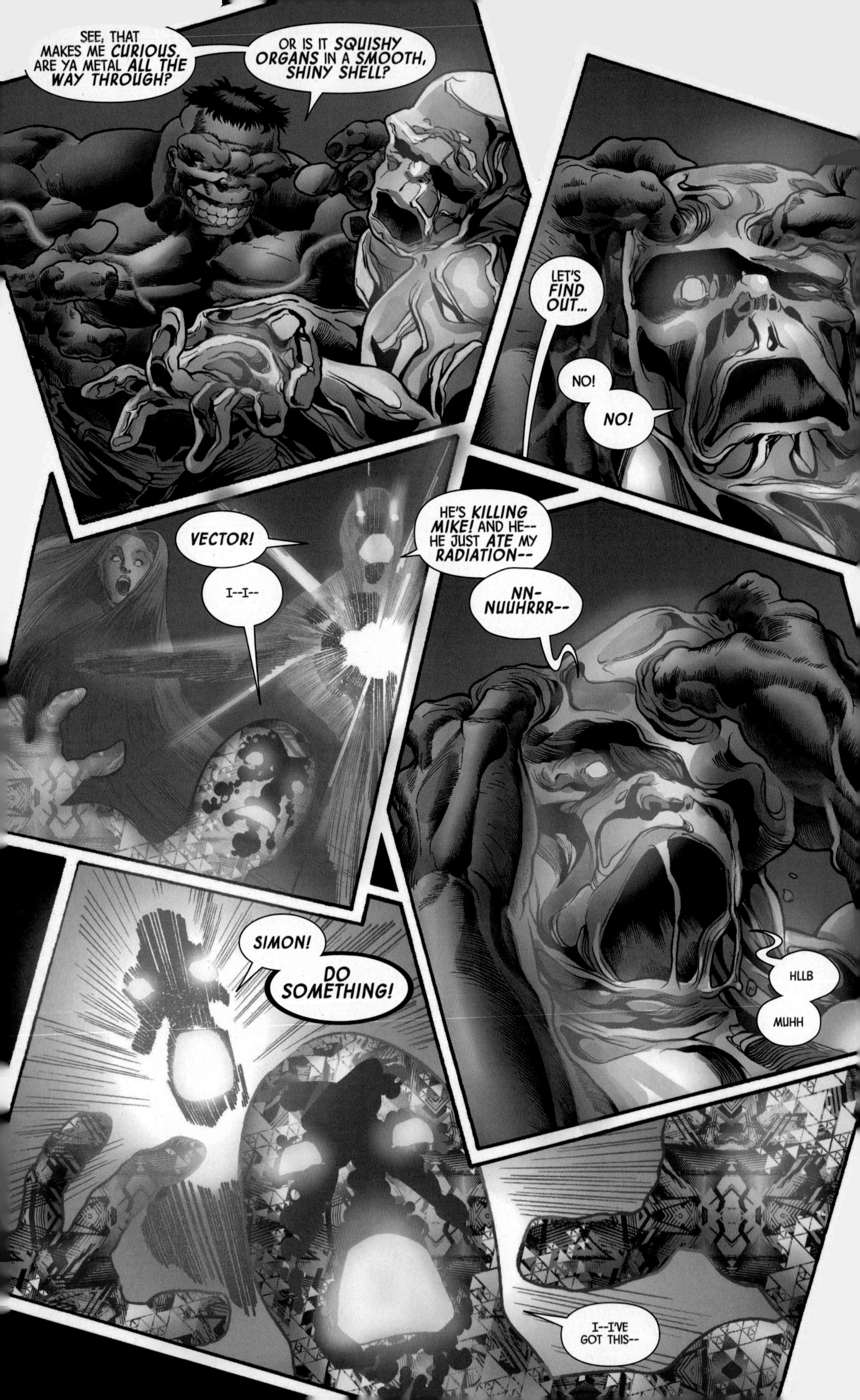
SEE, THAT MAKES ME CURIOUS. ARE YA METAL ALL THE WAY THROUGH?
OR IS IT SQUISHY ORGANS IN A SMOOTH, SHINY SHELL?
LET'S FIND OUT...
NO!
NO!
VECTOR!
I--I--
HE'S KILLING MIKE! AND HE-- HE JUST ATE MY RADIATION--
NN-NUUHRRR--
HLLB
MUHH
SIMON!
DO SOMETHING!
I--I'VE GOT THIS--

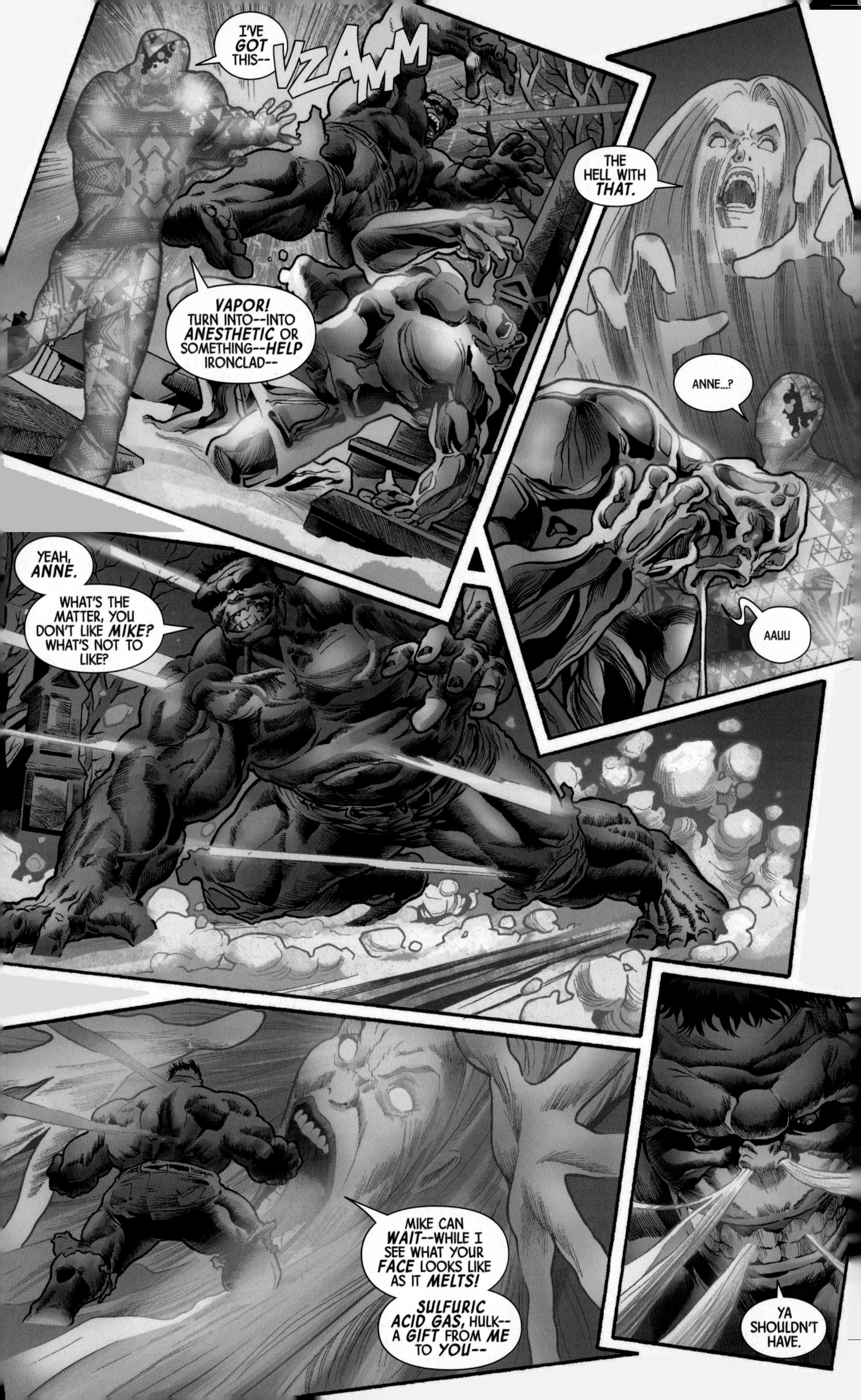

I'VE GOT THIS--
VZAMM
VAPOR! TURN INTO--INTO ANESTHETIC OR SOMETHING--HELP IRONCLAD--
THE HELL WITH THAT.
ANNE...?
AAUU
YEAH, ANNE.
WHAT'S THE MATTER, YOU DON'T LIKE MIKE? WHAT'S NOT TO LIKE?
MIKE CAN WAIT--WHILE I SEE WHAT YOUR FACE LOOKS LIKE AS IT MELTS!
SULFURIC ACID GAS, HULK--A GIFT FROM ME TO YOU--
YA SHOULDN'T HAVE.

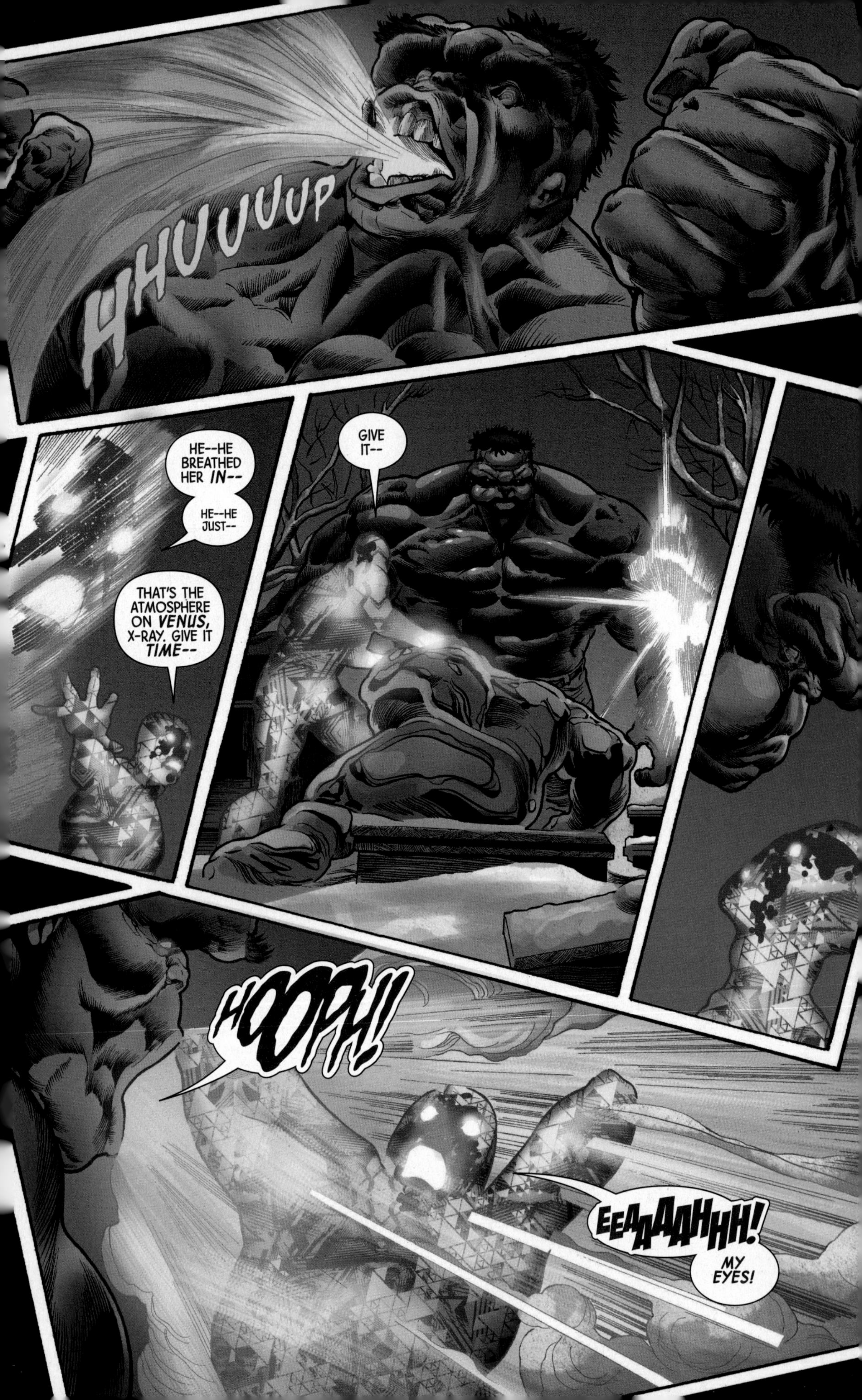
HHUUUUP
HE--HE BREATHED HER IN--
HE--HE JUST--
THAT'S THE ATMOSPHERE ON VENUS, X-RAY. GIVE IT TIME--
GIVE IT--
HOOPH!!
EEAAAAHHH!
MY EYES!

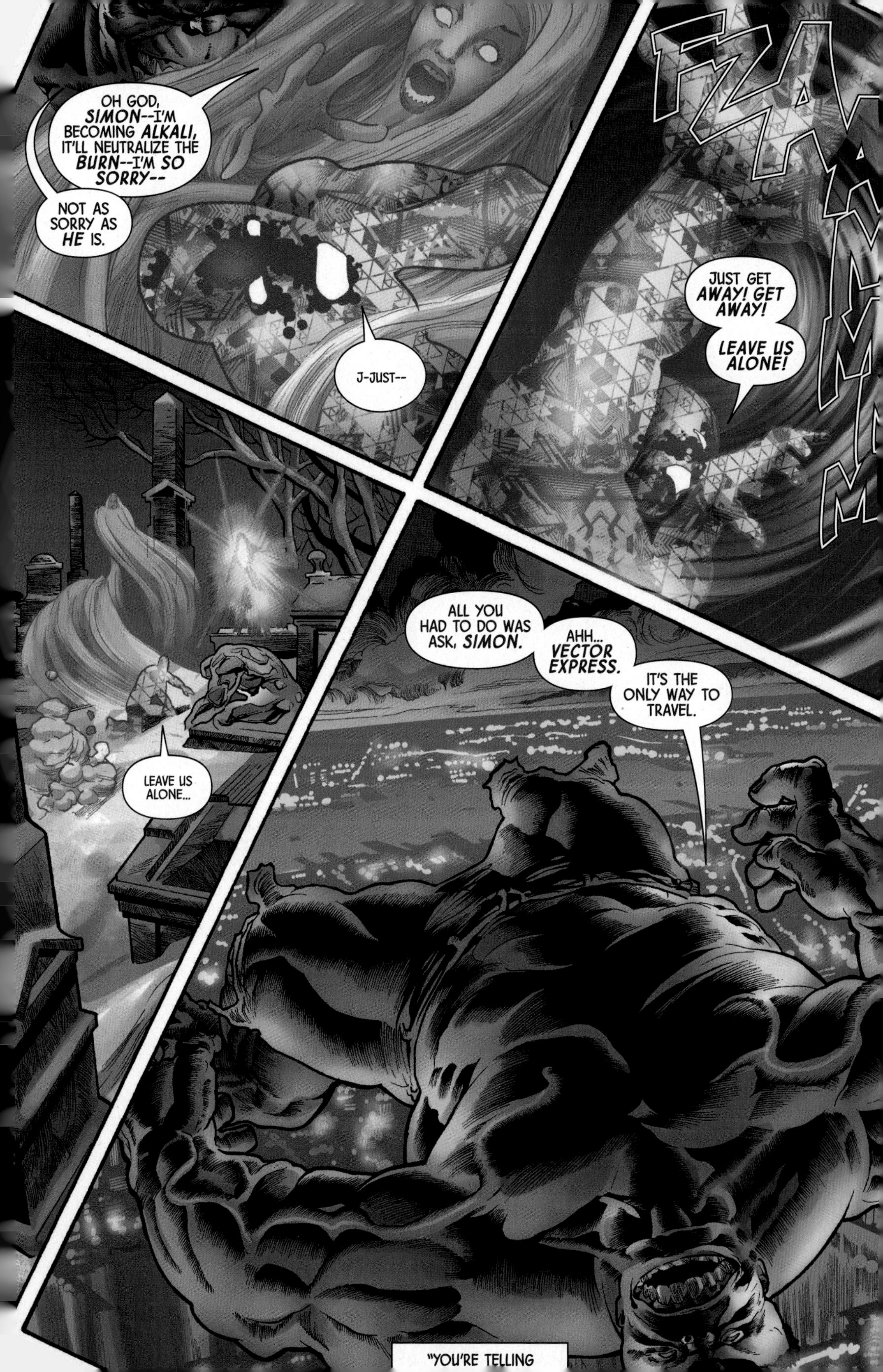
OH GOD, SIMON--I'M BECOMING ALKALI, IT'LL NEUTRALIZE THE BURN--I'M SO SORRY--
NOT AS SORRY AS HE IS.
J-JUST--
FZAMMMM
JUST GET AWAY! GET AWAY!
LEAVE US ALONE!
LEAVE US ALONE...
ALL YOU HAD TO DO WAS ASK, SIMON.
AHH... VECTOR EXPRESS.
IT'S THE ONLY WAY TO TRAVEL.
"YOU'RE TELLING

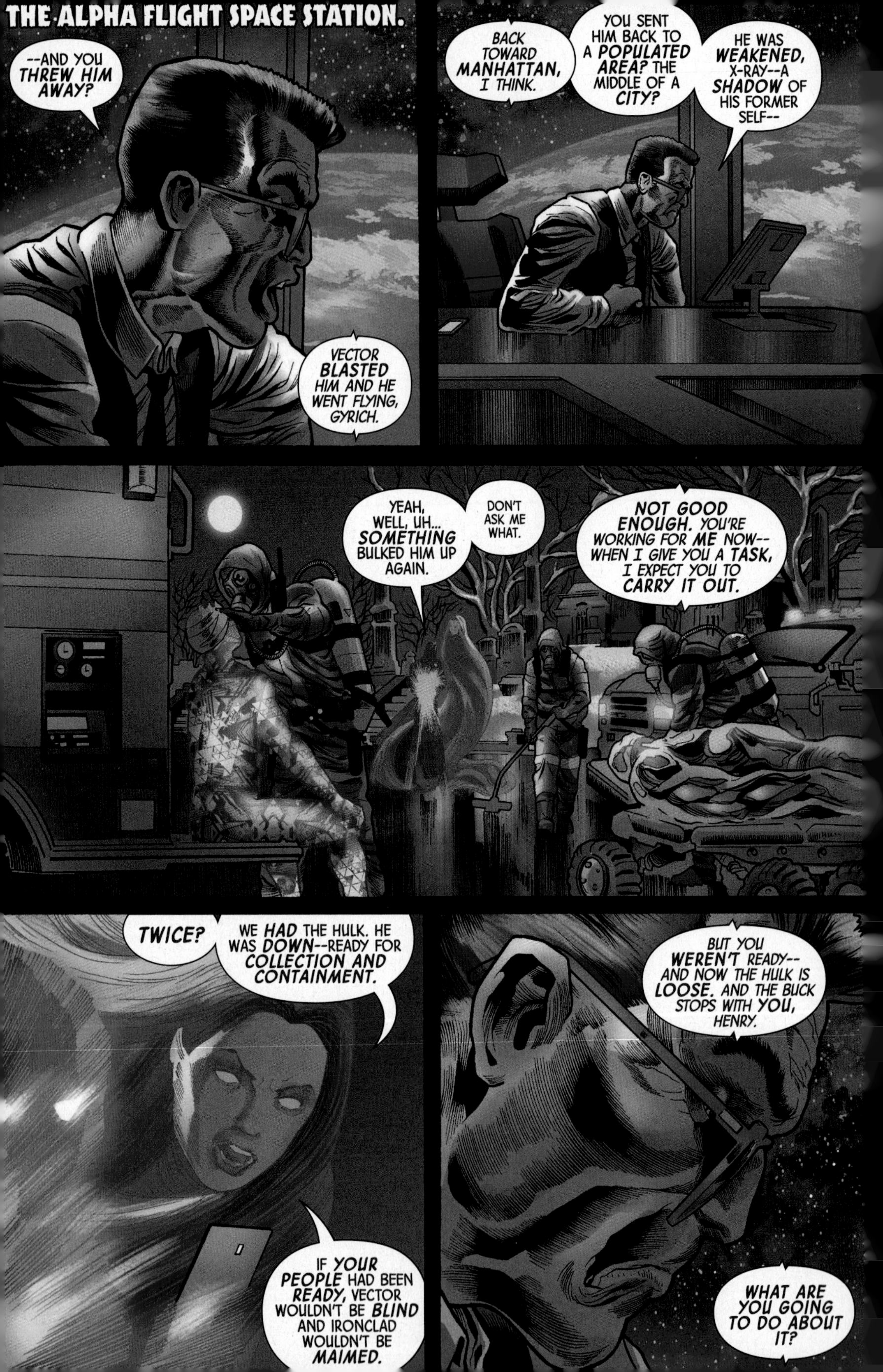

THE ALPHA FLIGHT SPACE STATION.
--AND YOU THREW HIM AWAY?
VECTOR BLASTED HIM AND HE WENT FLYING, GYRICH.
BACK TOWARD MANHATTAN, I THINK.
YOU SENT HIM BACK TO A POPULATED AREA? THE MIDDLE OF A CITY?
HE WAS WEAKENED, X-RAY--A SHADOW OF HIS FORMER SELF--
YEAH, WELL, UH... SOMETHING BULKED HIM UP AGAIN.
DON'T ASK ME WHAT.
NOT GOOD ENOUGH. YOU'RE WORKING FOR ME NOW-- WHEN I GIVE YOU A TASK, I EXPECT YOU TO CARRY IT OUT.
TWICE?
WE HAD THE HULK. HE WAS DOWN--READY FOR COLLECTION AND CONTAINMENT.
IF YOUR PEOPLE HAD BEEN READY, VECTOR WOULDN'T BE BLIND AND IRONCLAD WOULDN'T BE MAIMED.
BUT YOU WEREN'T READY-- AND NOW THE HULK IS LOOSE. AND THE BUCK STOPS WITH YOU, HENRY.
WHAT ARE YOU GOING TO DO ABOUT IT?

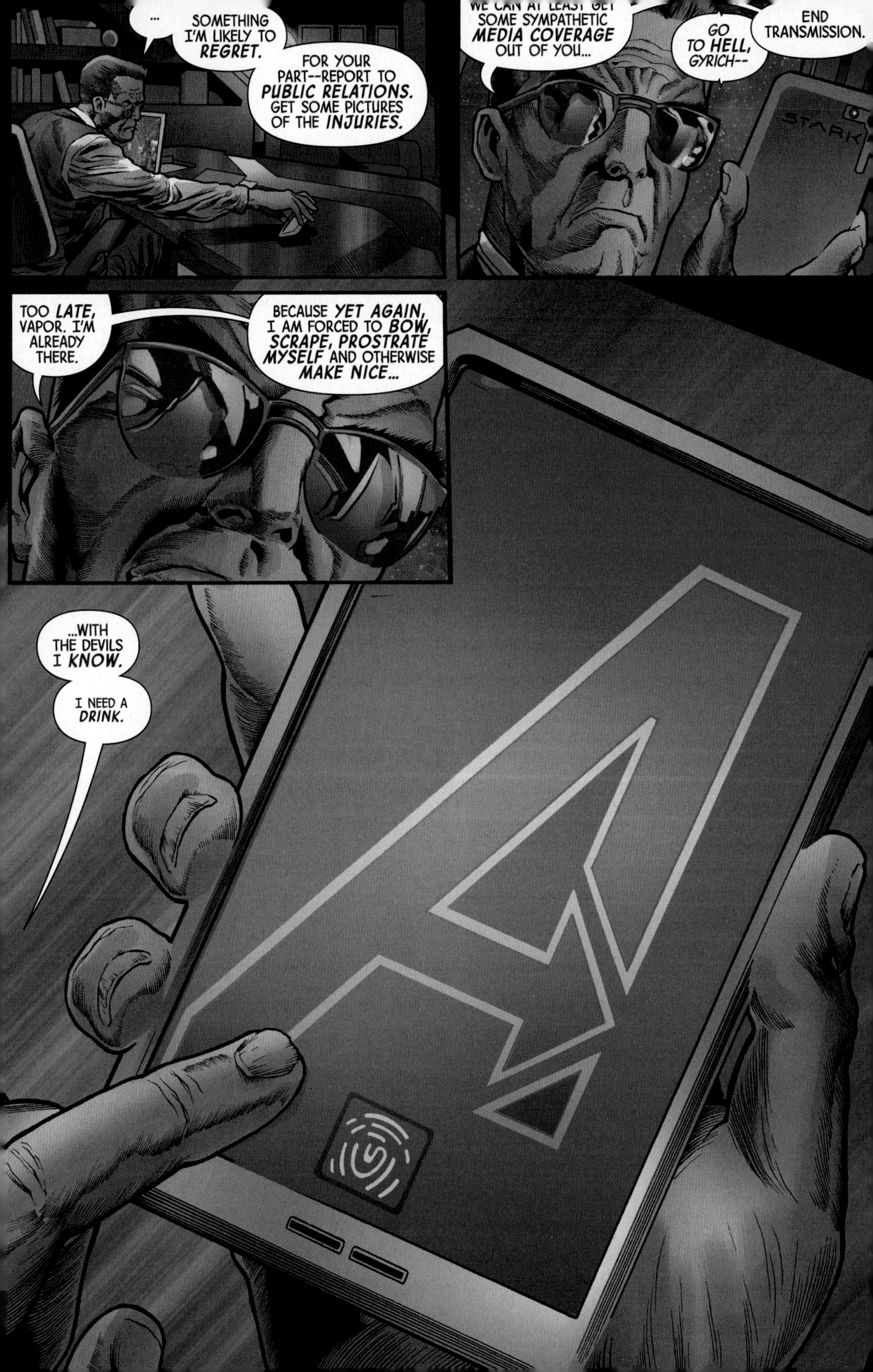

...
SOMETHING I'M LIKELY TO REGRET.
FOR YOUR PART--REPORT TO PUBLIC RELATIONS. GET SOME PICTURES OF THE INJURIES.
WE CAN AT LEAST GET SOME SYMPATHETIC MEDIA COVERAGE OUT OF YOU...
GO TO HELL, GYRICH--
END TRANSMISSION.
STARK
TOO LATE, VAPOR. I'M ALREADY THERE.
BECAUSE YET AGAIN, I AM FORCED TO BOW, SCRAPE, PROSTRATE MYSELF AND OTHERWISE MAKE NICE...
...WITH THE DEVILS I KNOW.
I NEED A DRINK.

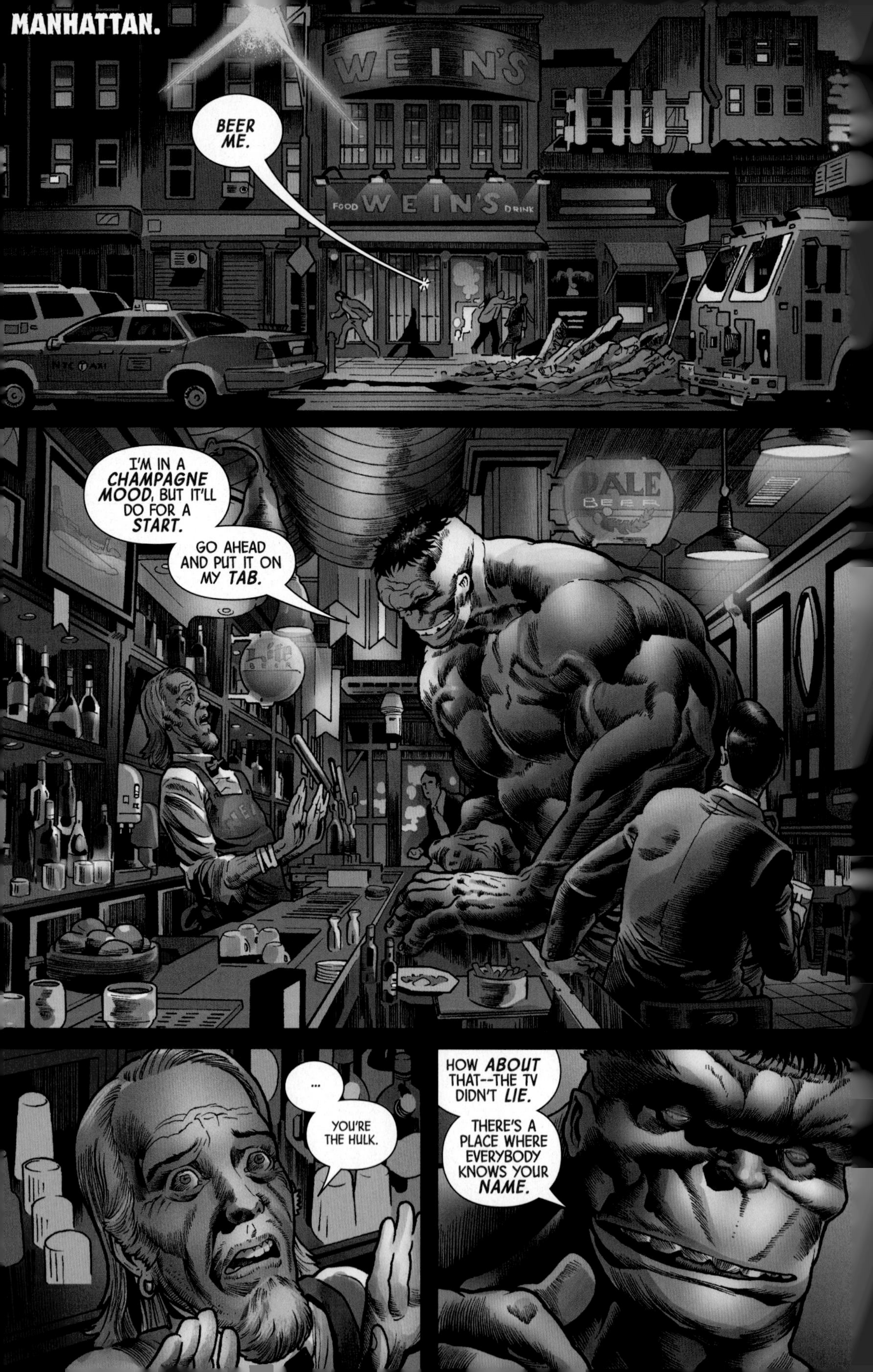
MANHATTAN.
WEIN'S
BEER ME.
FOOD WEIN'S DRINK
I'M IN A CHAMPAGNE MOOD, BUT IT'LL DO FOR A START.
GO AHEAD AND PUT IT ON MY TAB.
PALE BEER
...
YOU'RE THE HULK.
HOW ABOUT THAT--THE TV DIDN'T LIE.
THERE'S A PLACE WHERE EVERYBODY KNOWS YOUR NAME.

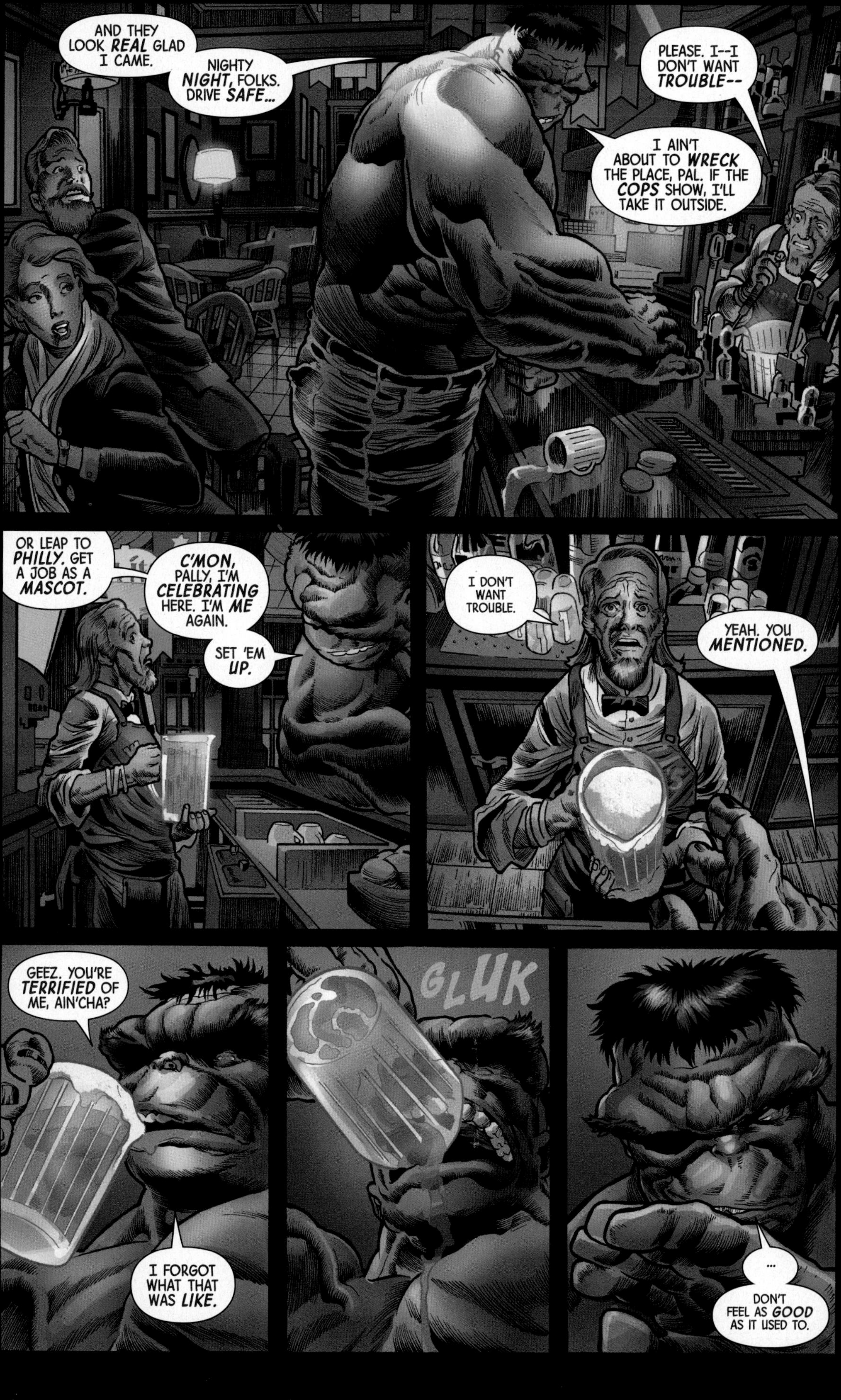
AND THEY LOOK REAL GLAD I CAME.
NIGHTY NIGHT, FOLKS. DRIVE SAFE...
PLEASE. I--I DON'T WANT TROUBLE--
I AIN'T ABOUT TO WRECK THE PLACE, PAL. IF THE COPS SHOW, I'LL TAKE IT OUTSIDE.
OR LEAP TO PHILLY. GET A JOB AS A MASCOT.
C'MON, PALLY, I'M CELEBRATING HERE. I'M ME AGAIN.
SET 'EM UP.
I DON'T WANT TROUBLE.
YEAH. YOU MENTIONED.
GEEZ. YOU'RE TERRIFIED OF ME, AIN'CHA?
I FORGOT WHAT THAT WAS LIKE.
GLUK
...
DON'T FEEL AS GOOD AS IT USED TO.

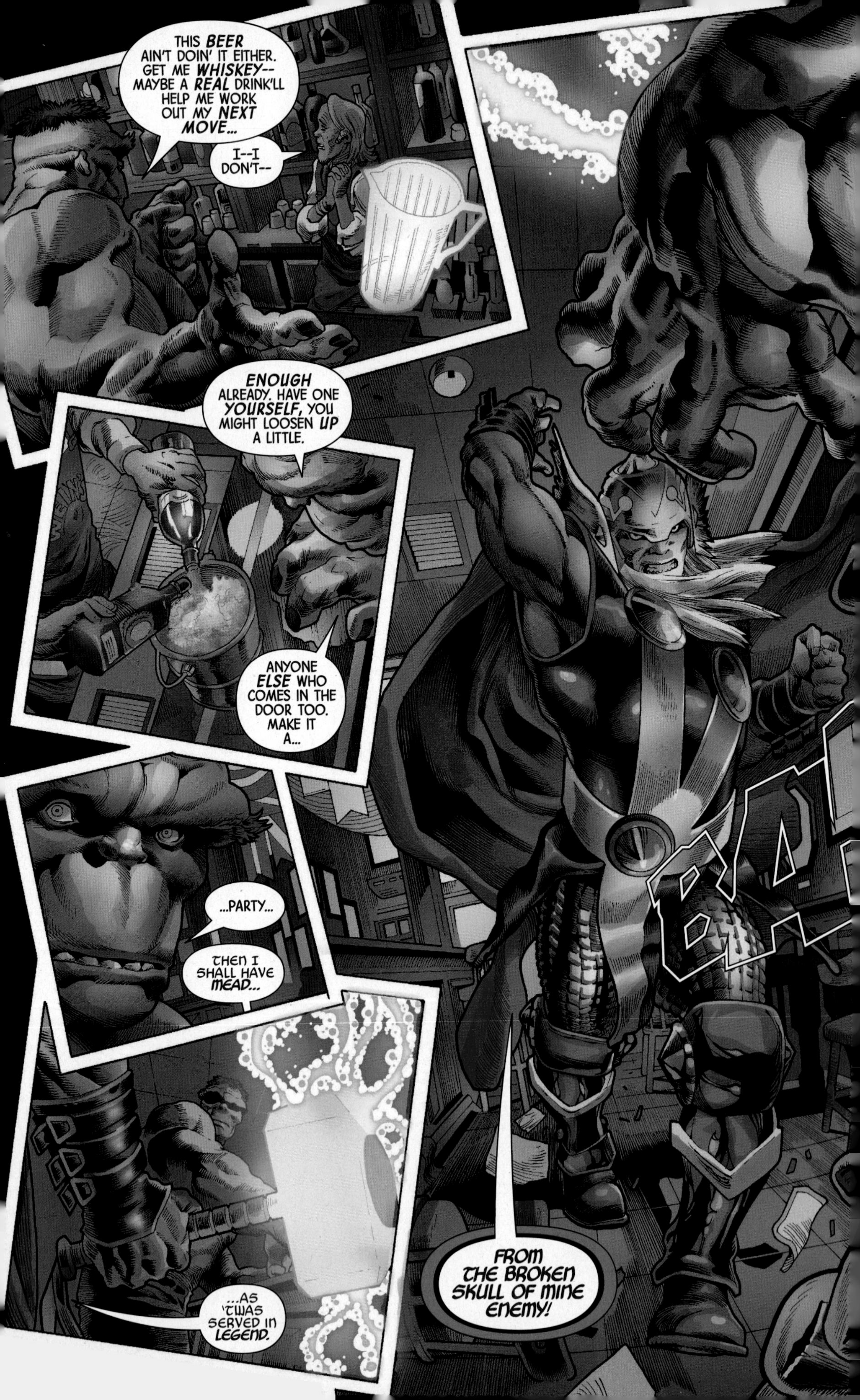

THIS BEER AIN'T DOIN' IT EITHER. GET ME WHISKEY-- MAYBE A REAL DRINK'LL HELP ME WORK OUT MY NEXT MOVE...
I--I DON'T--
ENOUGH ALREADY. HAVE ONE YOURSELF, YOU MIGHT LOOSEN UP A LITTLE.
ANYONE ELSE WHO COMES IN THE DOOR TOO. MAKE IT A...
...PARTY...
THEN I SHALL HAVE MEAD...
...AS 'TWAS SERVED IN LEGEND.
FROM THE BROKEN SKULL OF MINE ENEMY!

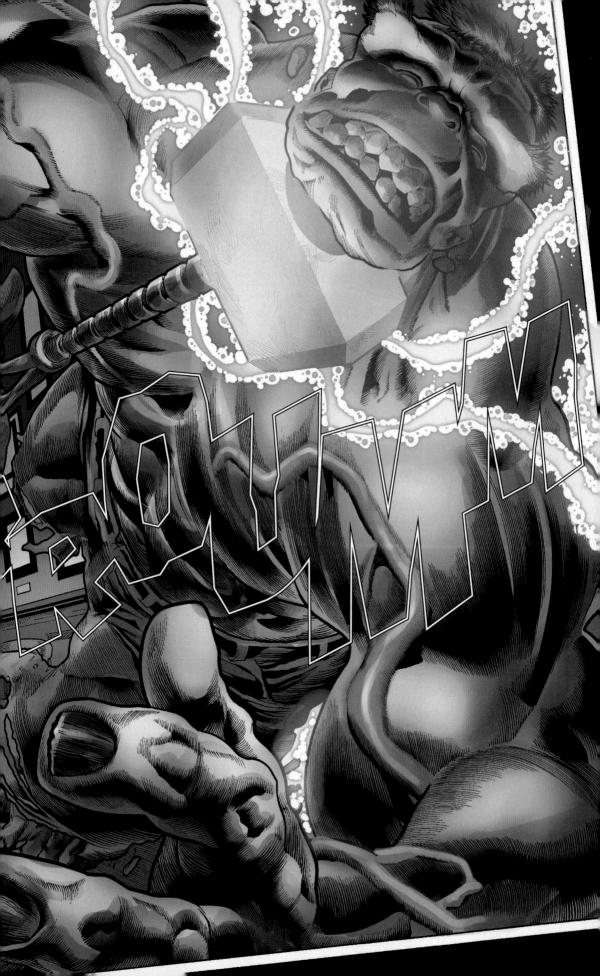

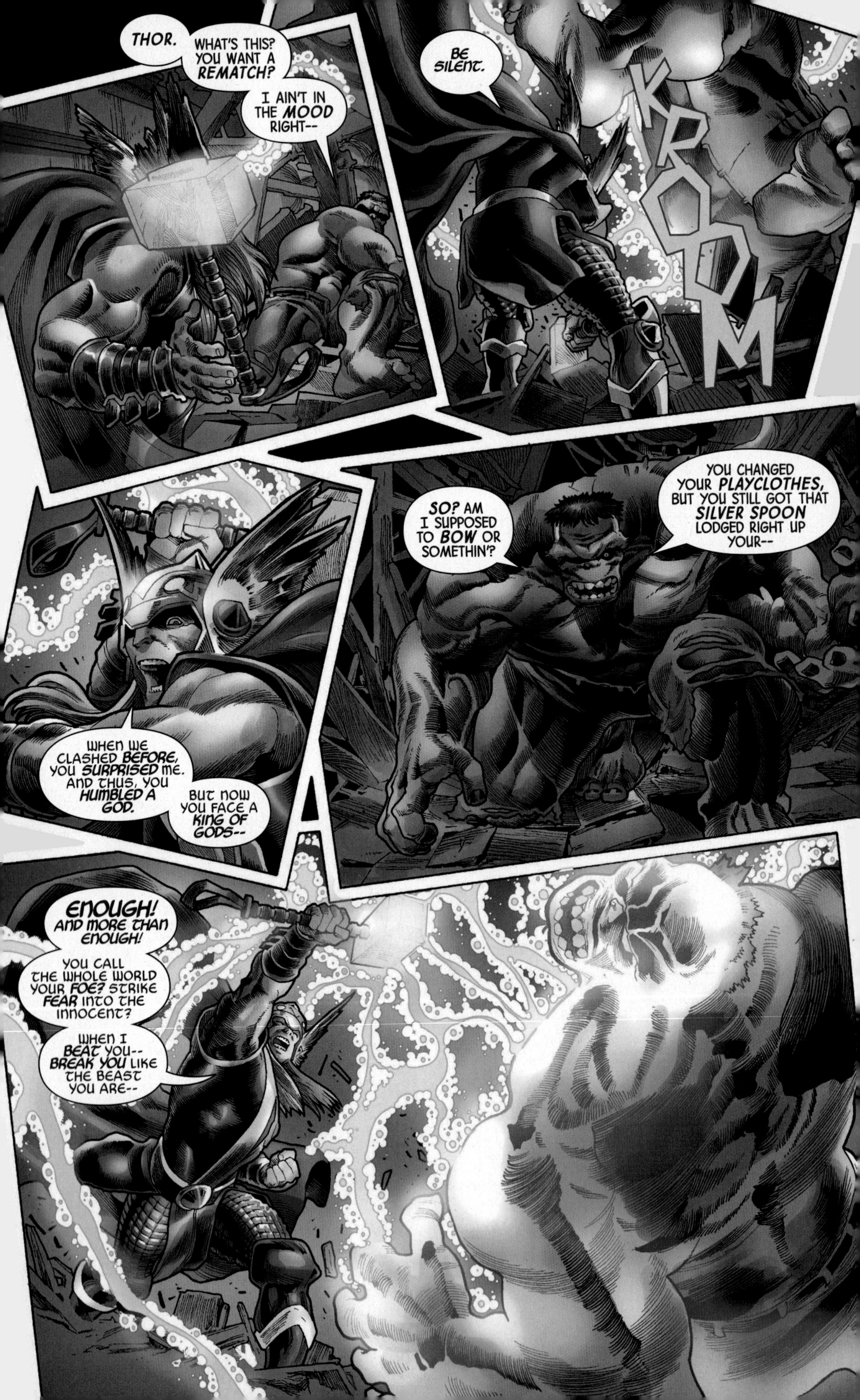
THOR.
WHAT'S THIS? YOU WANT A REMATCH?
I AIN'T IN THE MOOD RIGHT--
BE SILENT.
KROOM
WHEN WE CLASHED BEFORE, YOU SURPRISED ME. AND THUS, YOU HUMBLED A GOD.
BUT NOW YOU FACE A KING OF GODS--
SO? AM I SUPPOSED TO BOW OR SOMETHIN'?
YOU CHANGED YOUR PLAYCLOTHES, BUT YOU STILL GOT THAT SILVER SPOON LODGED RIGHT UP YOUR--
ENOUGH! AND MORE THAN ENOUGH!
YOU CALL THE WHOLE WORLD YOUR FOE? STRIKE FEAR INTO THE INNOCENT?
WHEN I BEAT YOU-- BREAK YOU LIKE THE BEAST YOU ARE--

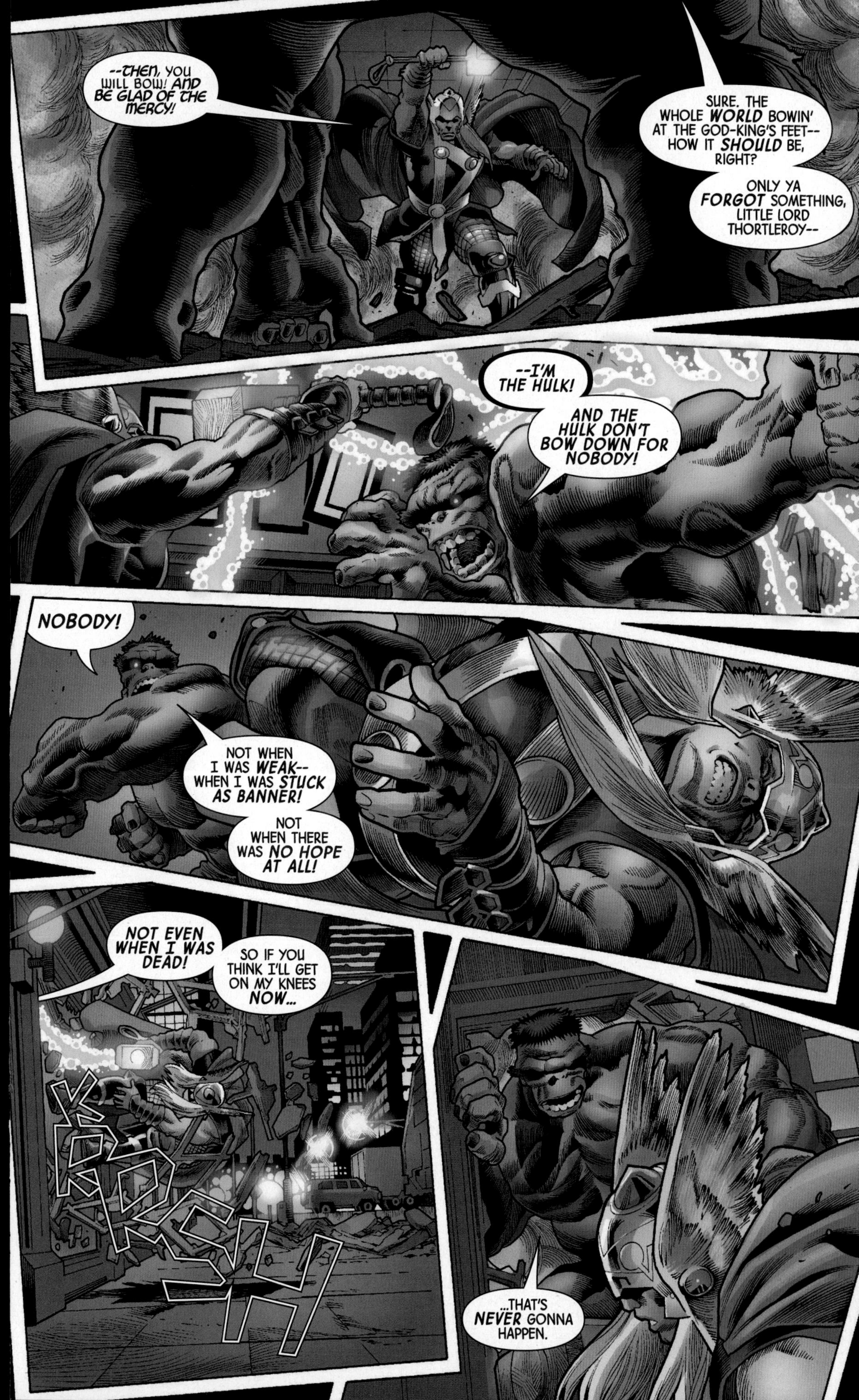
--THEN, YOU WILL BOW! AND BE GLAD OF THE MERCY!
SURE. THE WHOLE WORLD BOWIN' AT THE GOD-KING'S FEET-- HOW IT SHOULD BE, RIGHT?
ONLY YA FORGOT SOMETHING, LITTLE LORD THORTLEROY--
--I'M THE HULK!
AND THE HULK DON'T BOW DOWN FOR NOBODY!
NOBODY!
NOT WHEN I WAS WEAK-- WHEN I WAS STUCK AS BANNER!
NOT WHEN THERE WAS NO HOPE AT ALL!
NOT EVEN WHEN I WAS DEAD!
SO IF YOU THINK I'LL GET ON MY KNEES NOW...
KRRSH
...THAT'S NEVER GONNA HAPPEN.

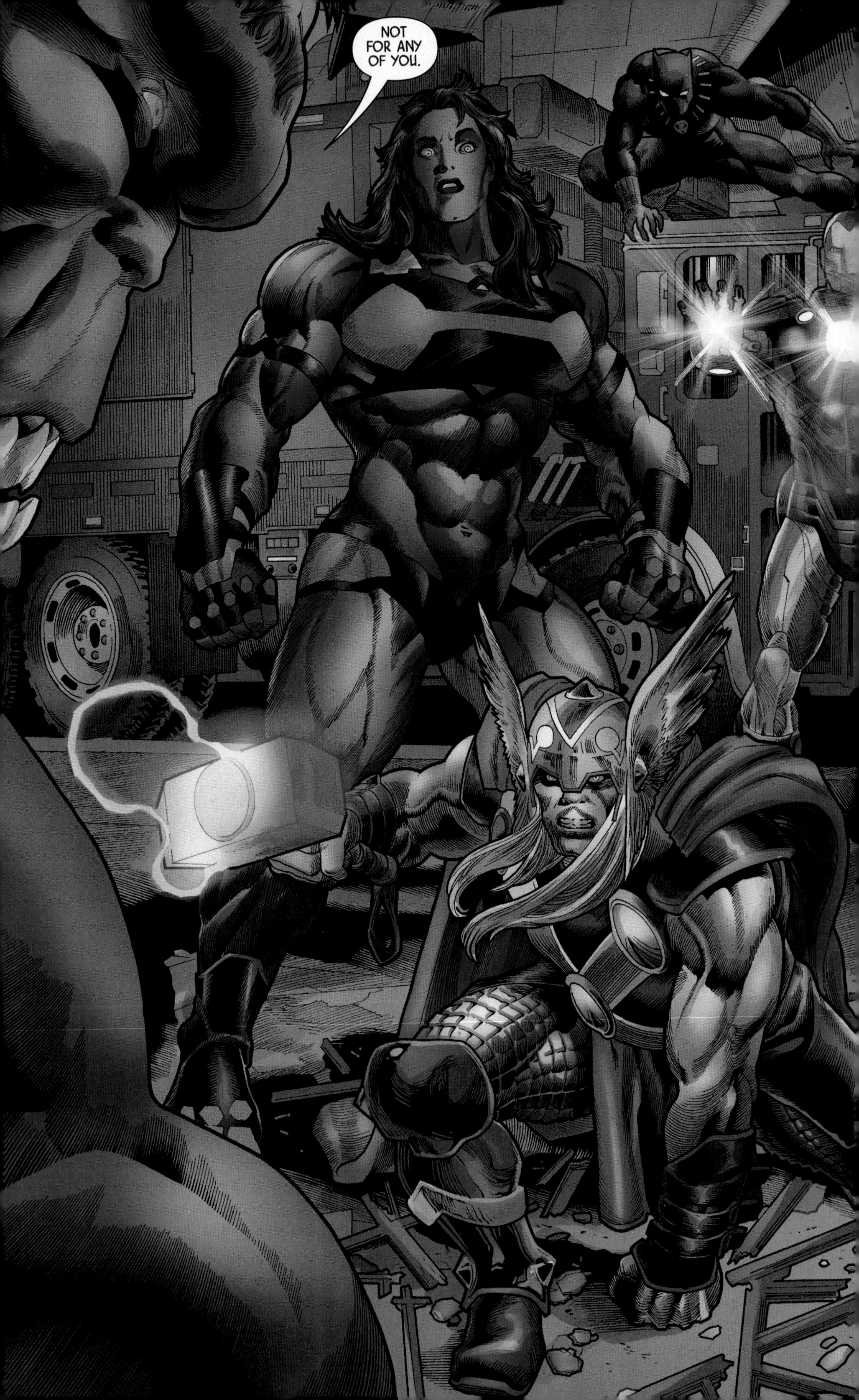
NOT FOR ANY OF YOU.

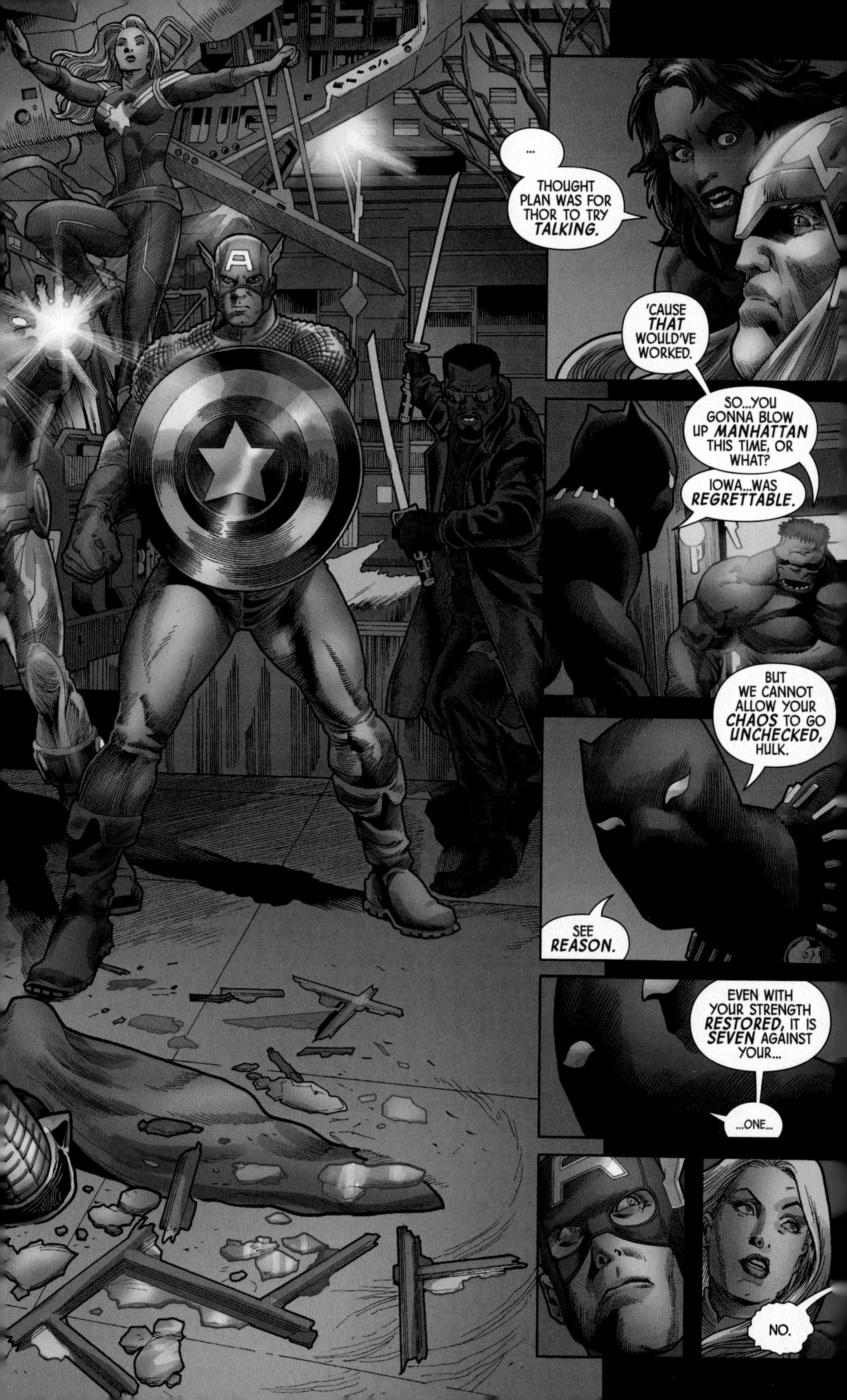
...
THOUGHT PLAN WAS FOR THOR TO TRY *TALKING.*
'CAUSE *THAT* WOULD'VE WORKED.
SO...YOU GONNA BLOW UP *MANHATTAN* THIS TIME, OR WHAT?
IOWA...WAS *REGRETTABLE.*
BUT WE CANNOT ALLOW YOUR *CHAOS* TO GO *UNCHECKED,* HULK.
SEE *REASON.*
EVEN WITH YOUR STRENGTH *RESTORED,* IT IS *SEVEN* AGAINST YOUR...
...ONE...
NO.

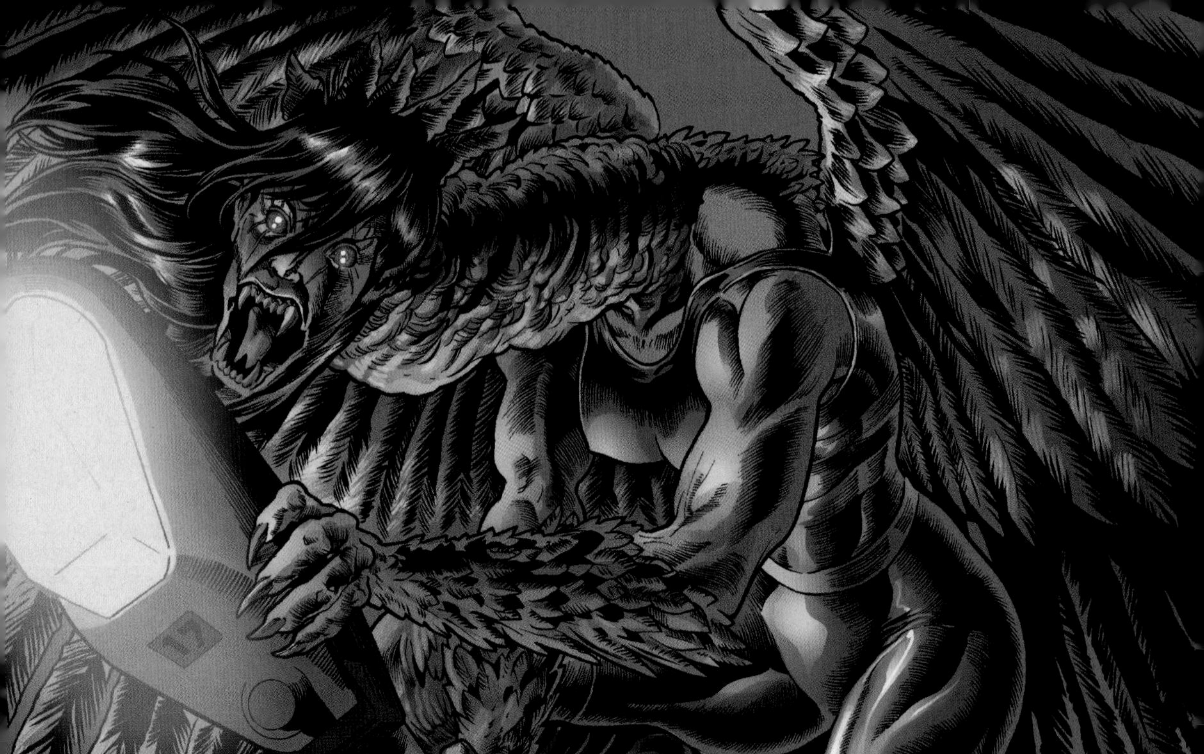
AGAINST TWO.

YOU AND ME AGAINST THE WORLD

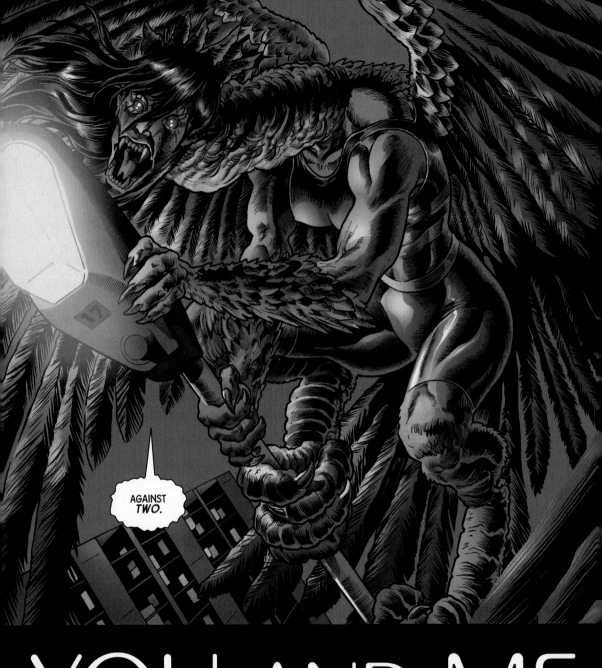

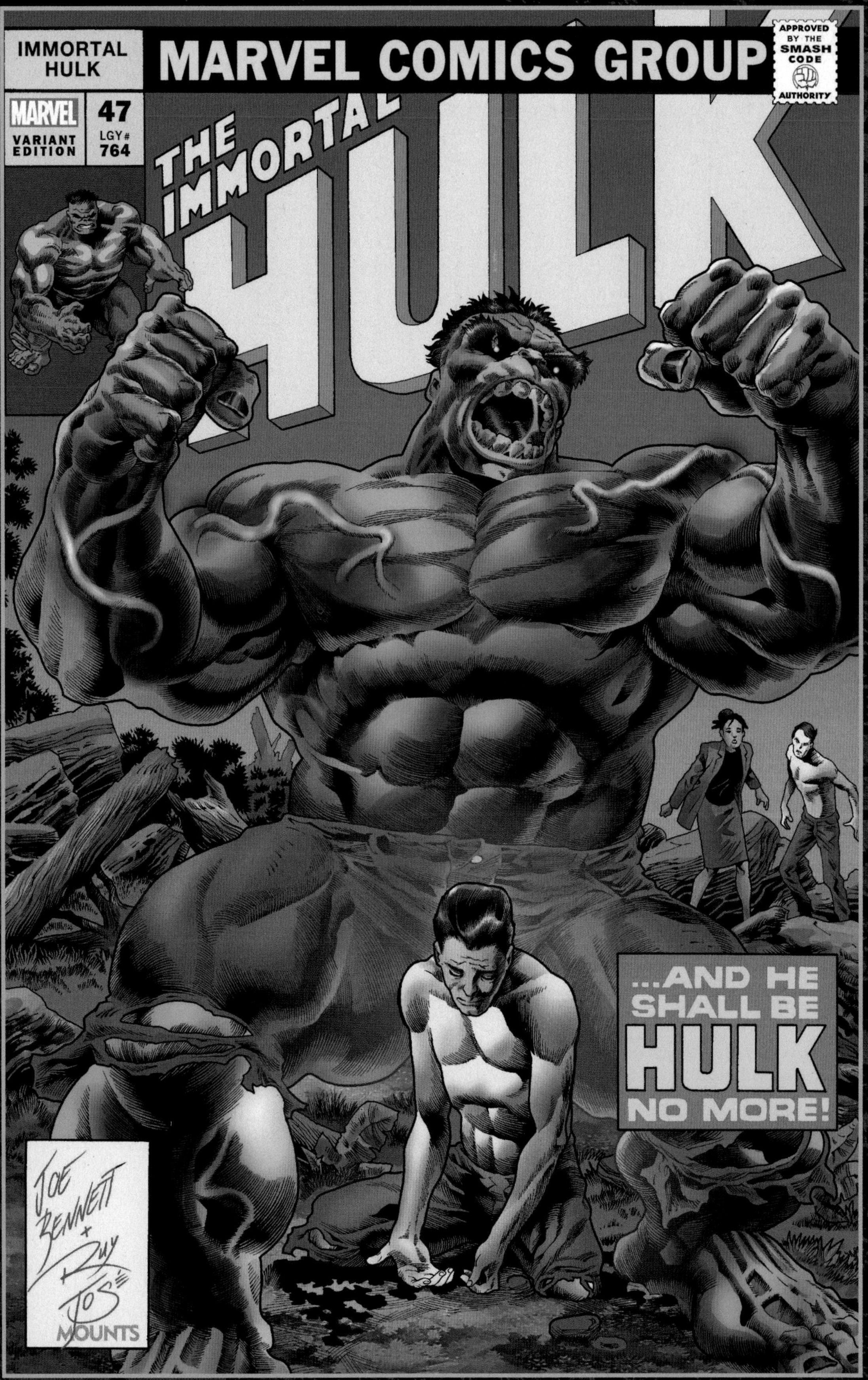
IMMORTAL HULK
MARVEL COMICS GROUP
APPROVED BY THE SMASH CODE AUTHORITY
MARVEL
47
LGY# 764
VARIANT EDITION
THE IMMORTAL HULK
...AND HE SHALL BE HULK NO MORE!
JOE BENNETT + RUY JOSÉ
MOUNTS

JOE BENNETT, RUY JOSÉ & PAUL MOUNTS
#47 HOMAGE VARIANT

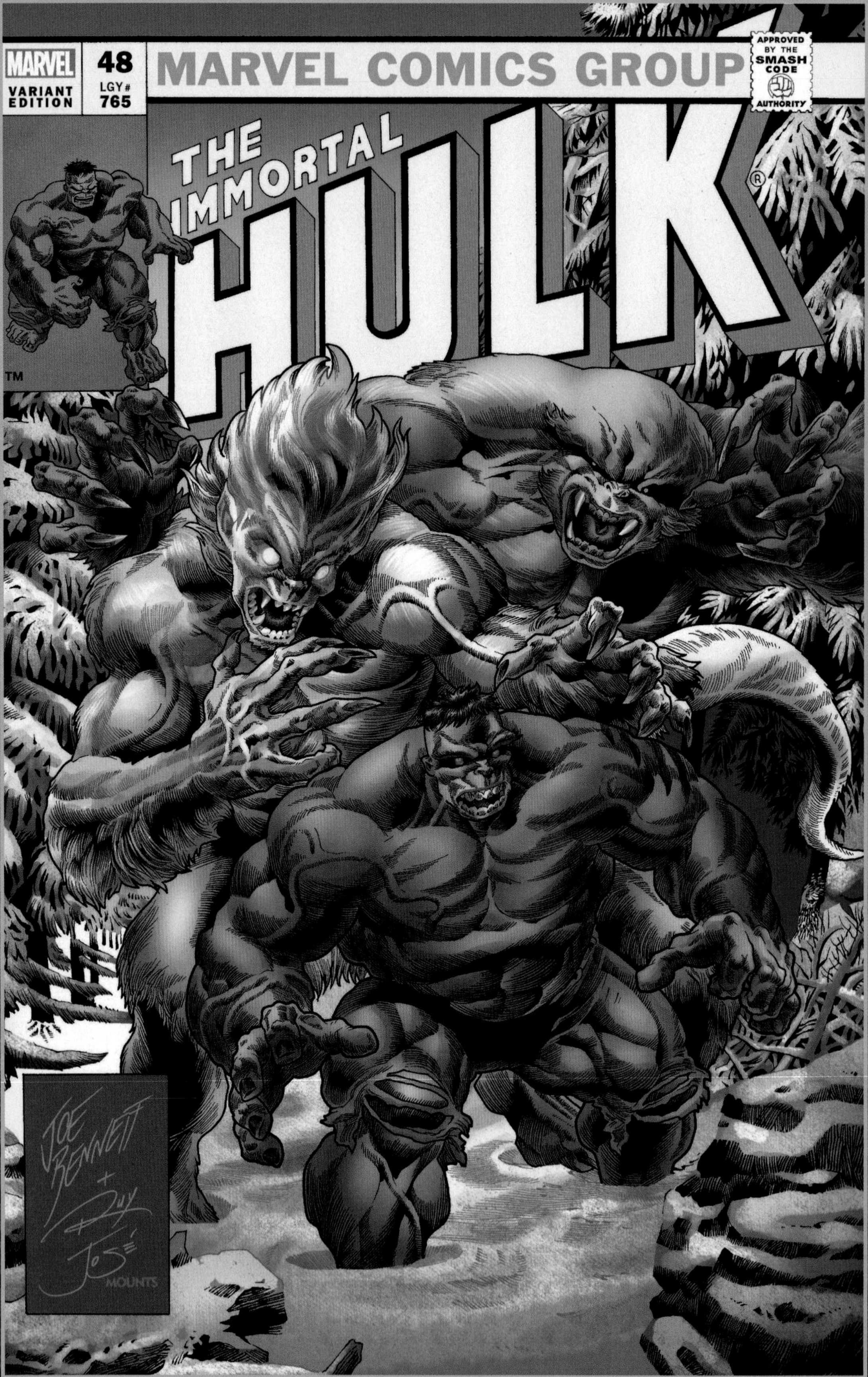
MARVEL
VARIANT EDITION
48
LGY# 765
MARVEL COMICS GROUP
APPROVED BY THE SMASH CODE AUTHORITY
THE IMMORTAL HULK
TM
JOE BENNETT + RUY JOSÉ
MOUNTS

JOE BENNETT, RUY JOSÉ & PAUL MOUNTS
#48 HOMAGE VARIANT

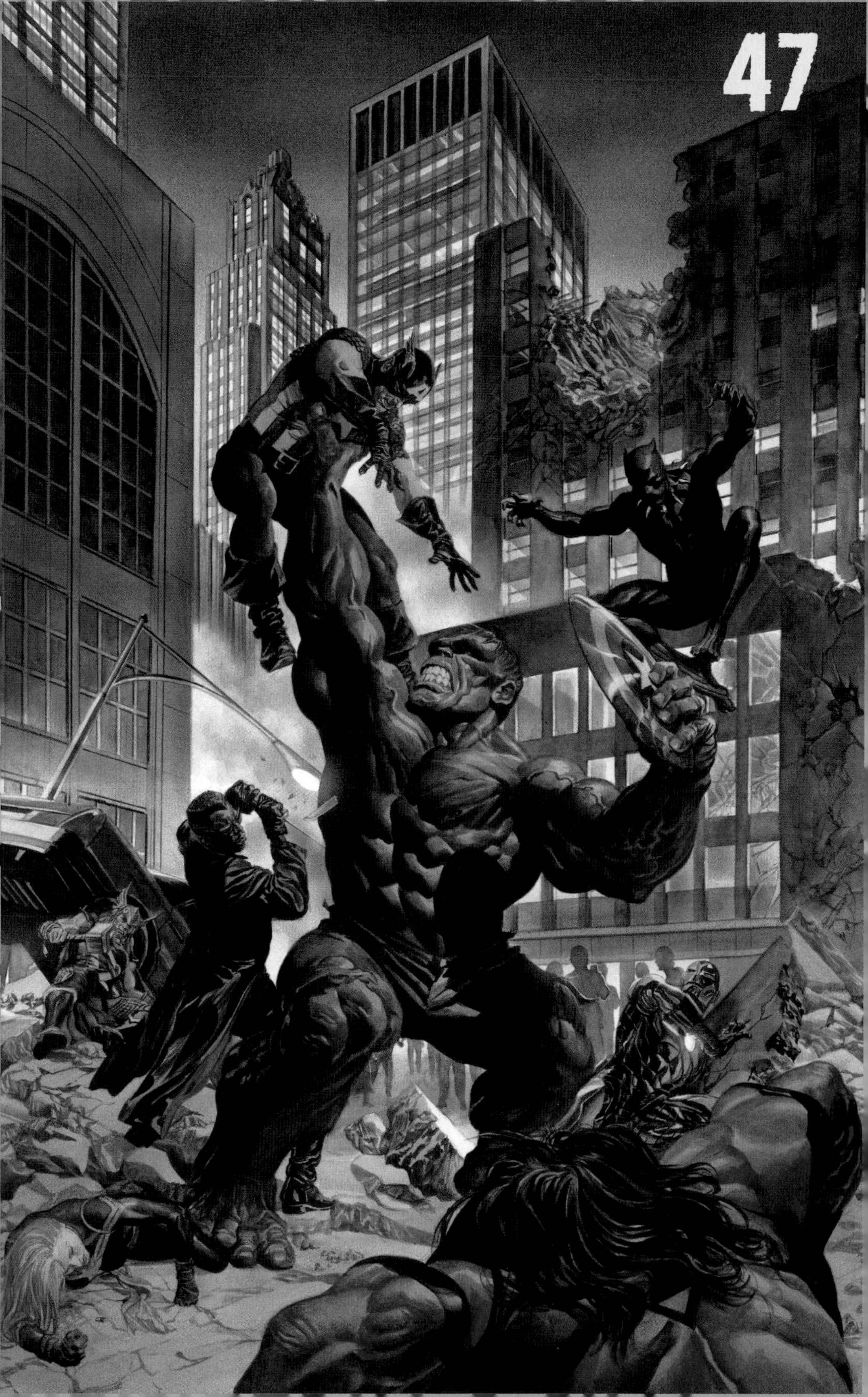
47

"I, LIKE THE ARCH-FIEND, BORE A HELL WITHIN ME, AND FINDING MYSELF UNSYMPATHISED WITH, WISHED TO TEAR UP THE TREES, SPREAD HAVOC AND DESTRUCTION AROUND ME, AND THEN TO HAVE SAT DOWN AND ENJOYED THE RUIN."

— MARY WOLLSTONECRAFT SHELLEY,
FRANKENSTEIN; OR, THE MODERN PROMETHEUS

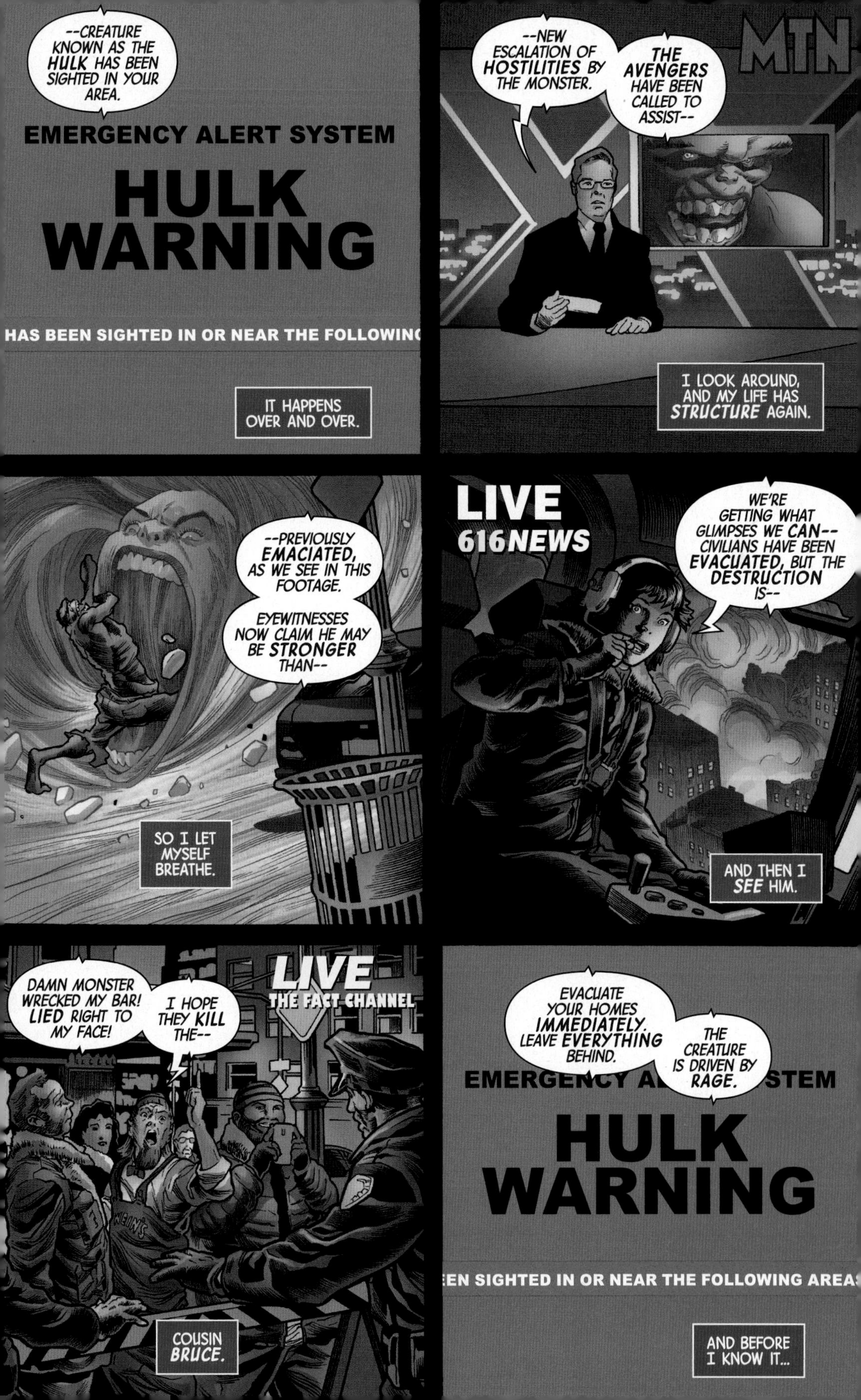
--CREATURE KNOWN AS THE HULK HAS BEEN SIGHTED IN YOUR AREA.
EMERGENCY ALERT SYSTEM
HULK WARNING
HAS BEEN SIGHTED IN OR NEAR THE FOLLOWIN
IT HAPPENS OVER AND OVER.
MTN
--NEW ESCALATION OF HOSTILITIES BY THE MONSTER.
THE AVENGERS HAVE BEEN CALLED TO ASSIST--
I LOOK AROUND, AND MY LIFE HAS STRUCTURE AGAIN.
--PREVIOUSLY EMACIATED, AS WE SEE IN THIS FOOTAGE.
EYEWITNESSES NOW CLAIM HE MAY BE STRONGER THAN--
SO I LET MYSELF BREATHE.
LIVE
616NEWS
WE'RE GETTING WHAT GLIMPSES WE CAN-- CIVILIANS HAVE BEEN EVACUATED, BUT THE DESTRUCTION IS--
AND THEN I SEE HIM.
LIVE
THE FACT CHANNEL
DAMN MONSTER WRECKED MY BAR! LIED RIGHT TO MY FACE!
I HOPE THEY KILL THE--
COUSIN BRUCE.
EVACUATE YOUR HOMES IMMEDIATELY. LEAVE EVERYTHING BEHIND.
THE CREATURE IS DRIVEN BY RAGE.
EMERGENCY A STEM
HULK WARNING
EEN SIGHTED IN OR NEAR THE FOLLOWING AREA
AND BEFORE I KNOW IT...

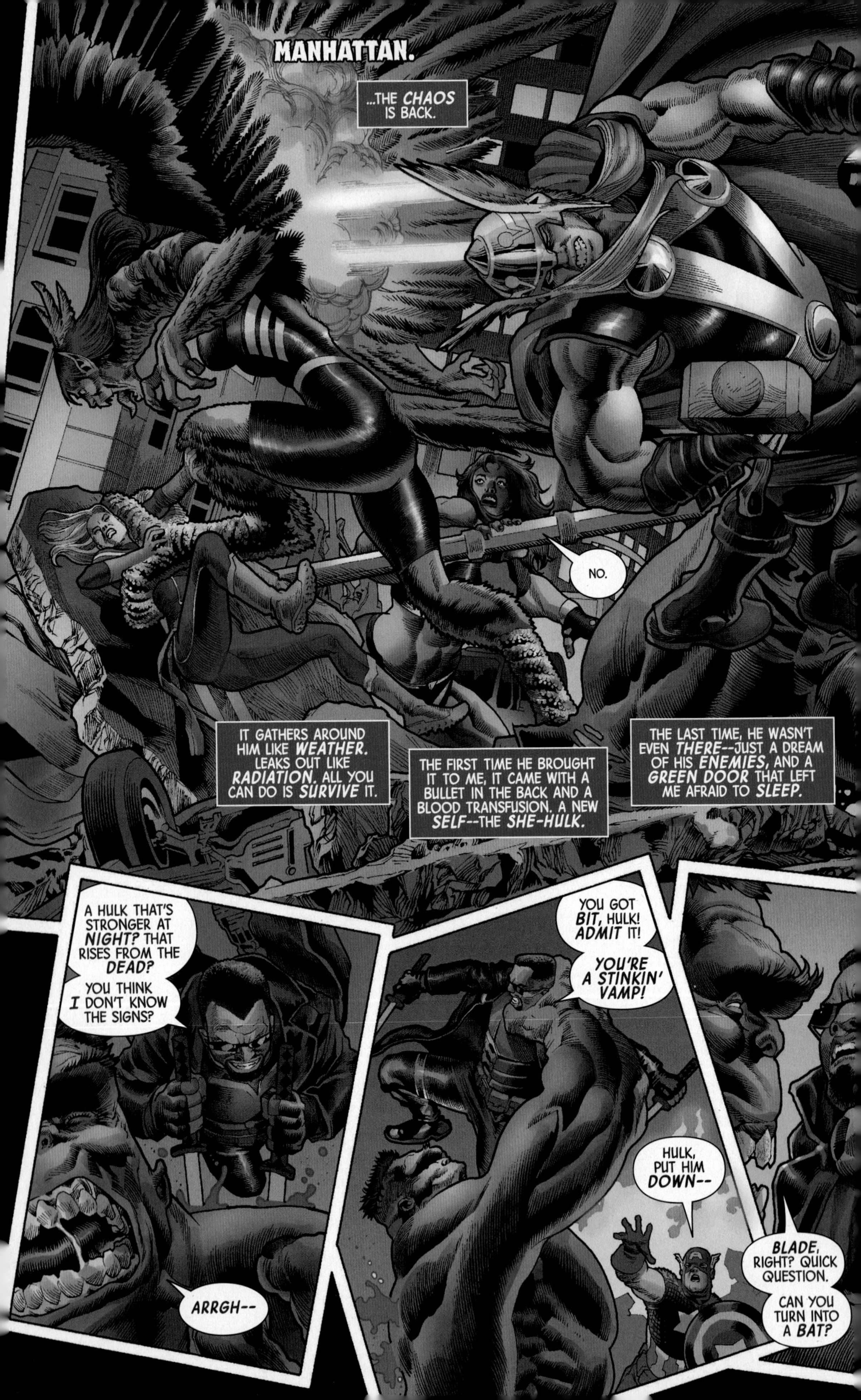
MANHATTAN.
...THE CHAOS IS BACK.
NO.
IT GATHERS AROUND HIM LIKE WEATHER. LEAKS OUT LIKE RADIATION. ALL YOU CAN DO IS SURVIVE IT.
THE FIRST TIME HE BROUGHT IT TO ME, IT CAME WITH A BULLET IN THE BACK AND A BLOOD TRANSFUSION. A NEW SELF--THE SHE-HULK.
THE LAST TIME, HE WASN'T EVEN THERE--JUST A DREAM OF HIS ENEMIES, AND A GREEN DOOR THAT LEFT ME AFRAID TO SLEEP.
A HULK THAT'S STRONGER AT NIGHT? THAT RISES FROM THE DEAD?
YOU THINK I DON'T KNOW THE SIGNS?
ARRGH--
YOU GOT BIT, HULK! ADMIT IT!
YOU'RE A STINKIN' VAMP!
HULK, PUT HIM DOWN--
BLADE, RIGHT? QUICK QUESTION.
CAN YOU TURN INTO A BAT?

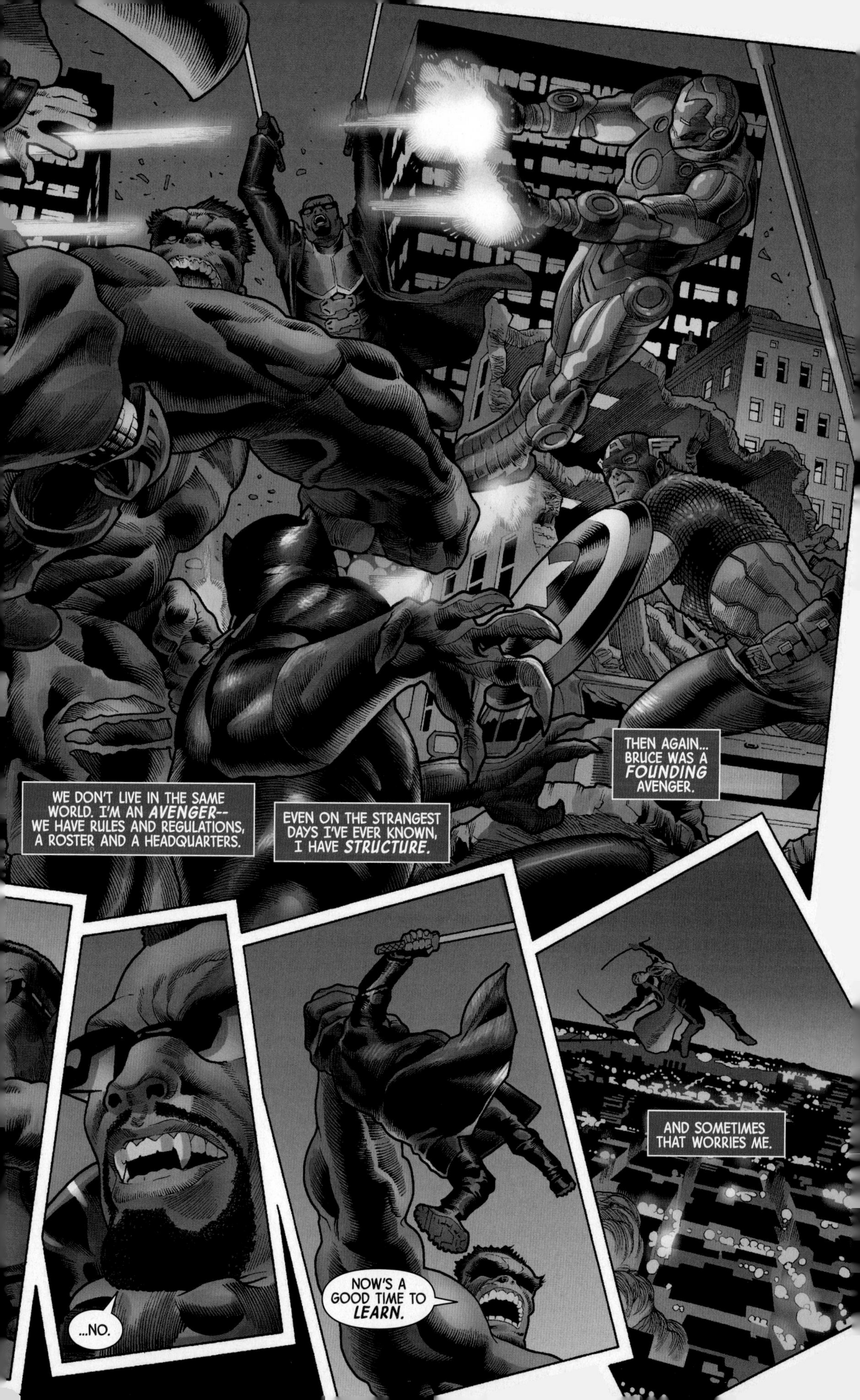

WE DON'T LIVE IN THE SAME WORLD. I'M AN AVENGER-- WE HAVE RULES AND REGULATIONS, A ROSTER AND A HEADQUARTERS.
EVEN ON THE STRANGEST DAYS I'VE EVER KNOWN, I HAVE STRUCTURE.
THEN AGAIN... BRUCE WAS A FOUNDING AVENGER.
...NO.
NOW'S A GOOD TIME TO LEARN.
AND SOMETIMES THAT WORRIES ME.

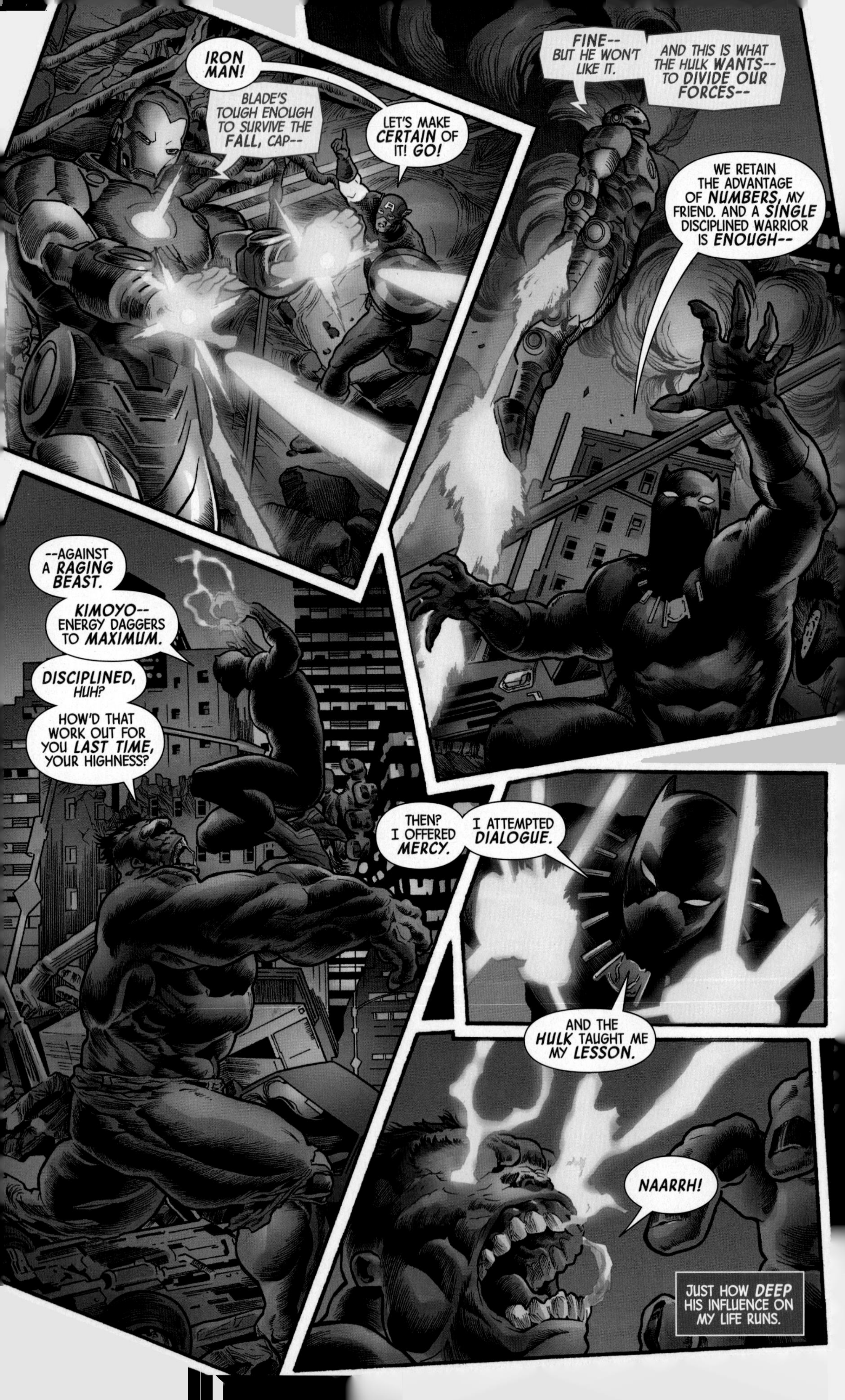
IRON MAN!
BLADE'S TOUGH ENOUGH TO SURVIVE THE FALL, CAP--
LET'S MAKE CERTAIN OF IT! GO!
FINE-- BUT HE WON'T LIKE IT.
AND THIS IS WHAT THE HULK WANTS-- TO DIVIDE OUR FORCES--
WE RETAIN THE ADVANTAGE OF NUMBERS, MY FRIEND. AND A SINGLE DISCIPLINED WARRIOR IS ENOUGH--
--AGAINST A RAGING BEAST.
KIMOYO-- ENERGY DAGGERS TO MAXIMUM.
DISCIPLINED, HUH?
HOW'D THAT WORK OUT FOR YOU LAST TIME, YOUR HIGHNESS?
THEN? I OFFERED MERCY.
I ATTEMPTED DIALOGUE.
AND THE HULK TAUGHT ME MY LESSON.
NAARRH!
JUST HOW DEEP HIS INFLUENCE ON MY LIFE RUNS.

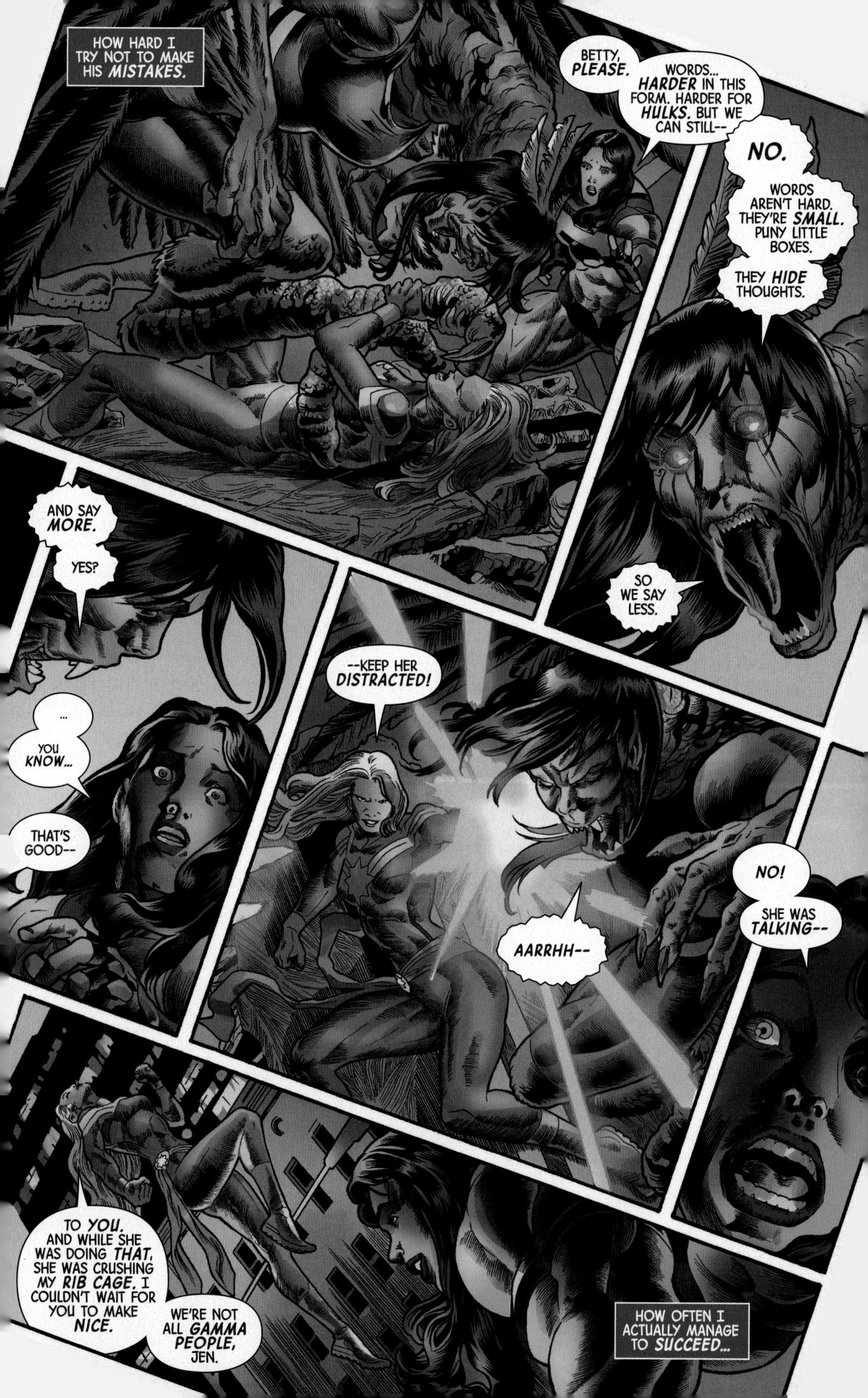
HOW HARD I TRY NOT TO MAKE HIS MISTAKES.
BETTY, PLEASE.
WORDS... HARDER IN THIS FORM. HARDER FOR HULKS. BUT WE CAN STILL--
NO.
WORDS AREN'T HARD. THEY'RE SMALL. PUNY LITTLE BOXES.
THEY HIDE THOUGHTS.
SO WE SAY LESS.
AND SAY MORE.
YES?
...
YOU KNOW...
THAT'S GOOD--
--KEEP HER DISTRACTED!
AARRHH--
NO!
SHE WAS TALKING--
TO YOU. AND WHILE SHE WAS DOING THAT, SHE WAS CRUSHING MY RIB CAGE. I COULDN'T WAIT FOR YOU TO MAKE NICE.
WE'RE NOT ALL GAMMA PEOPLE, JEN.
HOW OFTEN I ACTUALLY MANAGE TO SUCCEED...

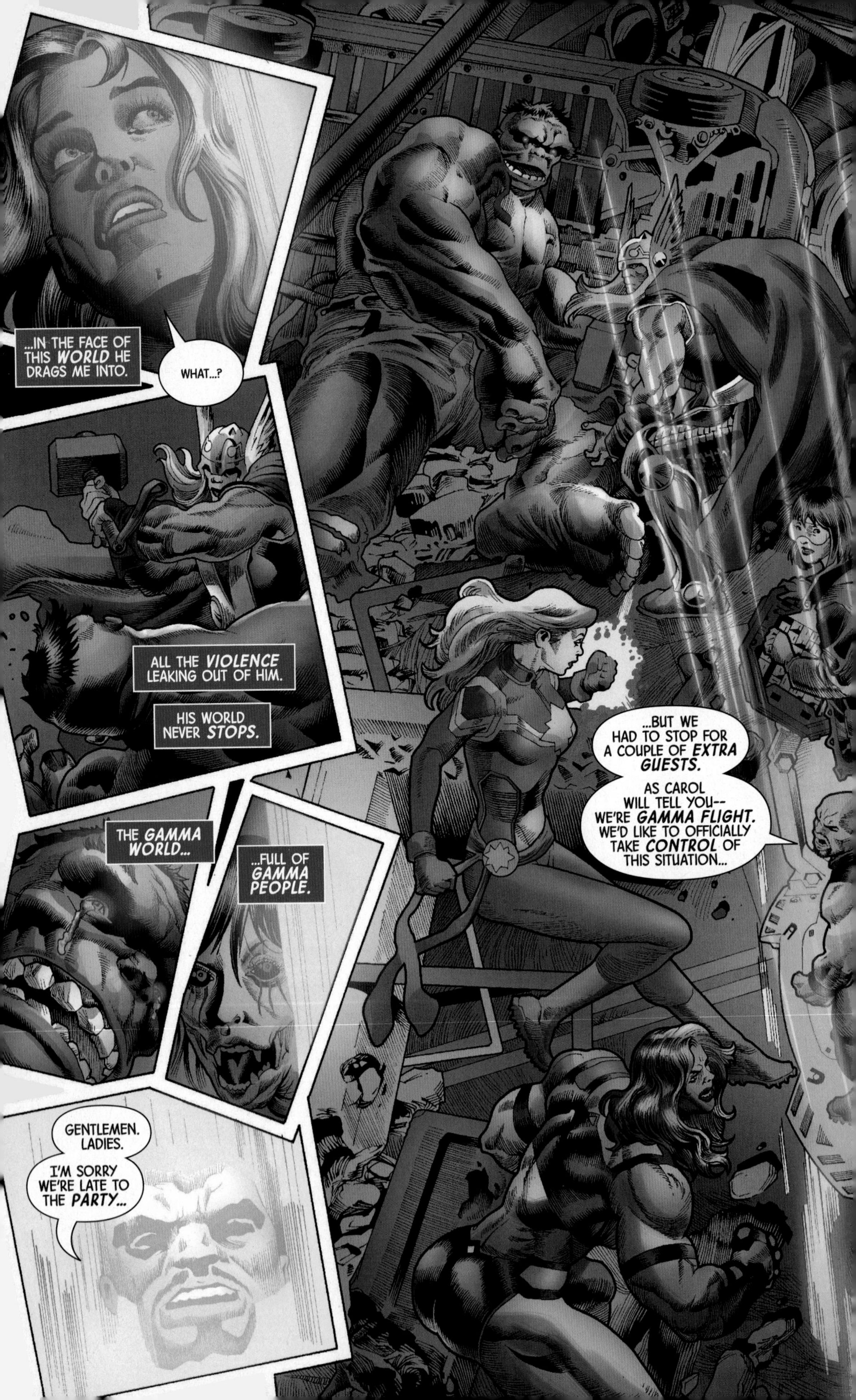

...IN THE FACE OF THIS WORLD HE DRAGS ME INTO.
WHAT...?
ALL THE VIOLENCE LEAKING OUT OF HIM.
HIS WORLD NEVER STOPS.
THE GAMMA WORLD...
...FULL OF GAMMA PEOPLE.
GENTLEMEN. LADIES.
I'M SORRY WE'RE LATE TO THE PARTY...
...BUT WE HAD TO STOP FOR A COUPLE OF EXTRA GUESTS.
AS CAROL WILL TELL YOU-- WE'RE GAMMA FLIGHT. WE'D LIKE TO OFFICIALLY TAKE CONTROL OF THIS SITUATION...

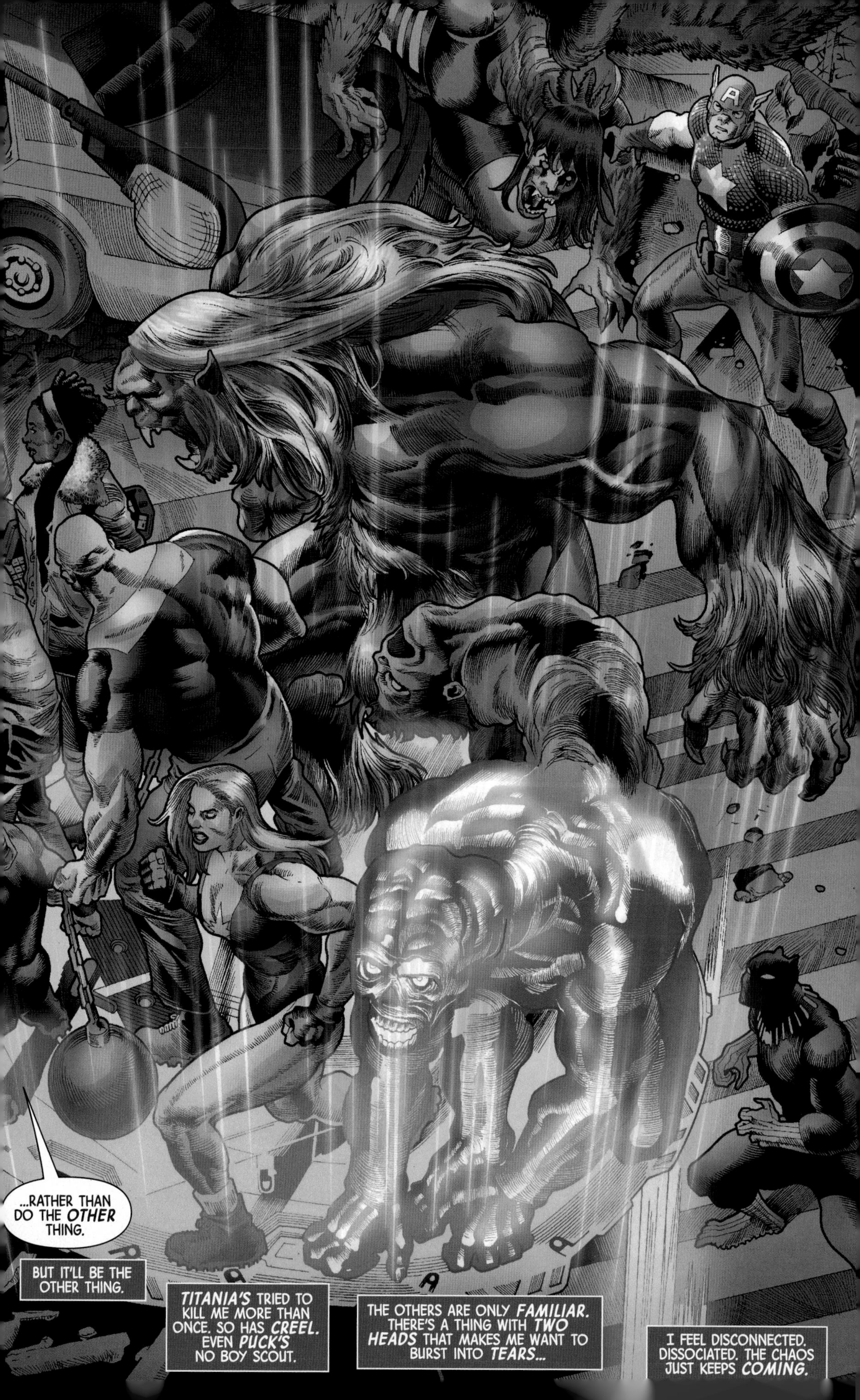
...RATHER THAN DO THE *OTHER* THING.
BUT IT'LL BE THE OTHER THING.
TITANIA'S TRIED TO KILL ME MORE THAN ONCE. SO HAS *CREEL.* EVEN *PUCK'S* NO BOY SCOUT.
THE OTHERS ARE ONLY *FAMILIAR.* THERE'S A THING WITH *TWO HEADS* THAT MAKES ME WANT TO BURST INTO *TEARS...*
I FEEL DISCONNECTED. DISSOCIATED. THE CHAOS JUST KEEPS *COMING.*

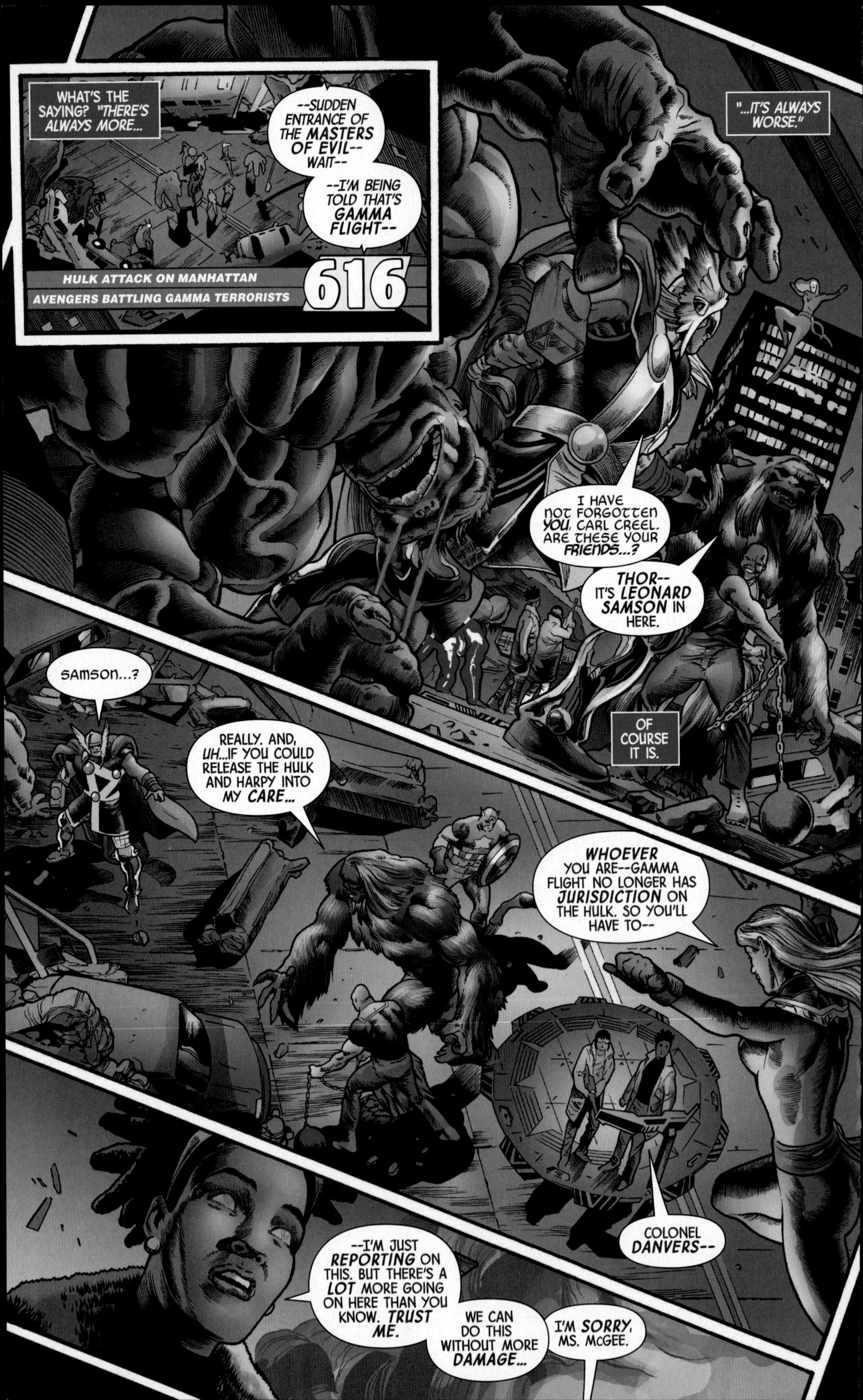
WHAT'S THE SAYING? "THERE'S ALWAYS MORE...
--SUDDEN ENTRANCE OF THE MASTERS OF EVIL-- WAIT--
--I'M BEING TOLD THAT'S GAMMA FLIGHT--
HULK ATTACK ON MANHATTAN
AVENGERS BATTLING GAMMA TERRORISTS
616
"...IT'S ALWAYS WORSE."
I HAVE NOT FORGOTTEN YOU, CARL CREEL. ARE THESE YOUR FRIENDS...?
THOR-- IT'S LEONARD SAMSON IN HERE.
OF COURSE IT IS.
SAMSON...?
REALLY. AND, UH...IF YOU COULD RELEASE THE HULK AND HARPY INTO MY CARE...
WHOEVER YOU ARE--GAMMA FLIGHT NO LONGER HAS JURISDICTION ON THE HULK. SO YOU'LL HAVE TO--
COLONEL DANVERS--
--I'M JUST REPORTING ON THIS. BUT THERE'S A LOT MORE GOING ON HERE THAN YOU KNOW. TRUST ME.
WE CAN DO THIS WITHOUT MORE DAMAGE...
I'M SORRY, MS. McGEE.

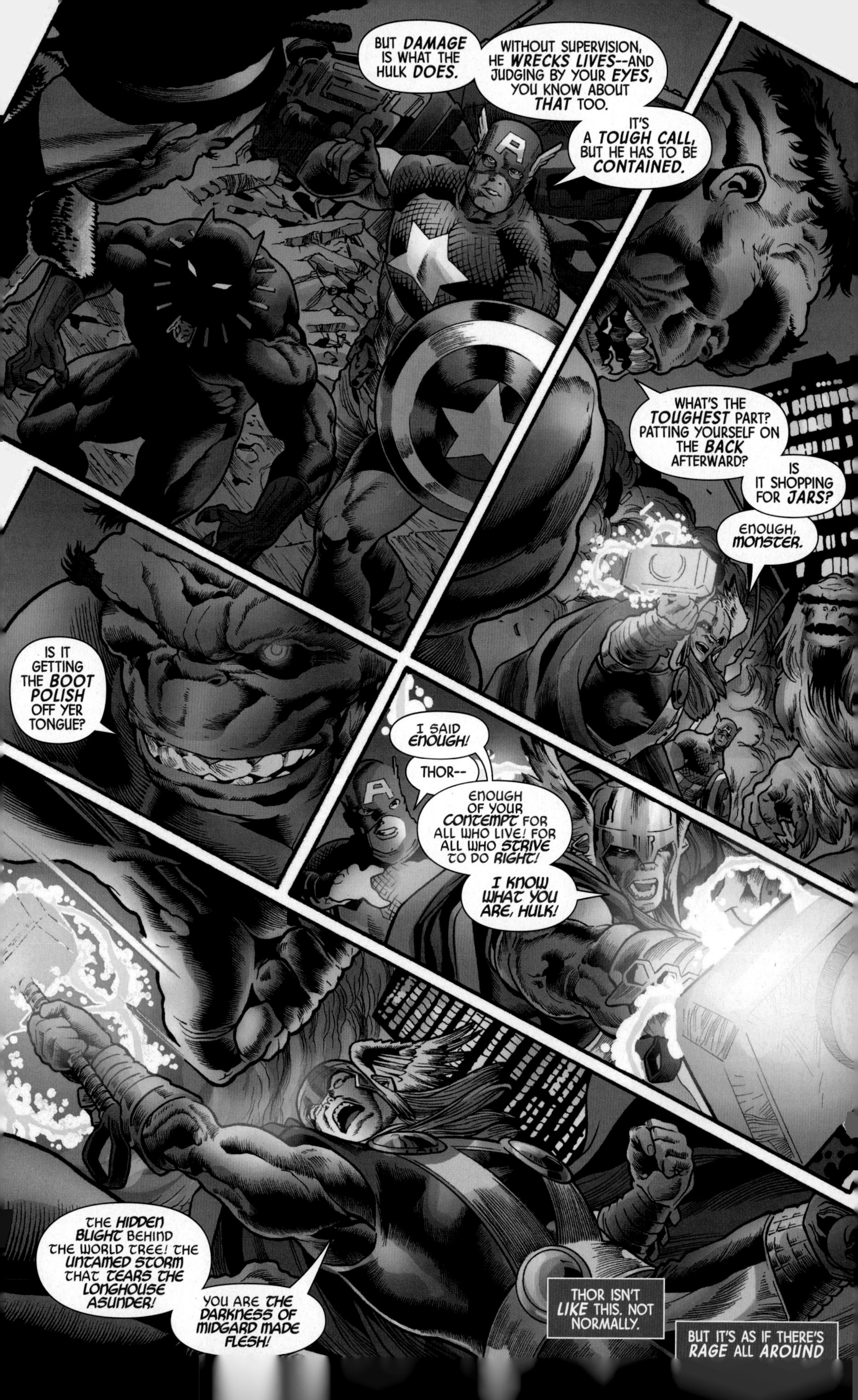
BUT DAMAGE IS WHAT THE HULK DOES.
WITHOUT SUPERVISION, HE WRECKS LIVES--AND JUDGING BY YOUR EYES, YOU KNOW ABOUT THAT TOO.
IT'S A TOUGH CALL, BUT HE HAS TO BE CONTAINED.
WHAT'S THE TOUGHEST PART? PATTING YOURSELF ON THE BACK AFTERWARD?
IS IT SHOPPING FOR JARS?
ENOUGH, MONSTER.
IS IT GETTING THE BOOT POLISH OFF YER TONGUE?
I SAID ENOUGH!
THOR--
ENOUGH OF YOUR CONTEMPT FOR ALL WHO LIVE! FOR ALL WHO STRIVE TO DO RIGHT!
I KNOW WHAT YOU ARE, HULK!
THE HIDDEN BLIGHT BEHIND THE WORLD TREE! THE UNTAMED STORM THAT TEARS THE LONGHOUSE ASUNDER!
YOU ARE THE DARKNESS OF MIDGARD MADE FLESH!
THOR ISN'T LIKE THIS. NOT NORMALLY.
BUT IT'S AS IF THERE'S RAGE ALL AROUND

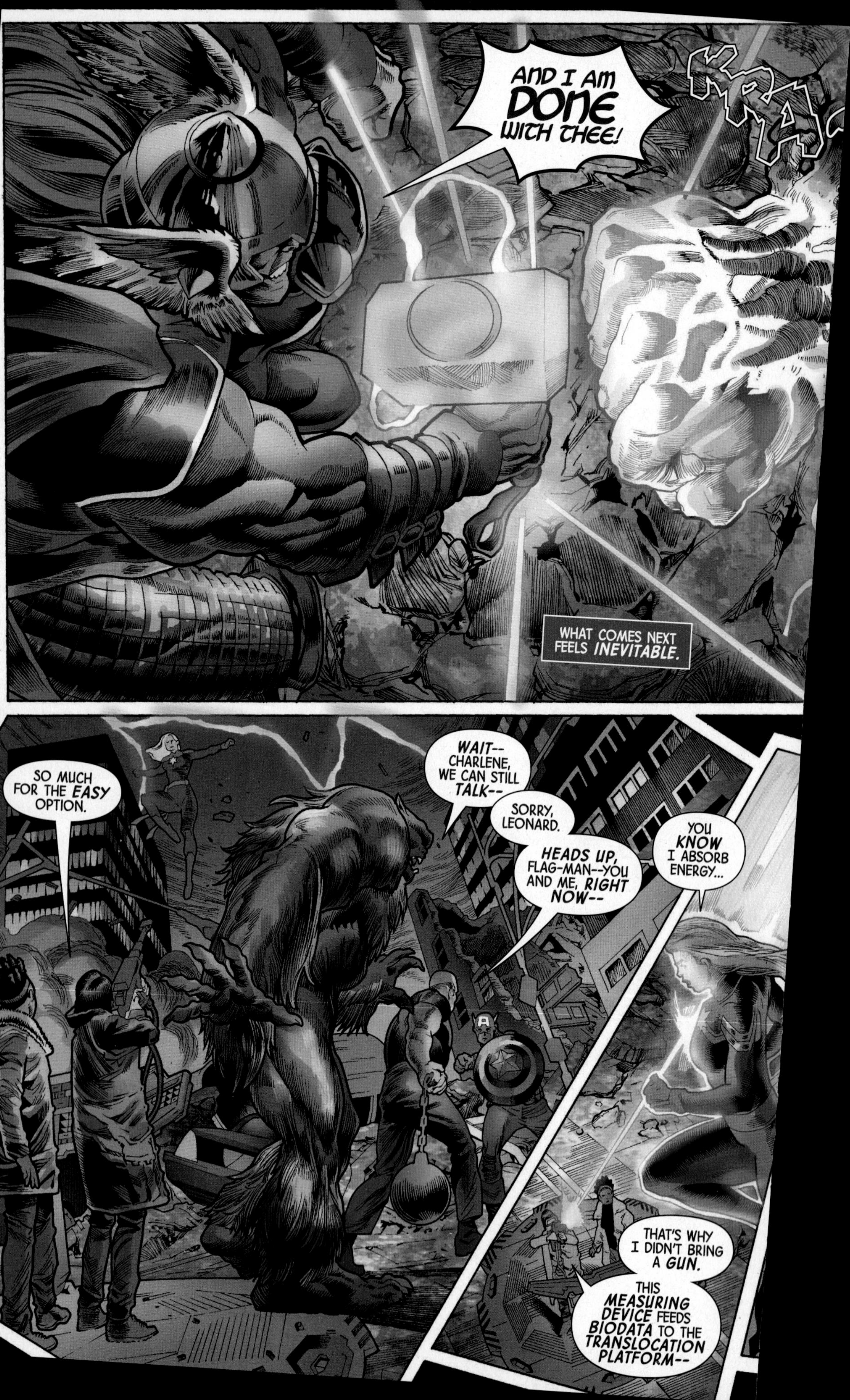
AND I AM DONE WITH THEE!
KRA...
WHAT COMES NEXT FEELS INEVITABLE.
SO MUCH FOR THE EASY OPTION.
WAIT-- CHARLENE, WE CAN STILL TALK--
SORRY, LEONARD.
HEADS UP, FLAG-MAN--YOU AND ME, RIGHT NOW--
YOU KNOW I ABSORB ENERGY...
THAT'S WHY I DIDN'T BRING A GUN.
THIS MEASURING DEVICE FEEDS BIODATA TO THE TRANSLOCATION PLATFORM--

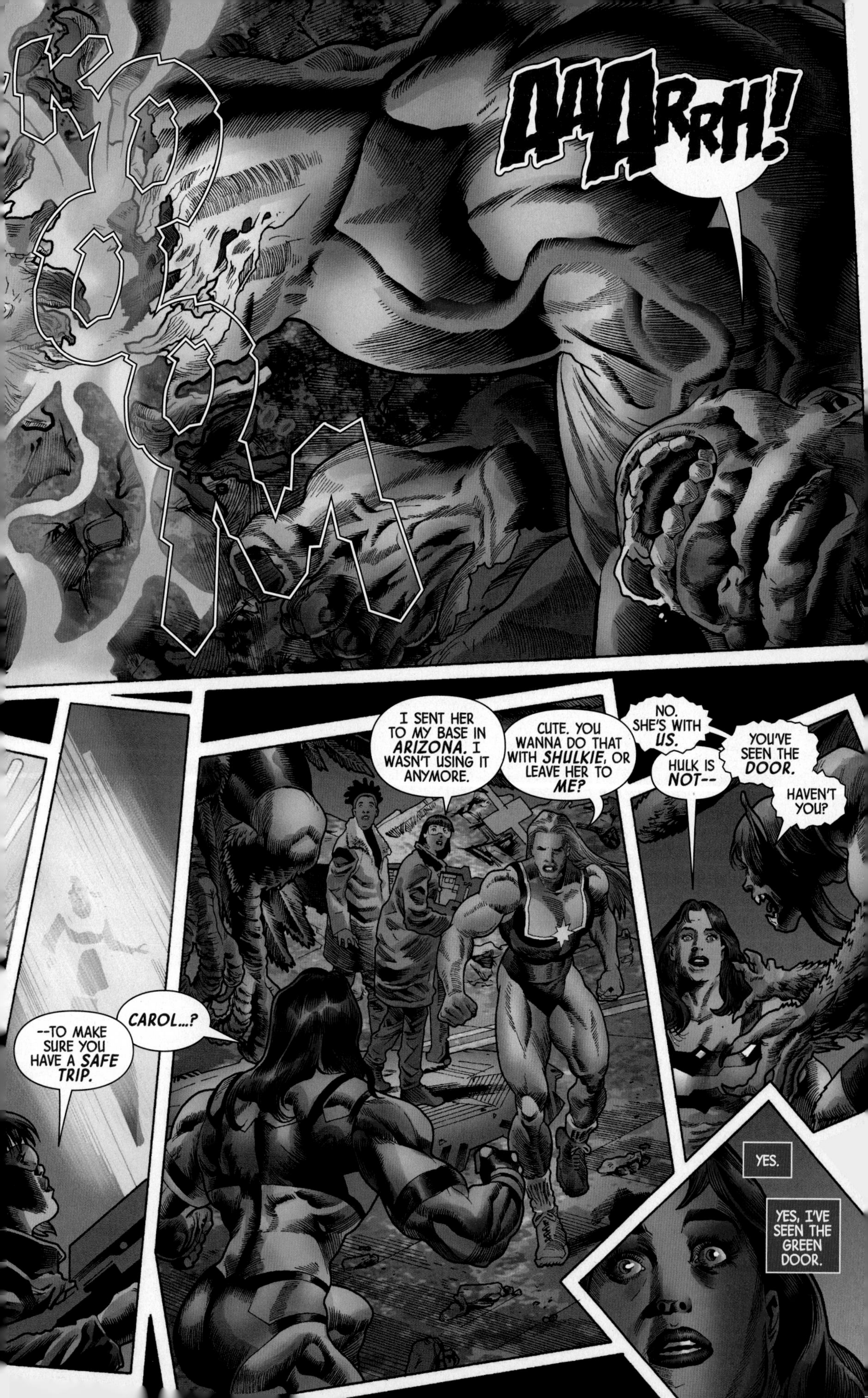
KRUMM
AAARRRH!
--TO MAKE SURE YOU HAVE A SAFE TRIP.
CAROL...?
I SENT HER TO MY BASE IN ARIZONA. I WASN'T USING IT ANYMORE.
CUTE. YOU WANNA DO THAT WITH SHULKIE, OR LEAVE HER TO ME?
NO. SHE'S WITH US.
HULK IS NOT--
YOU'VE SEEN THE DOOR.
HAVEN'T YOU?
YES.
YES, I'VE SEEN THE GREEN DOOR.

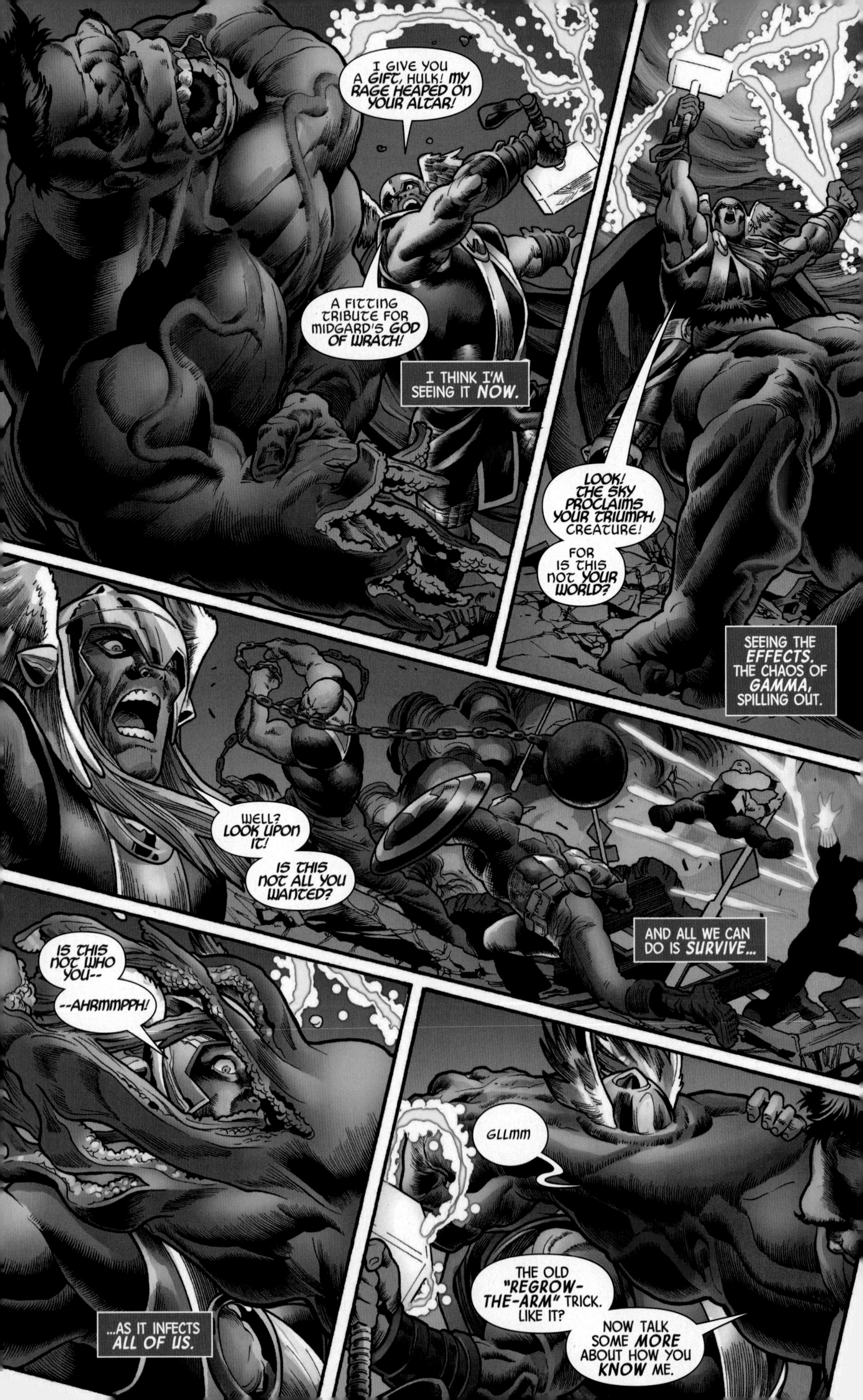
I GIVE YOU A GIFT, HULK! MY RAGE HEAPED ON YOUR ALTAR!
A FITTING TRIBUTE FOR MIDGARD'S GOD OF WRATH!
I THINK I'M SEEING IT NOW.
LOOK! THE SKY PROCLAIMS YOUR TRIUMPH, CREATURE!
FOR IS THIS NOT YOUR WORLD?
SEEING THE EFFECTS. THE CHAOS OF GAMMA, SPILLING OUT.
WELL? LOOK UPON IT!
IS THIS NOT ALL YOU WANTED?
AND ALL WE CAN DO IS SURVIVE...
IS THIS NOT WHO YOU--
--AHRMMPPH!
...AS IT INFECTS ALL OF US.
GLLMM
THE OLD "REGROW-THE-ARM" TRICK. LIKE IT?
NOW TALK SOME MORE ABOUT HOW YOU KNOW ME.

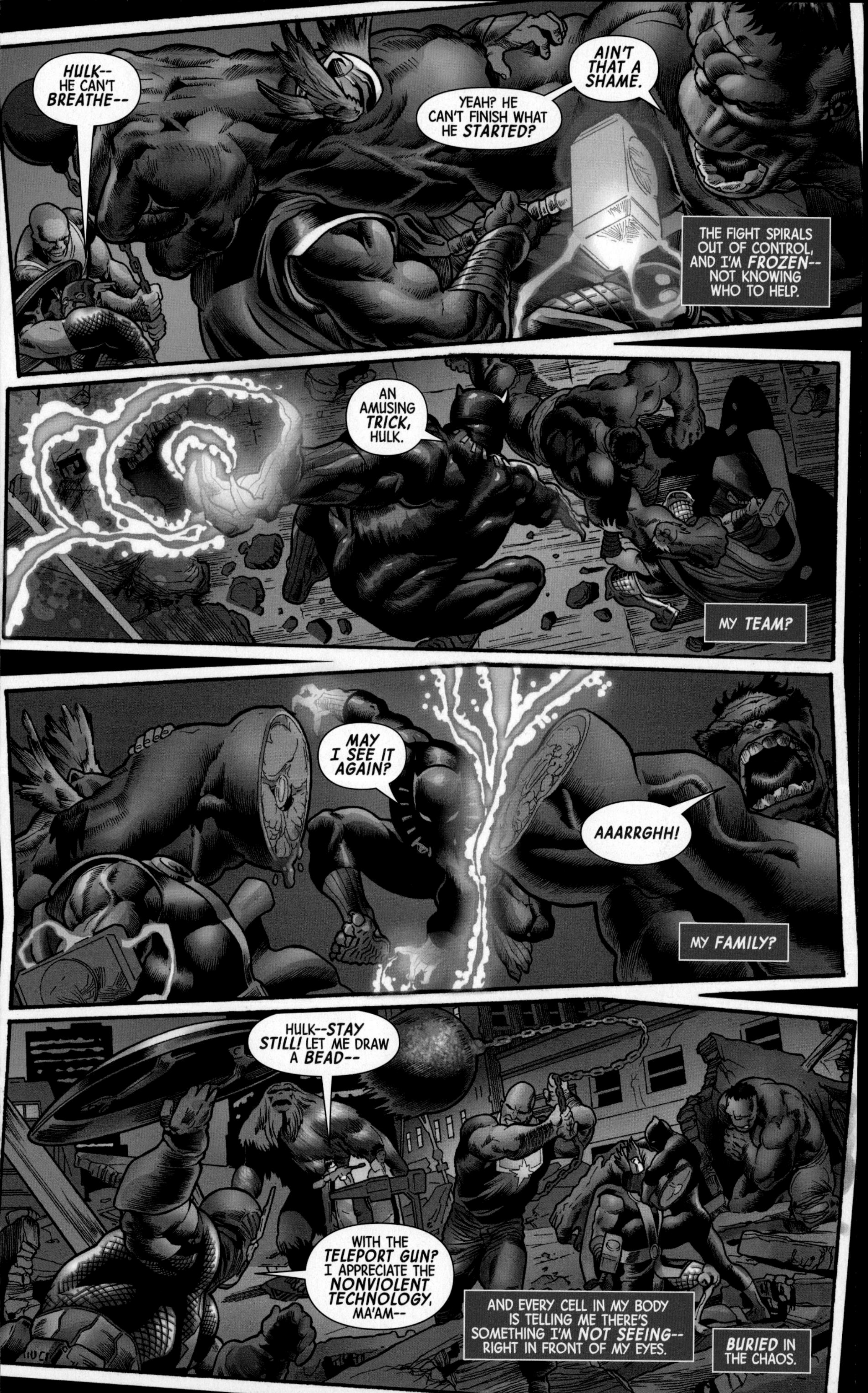
HULK-- HE CAN'T BREATHE--
YEAH? HE CAN'T FINISH WHAT HE STARTED?
AIN'T THAT A SHAME.
THE FIGHT SPIRALS OUT OF CONTROL, AND I'M FROZEN-- NOT KNOWING WHO TO HELP.
AN AMUSING TRICK, HULK.
MY TEAM?
MAY I SEE IT AGAIN?
AAARRGHH!
MY FAMILY?
HULK--STAY STILL! LET ME DRAW A BEAD--
WITH THE TELEPORT GUN? I APPRECIATE THE NONVIOLENT TECHNOLOGY, MA'AM--
AND EVERY CELL IN MY BODY IS TELLING ME THERE'S SOMETHING I'M NOT SEEING-- RIGHT IN FRONT OF MY EYES.
BURIED IN THE CHAOS.

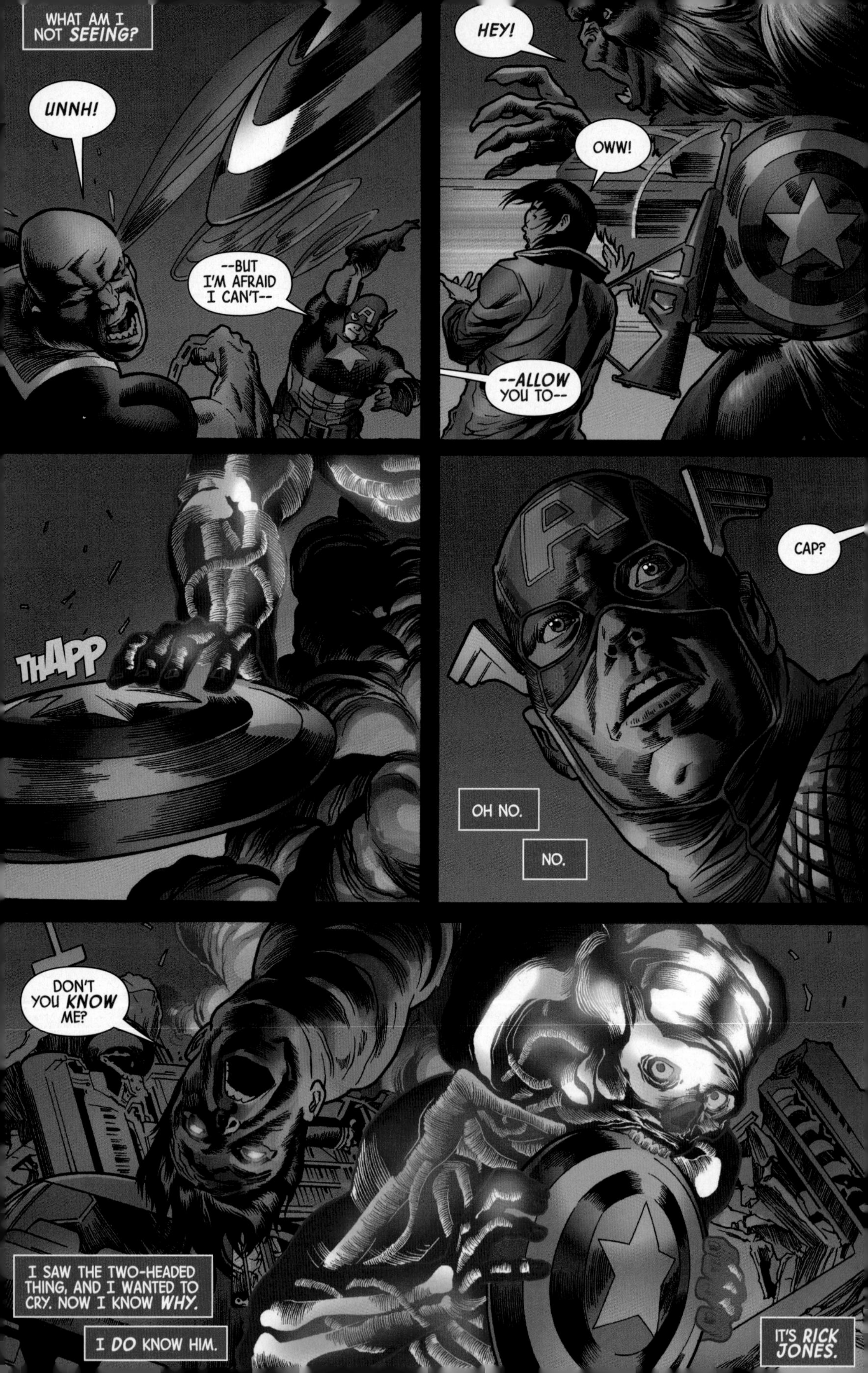

WHAT AM I NOT SEEING?
UNNH!
--BUT I'M AFRAID I CAN'T--
HEY!
OWW!
--ALLOW YOU TO--
THAPP
CAP?
OH NO.
NO.
DON'T YOU KNOW ME?
I SAW THE TWO-HEADED THING, AND I WANTED TO CRY. NOW I KNOW WHY.
I DO KNOW HIM.
IT'S RICK JONES.

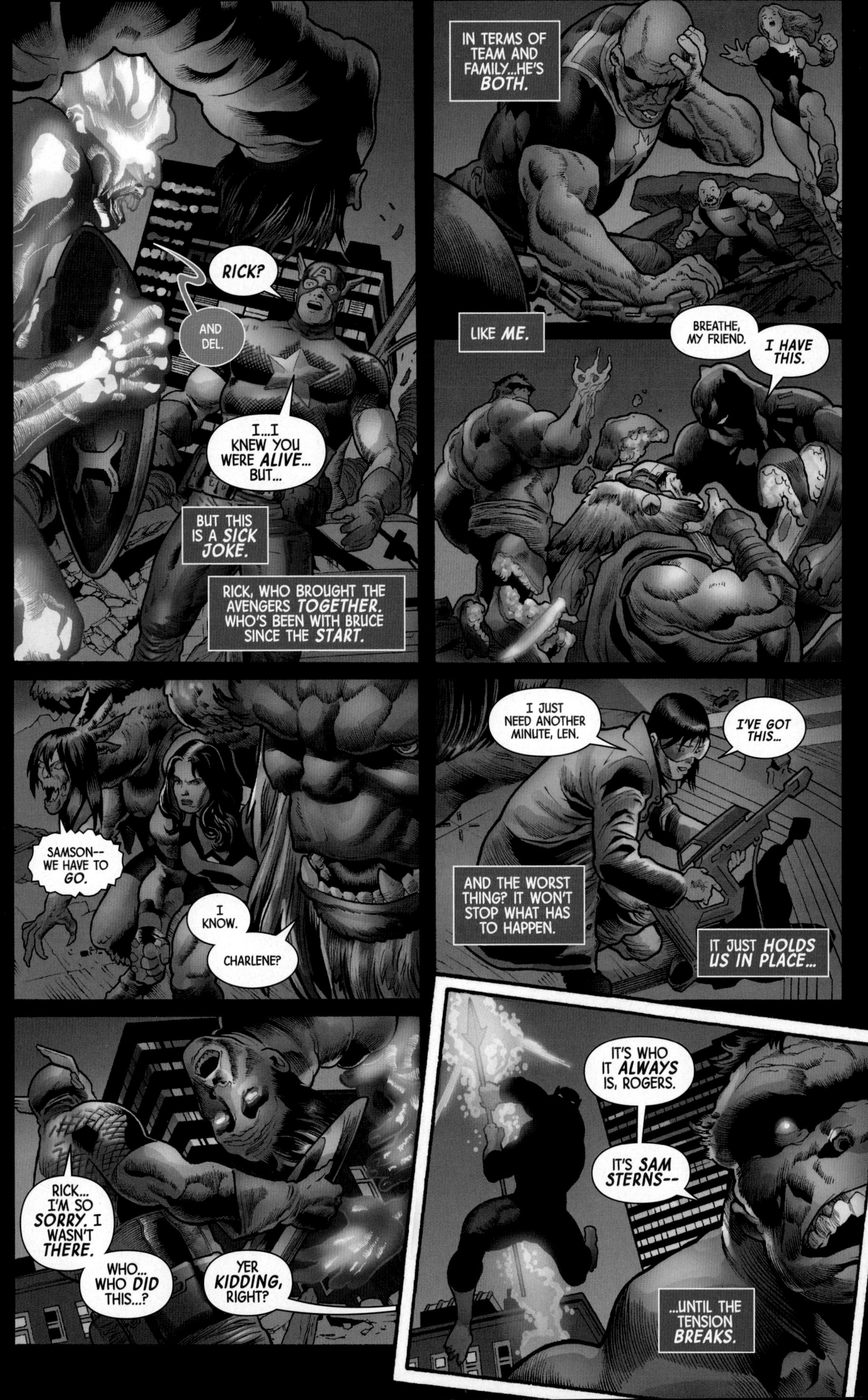
RICK?
AND DEL.
I...I KNEW YOU WERE ALIVE... BUT...
BUT THIS IS A SICK JOKE.
RICK, WHO BROUGHT THE AVENGERS TOGETHER. WHO'S BEEN WITH BRUCE SINCE THE START.
IN TERMS OF TEAM AND FAMILY...HE'S BOTH.
LIKE ME.
BREATHE, MY FRIEND.
I HAVE THIS.
SAMSON-- WE HAVE TO GO.
I KNOW.
CHARLENE?
I JUST NEED ANOTHER MINUTE, LEN.
I'VE GOT THIS...
AND THE WORST THING? IT WON'T STOP WHAT HAS TO HAPPEN.
IT JUST HOLDS US IN PLACE...
RICK... I'M SO SORRY. I WASN'T THERE.
WHO... WHO DID THIS...?
YER KIDDING, RIGHT?
IT'S WHO IT ALWAYS IS, ROGERS.
IT'S SAM STERNS--
...UNTIL THE TENSION BREAKS.

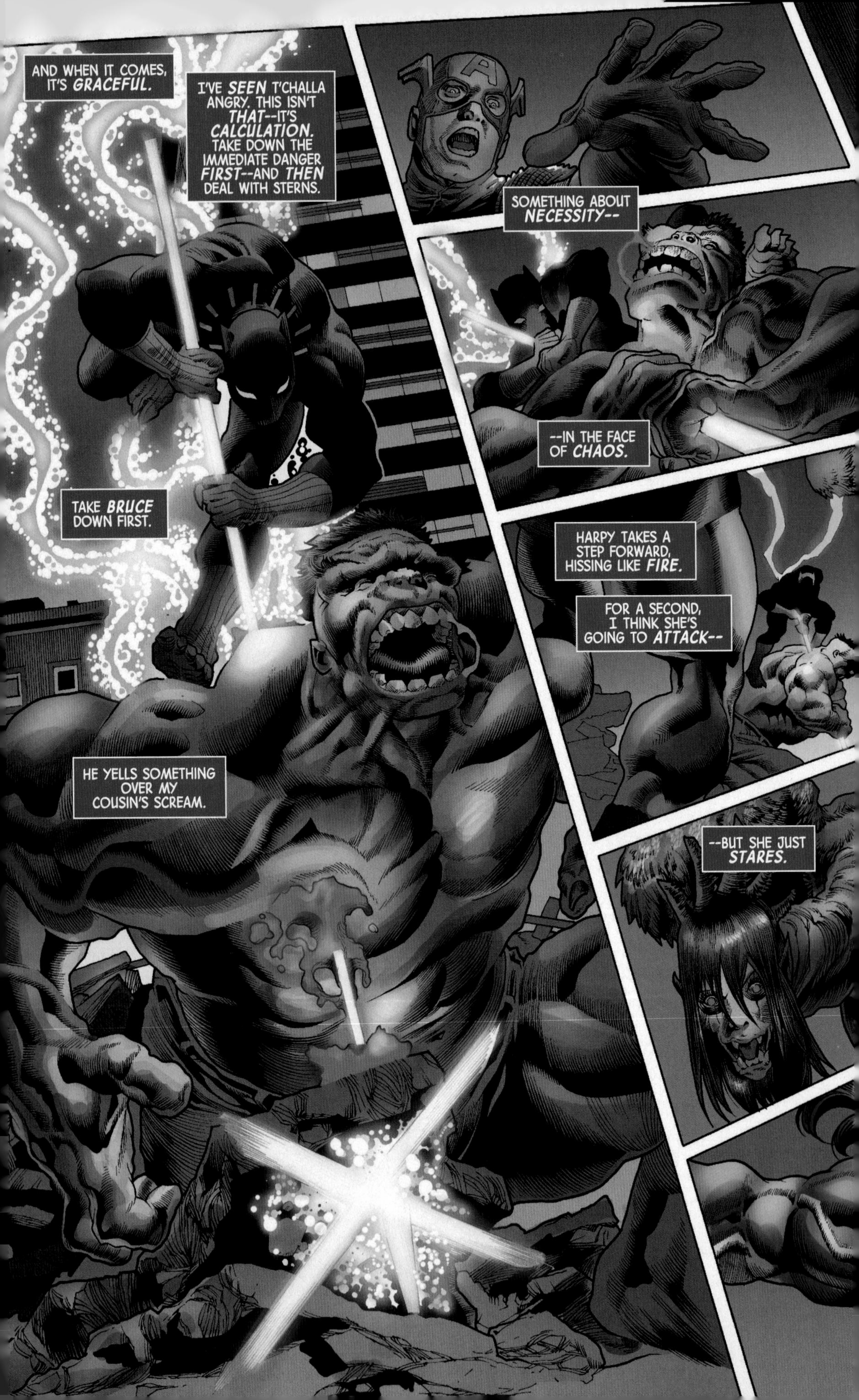

AND WHEN IT COMES, IT'S *GRACEFUL.*
I'VE *SEEN* T'CHALLA ANGRY. THIS ISN'T *THAT*--IT'S *CALCULATION.* TAKE DOWN THE IMMEDIATE DANGER *FIRST*--AND *THEN* DEAL WITH STERNS.
TAKE *BRUCE* DOWN FIRST.
HE YELLS SOMETHING OVER MY COUSIN'S SCREAM.
SOMETHING ABOUT *NECESSITY*--
--IN THE FACE OF *CHAOS.*
HARPY TAKES A STEP FORWARD, HISSING LIKE *FIRE.*
FOR A SECOND, I THINK SHE'S GOING TO *ATTACK*--
--BUT SHE JUST *STARES.*

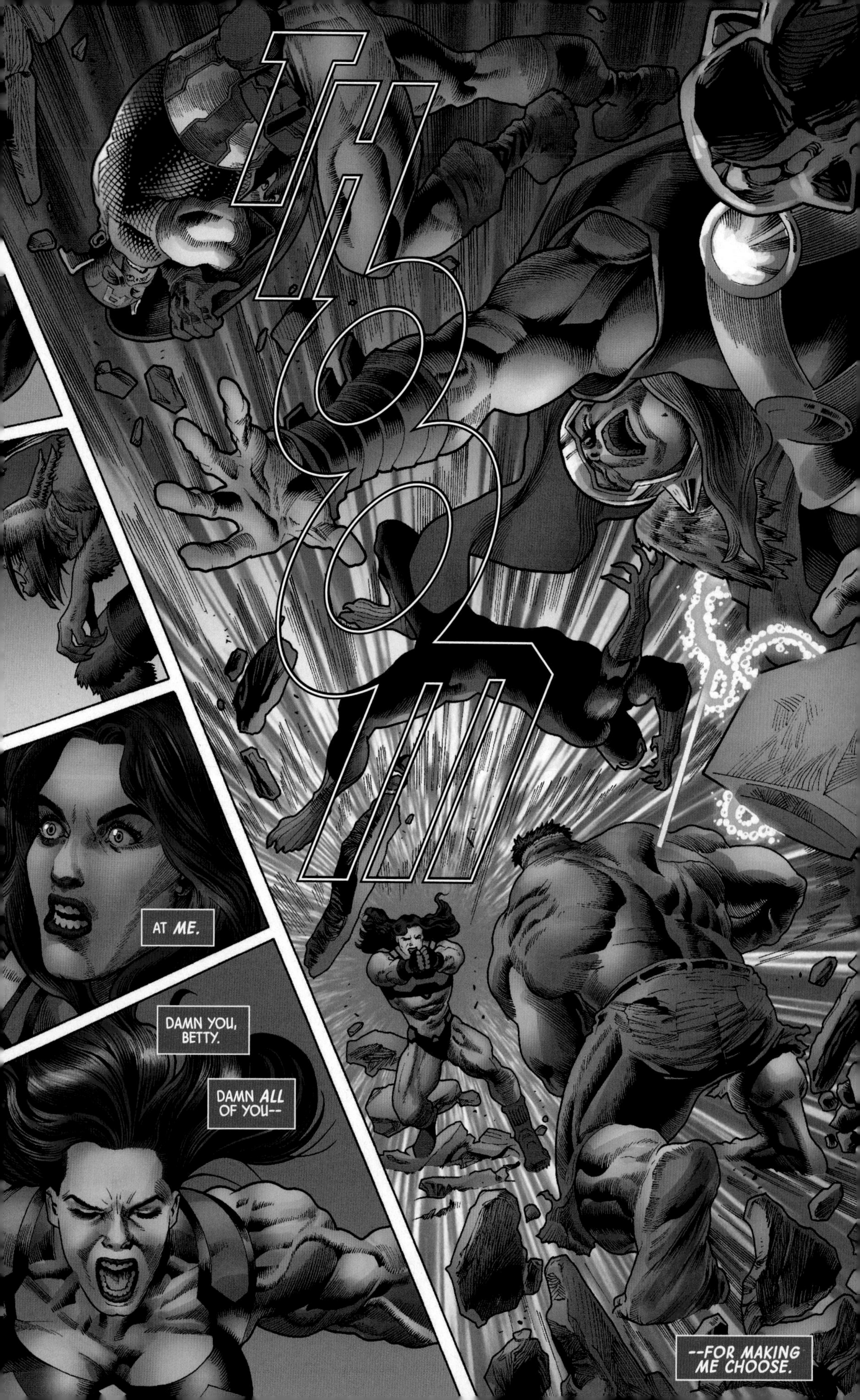
THOOM
AT ME.
DAMN YOU, BETTY.
DAMN ALL OF YOU--
--FOR MAKING ME CHOOSE.

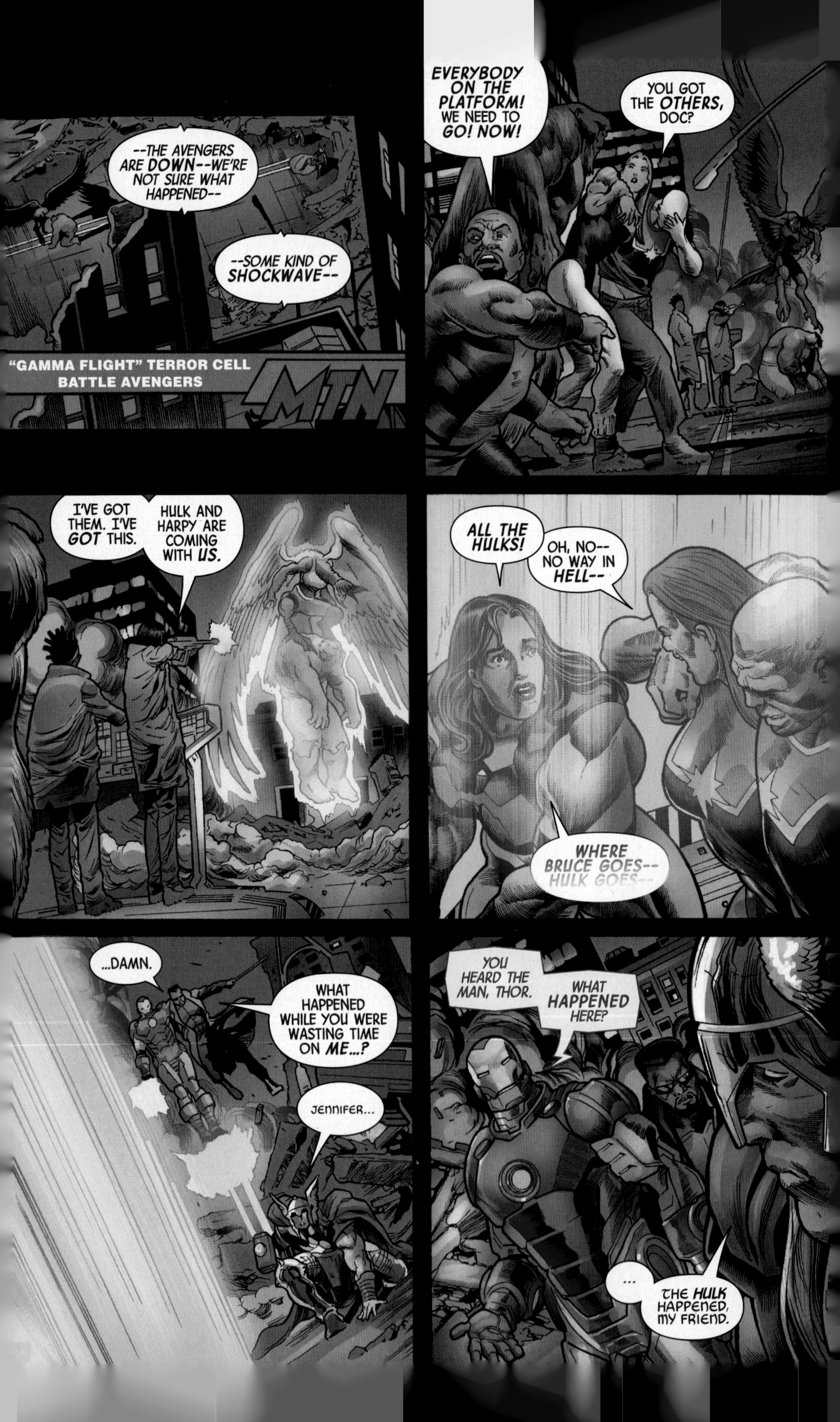
--THE AVENGERS ARE DOWN--WE'RE NOT SURE WHAT HAPPENED--
--SOME KIND OF SHOCKWAVE--
"GAMMA FLIGHT" TERROR CELL BATTLE AVENGERS
MTN
EVERYBODY ON THE PLATFORM! WE NEED TO GO! NOW!
YOU GOT THE OTHERS, DOC?
I'VE GOT THEM. I'VE GOT THIS.
HULK AND HARPY ARE COMING WITH US.
ALL THE HULKS!
OH, NO-- NO WAY IN HELL--
WHERE BRUCE GOES-- HULK GOES--
...DAMN.
WHAT HAPPENED WHILE YOU WERE WASTING TIME ON ME...?
JENNIFER...
YOU HEARD THE MAN, THOR.
WHAT HAPPENED HERE?
...
THE HULK HAPPENED, MY FRIEND.

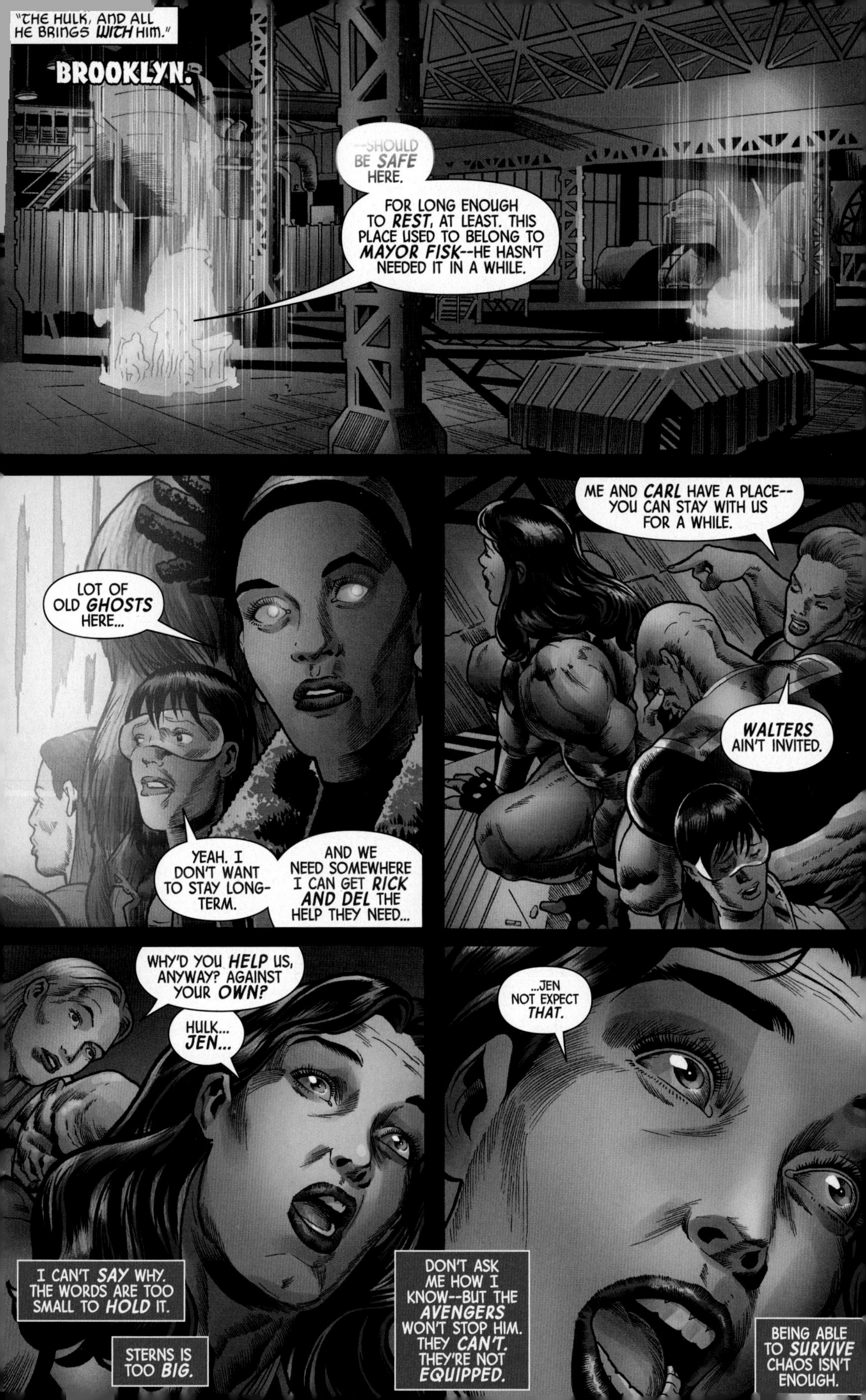
"THE HULK, AND ALL HE BRINGS WITH HIM."
BROOKLYN.
--SHOULD BE SAFE HERE.
FOR LONG ENOUGH TO REST, AT LEAST. THIS PLACE USED TO BELONG TO MAYOR FISK--HE HASN'T NEEDED IT IN A WHILE.
LOT OF OLD GHOSTS HERE...
YEAH. I DON'T WANT TO STAY LONG-TERM.
AND WE NEED SOMEWHERE I CAN GET RICK AND DEL THE HELP THEY NEED...
ME AND CARL HAVE A PLACE--YOU CAN STAY WITH US FOR A WHILE.
WALTERS AIN'T INVITED.
WHY'D YOU HELP US, ANYWAY? AGAINST YOUR OWN?
HULK... JEN...
I CAN'T SAY WHY. THE WORDS ARE TOO SMALL TO HOLD IT.
STERNS IS TOO BIG.
...JEN NOT EXPECT THAT.
DON'T ASK ME HOW I KNOW--BUT THE AVENGERS WON'T STOP HIM. THEY CAN'T. THEY'RE NOT EQUIPPED.
BEING ABLE TO SURVIVE CHAOS ISN'T ENOUGH.

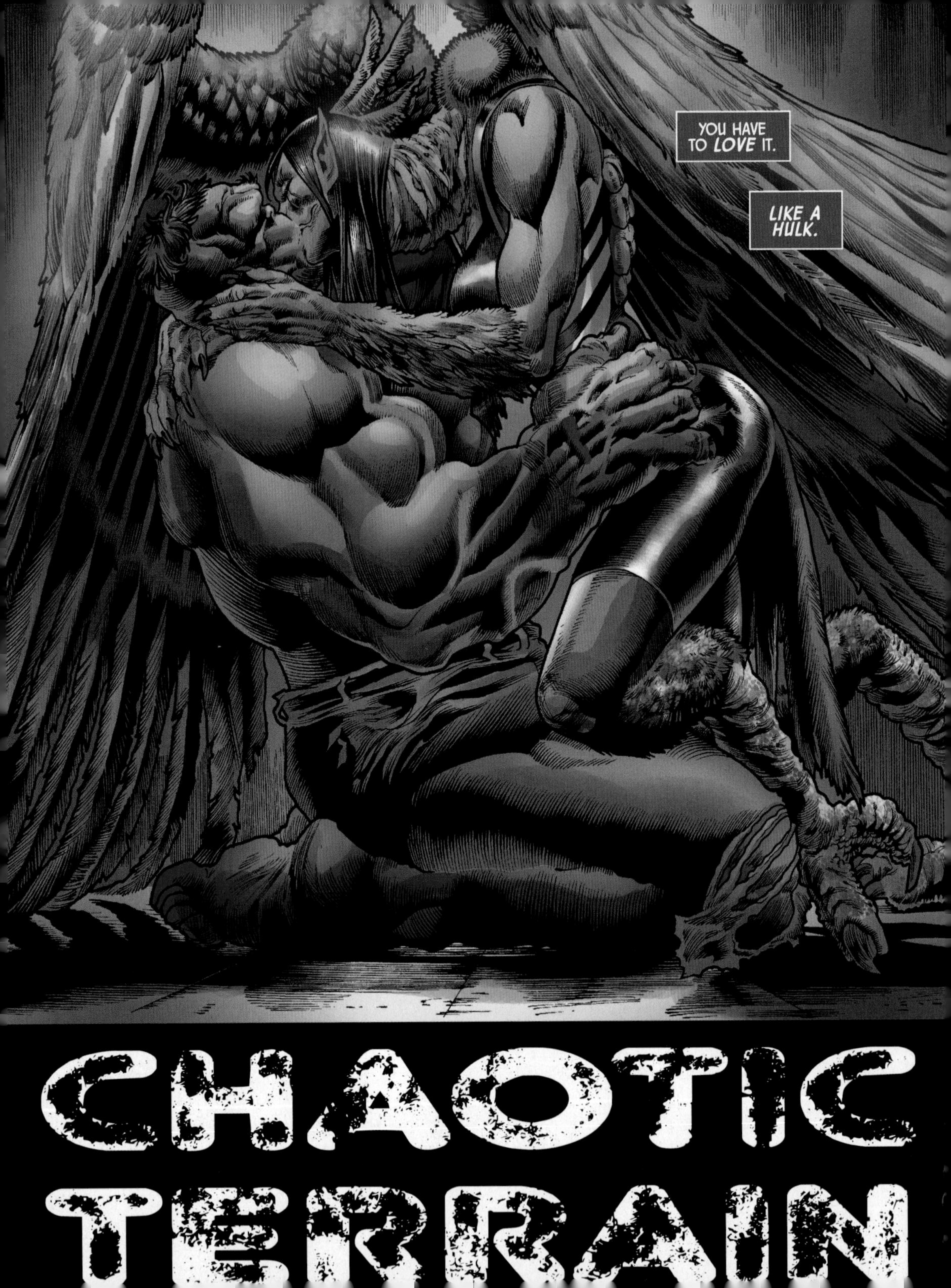
YOU HAVE TO LOVE IT.
LIKE A HULK.
CHAOTIC TERRAIN

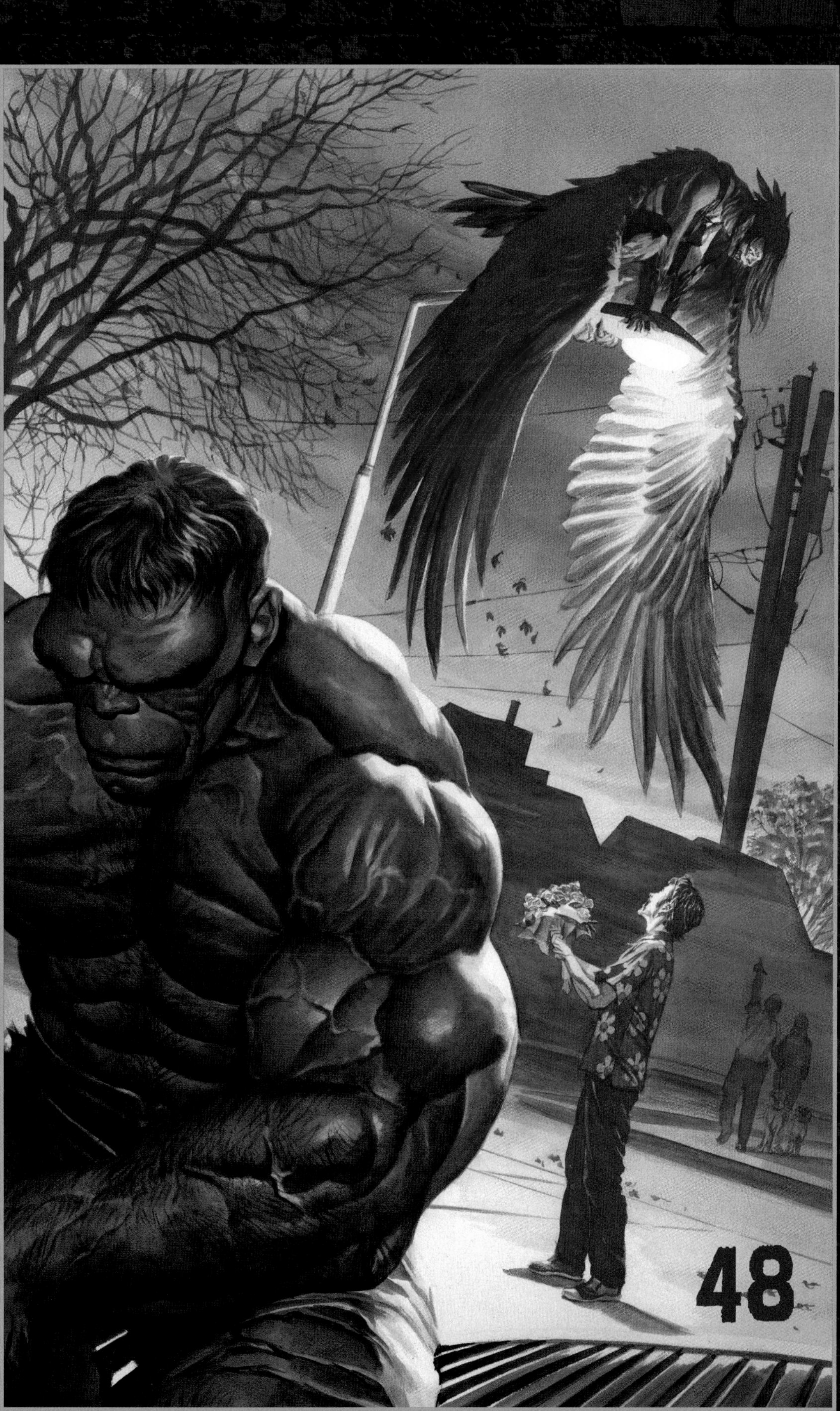
48

"AND I DREAM OF A GRAVE, DEEP AND NARROW, WHERE WE COULD CLASP EACH OTHER IN OUR ARMS AS WITH IRON BARS, AND I WOULD HIDE MY FACE IN YOU AND YOU WOULD HIDE YOUR FACE IN ME, AND NOBODY WOULD EVER SEE US ANY MORE."

— FRANZ KAFKA,
THE CASTLE

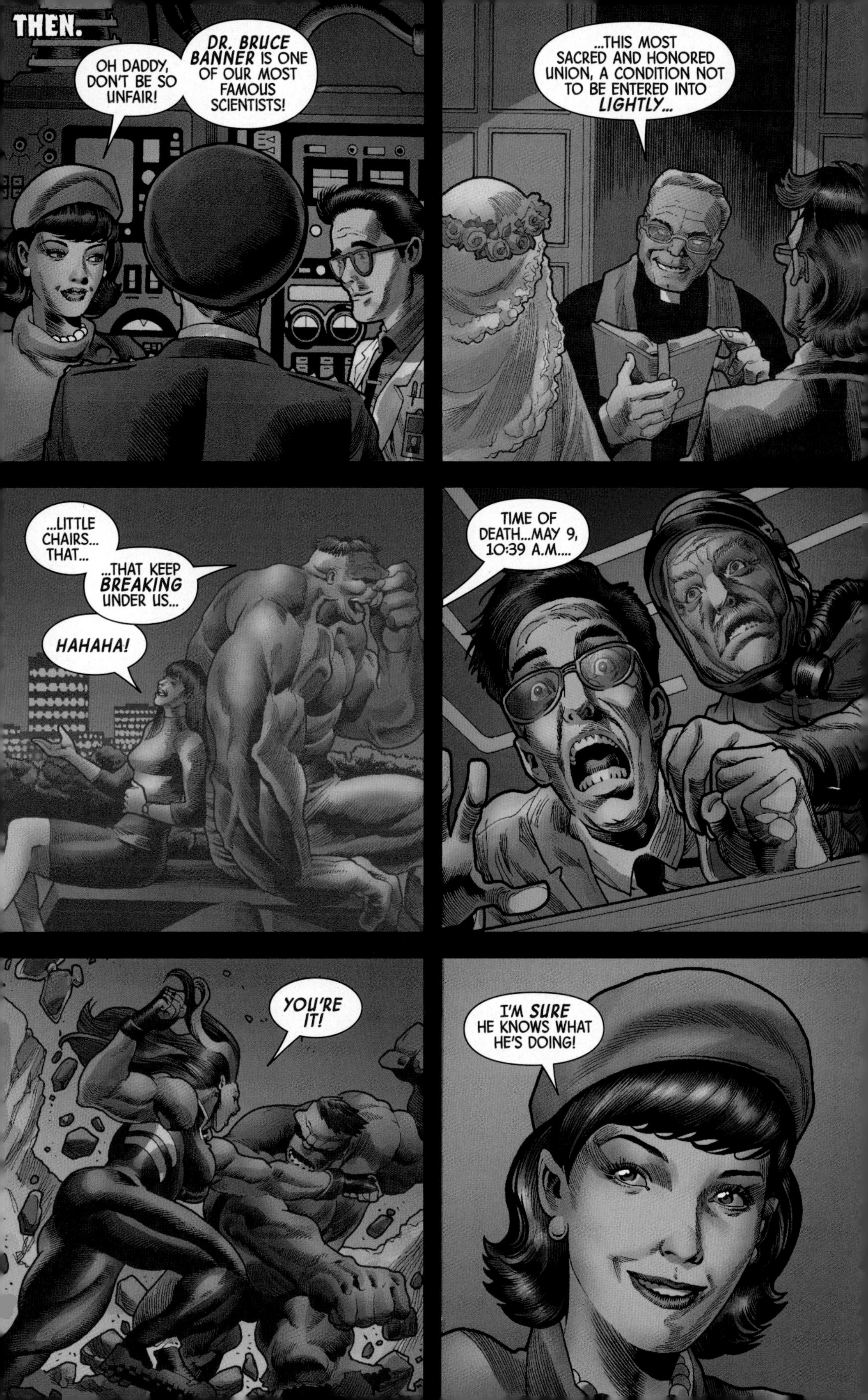
THEN.
OH DADDY, DON'T BE SO UNFAIR!
DR. BRUCE BANNER IS ONE OF OUR MOST FAMOUS SCIENTISTS!
...THIS MOST SACRED AND HONORED UNION, A CONDITION NOT TO BE ENTERED INTO LIGHTLY...
...LITTLE CHAIRS... THAT...
...THAT KEEP BREAKING UNDER US...
HAHAHA!
TIME OF DEATH...MAY 9, 10:39 A.M....
YOU'RE IT!
I'M SURE HE KNOWS WHAT HE'S DOING!

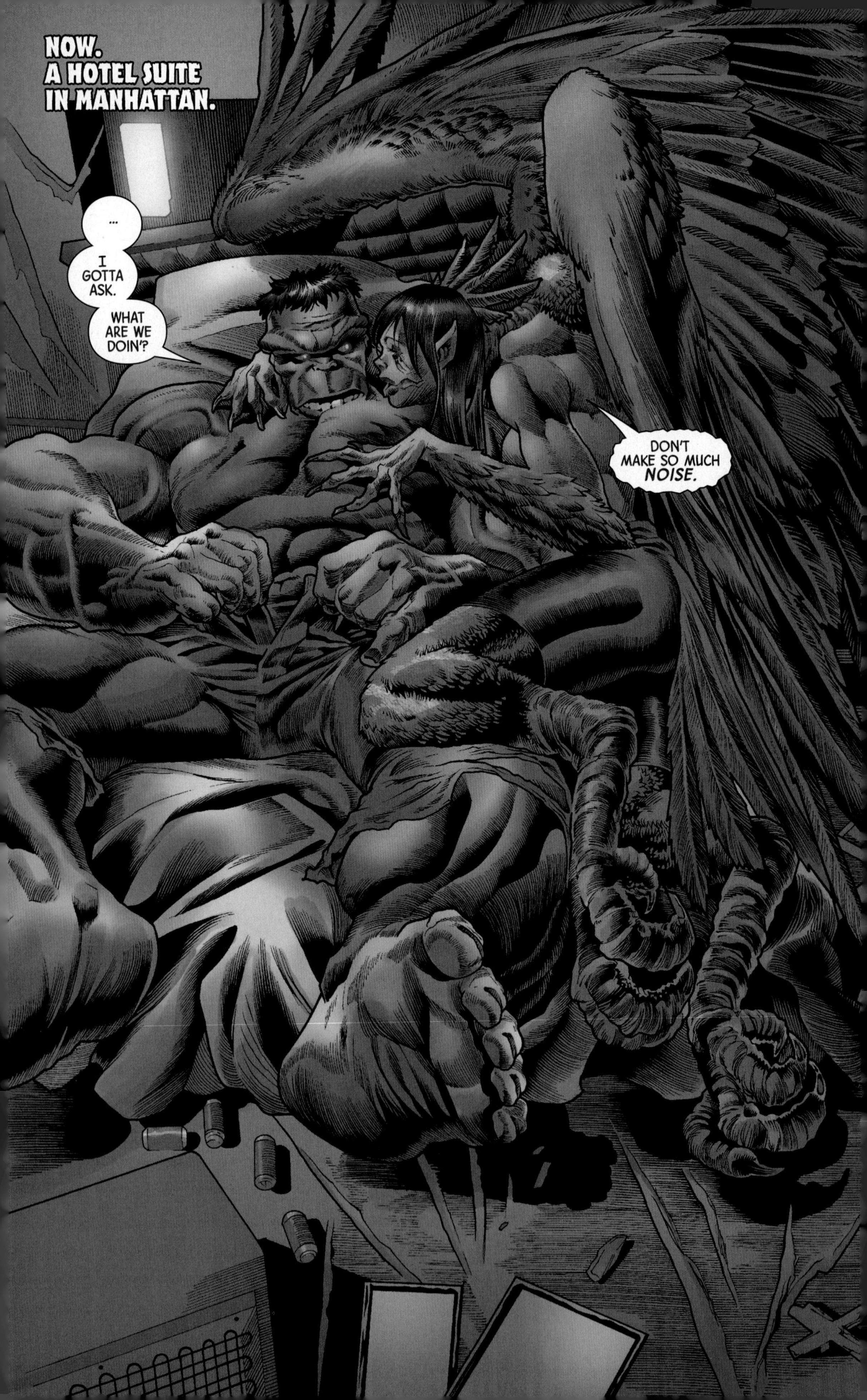
NOW.
A HOTEL SUITE IN MANHATTAN.
...
I GOTTA ASK.
WHAT ARE WE DOIN'?
DON'T MAKE SO MUCH NOISE.

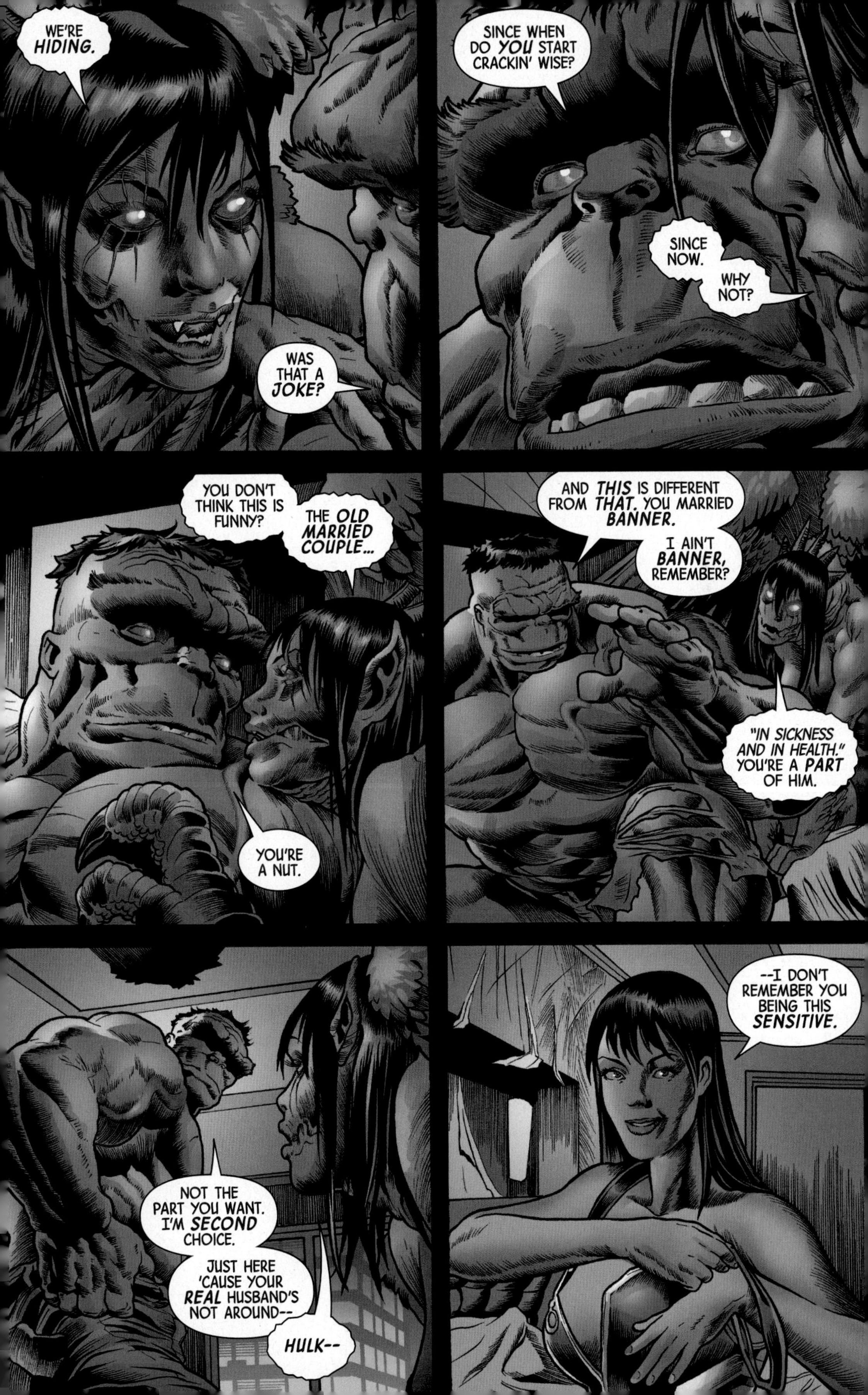
WE'RE HIDING.
WAS THAT A JOKE?
SINCE WHEN DO YOU START CRACKIN' WISE?
SINCE NOW.
WHY NOT?
YOU DON'T THINK THIS IS FUNNY?
THE OLD MARRIED COUPLE...
YOU'RE A NUT.
AND THIS IS DIFFERENT FROM THAT. YOU MARRIED BANNER.
I AIN'T BANNER, REMEMBER?
"IN SICKNESS AND IN HEALTH." YOU'RE A PART OF HIM.
NOT THE PART YOU WANT. I'M SECOND CHOICE.
JUST HERE 'CAUSE YOUR REAL HUSBAND'S NOT AROUND--
HULK--
--I DON'T REMEMBER YOU BEING THIS SENSITIVE.

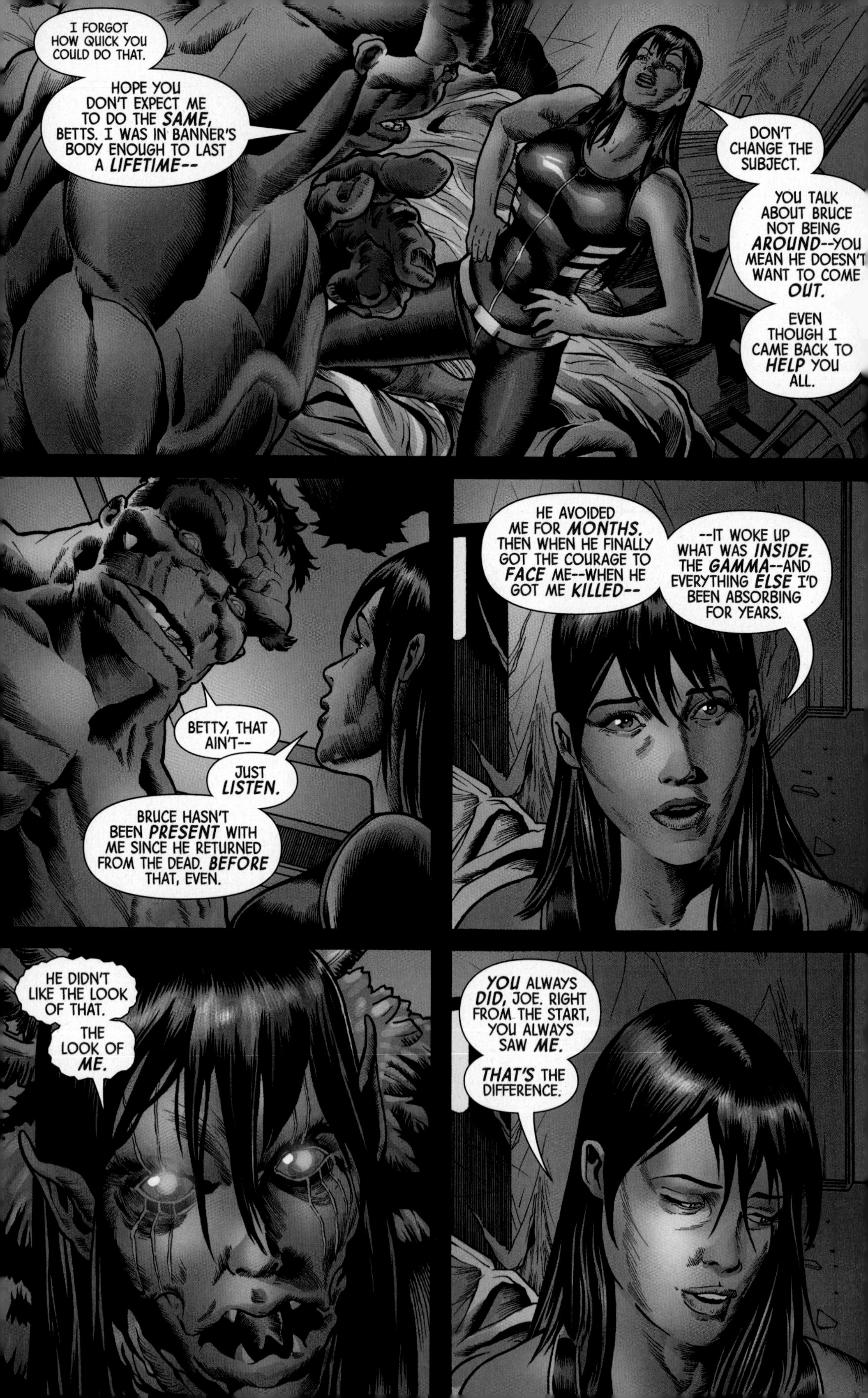
I FORGOT HOW QUICK YOU COULD DO THAT.
HOPE YOU DON'T EXPECT ME TO DO THE SAME, BETTS. I WAS IN BANNER'S BODY ENOUGH TO LAST A LIFETIME--
DON'T CHANGE THE SUBJECT.
YOU TALK ABOUT BRUCE NOT BEING AROUND--YOU MEAN HE DOESN'T WANT TO COME OUT.
EVEN THOUGH I CAME BACK TO HELP YOU ALL.
BETTY, THAT AIN'T--
JUST LISTEN.
BRUCE HASN'T BEEN PRESENT WITH ME SINCE HE RETURNED FROM THE DEAD. BEFORE THAT, EVEN.
HE AVOIDED ME FOR MONTHS. THEN WHEN HE FINALLY GOT THE COURAGE TO FACE ME--WHEN HE GOT ME KILLED--
--IT WOKE UP WHAT WAS INSIDE. THE GAMMA--AND EVERYTHING ELSE I'D BEEN ABSORBING FOR YEARS.
HE DIDN'T LIKE THE LOOK OF THAT.
THE LOOK OF ME.
YOU ALWAYS DID, JOE. RIGHT FROM THE START, YOU ALWAYS SAW ME.
THAT'S THE DIFFERENCE.

THIS *IS* ME. THIS IS *US*. IT'S *OURS*.

DON'T BE *YOU*, HULK.

DON'T SMASH IT UP.

"THIS IS ME," HUH?

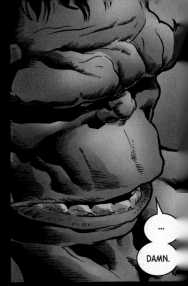

...

DAMN.

BANNER AIN'T *HIDIN'* FROM YOU, BETTS. HE'S *GONE*. HE'S IN *HELL*, OR... SOMEPLACE *BELOW* IT...

IT'S *LEADER* STUFF. STERNS IS *BACK*, AND HE'S *THERE*, AND...HE'S GOT *BANNER*.

WHEN STERNS TOOK HIM--I WAS WEAK. IN *CHAINS* IN BANNER'S HEAD. I COULDN'T HAVE STOPPED IT.

BUT I WAS DOWN THERE *AGAIN* JUST BEFORE YOU SHOWED UP. DOWN IN *HELL*, AS A HULK-- STRONG AS I EVER WAS.

AND I DIDN'T LOOK FOR BANNER.

I JUST LOOKED OUT FOR ME.

YOU LEFT BRUCE IN *HELL*?

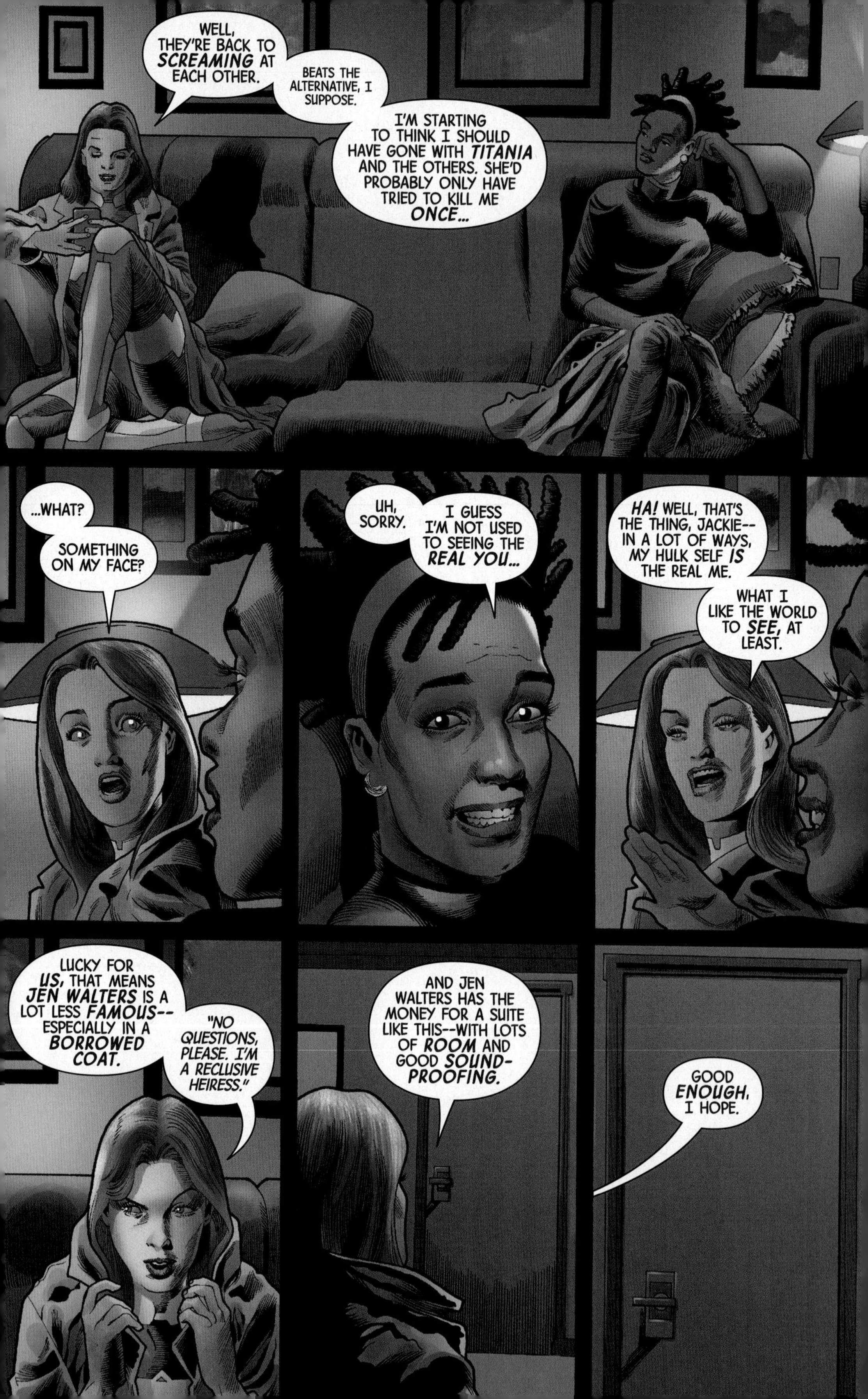
WELL, THEY'RE BACK TO SCREAMING AT EACH OTHER.
BEATS THE ALTERNATIVE, I SUPPOSE.
I'M STARTING TO THINK I SHOULD HAVE GONE WITH TITANIA AND THE OTHERS. SHE'D PROBABLY ONLY HAVE TRIED TO KILL ME ONCE...
...WHAT?
SOMETHING ON MY FACE?
UH, SORRY.
I GUESS I'M NOT USED TO SEEING THE REAL YOU...
HA! WELL, THAT'S THE THING, JACKIE-- IN A LOT OF WAYS, MY HULK SELF IS THE REAL ME.
WHAT I LIKE THE WORLD TO SEE, AT LEAST.
LUCKY FOR US, THAT MEANS JEN WALTERS IS A LOT LESS FAMOUS-- ESPECIALLY IN A BORROWED COAT.
"NO QUESTIONS, PLEASE. I'M A RECLUSIVE HEIRESS."
AND JEN WALTERS HAS THE MONEY FOR A SUITE LIKE THIS--WITH LOTS OF ROOM AND GOOD SOUND-PROOFING.
GOOD ENOUGH, I HOPE.

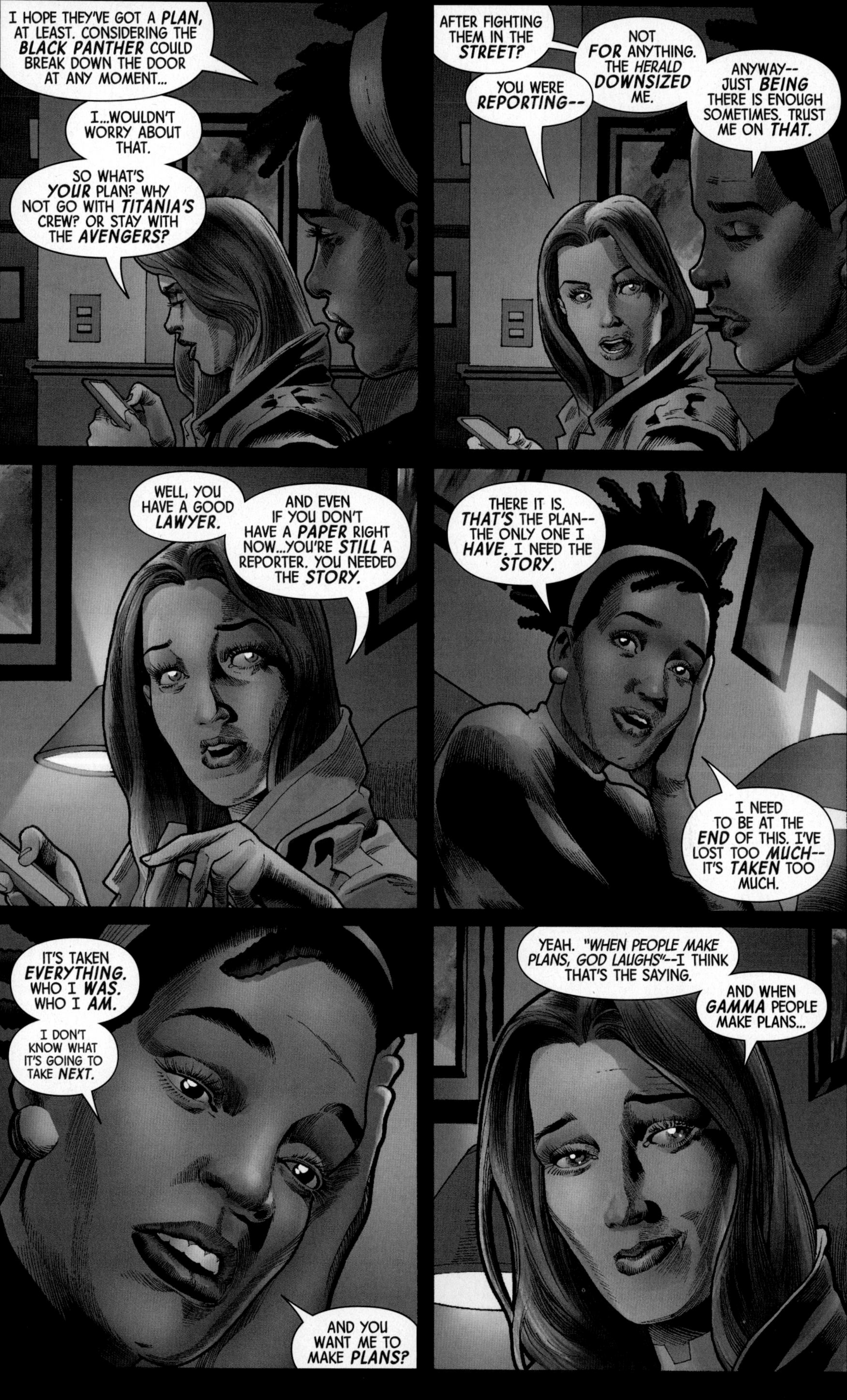

I HOPE THEY'VE GOT A PLAN, AT LEAST. CONSIDERING THE BLACK PANTHER COULD BREAK DOWN THE DOOR AT ANY MOMENT...
I...WOULDN'T WORRY ABOUT THAT.
SO WHAT'S YOUR PLAN? WHY NOT GO WITH TITANIA'S CREW? OR STAY WITH THE AVENGERS?
AFTER FIGHTING THEM IN THE STREET?
YOU WERE REPORTING--
NOT FOR ANYTHING. THE HERALD DOWNSIZED ME.
ANYWAY-- JUST BEING THERE IS ENOUGH SOMETIMES. TRUST ME ON THAT.
WELL, YOU HAVE A GOOD LAWYER.
AND EVEN IF YOU DON'T HAVE A PAPER RIGHT NOW...YOU'RE STILL A REPORTER. YOU NEEDED THE STORY.
THERE IT IS. THAT'S THE PLAN-- THE ONLY ONE I HAVE. I NEED THE STORY.
I NEED TO BE AT THE END OF THIS. I'VE LOST TOO MUCH-- IT'S TAKEN TOO MUCH.
IT'S TAKEN EVERYTHING. WHO I WAS. WHO I AM.
I DON'T KNOW WHAT IT'S GOING TO TAKE NEXT.
AND YOU WANT ME TO MAKE PLANS?
YEAH. "WHEN PEOPLE MAKE PLANS, GOD LAUGHS"--I THINK THAT'S THE SAYING.
AND WHEN GAMMA PEOPLE MAKE PLANS...

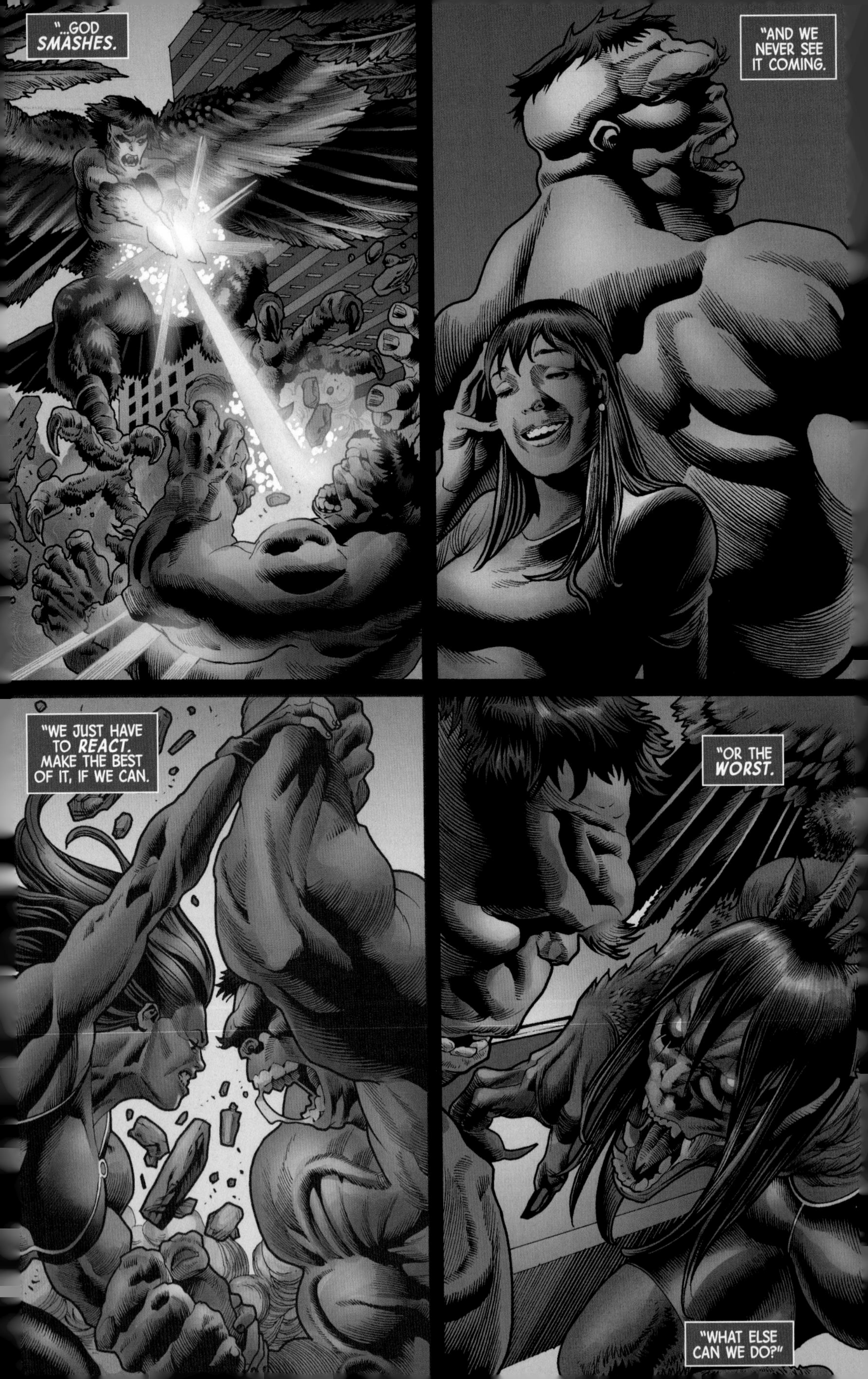
"...GOD SMASHES.
"AND WE NEVER SEE IT COMING.
"WE JUST HAVE TO REACT. MAKE THE BEST OF IT, IF WE CAN.
"OR THE WORST.
"WHAT ELSE CAN WE DO?"

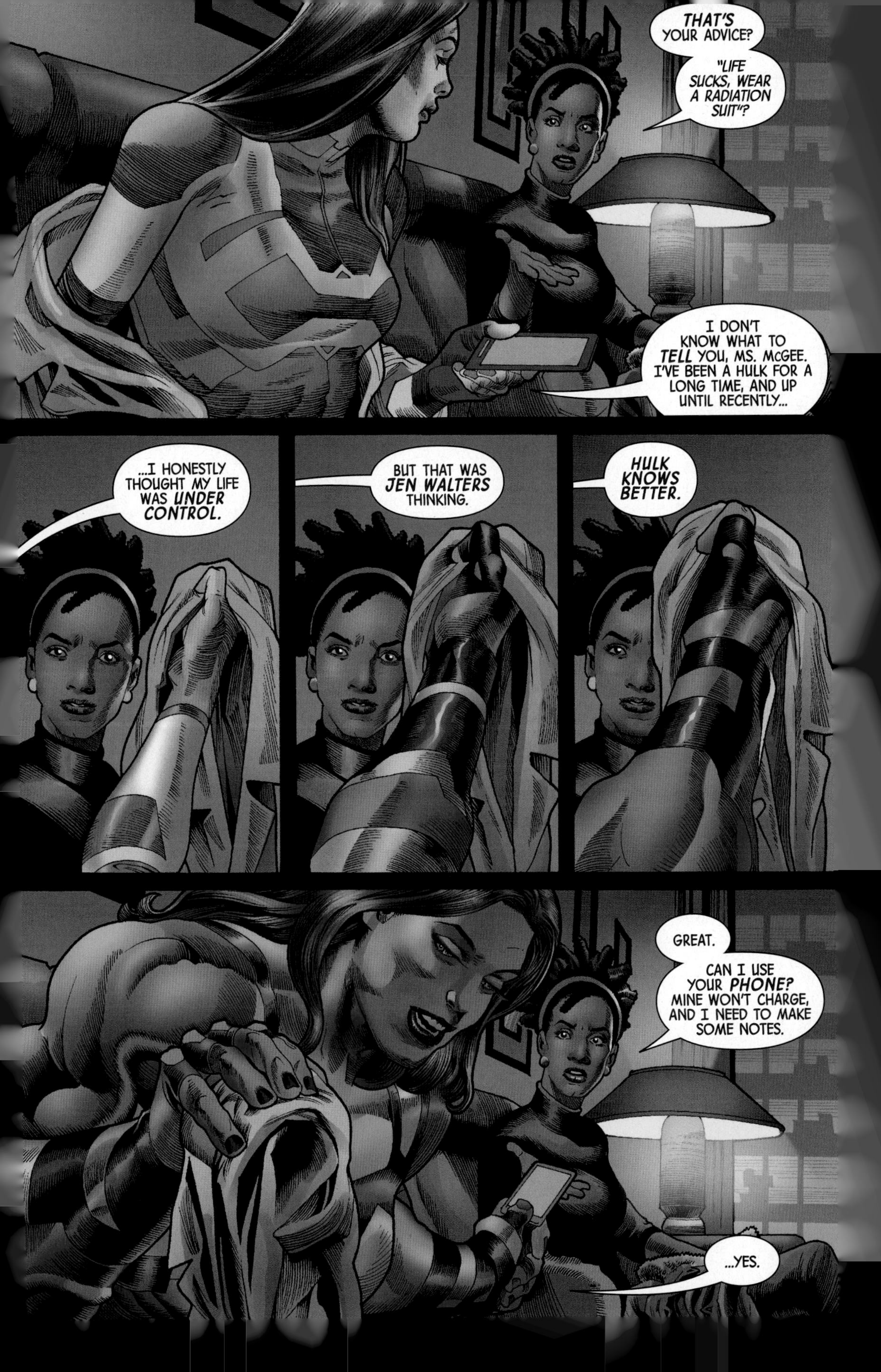
THAT'S YOUR ADVICE?
"LIFE SUCKS, WEAR A RADIATION SUIT"?
I DON'T KNOW WHAT TO TELL YOU, MS. McGEE. I'VE BEEN A HULK FOR A LONG TIME, AND UP UNTIL RECENTLY...
...I HONESTLY THOUGHT MY LIFE WAS UNDER CONTROL.
BUT THAT WAS JEN WALTERS THINKING.
HULK KNOWS BETTER.
GREAT.
CAN I USE YOUR PHONE? MINE WON'T CHARGE, AND I NEED TO MAKE SOME NOTES.
...YES.

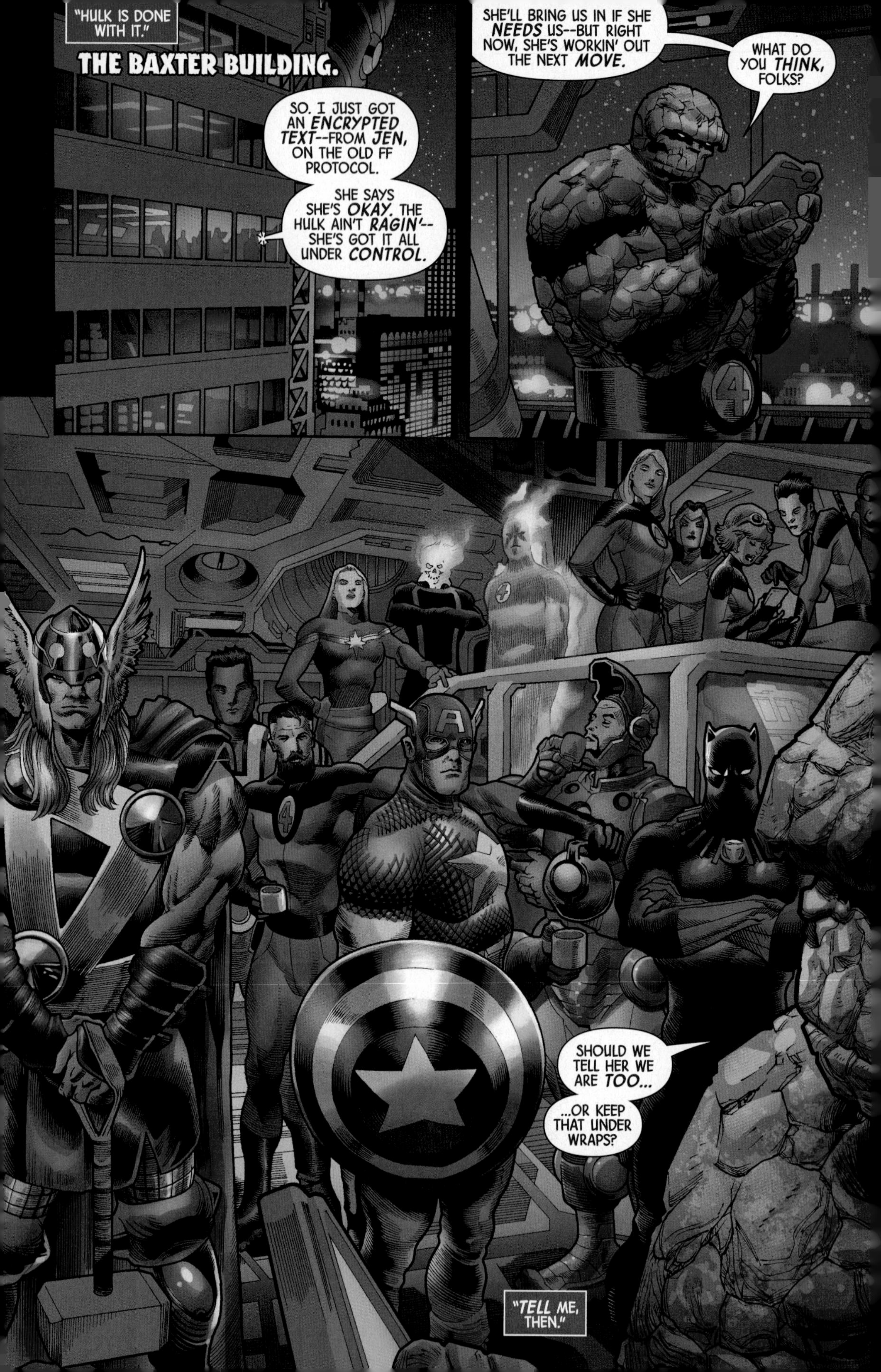
"HULK IS DONE WITH IT."
THE BAXTER BUILDING.
SO. I JUST GOT AN ENCRYPTED TEXT--FROM JEN, ON THE OLD FF PROTOCOL.
SHE SAYS SHE'S OKAY. THE HULK AIN'T RAGIN'--SHE'S GOT IT ALL UNDER CONTROL.
SHE'LL BRING US IN IF SHE NEEDS US--BUT RIGHT NOW, SHE'S WORKIN' OUT THE NEXT MOVE.
WHAT DO YOU THINK, FOLKS?
SHOULD WE TELL HER WE ARE TOO...
...OR KEEP THAT UNDER WRAPS?
"TELL ME, THEN."

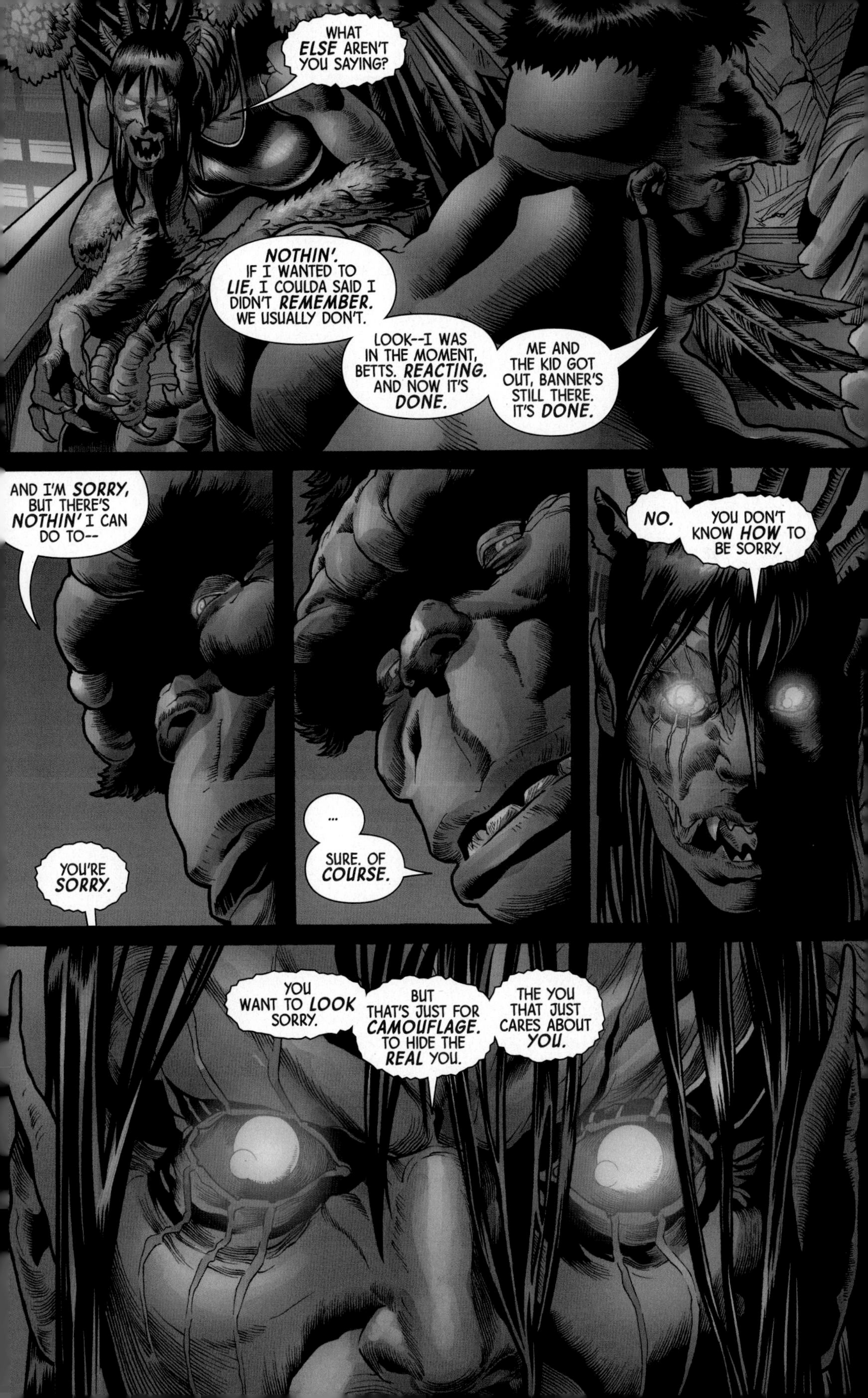
WHAT ELSE AREN'T YOU SAYING?
NOTHIN'. IF I WANTED TO LIE, I COULDA SAID I DIDN'T REMEMBER. WE USUALLY DON'T.
LOOK--I WAS IN THE MOMENT, BETTS. REACTING. AND NOW IT'S DONE.
ME AND THE KID GOT OUT, BANNER'S STILL THERE. IT'S DONE.
AND I'M SORRY, BUT THERE'S NOTHIN' I CAN DO TO--
YOU'RE SORRY.
...
SURE. OF COURSE.
NO.
YOU DON'T KNOW HOW TO BE SORRY.
YOU WANT TO LOOK SORRY.
BUT THAT'S JUST FOR CAMOUFLAGE. TO HIDE THE REAL YOU.
THE YOU THAT JUST CARES ABOUT YOU.

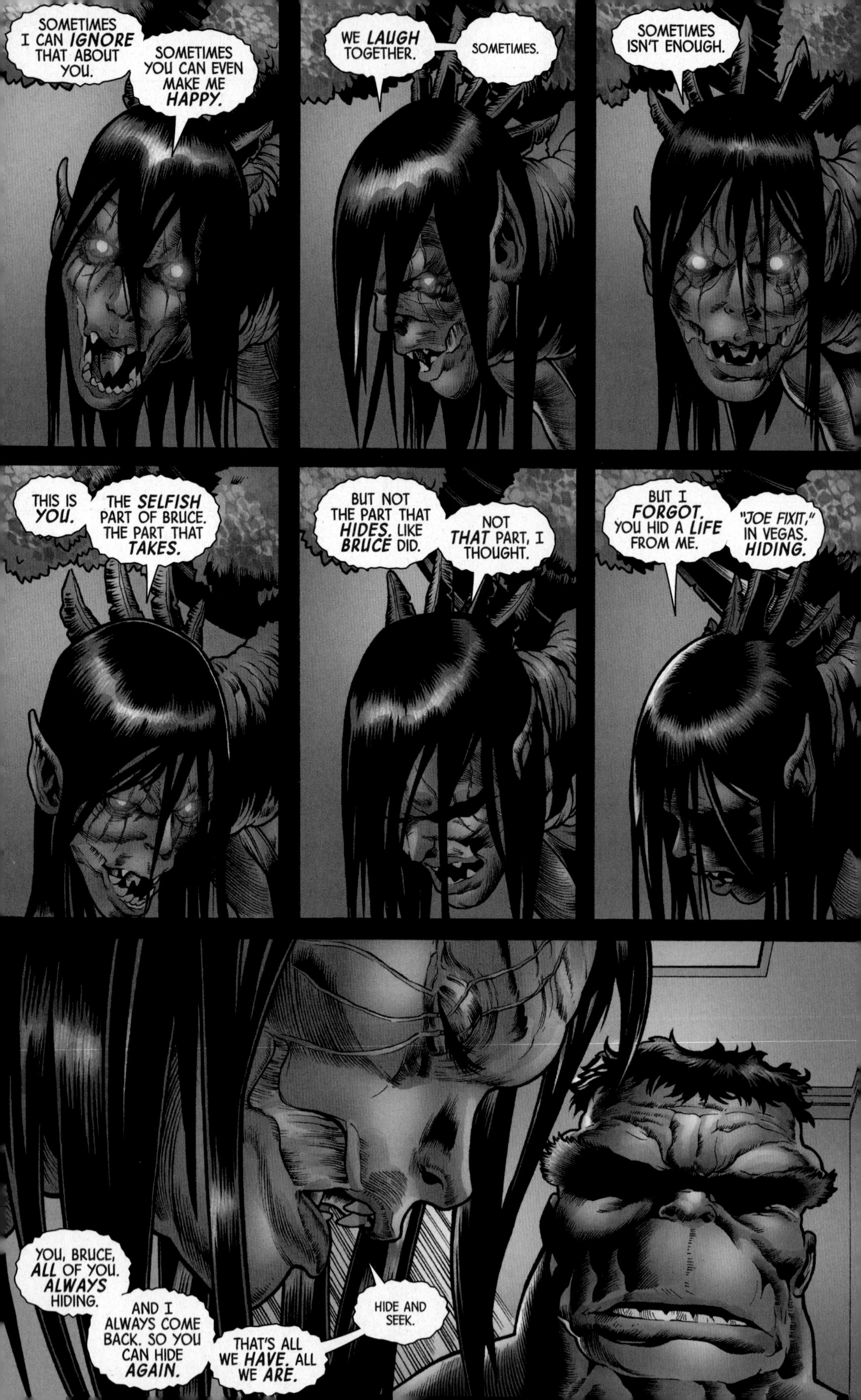
SOMETIMES I CAN IGNORE THAT ABOUT YOU.
SOMETIMES YOU CAN EVEN MAKE ME HAPPY.
WE LAUGH TOGETHER.
SOMETIMES.
SOMETIMES ISN'T ENOUGH.
THIS IS YOU.
THE SELFISH PART OF BRUCE. THE PART THAT TAKES.
BUT NOT THE PART THAT HIDES, LIKE BRUCE DID.
NOT THAT PART, I THOUGHT.
BUT I FORGOT. YOU HID A LIFE FROM ME.
"JOE FIXIT," IN VEGAS. HIDING.
YOU, BRUCE, ALL OF YOU. ALWAYS HIDING.
AND I ALWAYS COME BACK. SO YOU CAN HIDE AGAIN.
THAT'S ALL WE HAVE. ALL WE ARE.
HIDE AND SEEK.

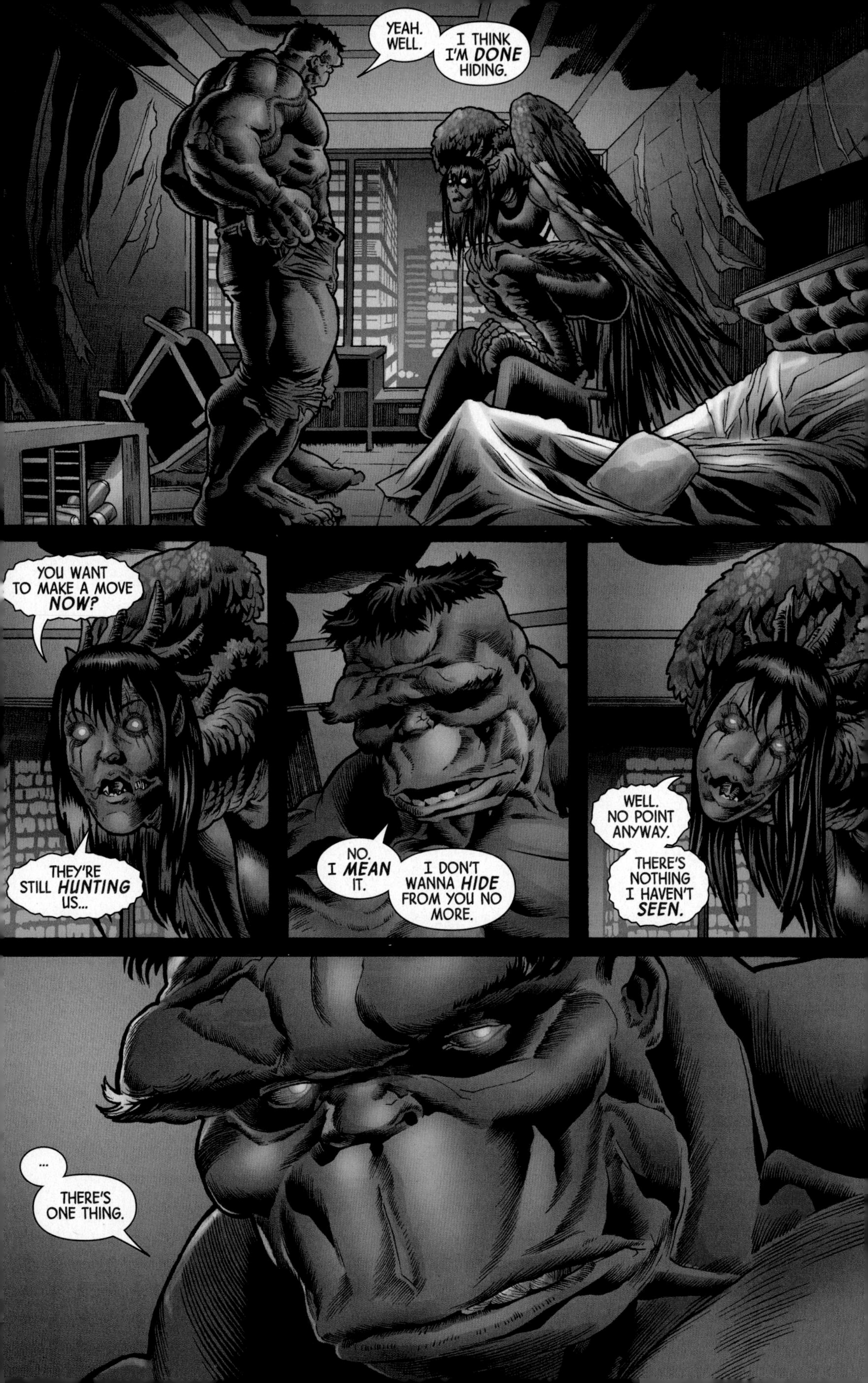
YEAH. WELL.
I THINK I'M DONE HIDING.
YOU WANT TO MAKE A MOVE NOW?
THEY'RE STILL HUNTING US...
NO. I MEAN IT.
I DON'T WANNA HIDE FROM YOU NO MORE.
WELL. NO POINT ANYWAY.
THERE'S NOTHING I HAVEN'T SEEN.
...
THERE'S ONE THING.

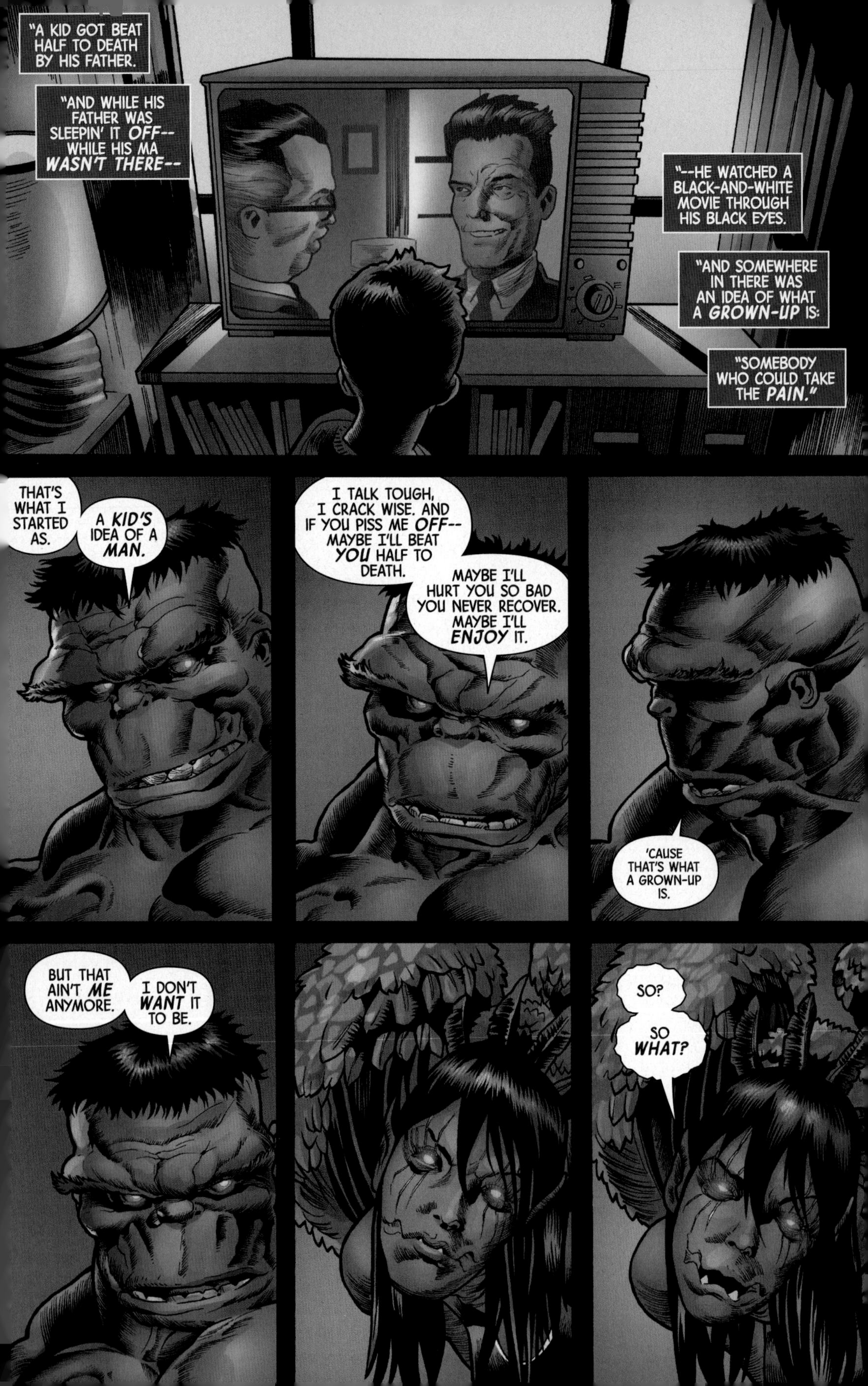
"A KID GOT BEAT HALF TO DEATH BY HIS FATHER.
"AND WHILE HIS FATHER WAS SLEEPIN' IT OFF-- WHILE HIS MA WASN'T THERE--
"--HE WATCHED A BLACK-AND-WHITE MOVIE THROUGH HIS BLACK EYES.
"AND SOMEWHERE IN THERE WAS AN IDEA OF WHAT A GROWN-UP IS:
"SOMEBODY WHO COULD TAKE THE PAIN."
THAT'S WHAT I STARTED AS.
A KID'S IDEA OF A MAN.
I TALK TOUGH, I CRACK WISE. AND IF YOU PISS ME OFF-- MAYBE I'LL BEAT YOU HALF TO DEATH.
MAYBE I'LL HURT YOU SO BAD YOU NEVER RECOVER. MAYBE I'LL ENJOY IT.
'CAUSE THAT'S WHAT A GROWN-UP IS.
BUT THAT AIN'T ME ANYMORE.
I DON'T WANT IT TO BE.
SO?
SO WHAT?

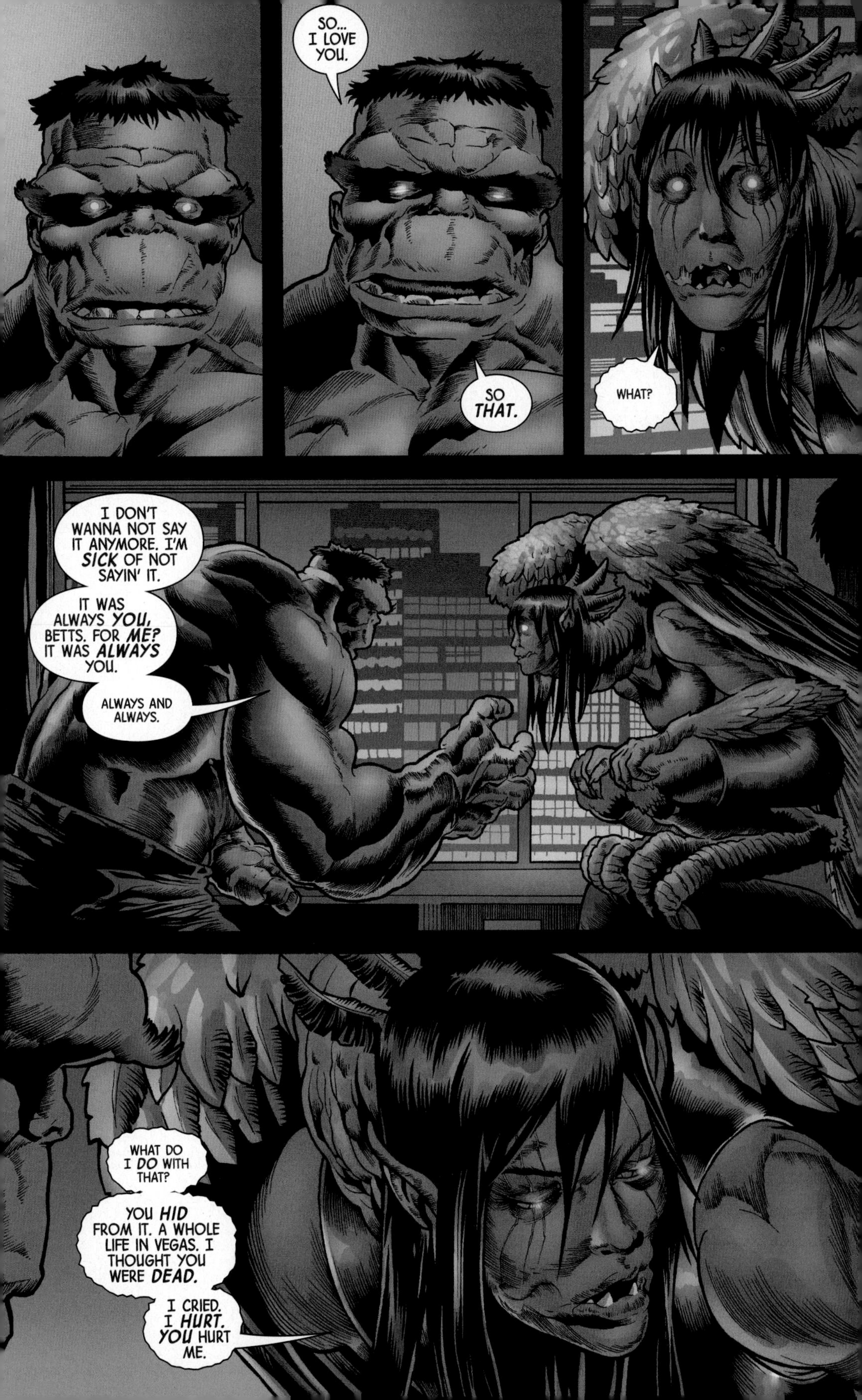
SO... I LOVE YOU.
SO THAT.
WHAT?
I DON'T WANNA NOT SAY IT ANYMORE. I'M SICK OF NOT SAYIN' IT.
IT WAS ALWAYS YOU, BETTS. FOR ME? IT WAS ALWAYS YOU.
ALWAYS AND ALWAYS.
WHAT DO I DO WITH THAT?
YOU HID FROM IT. A WHOLE LIFE IN VEGAS. I THOUGHT YOU WERE DEAD.
I CRIED. I HURT. YOU HURT ME.

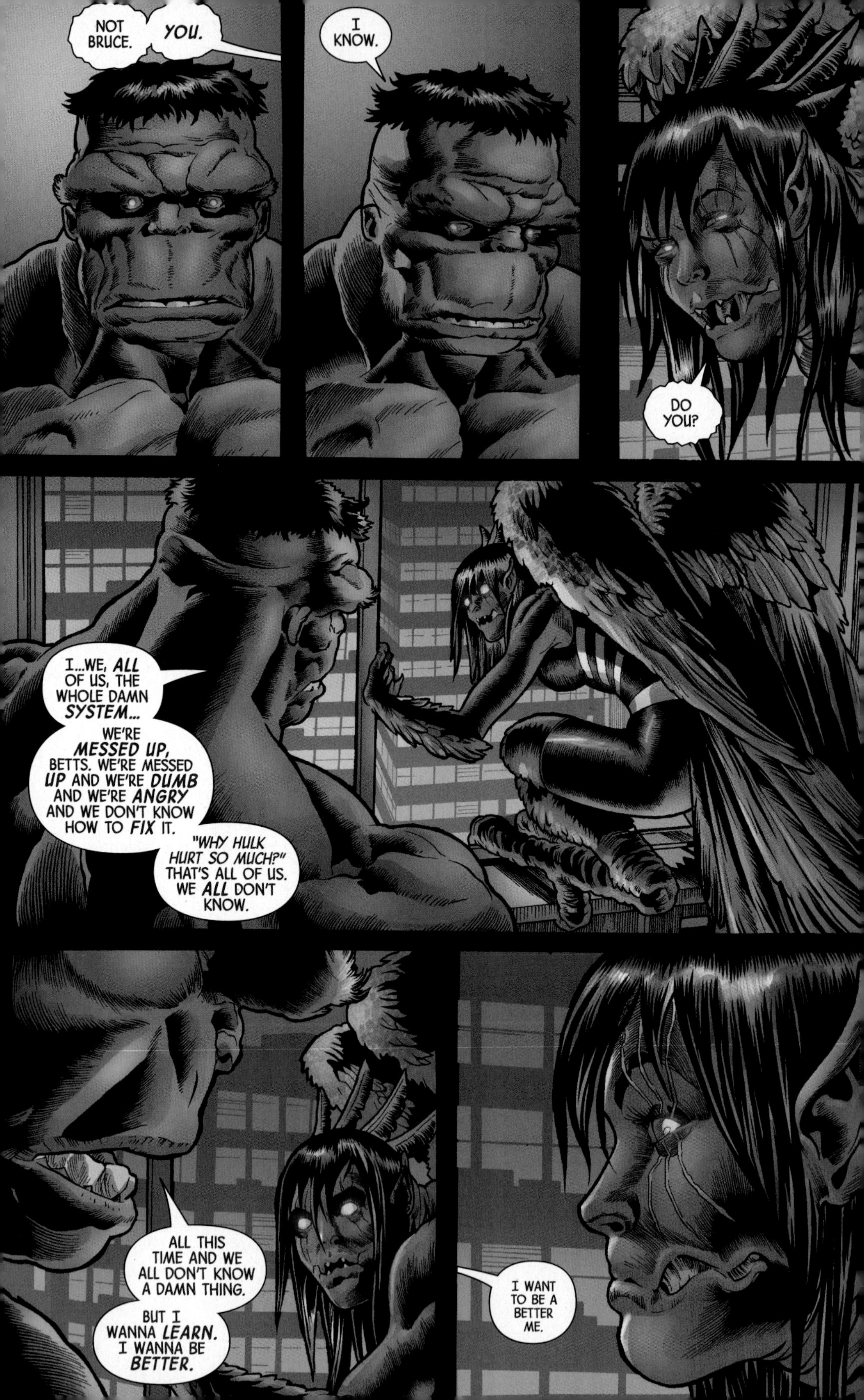
NOT BRUCE.
YOU.
I KNOW.
DO YOU?
I...WE, ALL OF US, THE WHOLE DAMN SYSTEM...
WE'RE MESSED UP, BETTS. WE'RE MESSED UP AND WE'RE DUMB AND WE'RE ANGRY AND WE DON'T KNOW HOW TO FIX IT.
"WHY HULK HURT SO MUCH?" THAT'S ALL OF US. WE ALL DON'T KNOW.
ALL THIS TIME AND WE ALL DON'T KNOW A DAMN THING.
BUT I WANNA LEARN. I WANNA BE BETTER.
I WANT TO BE A BETTER ME.

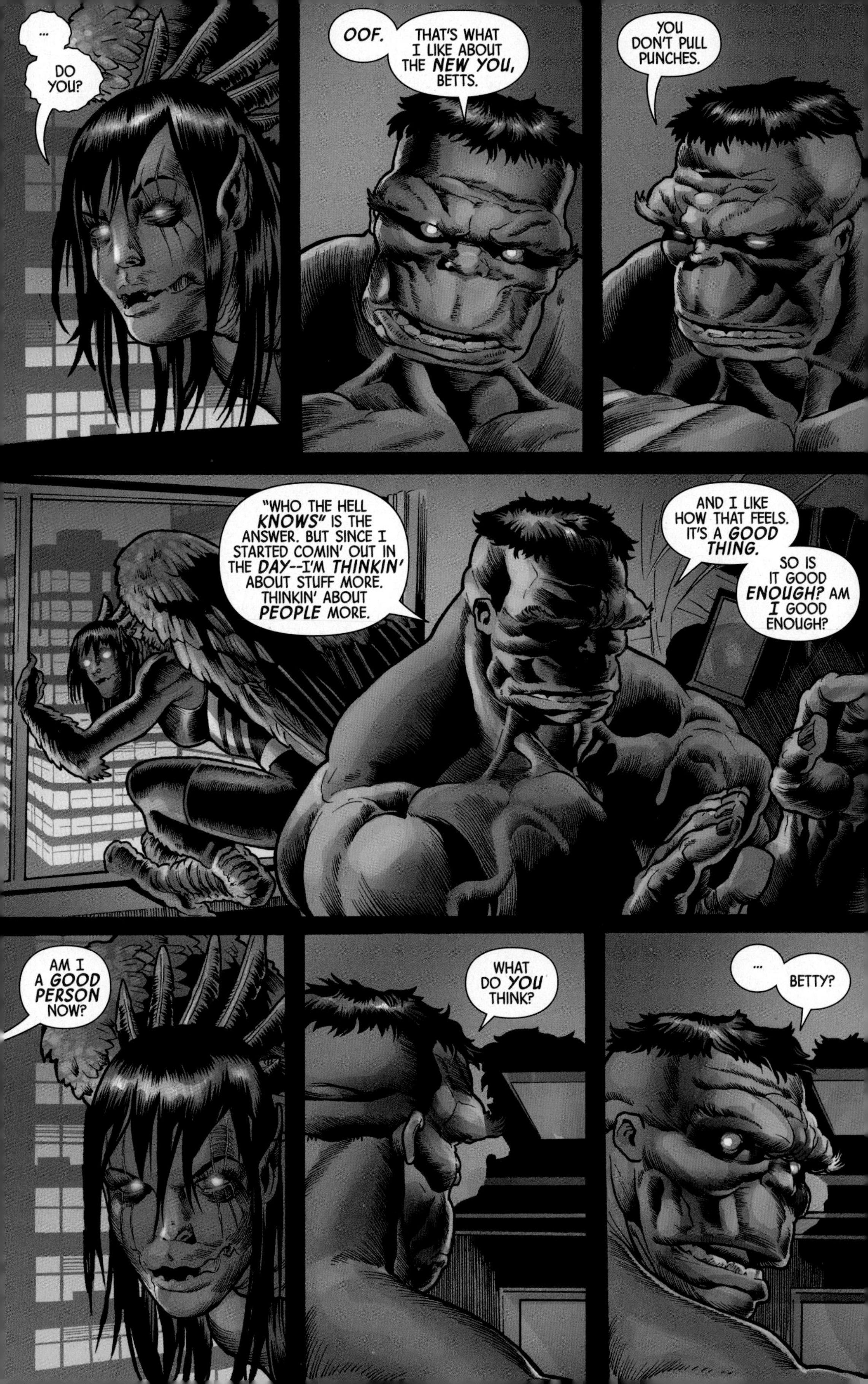
...
DO YOU?
OOF.
THAT'S WHAT I LIKE ABOUT THE NEW YOU, BETTS.
YOU DON'T PULL PUNCHES.
"WHO THE HELL KNOWS" IS THE ANSWER. BUT SINCE I STARTED COMIN' OUT IN THE DAY--I'M THINKIN' ABOUT STUFF MORE. THINKIN' ABOUT PEOPLE MORE.
AND I LIKE HOW THAT FEELS. IT'S A GOOD THING.
SO IS IT GOOD ENOUGH? AM I GOOD ENOUGH?
AM I A GOOD PERSON NOW?
WHAT DO YOU THINK?
...
BETTY?

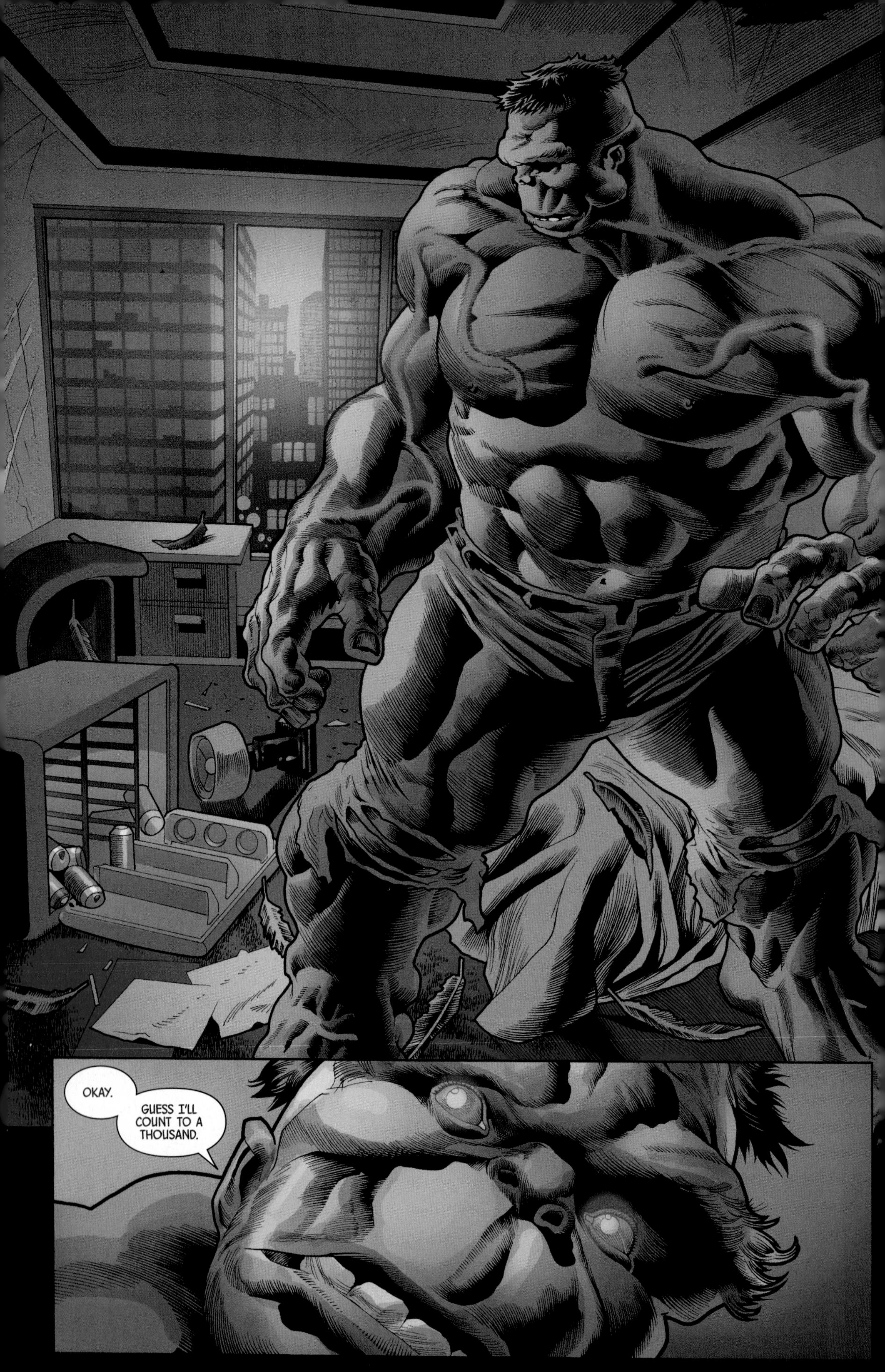
OKAY.
GUESS I'LL COUNT TO A THOUSAND.

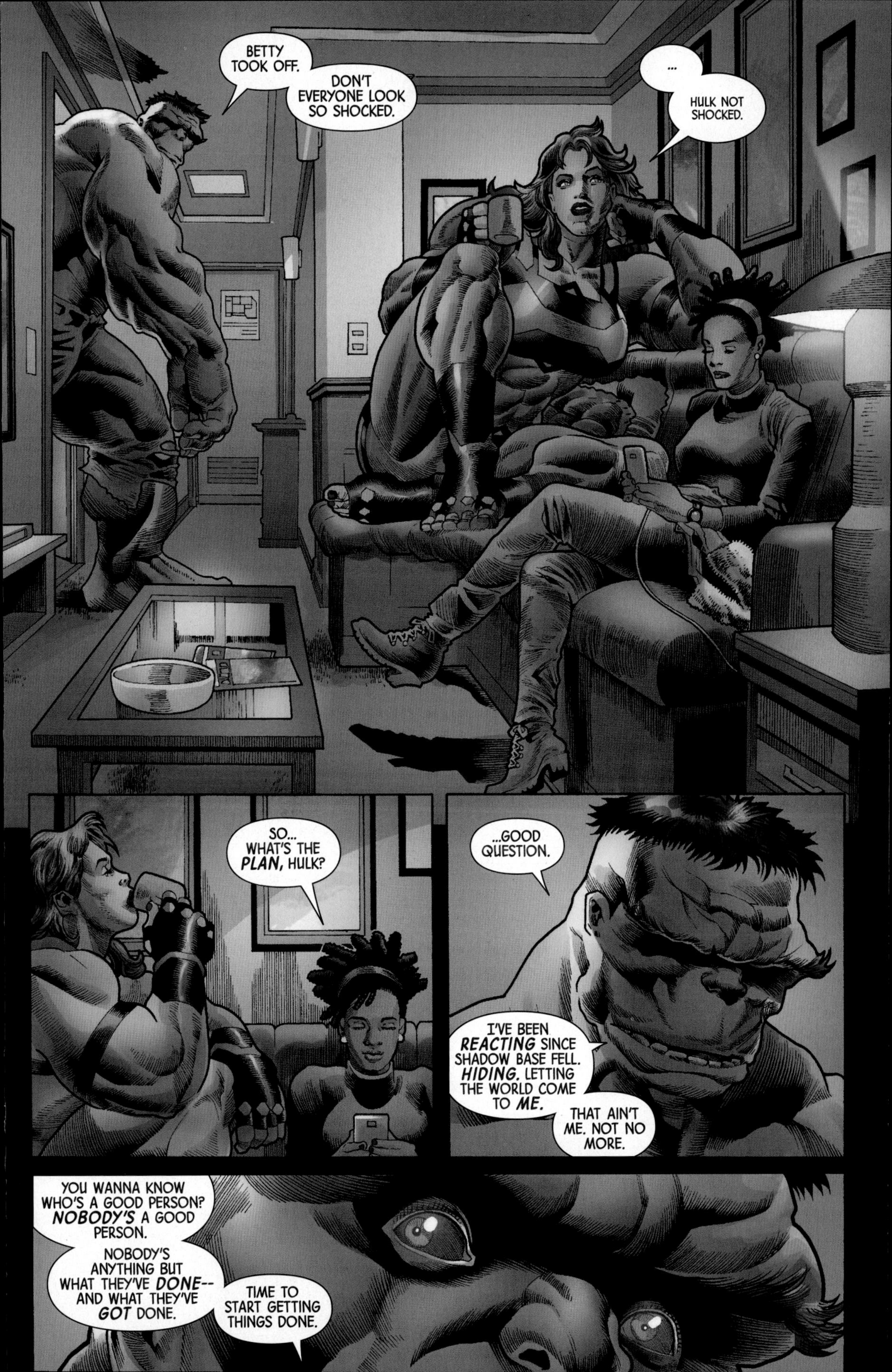
BETTY TOOK OFF.
DON'T EVERYONE LOOK SO SHOCKED.
...
HULK NOT SHOCKED.
SO... WHAT'S THE *PLAN*, HULK?
...GOOD QUESTION.
I'VE BEEN *REACTING* SINCE SHADOW BASE FELL. *HIDING*. LETTING THE WORLD COME TO *ME*.
THAT AIN'T ME. NOT NO MORE.
YOU WANNA KNOW WHO'S A GOOD PERSON? *NOBODY'S* A GOOD PERSON.
NOBODY'S ANYTHING BUT WHAT THEY'VE *DONE*-- AND WHAT THEY'VE *GOT* DONE.
TIME TO START GETTING THINGS DONE.

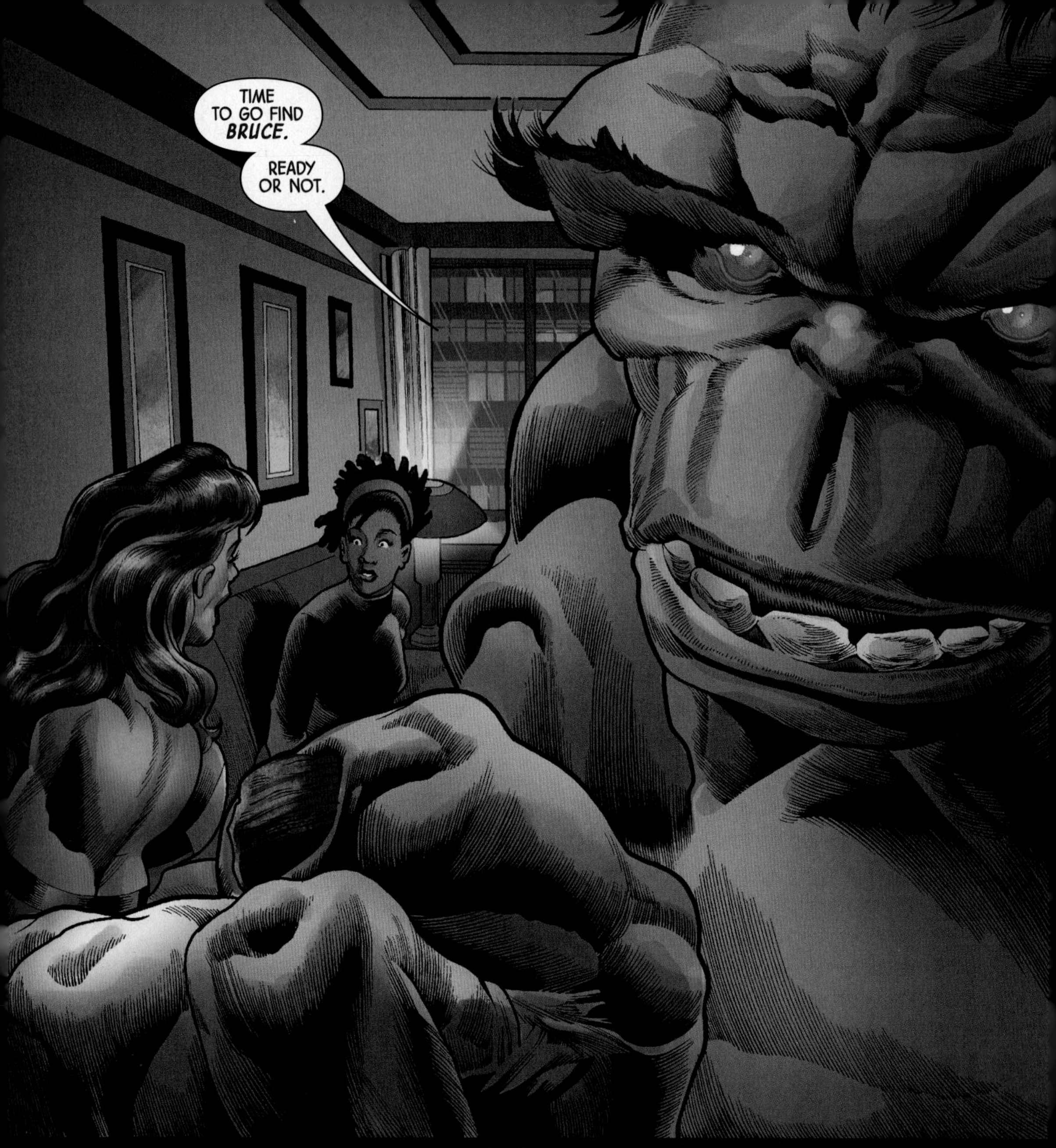
TIME TO GO FIND BRUCE.
READY OR NOT.

HIDING PLACES

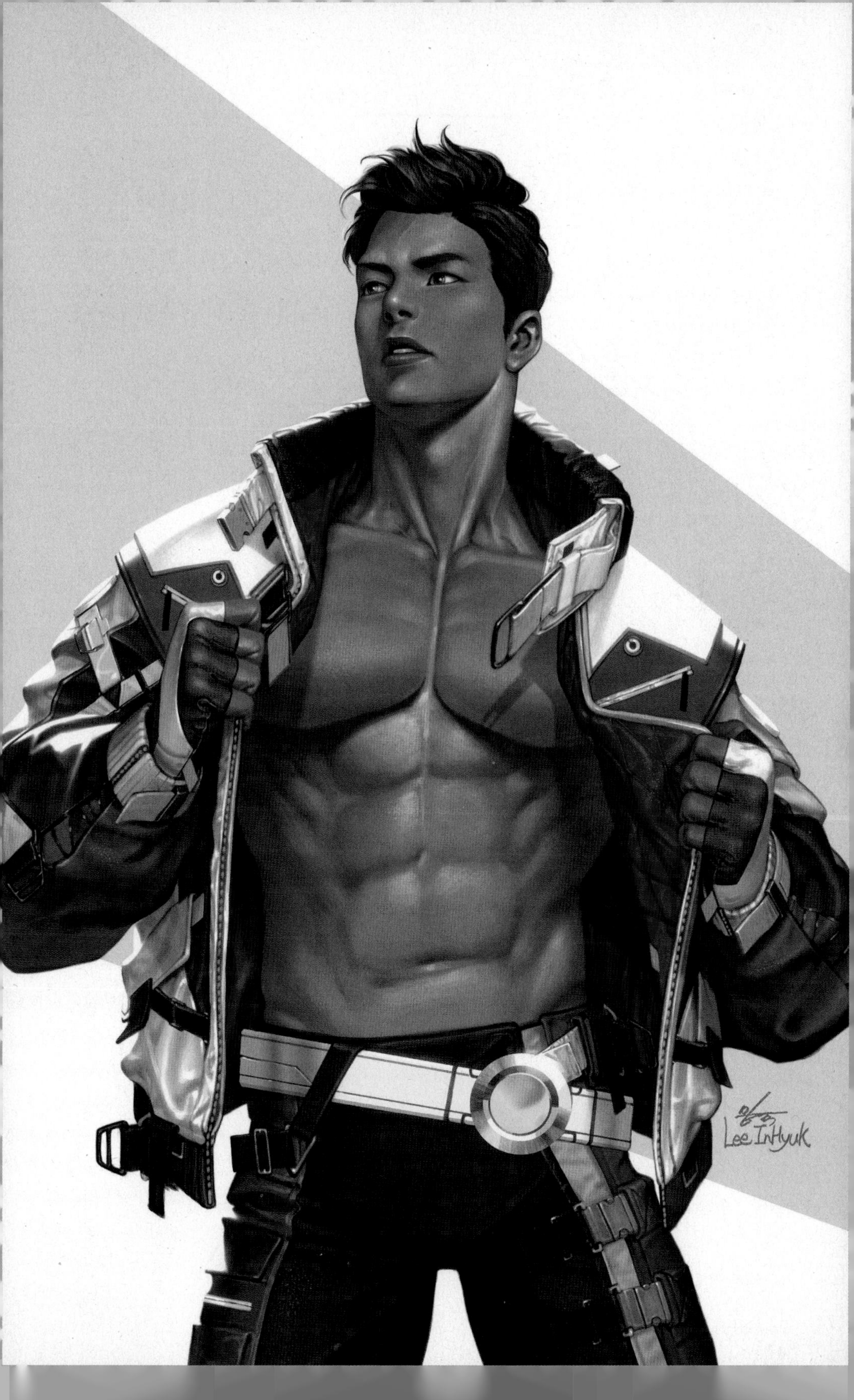
Lee InHyuk

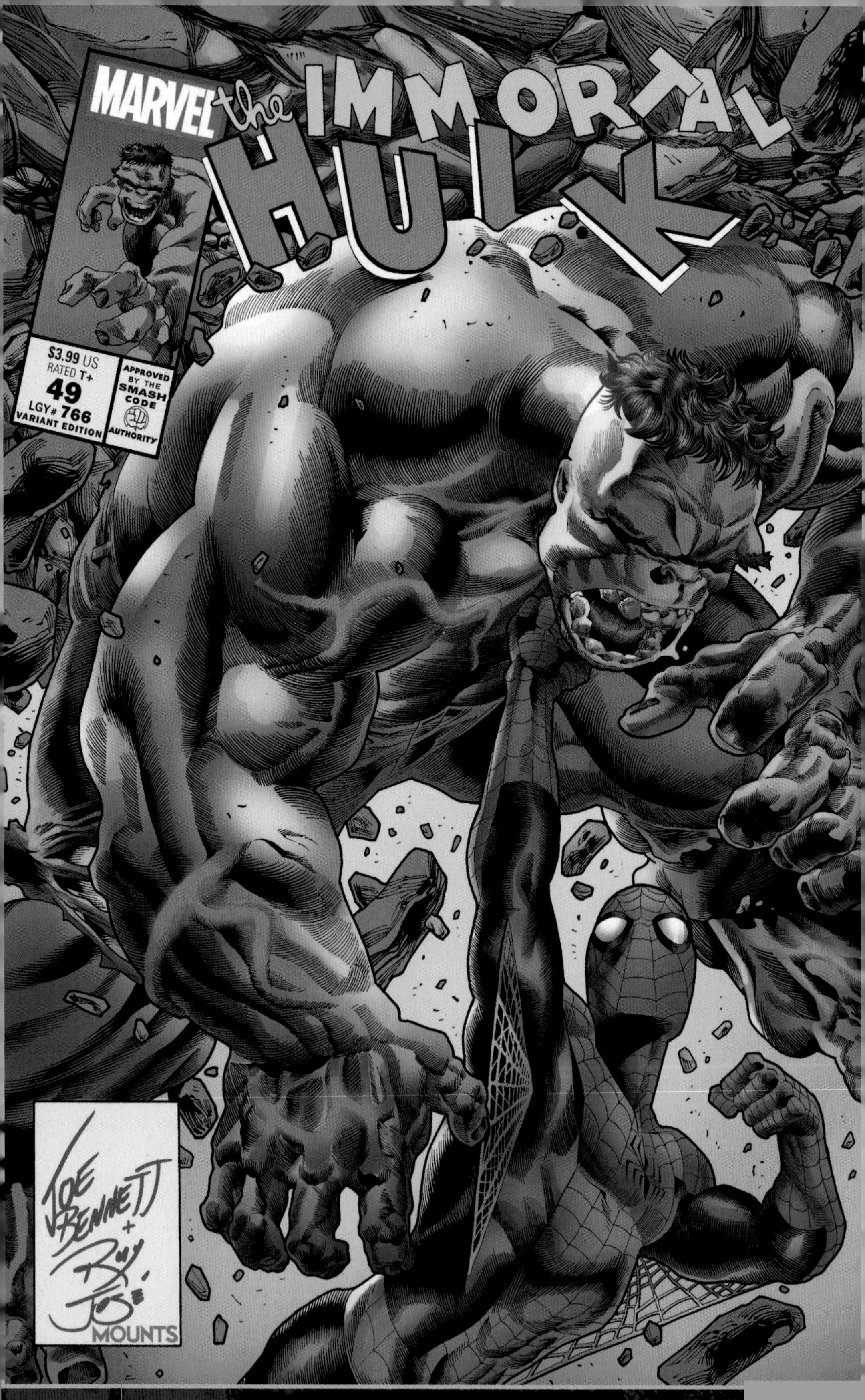
MARVEL
the IMMORTAL HULK
$3.99 US
RATED T+
49
LGY# 766
VARIANT EDITION
APPROVED BY THE SMASH CODE AUTHORITY
JOE BENNETT + RUY JOSÉ
MOUNTS

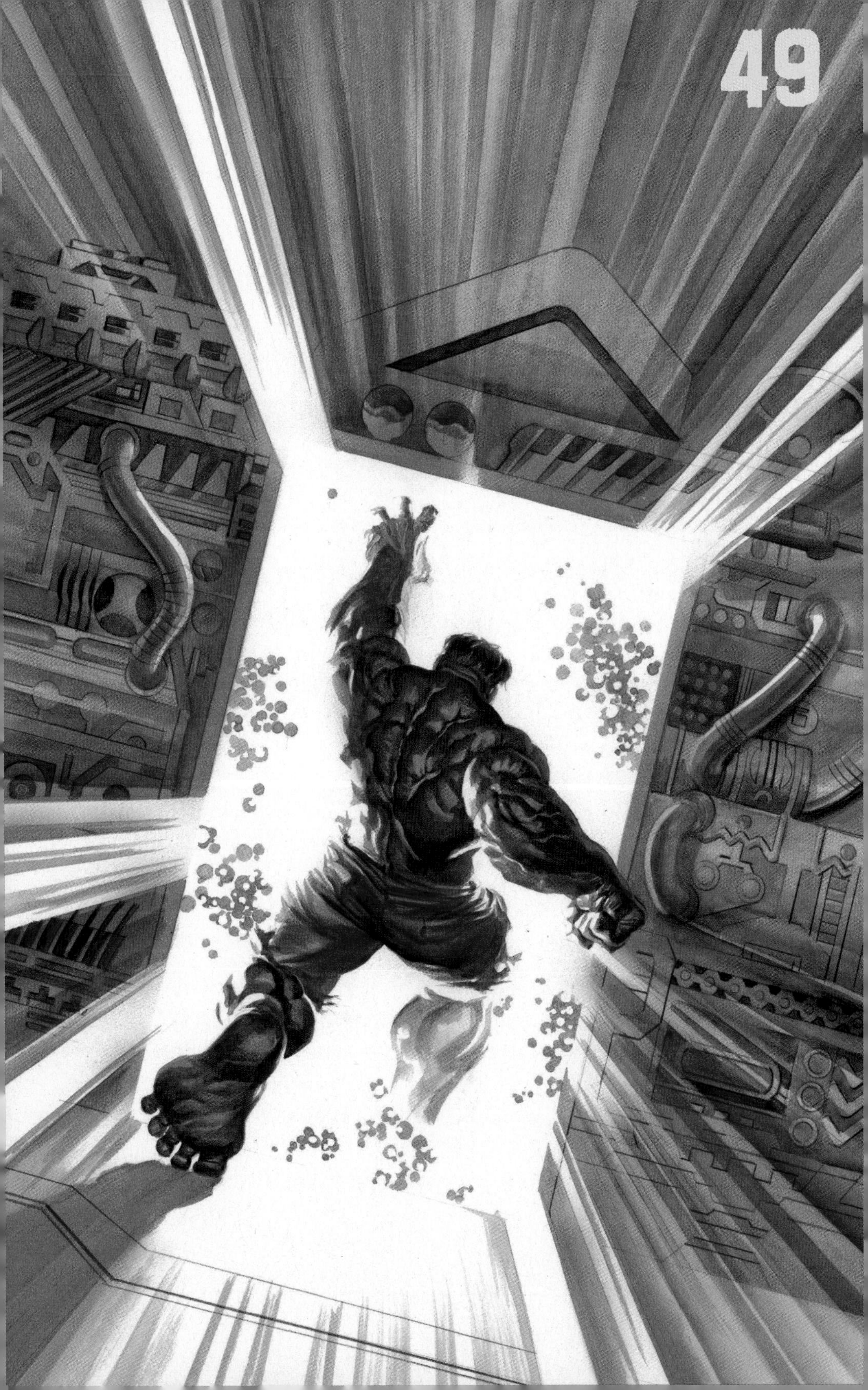
49

"THROUGH ME YOU PASS INTO THE CITY OF WOE:
THROUGH ME YOU PASS INTO ETERNAL PAIN:
THROUGH ME AMONG THE PEOPLE LOST FOR AYE.
JUSTICE THE FOUNDER OF MY FABRIC MOV'D:
TO REAR ME WAS THE TASK OF POWER DIVINE,
SUPREMEST WISDOM, AND PRIMEVAL LOVE.
BEFORE ME THINGS CREATE WERE NONE, SAVE THINGS
ETERNAL, AND ETERNAL I ENDURE."

– DANTE ALIGHIERI,
THE VISION OF HELL

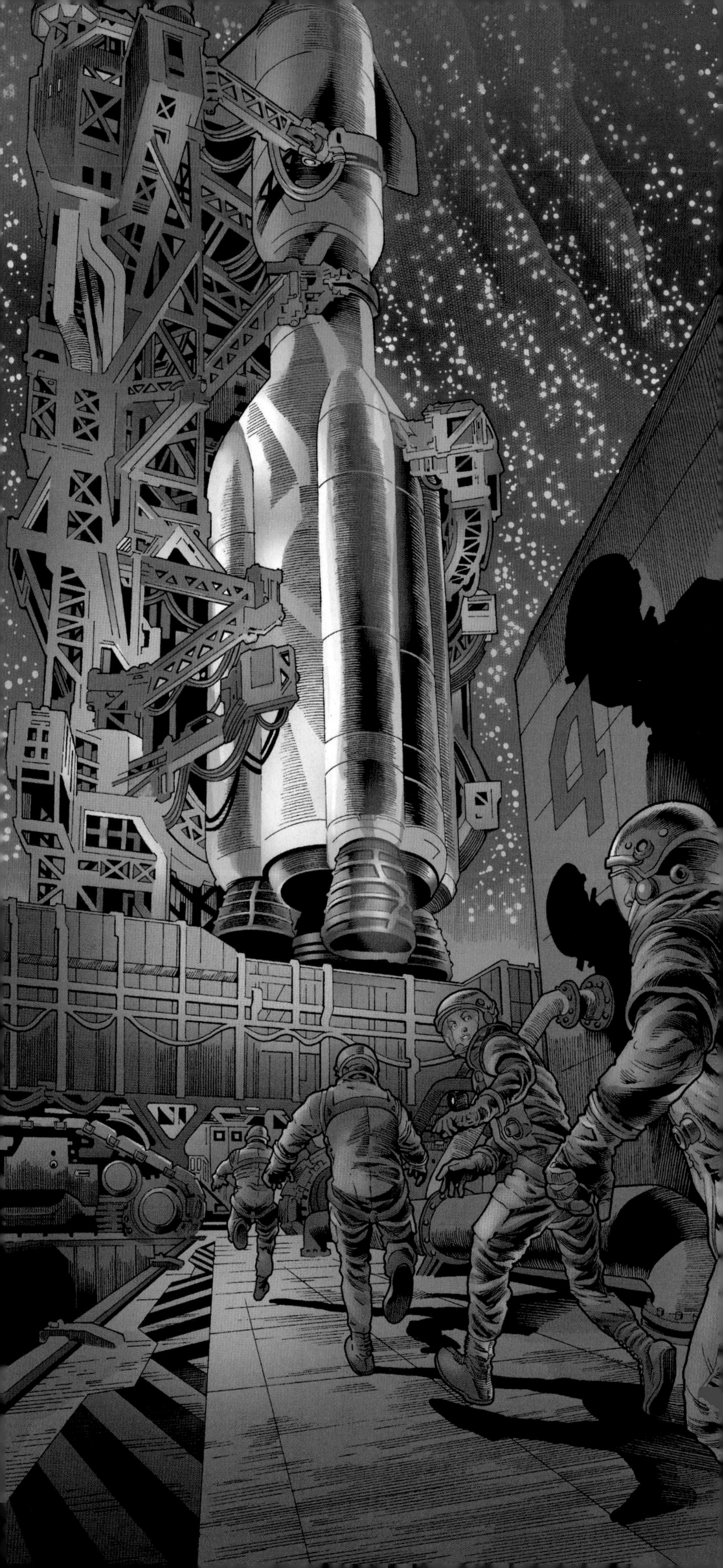
4

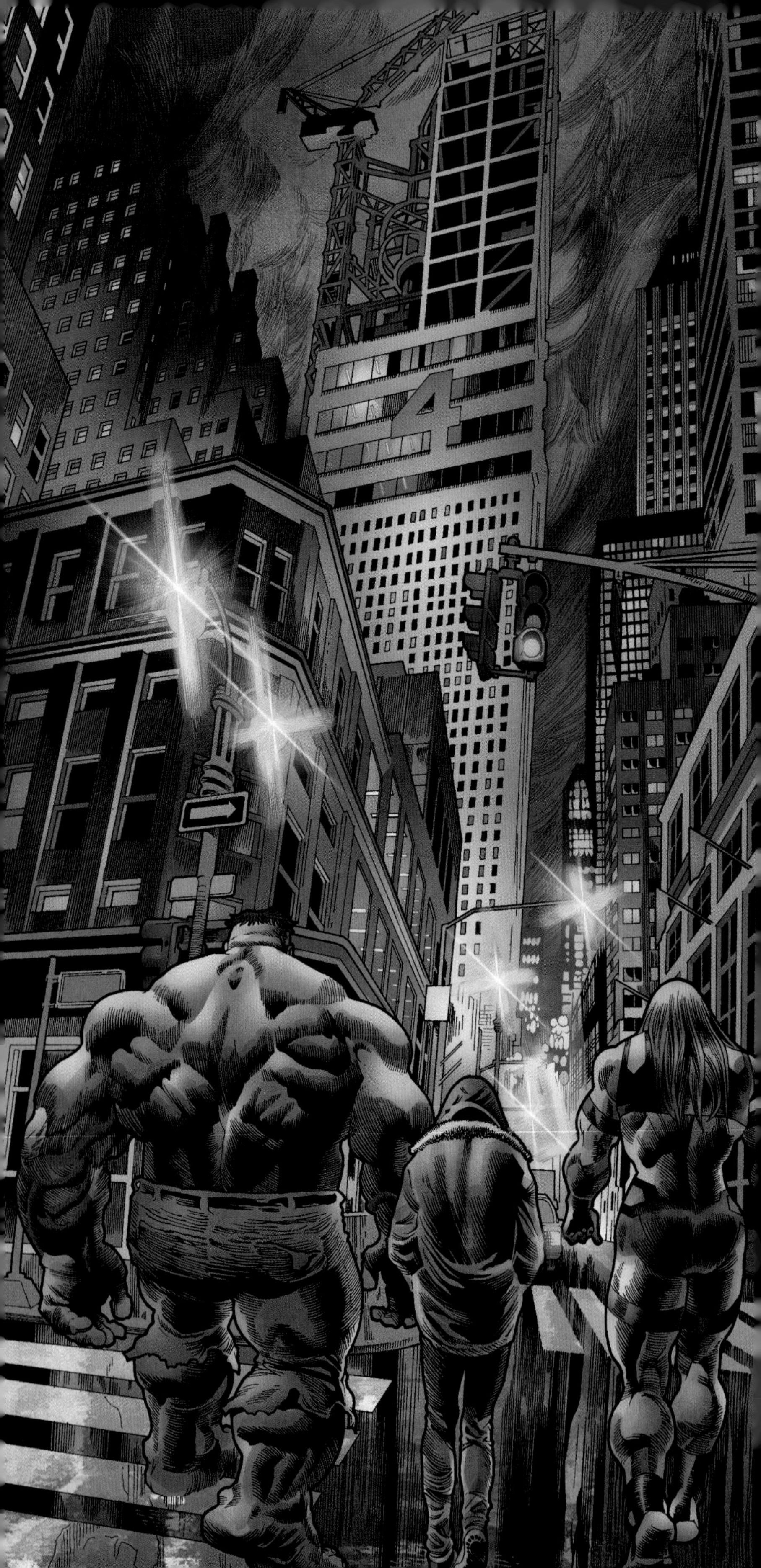
4

IN THE WORLD OF THE SUPER HEROES, WHEN SOMETHING SMASHES YOUR HOME TO RUBBLE, THEY JUST BUILD IT BACK AGAIN, BETTER THAN NEW.

NOTHING EVER REALLY CHANGES.

THE LOBBY WAS BEAUTIFUL, AS QUIET AND SERENE AS A CHURCH. IT WAS A PLACE FOR PEOPLE TO WAIT IN COMFORT--AND A LITTLE AWE--FOR THE ATTENTIONS OF THE MIGHTY. TO PRAY FOR THEIR AID.

AS WE ENTERED, JEN EXHALED, AND I COULDN'T TELL IF THAT WAS RELIEF OR SOME DEEP SADNESS. SHE WAS IN HER PLACE OF POWER, BUT SHE DIDN'T QUITE FIT THERE ANYMORE.

THE HULK DIDN'T FIT AT ALL. HE LOOKED *WRONG* HERE--SOMETHING PROFANE, AN UNHOLY THING IN A HOLY PLACE.

HE KEPT WALKING.

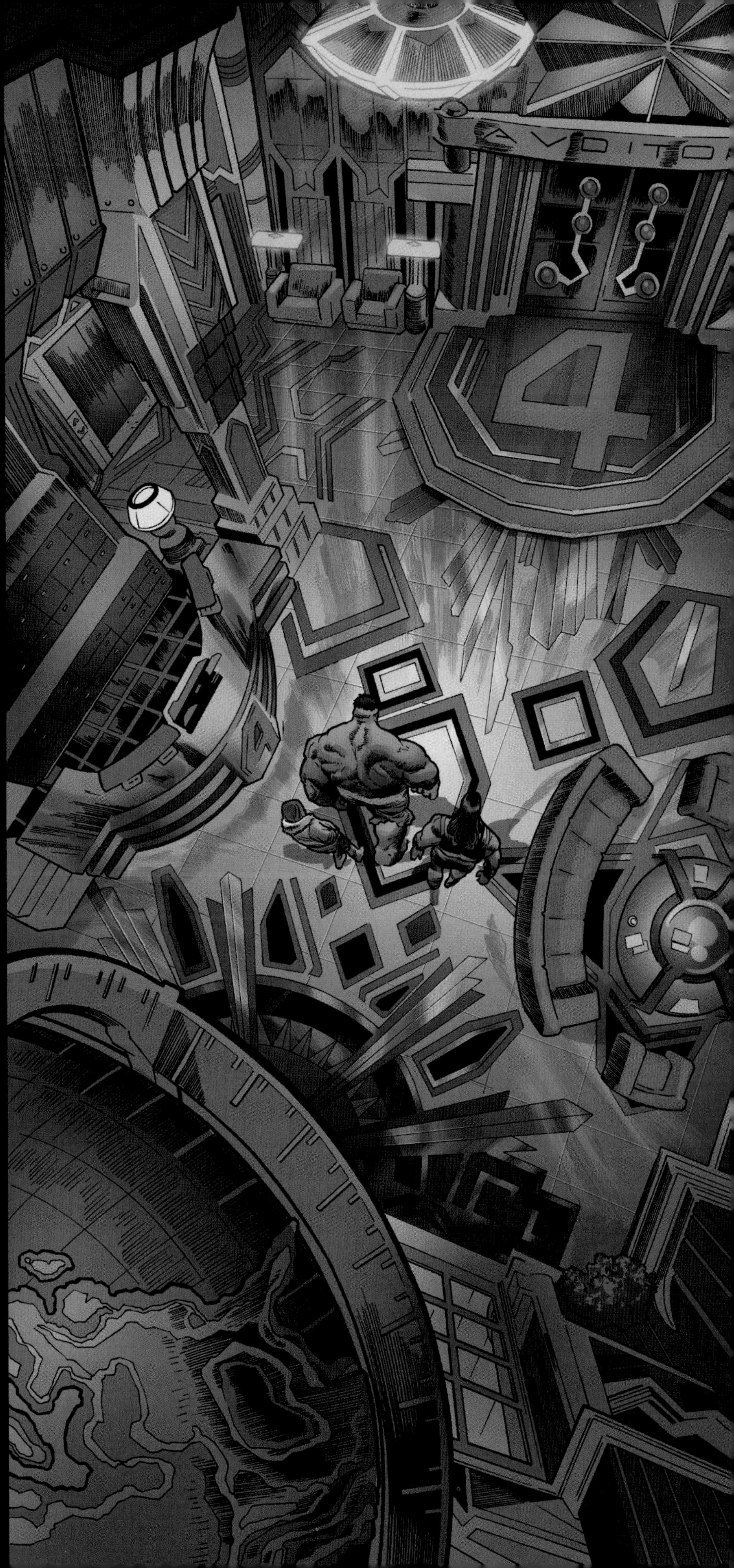

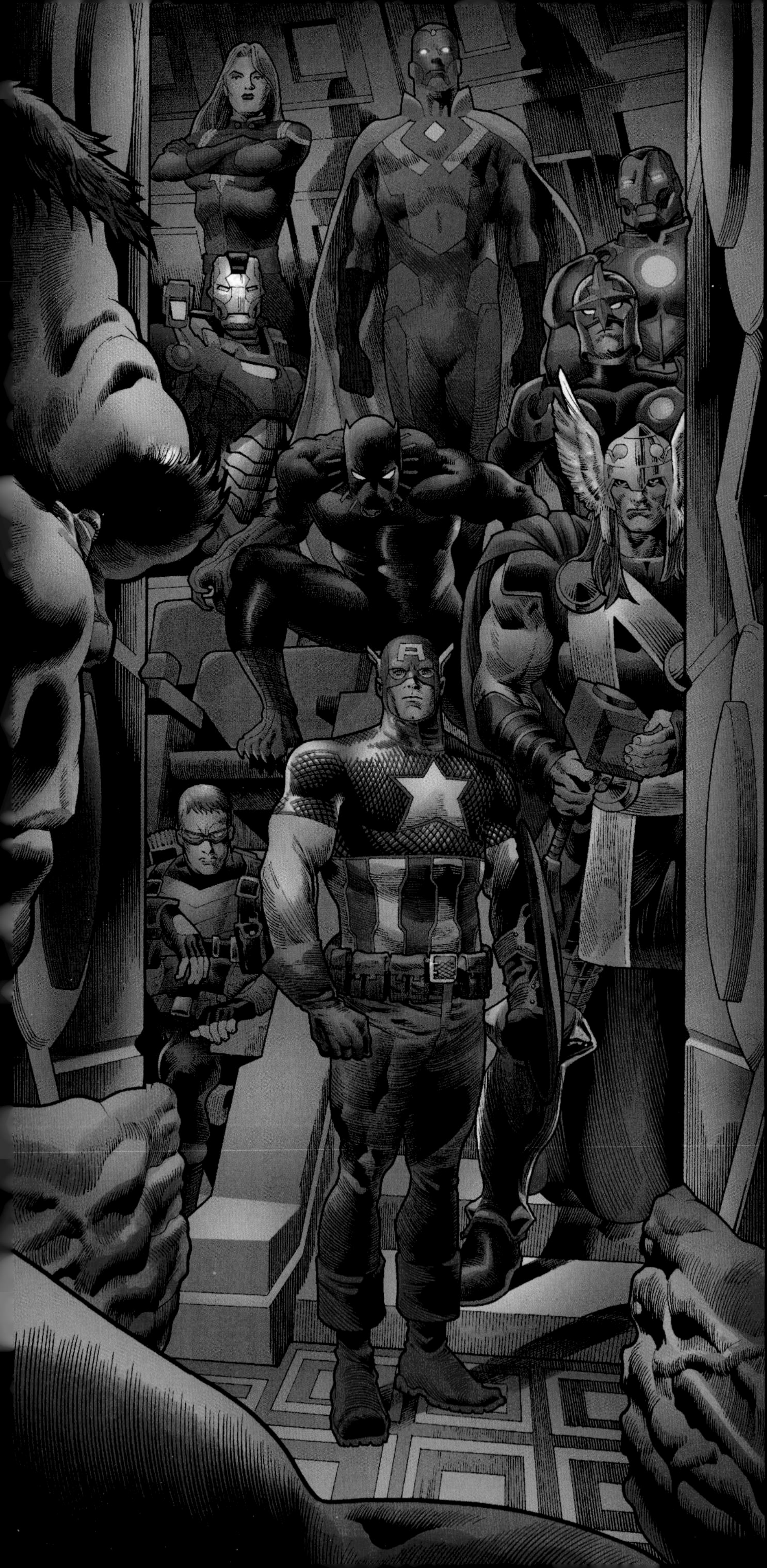
AND THEN--
THERE THEY WERE. WAITING FOR US, FACES WREATHED IN JUDGMENT.
THE SUPER HEROES.

JEN PUT HER ARM UP--A GREEN STEEL BAR, PADDED WITH MUSCLE. FOR A MOMENT, I FELT LIKE I WAS ON A ROLLER-COASTER, READYING FOR THE DROP.

THE HULK STEPPED FORWARD.

THE ROOM BRISTLED. HE MADE THEM ANGRY JUST BY STANDING THERE, NOT SAYING A WORD-- AS IF THE ANGER WAS FLOWING OUT OF HIM AND INTO THEM.

HE DIDN'T SPEAK.

HE ONLY SMILED.

THE ROOM ERUPTED.

STEVE ROGERS TRIED TO CALM THINGS, BUT THE ANGER WAS FLOWING NOW-- A FLOOD TIDE HEADING FOR US. THOR LAUNCHED INTO A SPEECH, BUT I COULDN'T HEAR HIM ABOVE ALL THE OTHER SPEECHES, ALL THE OTHER PROCLAMATIONS AND PRONOUNCEMENTS

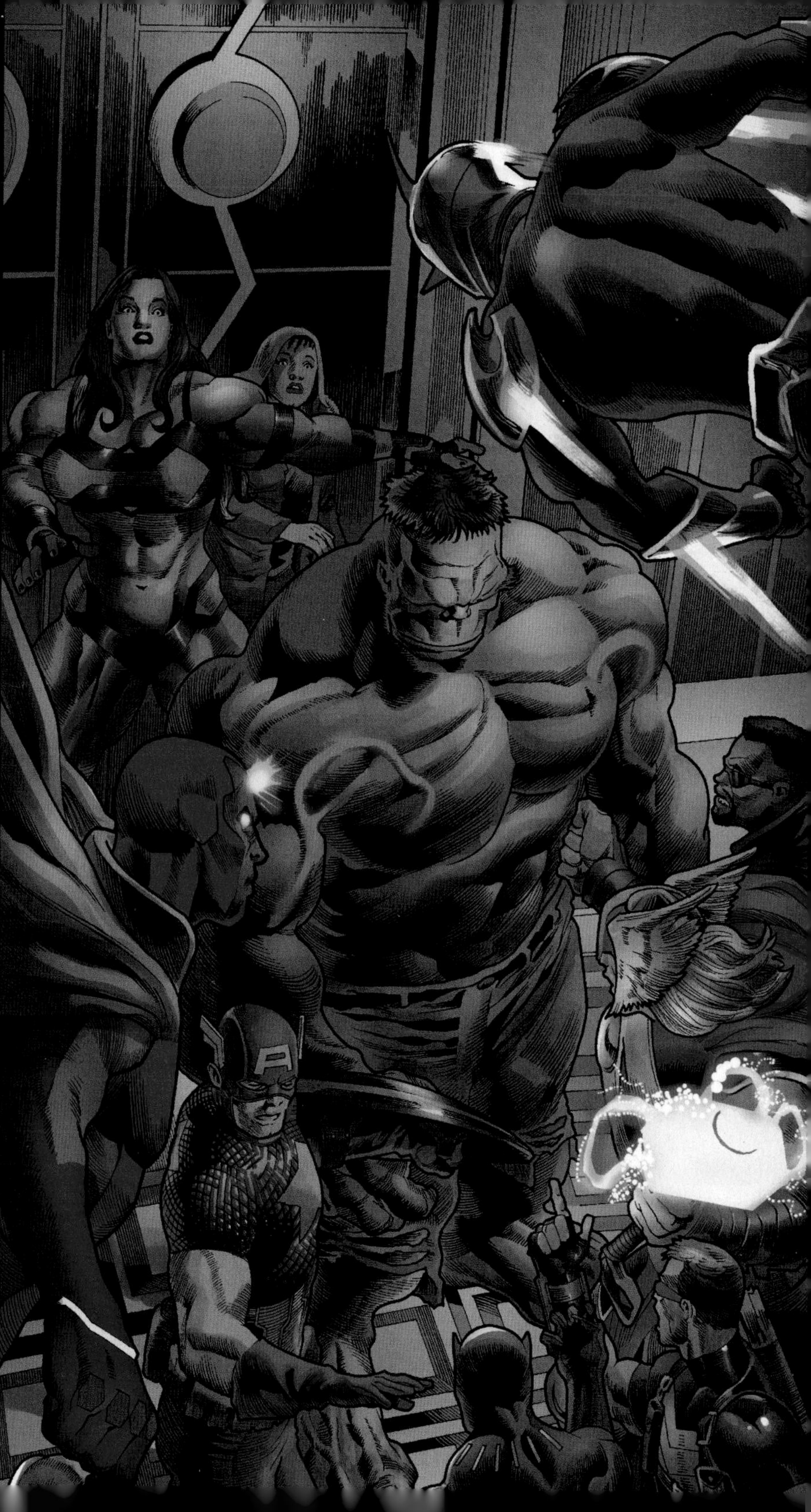

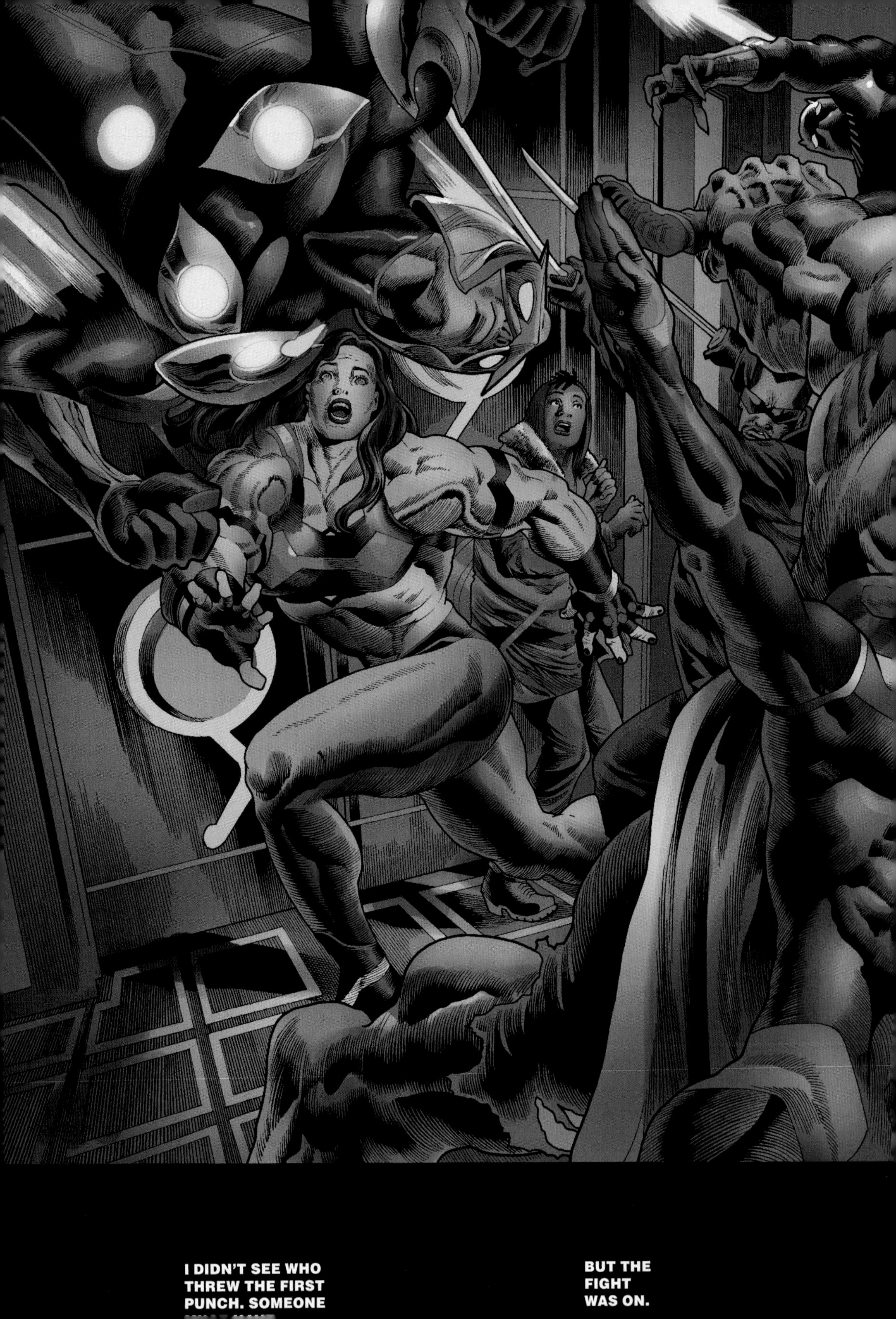
I DIDN'T SEE WHO THREW THE FIRST PUNCH. SOMEONE
BUT THE FIGHT WAS ON.

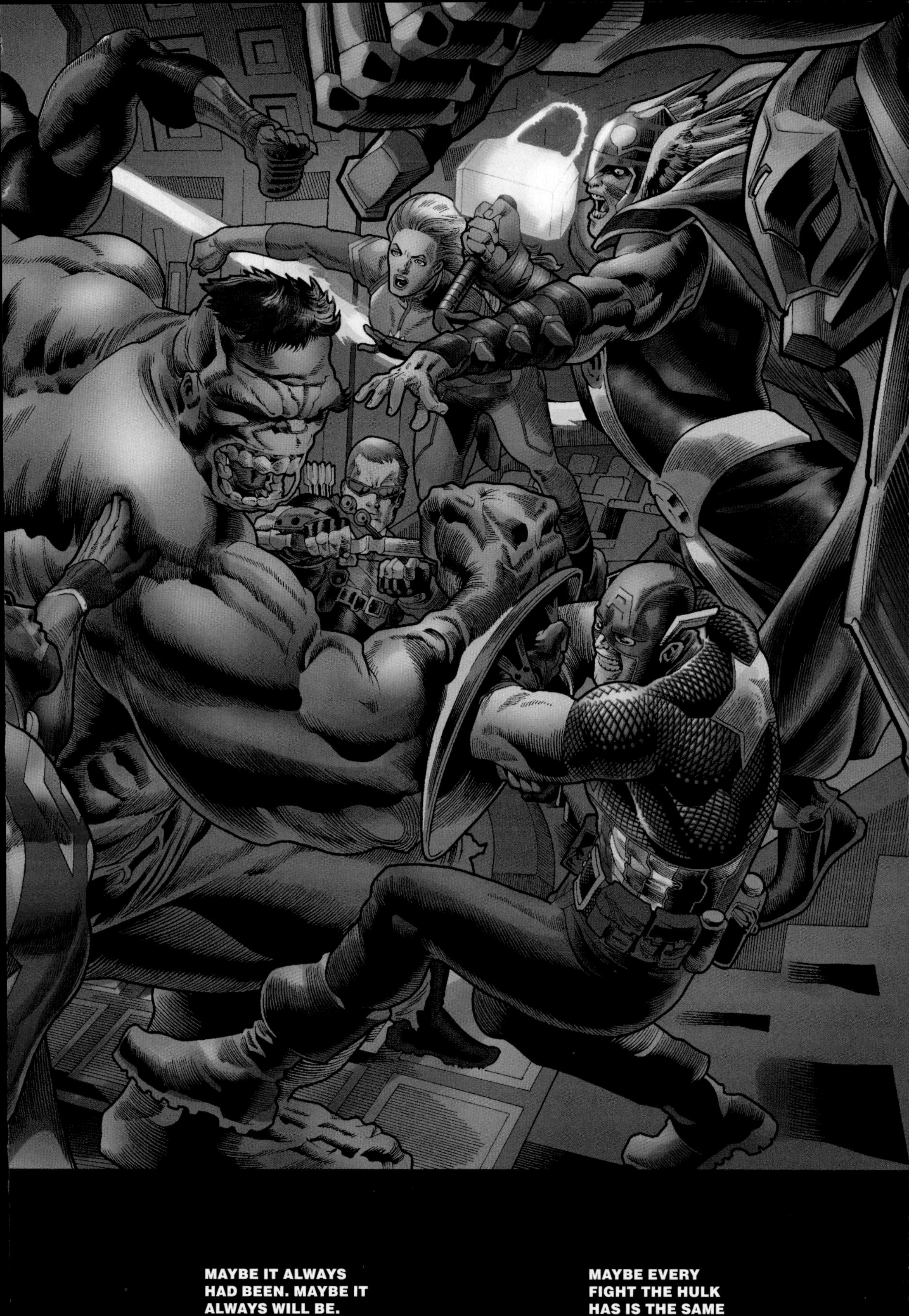
MAYBE IT ALWAYS HAD BEEN. MAYBE IT ALWAYS WILL BE.
MAYBE EVERY FIGHT THE HULK HAS IS THE SAME

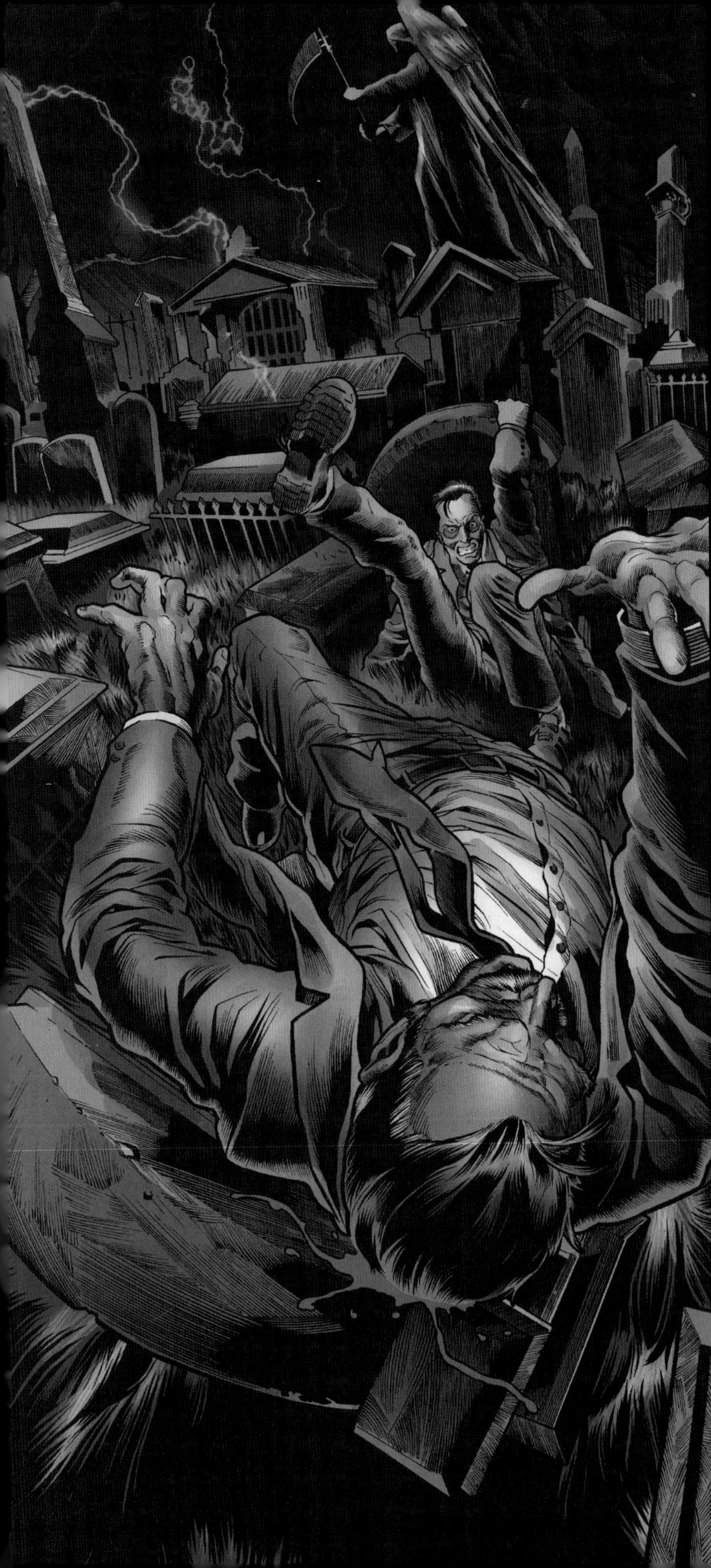

...EVER SINCE THE BEGINNING.

THE NIGHT BEFORE THE FIRST GAMMA BOMB TEST, BRIAN BANNER DIED FROM A VIOLENT ASSAULT IN THE GRAVEYARD WHERE HIS WIFE REBECCA WAS BURIED. IT WAS THE ANNIVERSARY OF THE DAY SHE HAD DIED.

BRIAN MURDERED HER.

HE FORCED HIS SON BRUCE TO LIE ABOUT IT IN COURT--TO BE COMPLICIT IN HIS OWN MOTHER'S KILLING--BUT THE TRUTH CAME OUT. SOMETIMES IT WORKS THAT WAY. BUT HE PLED INSANITY AND WAS COMMITTED, RATHER THAN JAILED, AND RELEASED INTO BRUCE'S CARE.

THE OFFICIAL STORY OF HIS DEATH WAS THAT HE WAS THE VICTIM OF A MUGGING--BUT FOOTPRINTS ON THE GRAVES MATCHED BRUCE'S SHOE SIZE, AND A PLASTIC STAR LEFT AT THE SCENE CAN ALSO BE SPOTTED HANGING ABOVE BRUCE'S CRIB IN FAMILY PHOTOS.

THIS EVIDENCE WAS IGNORED BY THE DAYTON POLICE--WHO WOULD HAVE KNOWN REBECCA, AND PERHAPS EVEN KNOWN HER BROTHER-IN-LAW, SHERIFF MORRIS WALTERS.

SOMETIMES IT WORKS THAT WAY TOO.

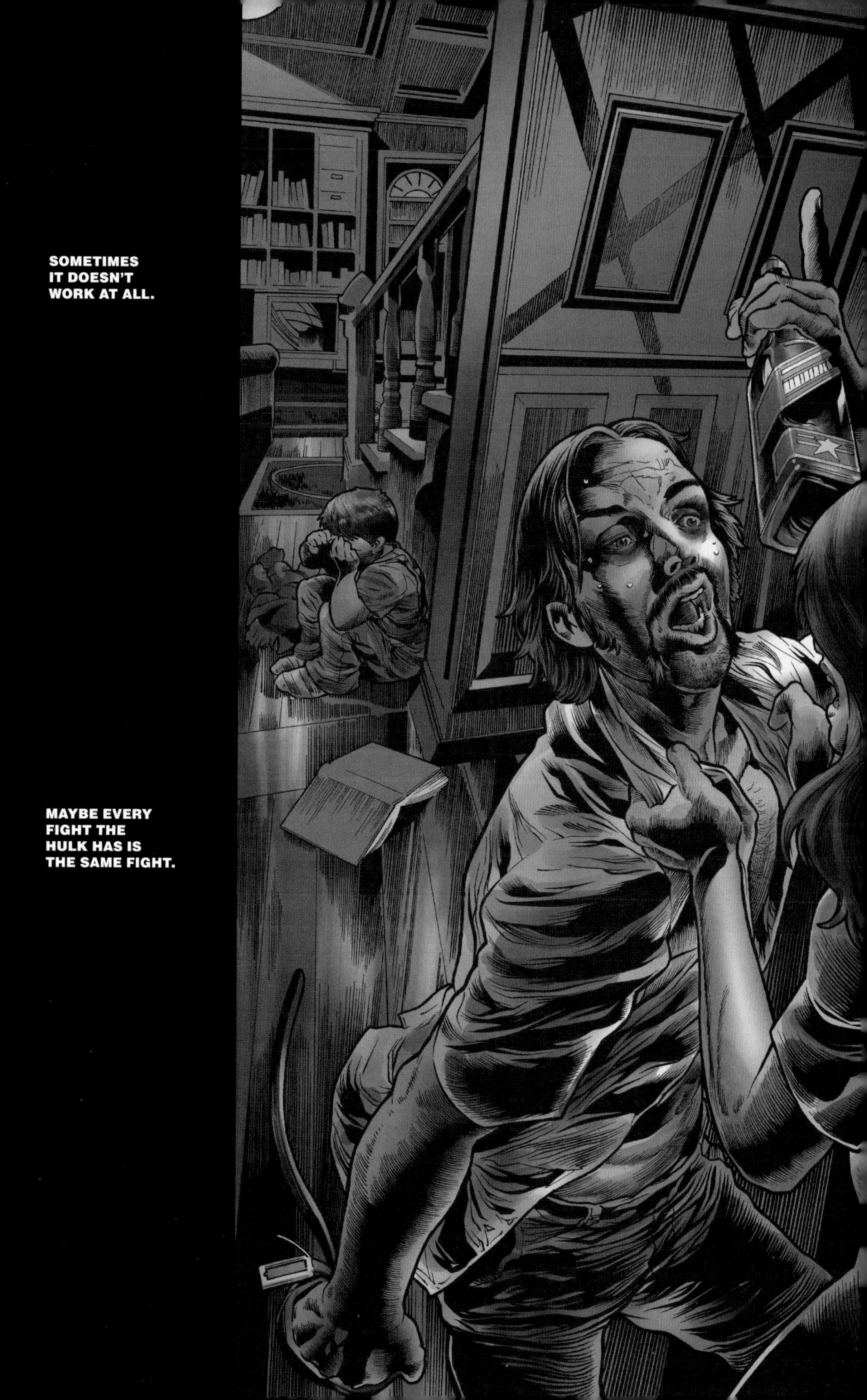
SOMETIMES IT DOESN'T WORK AT ALL.
MAYBE EVERY FIGHT THE HULK HAS IS THE SAME FIGHT.

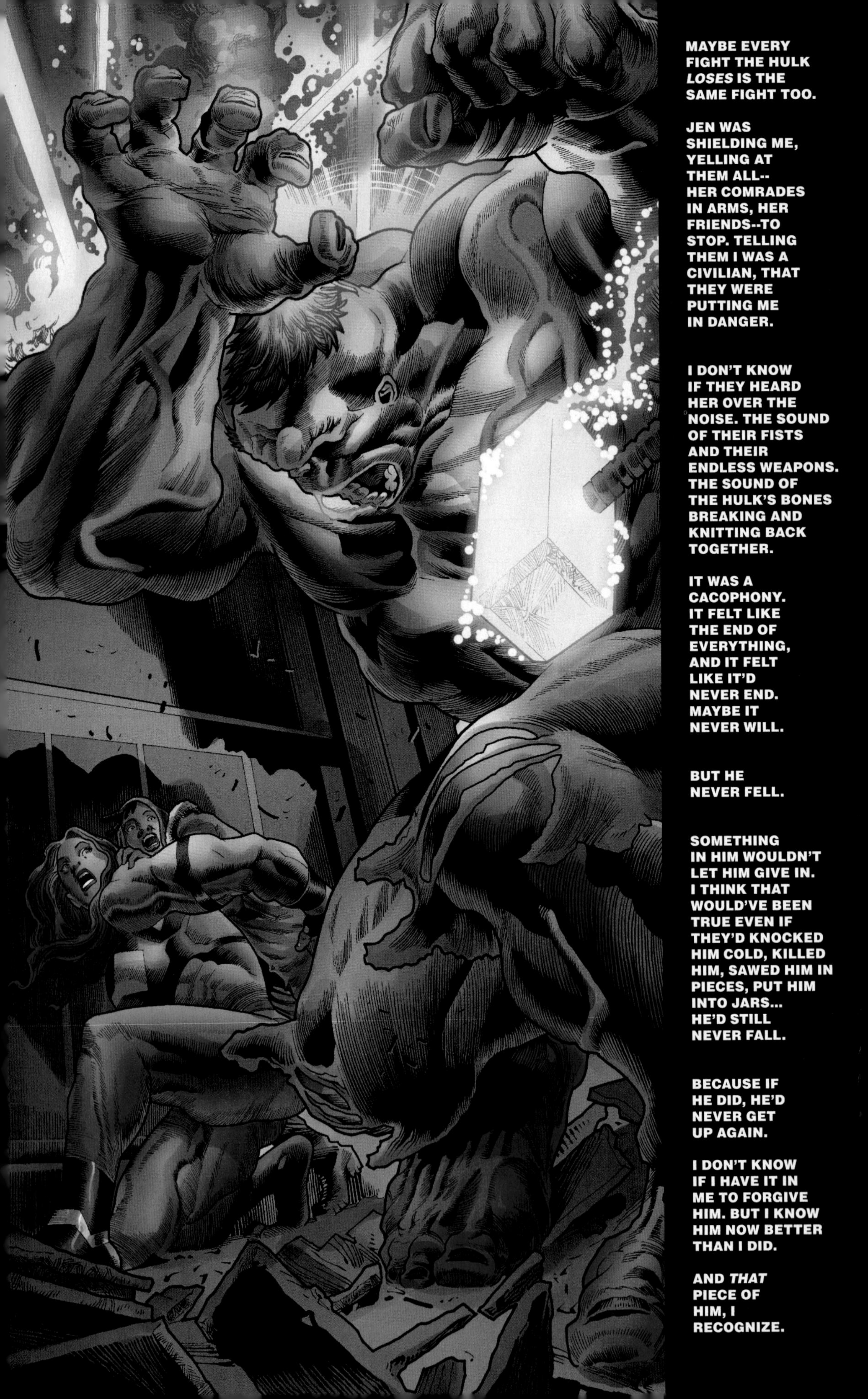
MAYBE EVERY FIGHT THE HULK *LOSES* IS THE SAME FIGHT TOO.
JEN WAS SHIELDING ME, YELLING AT THEM ALL-- HER COMRADES IN ARMS, HER FRIENDS--TO STOP. TELLING THEM I WAS A CIVILIAN, THAT THEY WERE PUTTING ME IN DANGER.
I DON'T KNOW IF THEY HEARD HER OVER THE NOISE. THE SOUND OF THEIR FISTS AND THEIR ENDLESS WEAPONS. THE SOUND OF THE HULK'S BONES BREAKING AND KNITTING BACK TOGETHER.
IT WAS A CACOPHONY. IT FELT LIKE THE END OF EVERYTHING, AND IT FELT LIKE IT'D NEVER END. MAYBE IT NEVER WILL.
BUT HE NEVER FELL.
SOMETHING IN HIM WOULDN'T LET HIM GIVE IN. I THINK THAT WOULD'VE BEEN TRUE EVEN IF THEY'D KNOCKED HIM COLD, KILLED HIM, SAWED HIM IN PIECES, PUT HIM INTO JARS... HE'D STILL NEVER FALL.
BECAUSE IF HE DID, HE'D NEVER GET UP AGAIN.
I DON'T KNOW IF I HAVE IT IN ME TO FORGIVE HIM. BUT I KNOW HIM NOW BETTER THAN I DID.
AND *THAT* PIECE OF HIM, I RECOGNIZE.

DID THEY SEE THEMSELVES IN HIM AS WELL?

WAS THAT WHY THEY COULDN'T HELP ATTACKING? BANNER SAW THE HULK IN MIRRORS, BUT THE HULK IS A MIRROR TOO-- A REFLECTION THAT REFLECTS BACK AT YOU. AND THESE WEREN'T GAMMA PEOPLE--DID THE HULK SEEM LIKE A CONTAGION TO THEM? WAS HE UNCLEAN?

WE'LL NEVER KNOW.

THE NOISE STOPPED. THOR'S HAMMER KEPT FALLING, BUT IT ONLY HIT SILENCE. AN INVISIBLE SPACE AROUND THE HULK TOOK SHAPE, AND WIDENED.

THE SHOUTING AND YELLING FELL TO GRUMBLING, THEN TO NOTHING. MAYBE THE FORCE-FIELD WAS BLOCKING WHATEVER EFFECT THE HULK WAS HAVING. OR MAYBE IT WAS JUST DOING WHAT THEY ALL WANTED--KEEPING THE HORROR AWAY FROM THOSE UNTOUCHED BY IT.

THE DOORS OPENED BEHIND US.

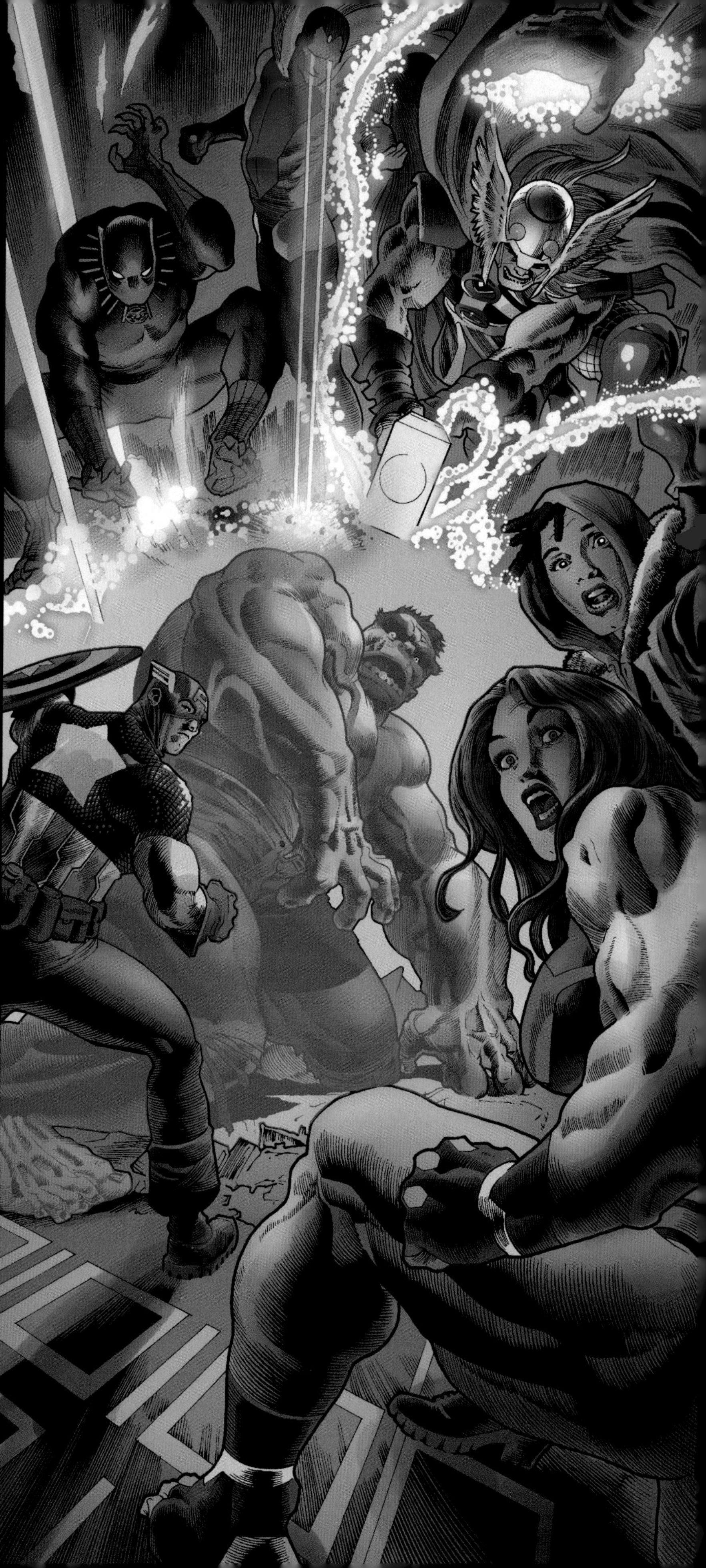

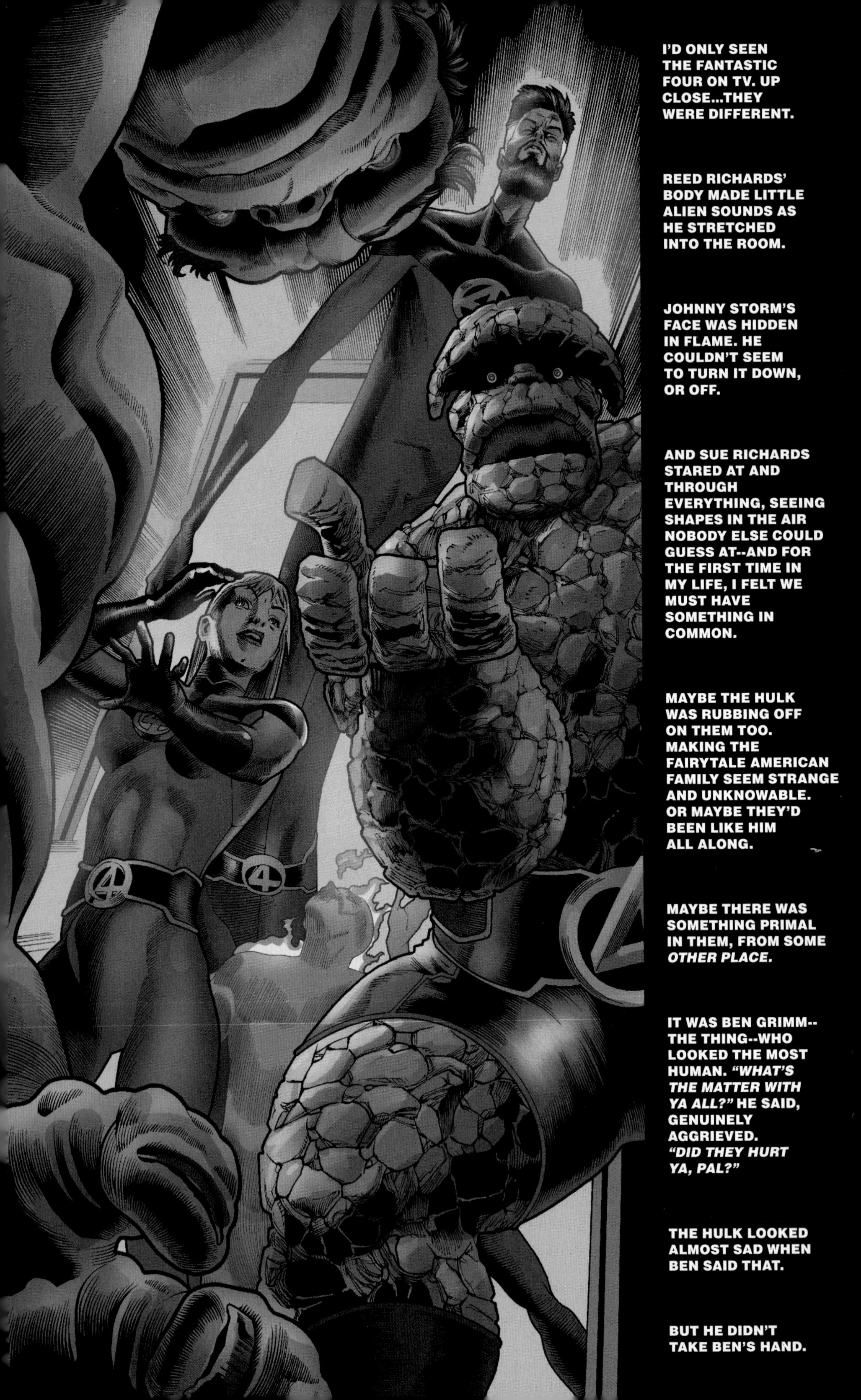
I'D ONLY SEEN THE FANTASTIC FOUR ON TV. UP CLOSE...THEY WERE DIFFERENT.
REED RICHARDS' BODY MADE LITTLE ALIEN SOUNDS AS HE STRETCHED INTO THE ROOM.
JOHNNY STORM'S FACE WAS HIDDEN IN FLAME. HE COULDN'T SEEM TO TURN IT DOWN, OR OFF.
AND SUE RICHARDS STARED AT AND THROUGH EVERYTHING, SEEING SHAPES IN THE AIR NOBODY ELSE COULD GUESS AT--AND FOR THE FIRST TIME IN MY LIFE, I FELT WE MUST HAVE SOMETHING IN COMMON.
MAYBE THE HULK WAS RUBBING OFF ON THEM TOO. MAKING THE FAIRYTALE AMERICAN FAMILY SEEM STRANGE AND UNKNOWABLE. OR MAYBE THEY'D BEEN LIKE HIM ALL ALONG.
MAYBE THERE WAS SOMETHING PRIMAL IN THEM, FROM SOME *OTHER PLACE.*
IT WAS BEN GRIMM--THE THING--WHO LOOKED THE MOST HUMAN. *"WHAT'S THE MATTER WITH YA ALL?"* HE SAID, GENUINELY AGGRIEVED. *"DID THEY HURT YA, PAL?"*
THE HULK LOOKED ALMOST SAD WHEN BEN SAID THAT.
BUT HE DIDN'T TAKE BEN'S HAND.

HE NEVER SAID A WORD AS WE LEFT THE WORLD OF THE SUPER HEROES BEHIND US. HE HADN'T BEATEN IT, IN THE END.

BUT IT HADN'T BEATEN HIM, EITHER.

BEN GRIMM'S VOICE SEEMED TO COME FROM FAR AWAY. *"YER OKAY, PAL. YER OKAY."*

IT WAS A VOICE WITH ALL THE DEEP GRAVEL OF THE HULK'S AND MORE--BUT WARMER SOMEHOW. I THOUGHT OF MY GRANDFATHER, AT MY MOTHER'S FUNERAL. HE'D SPOKEN OF THE LAST DAY, WHEN GOD WOULD CALL THE SOULS OF THE DEAD. CALL THEM AND JUDGE THEM.

"YER OKAY, PAL. YER OKAY."

WE WALKED DEEPER INTO THE BUILDING, PASSING THROUGH CORRIDORS OF FLASHING LIGHT AND SOUND. SECURITY SYSTEMS AND STRANGE EXPERIMENTS. WONDERS AND PORTENTS.

UNTIL FINALLY, WE CAME TO THE GATE.

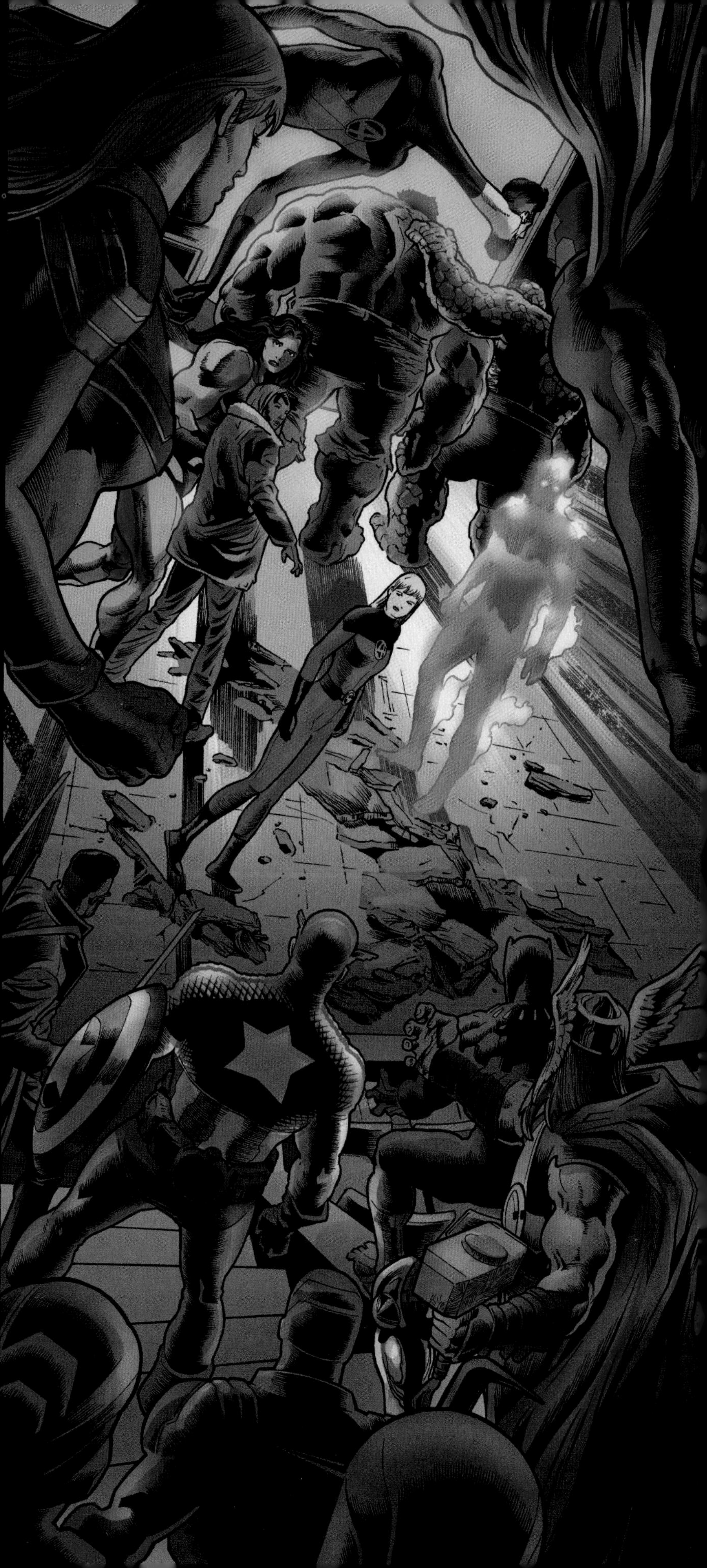

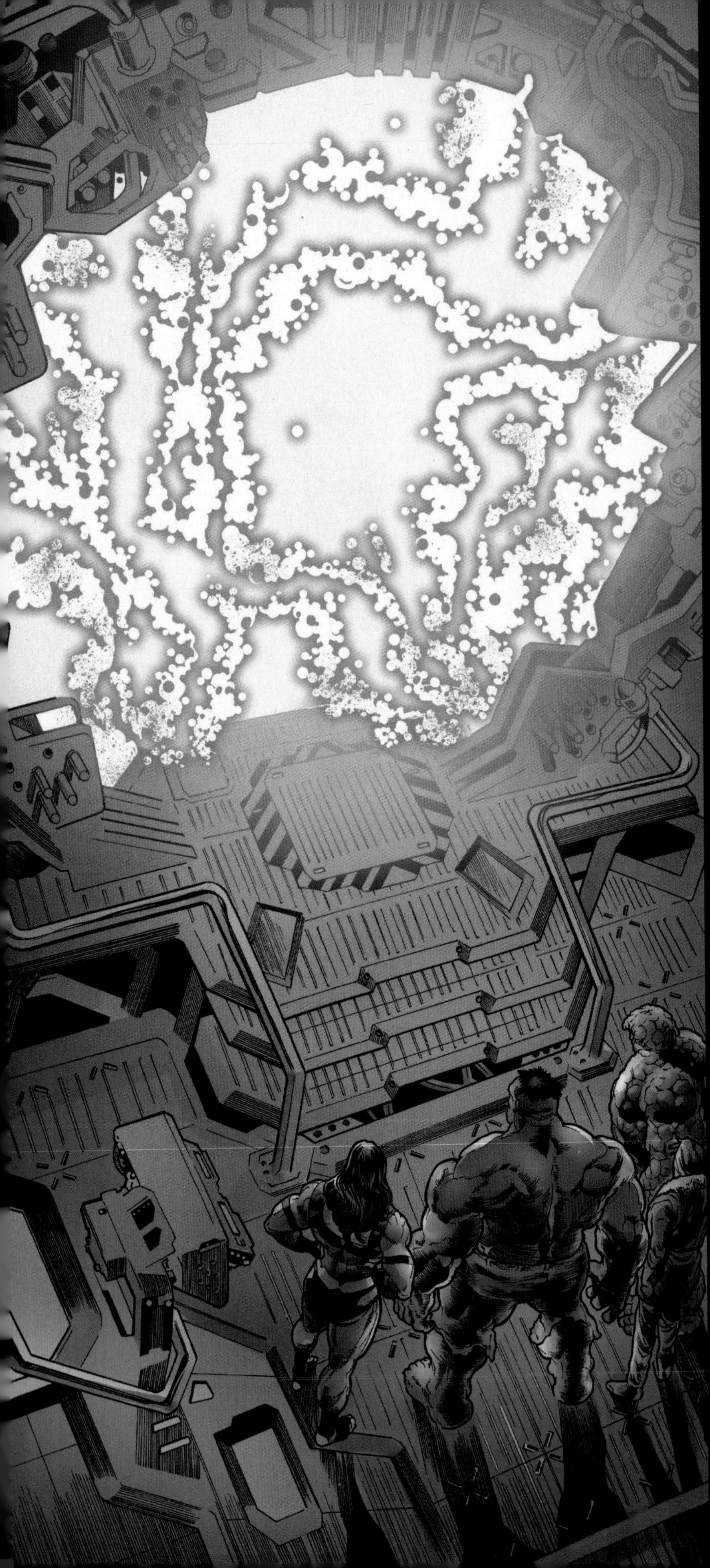

THE FOREVER GATE.

IT WAS A PORTAL TO WHEREVER YOU WANTED TO GO, BEN SAID. A JUNCTION TO ANYWHERE. THE KIND OF CASUAL MIRACLE THE FANTASTIC FOUR DEALT WITH EVERY DAY.

DR. RICHARDS TRIED TO EXPLAIN IT. HIS VOICE FALTERED AS HE SPOKE OF PARTICLES, WAVES, FREQUENCIES, GAMMA AND COSMIC RADIATION--AS IF HE WAS TRYING TO SPEAK, IN THE ONLY LANGUAGE HE KNEW, OF THINGS EVEN HE HAD NO WORDS FOR. EVENTUALLY, HE FALTERED, SHOOK HIS HEAD AND LET BEN TALK FOR HIM.

IT WAS SIMPLE, BEN SAID. THE GATE WOULD SCAN THE HULK, EVERY CELL OF HIM, AND USE WHAT IT FOUND IN HIM TO FIND WHERE WE WERE GOING. IT MIGHT NOT BRING THE HULK TO THE LEADER'S DOOR, BUT IT'D AT LEAST TAKE HIM TO THE LEADER'S BACKYARD--AND MAYBE THAT WAY, HULK COULD SURPRISE HIM. IT WAS A FAIR CHANCE--NOTHING MORE, NOTHING LESS.

WHEN HE SAID IT, IT MADE SENSE. WE WAITED FOR THE HULK TO SAY SOMETHING BACK.

THE MACHINE BEGAN TO HUM.

THE HULK LOOKED INTO THE GATE.

AND THE GATE LOOKED INTO THE HULK.

AS THE MACHINE ANALYZED THE DATA, SEARCHING THROUGH POSSIBILITIES, IMAGES FLICKERED AND FLOWED IN THE CRACKLING RED PLASMA.

FOR A MOMENT, I SAW FOUR FIGURES TAKE SHAPE--A BIG-HEARTED SCIENTIST AND HIS LOVING WIFE, A GRUFF EX-MILITARY MAN, A CAREFREE TEENAGER. A FAMILY OF FOUR. YOU COULD SEE THE LOVE BETWEEN THEM ALL.

THEY'D NEVER TRIED TO KILL EACH OTHER.

THEY WERE WHAT COULD HAVE BEEN, IF THE ORDER OF EVENTS HAD BEEN JUST A LITTLE DIFFERENT, IF THE COIN HAD LANDED THE OTHER WAY UP.

SOMEONE HAD TO FLY THE ROCKET.

SOMEONE HAD TO BUILD THE BOMB.

THE HULK SAW THEM TOO.

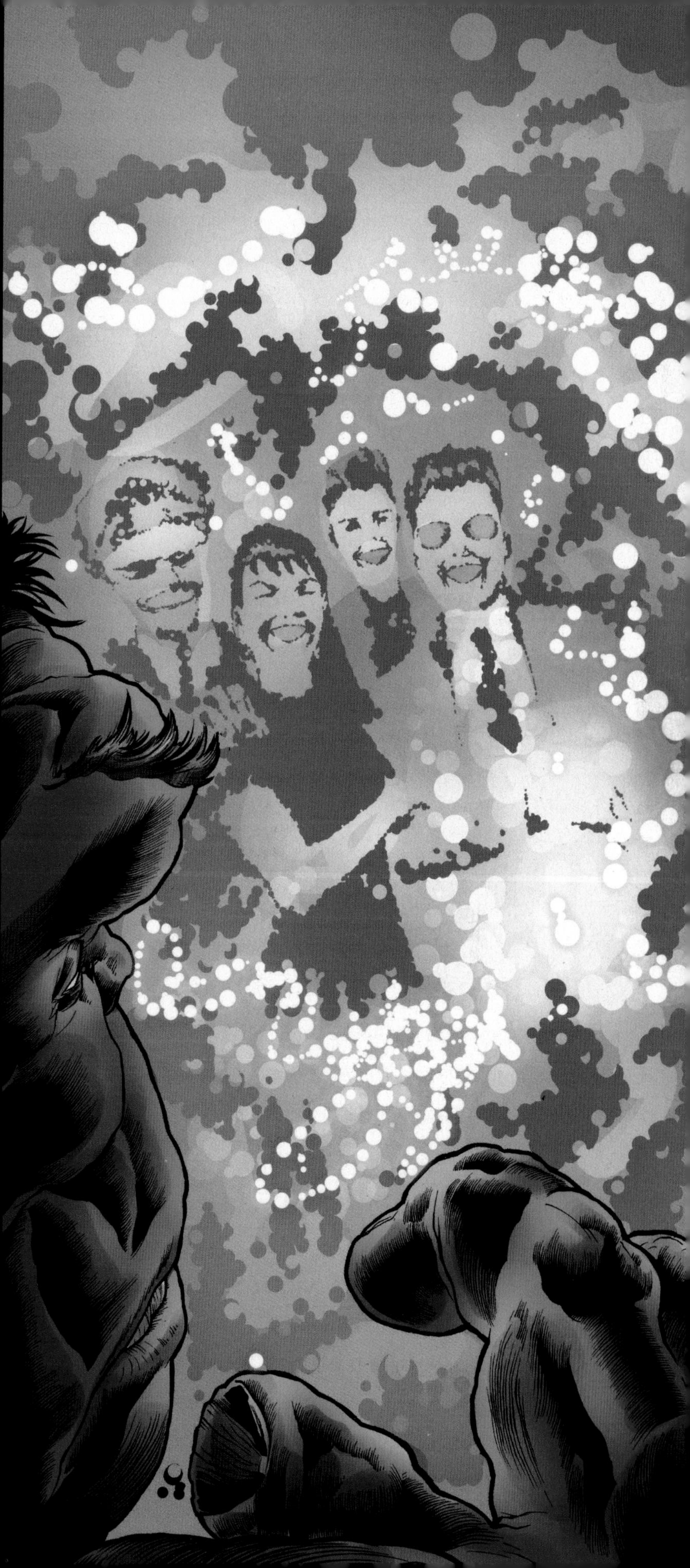

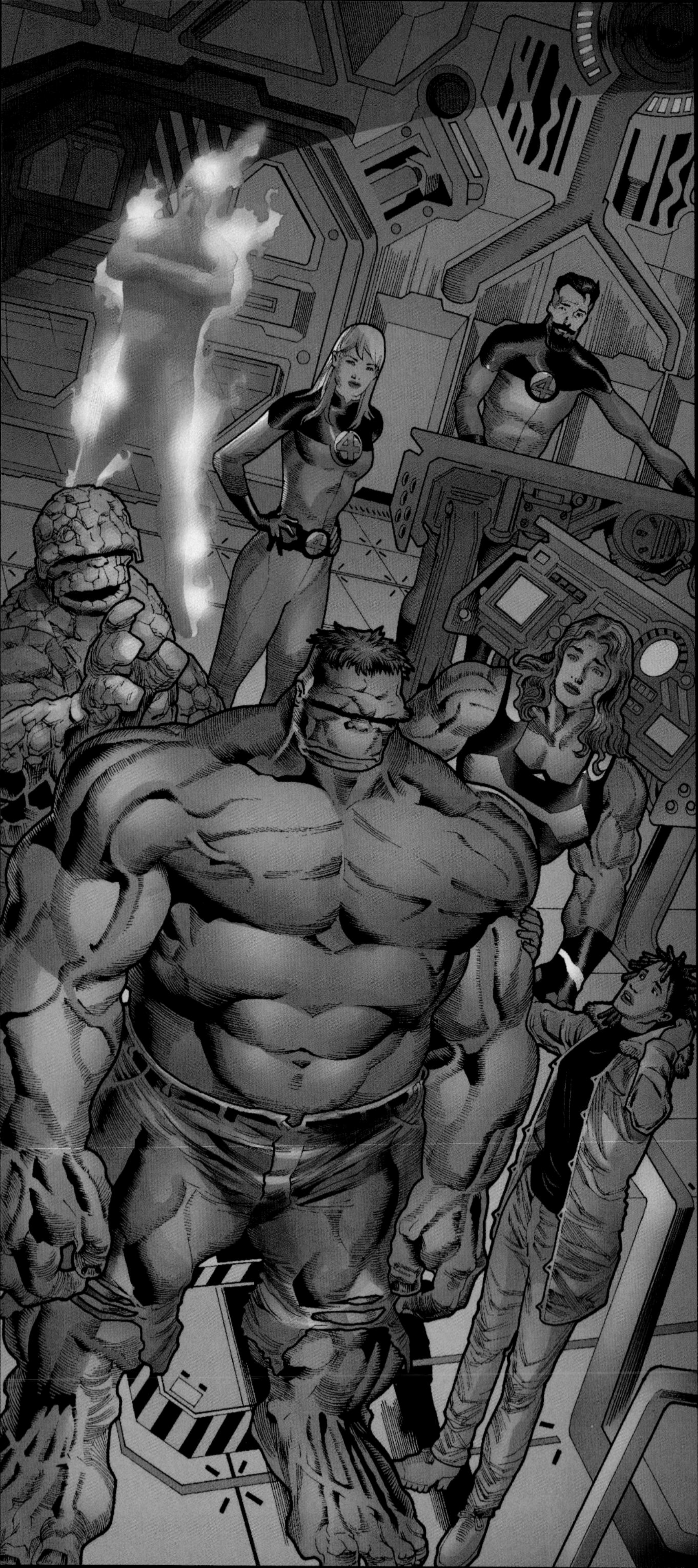

HE KEPT STARING, AS THE IMAGES MERGED BACK INTO STATIC. HE DIDN'T SPEAK.

BEFORE, HIS SILENCE FELT STUBBORN, SINGLE-MINDED--BLOODY-MINDED, EVEN. NOW, AS THE GATE OF HELL YAWNED IN FRONT OF HIM...IT WAS SOMETHING ELSE.

SOMETHING LIKE *FEAR.*

BEN SPOKE, GENTLY. THE FOUR WOULD BACK THE HULK UP WHEN THEY COULD, HE SAID--BUT THIS GATE, RIGHT HERE AND NOW, WAS JUST FOR HIM. HE'D OPEN IT WHEN HE WENT THROUGH, AND HE'D CLOSE IT BEHIND HIM.

DR. RICHARDS LOOKED QUIETLY APOLOGETIC. HE'D DONE HIS BEST.

RED PLASMA BOILED IN FRONT OF US. BRUCE BANNER WAS WAITING ON THE OTHER SIDE OF IT. SO WAS THE LEADER.

SO WAS THE STORY.

THE STORY THAT WAS PART OF ME. THAT HAD BROUGHT ME FROM ARIZONA TO THE EDGE OF SPACE, THAT HAD BROKEN MY LIFE AND BECOME IT. THE ANSWER TO ALL THE QUESTIONS I COULDN'T WALK AWAY FROM.

SO I REACHED OUT...

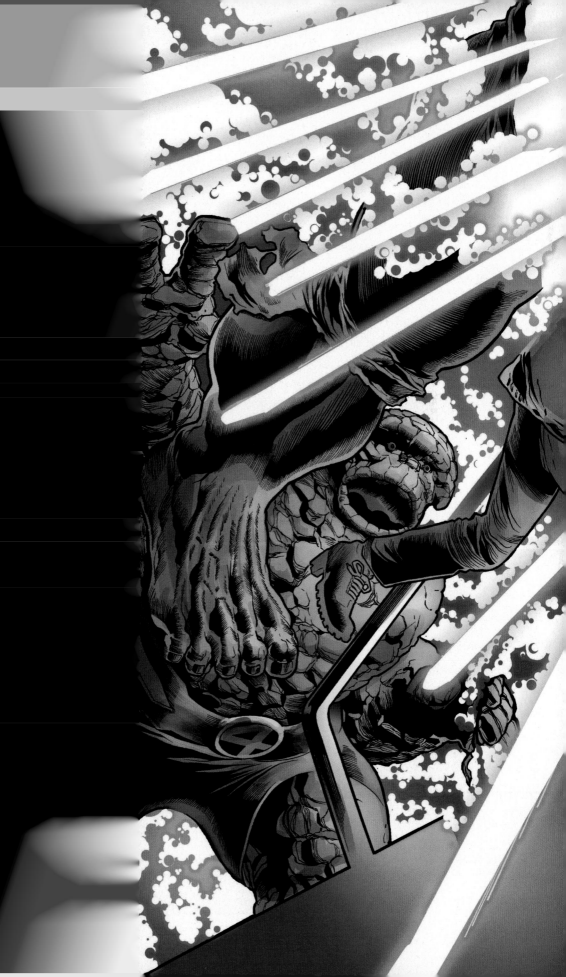

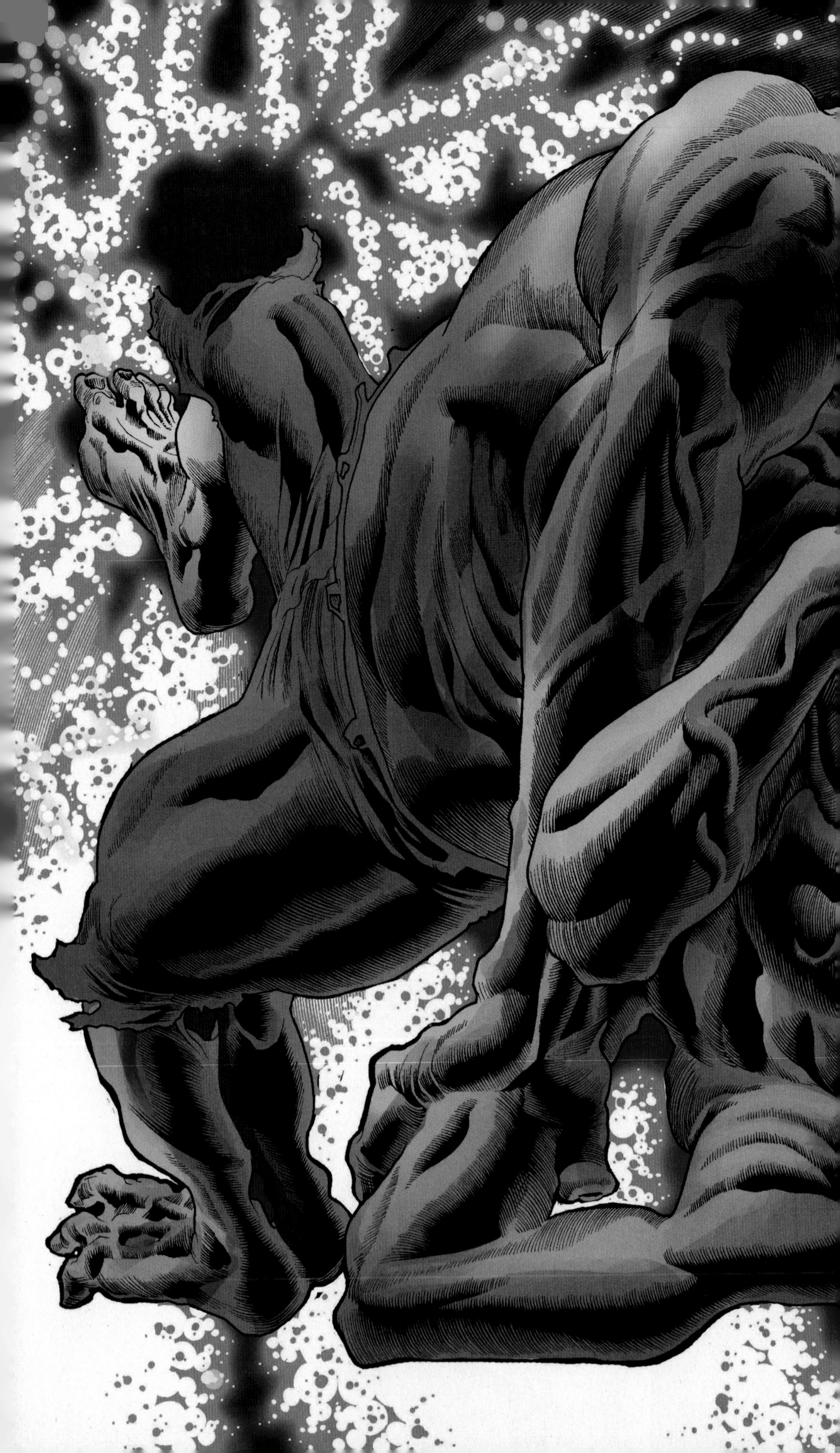

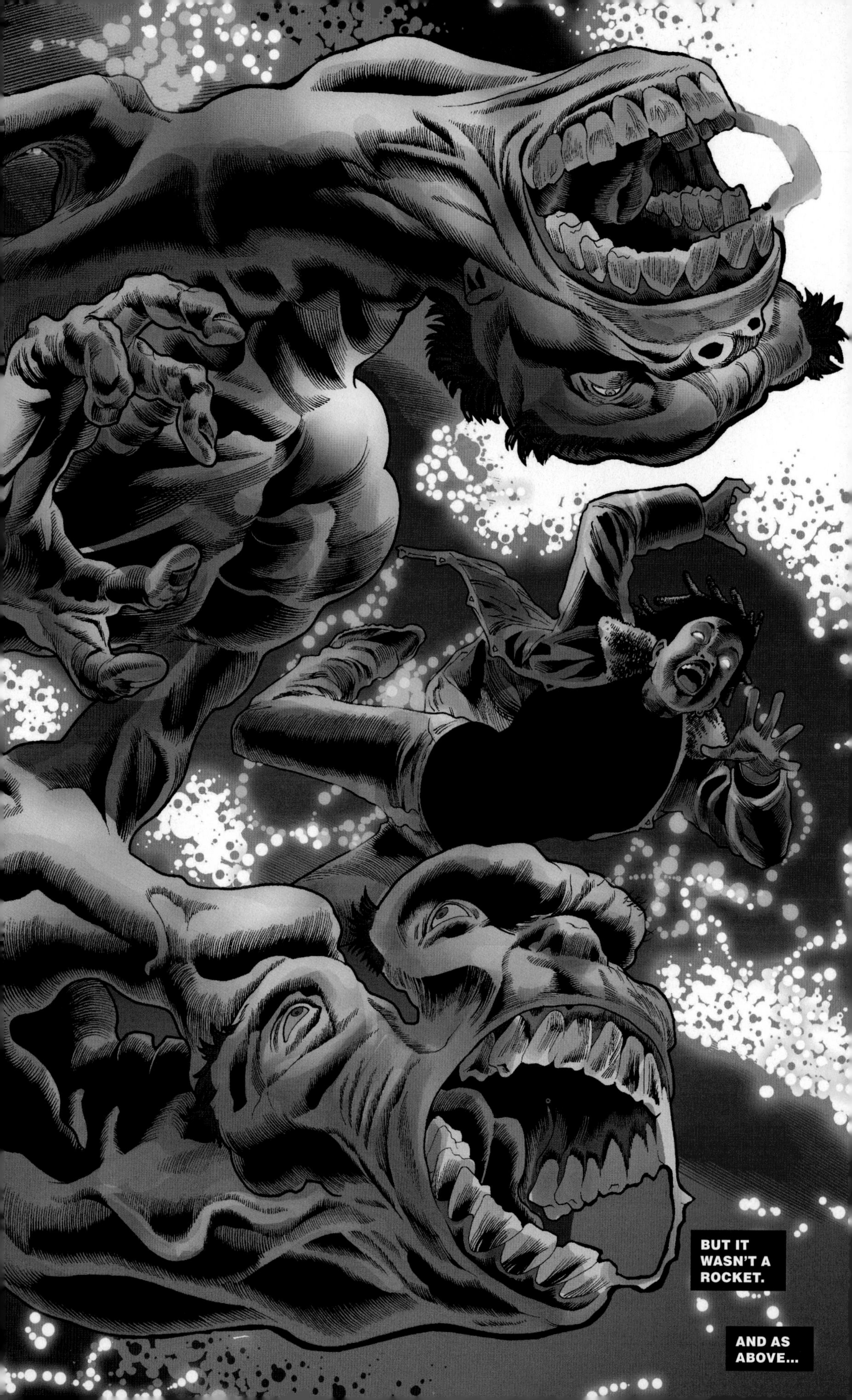

BUT IT WASN'T A ROCKET.
AND AS ABOVE...

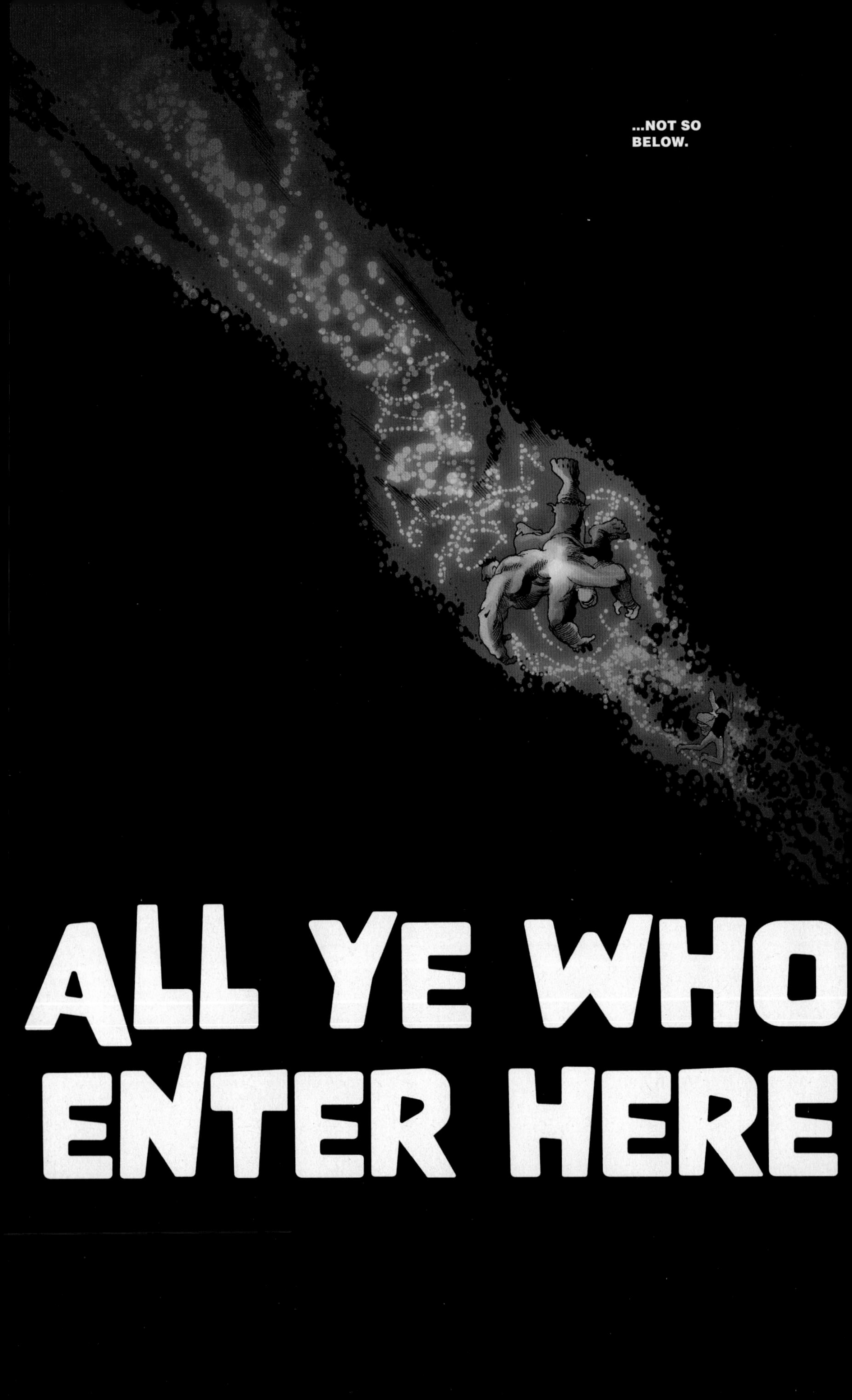
...NOT SO BELOW.
ALL YE WHO ENTER HERE

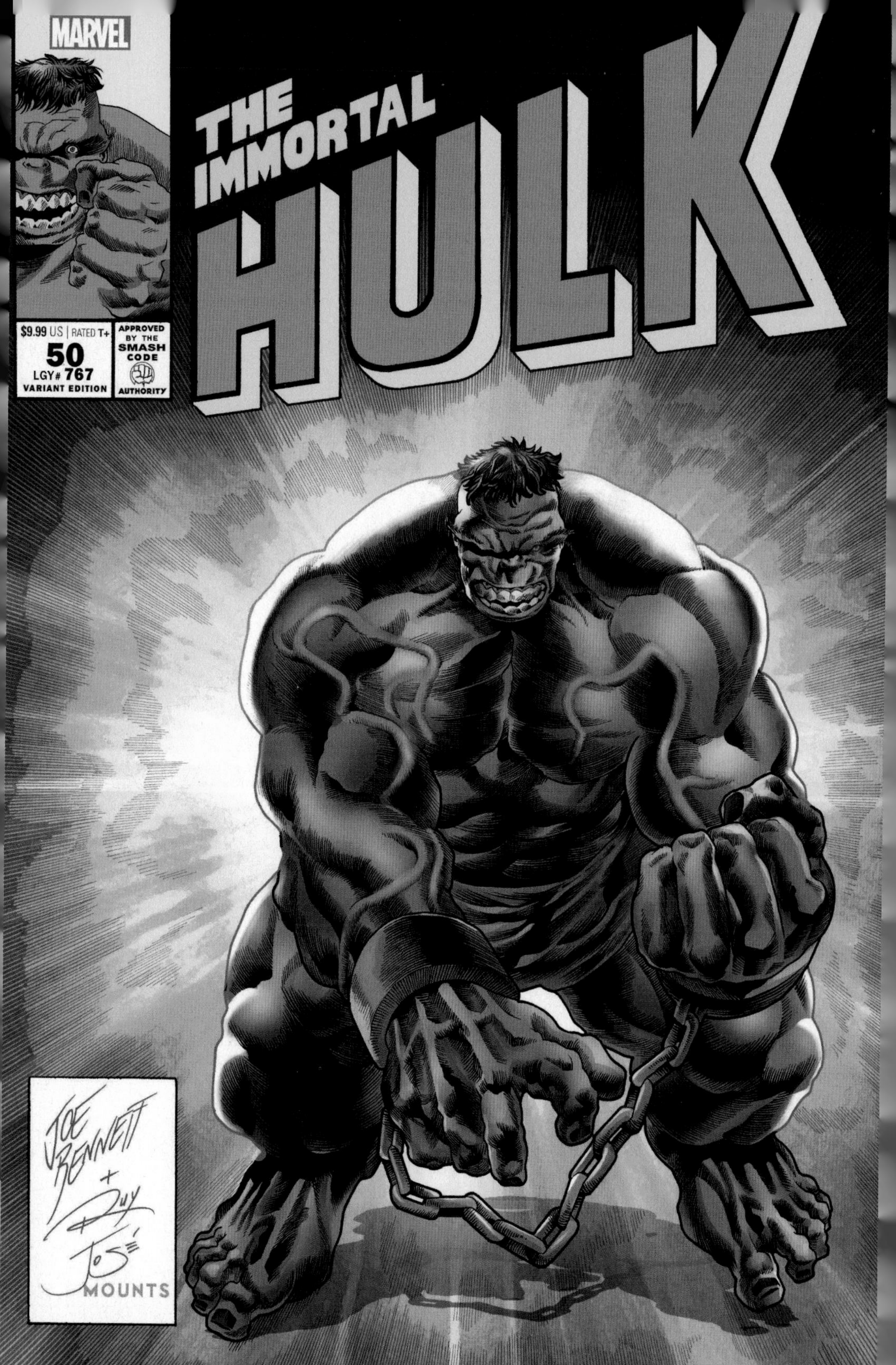
MARVEL
THE IMMORTAL
HULK
$9.99 US | RATED T+
50
LGY# 767
VARIANT EDITION
APPROVED BY THE SMASH CODE AUTHORITY
JOE BENNETT + RUY JOSÉ
MOUNTS

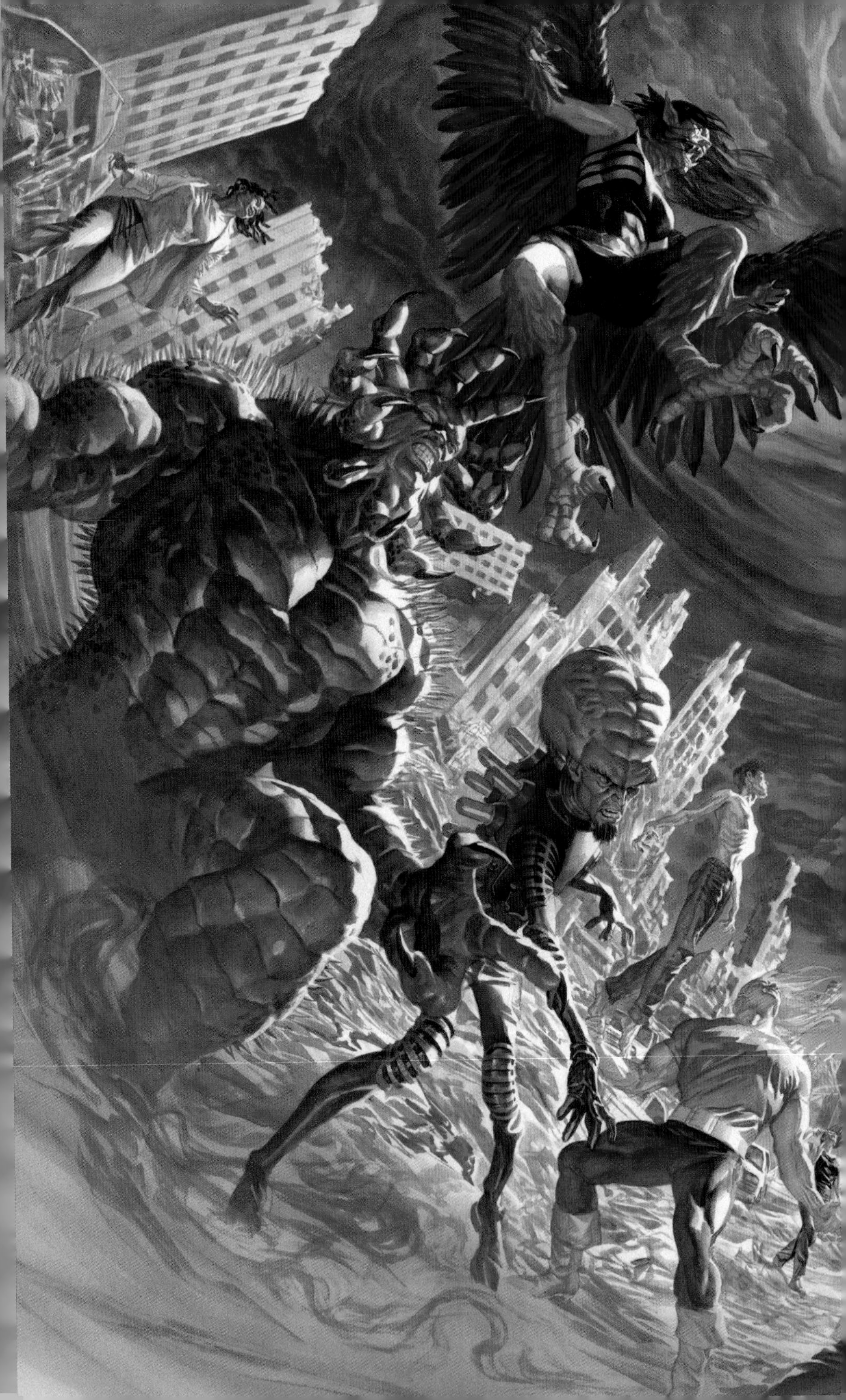

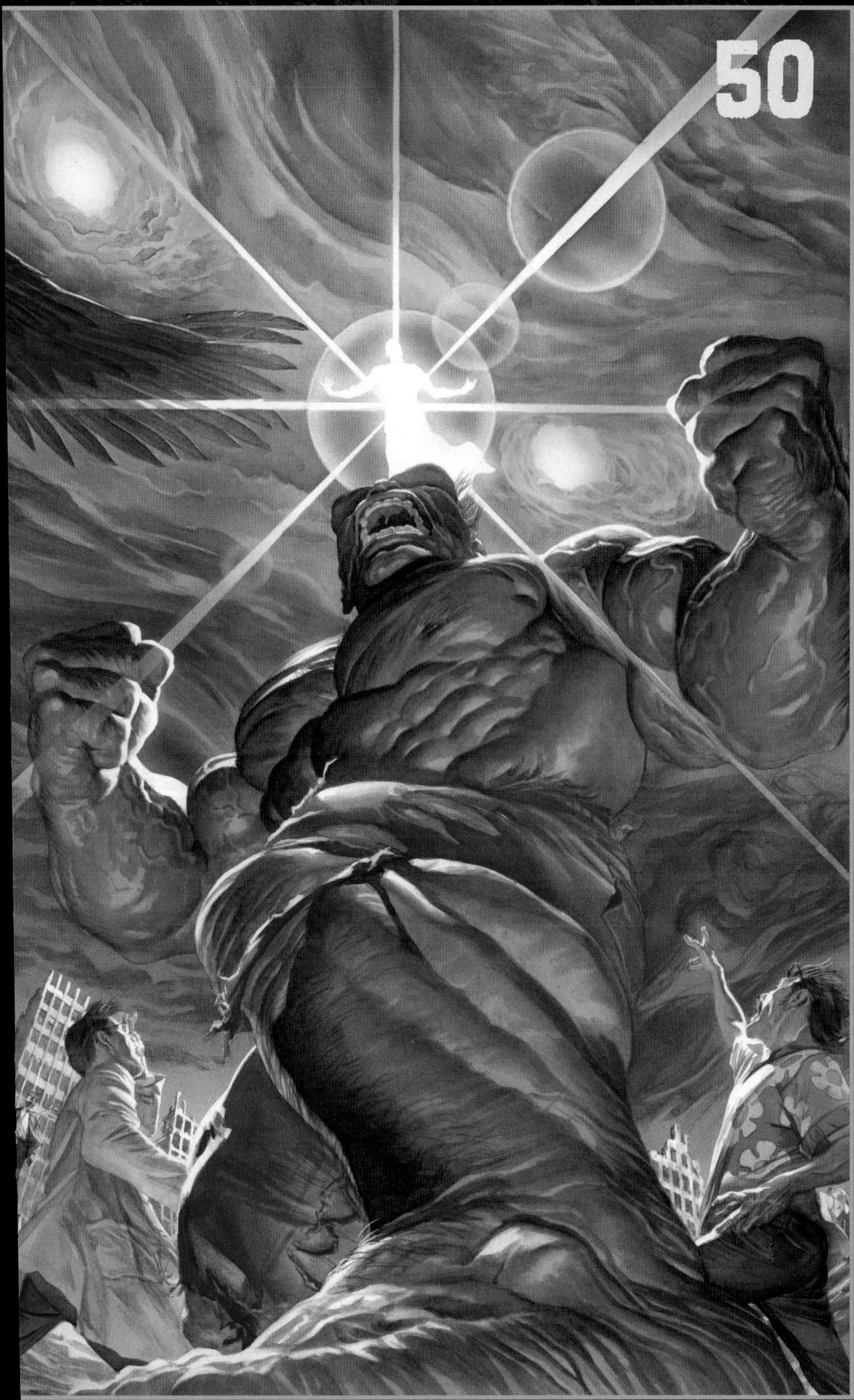
50

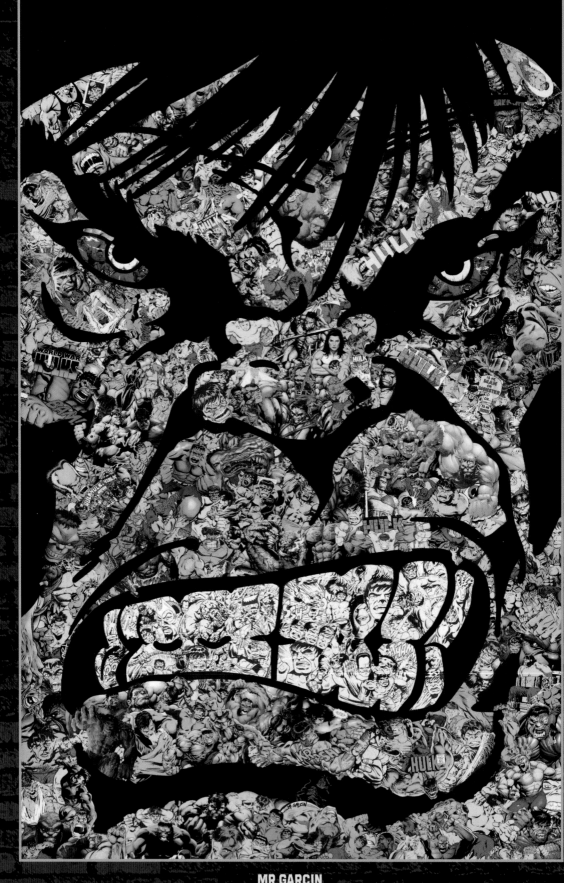

MR GARCIN
#50 VARIANT

"I AM HE THAT LIVETH, AND WAS DEAD; AND, BEHOLD, I AM ALIVE FOR EVERMORE, AMEN; AND HAVE THE KEYS OF HELL AND OF DEATH."

— REVELATION 1:18

OHIO
1901

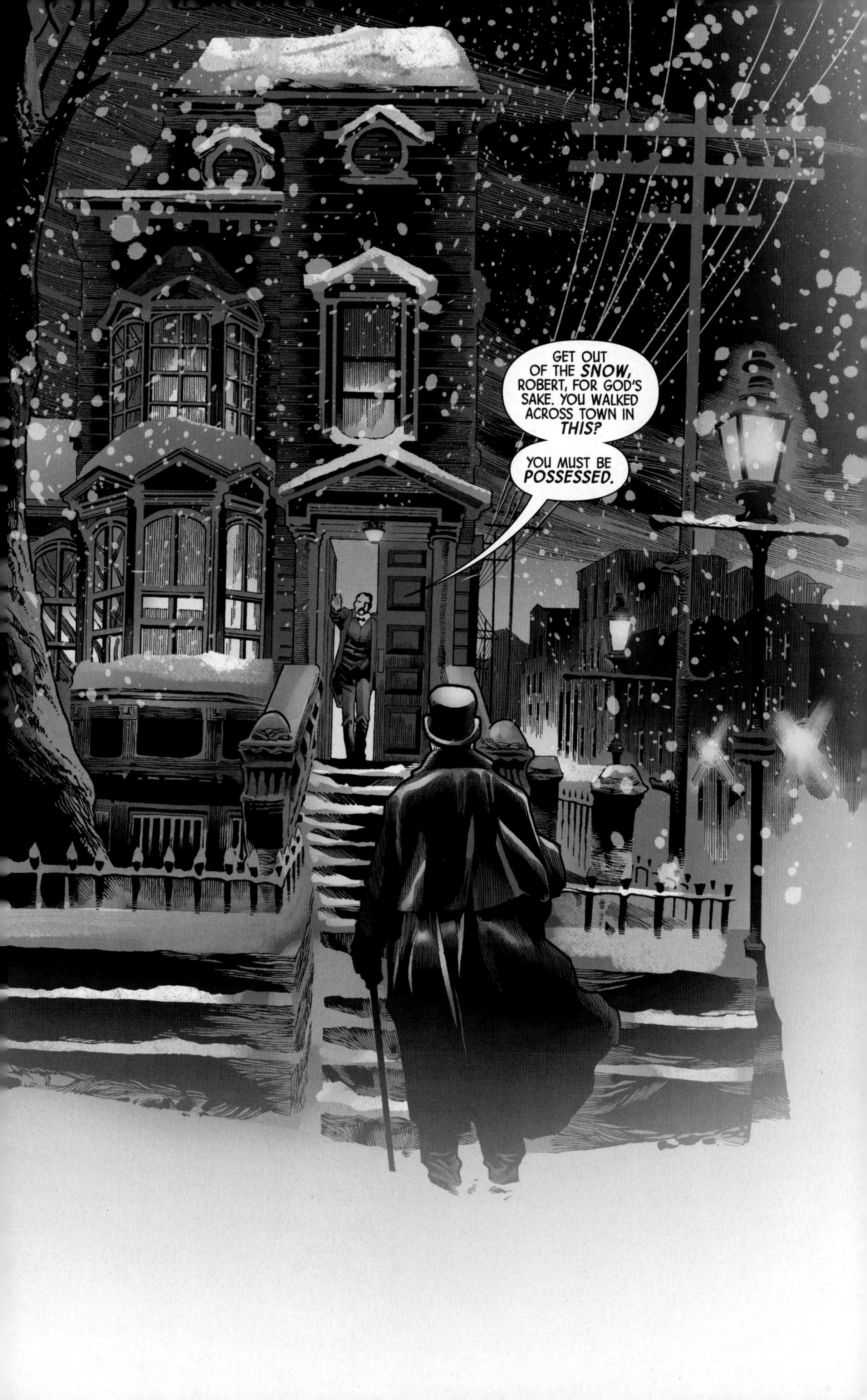
GET OUT OF THE SNOW, ROBERT, FOR GOD'S SAKE. YOU WALKED ACROSS TOWN IN THIS?
YOU MUST BE POSSESSED.

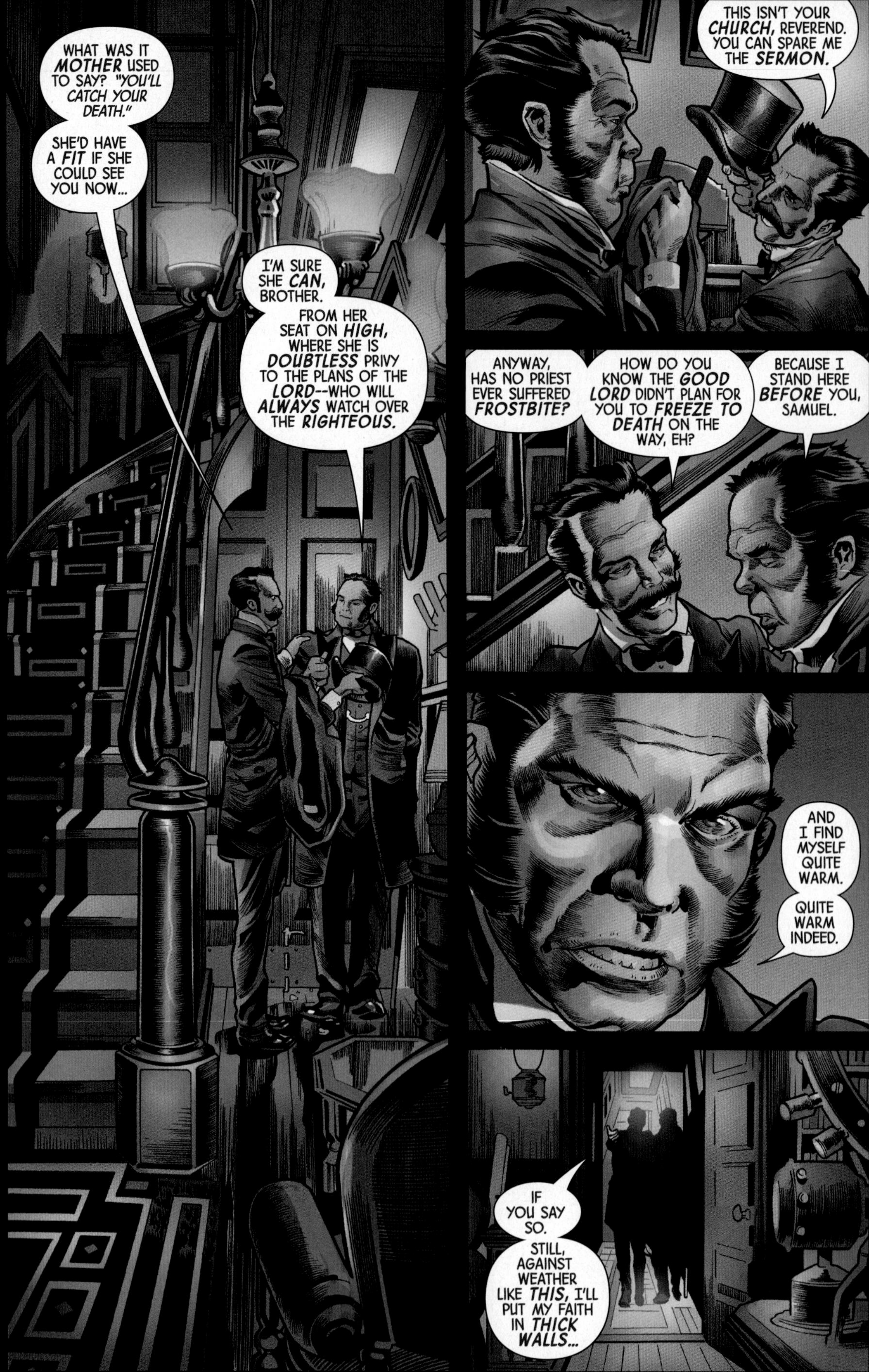
WHAT WAS IT MOTHER USED TO SAY? "YOU'LL CATCH YOUR DEATH."
SHE'D HAVE A FIT IF SHE COULD SEE YOU NOW...
I'M SURE SHE CAN, BROTHER.
FROM HER SEAT ON HIGH, WHERE SHE IS DOUBTLESS PRIVY TO THE PLANS OF THE LORD--WHO WILL ALWAYS WATCH OVER THE RIGHTEOUS.
THIS ISN'T YOUR CHURCH, REVEREND. YOU CAN SPARE ME THE SERMON.
ANYWAY, HAS NO PRIEST EVER SUFFERED FROSTBITE?
HOW DO YOU KNOW THE GOOD LORD DIDN'T PLAN FOR YOU TO FREEZE TO DEATH ON THE WAY, EH?
BECAUSE I STAND HERE BEFORE YOU, SAMUEL.
AND I FIND MYSELF QUITE WARM.
QUITE WARM INDEED.
IF YOU SAY SO.
STILL, AGAINST WEATHER LIKE THIS, I'LL PUT MY FAITH IN THICK WALLS...

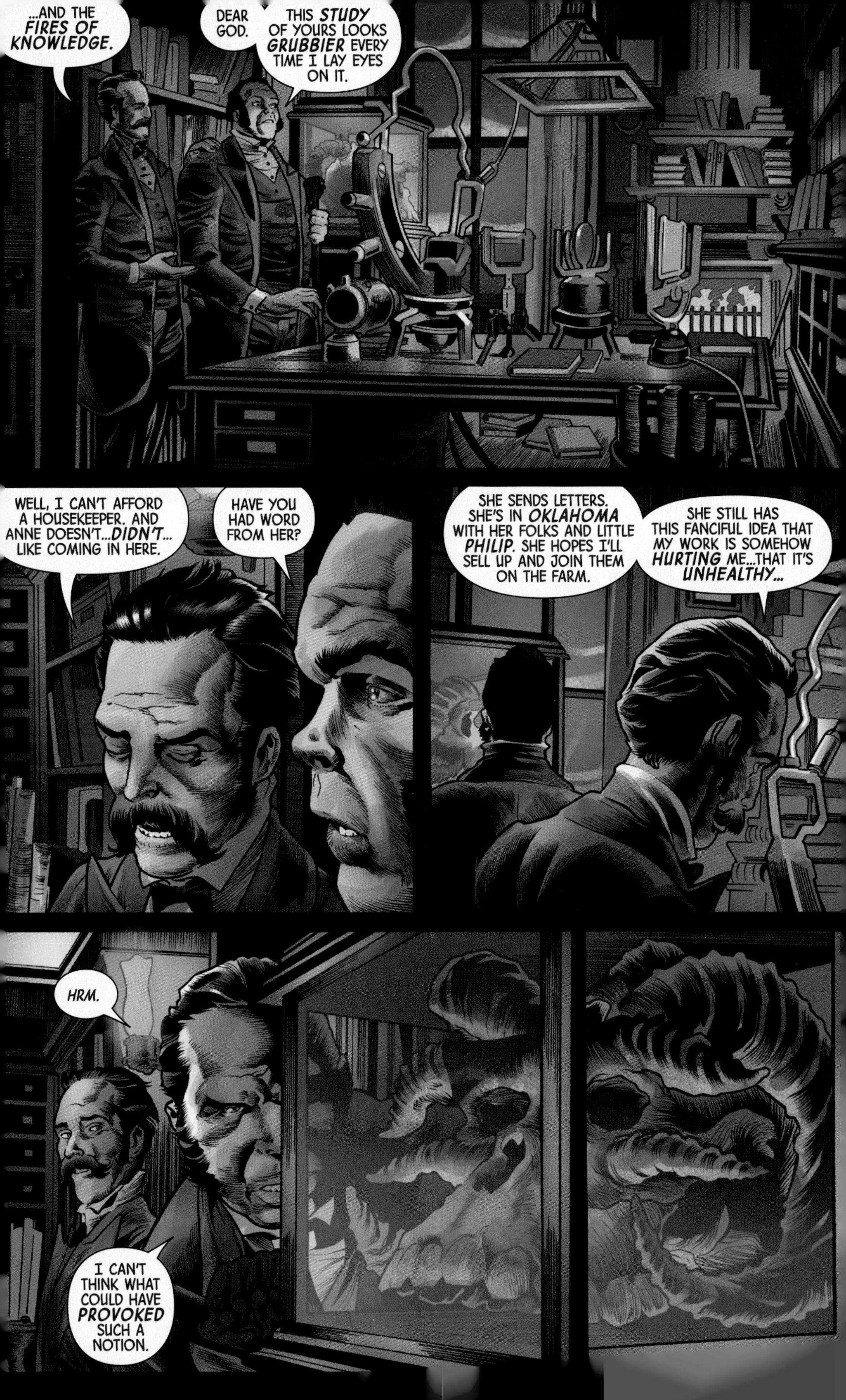
...AND THE FIRES OF KNOWLEDGE.
DEAR GOD.
THIS STUDY OF YOURS LOOKS GRUBBIER EVERY TIME I LAY EYES ON IT.
WELL, I CAN'T AFFORD A HOUSEKEEPER. AND ANNE DOESN'T...DIDN'T... LIKE COMING IN HERE.
HAVE YOU HAD WORD FROM HER?
SHE SENDS LETTERS. SHE'S IN OKLAHOMA WITH HER FOLKS AND LITTLE PHILIP. SHE HOPES I'LL SELL UP AND JOIN THEM ON THE FARM.
SHE STILL HAS THIS FANCIFUL IDEA THAT MY WORK IS SOMEHOW HURTING ME...THAT IT'S UNHEALTHY...
HRM.
I CAN'T THINK WHAT COULD HAVE PROVOKED SUCH A NOTION.

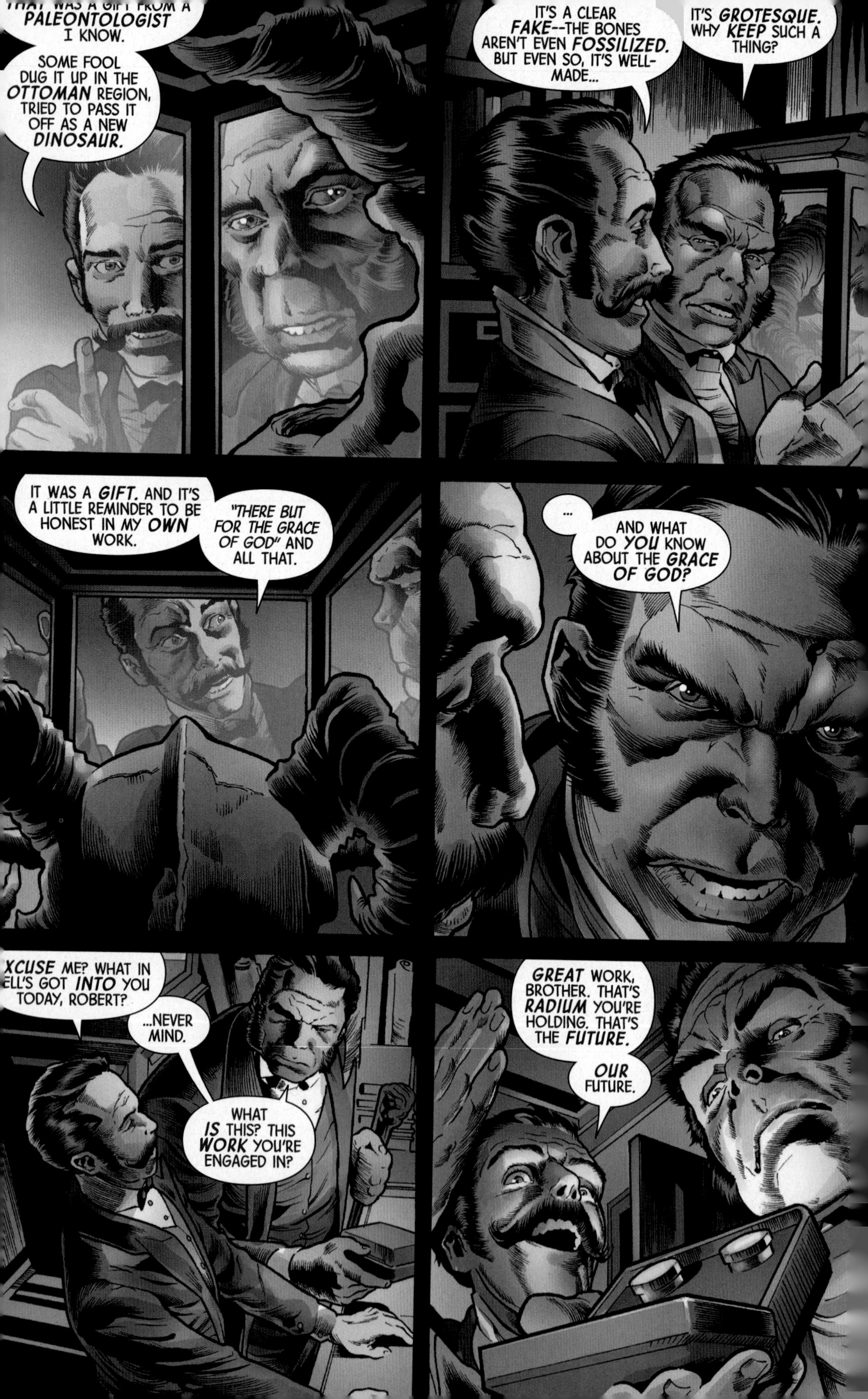
PALEONTOLOGIST I KNOW.
SOME FOOL DUG IT UP IN THE OTTOMAN REGION, TRIED TO PASS IT OFF AS A NEW DINOSAUR.
IT'S A CLEAR FAKE--THE BONES AREN'T EVEN FOSSILIZED. BUT EVEN SO, IT'S WELL-MADE...
IT'S GROTESQUE. WHY KEEP SUCH A THING?
IT WAS A GIFT. AND IT'S A LITTLE REMINDER TO BE HONEST IN MY OWN WORK.
"THERE BUT FOR THE GRACE OF GOD" AND ALL THAT.
...
AND WHAT DO YOU KNOW ABOUT THE GRACE OF GOD?
XCUSE ME? WHAT IN ELL'S GOT INTO YOU TODAY, ROBERT?
...NEVER MIND.
WHAT IS THIS? THIS WORK YOU'RE ENGAGED IN?
GREAT WORK, BROTHER. THAT'S RADIUM YOU'RE HOLDING. THAT'S THE FUTURE.
OUR FUTURE.

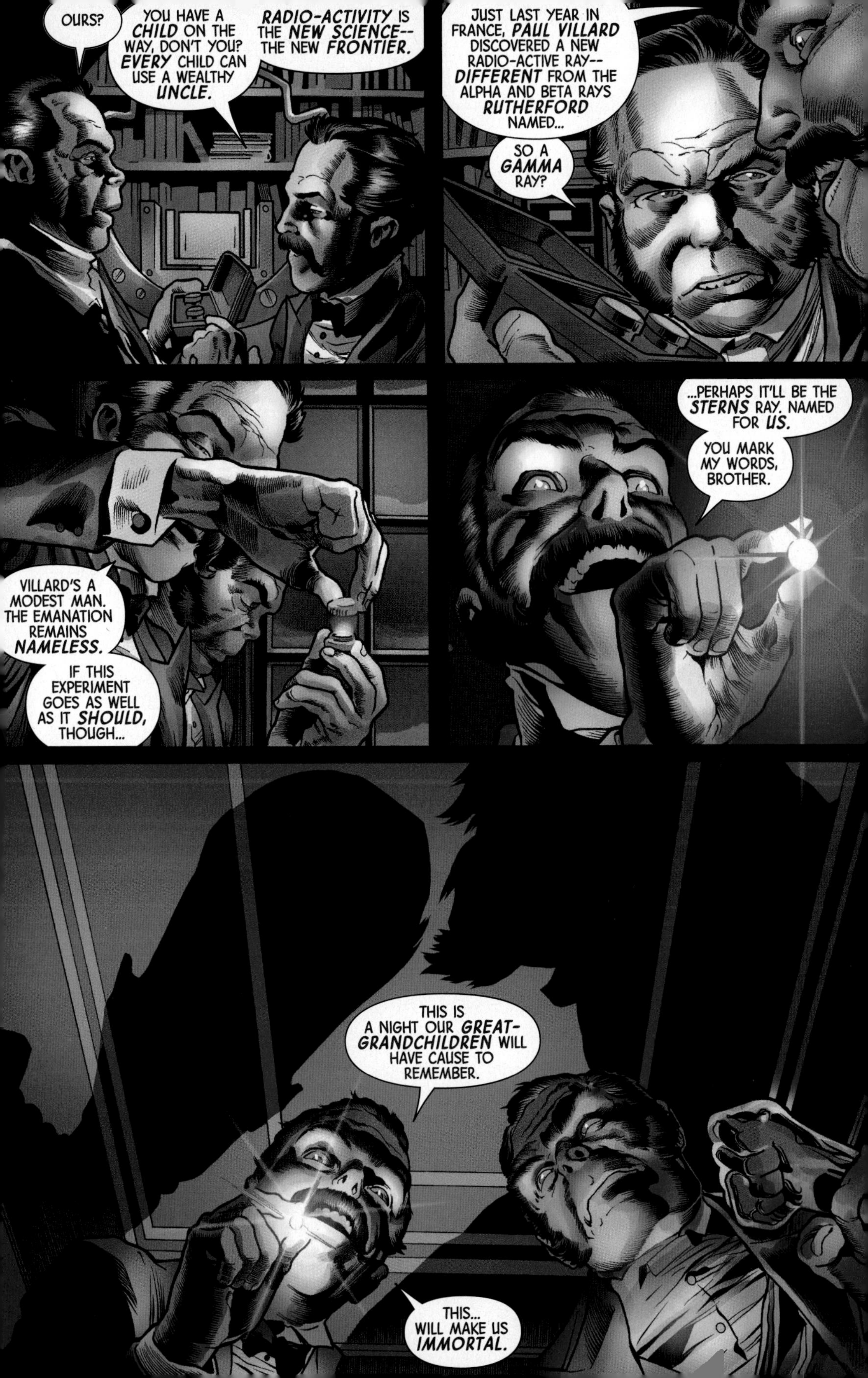
OURS?
YOU HAVE A CHILD ON THE WAY, DON'T YOU? EVERY CHILD CAN USE A WEALTHY UNCLE.
RADIO-ACTIVITY IS THE NEW SCIENCE-- THE NEW FRONTIER.
JUST LAST YEAR IN FRANCE, PAUL VILLARD DISCOVERED A NEW RADIO-ACTIVE RAY-- DIFFERENT FROM THE ALPHA AND BETA RAYS RUTHERFORD NAMED...
SO A GAMMA RAY?
VILLARD'S A MODEST MAN. THE EMANATION REMAINS NAMELESS.
IF THIS EXPERIMENT GOES AS WELL AS IT SHOULD, THOUGH...
...PERHAPS IT'LL BE THE STERNS RAY. NAMED FOR US.
YOU MARK MY WORDS, BROTHER.
THIS IS A NIGHT OUR GREAT-GRANDCHILDREN WILL HAVE CAUSE TO REMEMBER.
THIS... WILL MAKE US IMMORTAL.

OF HELL AND

OF

DEATH

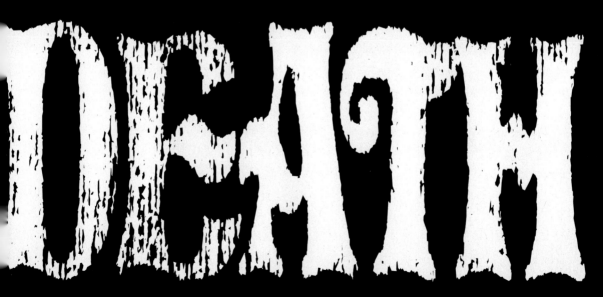

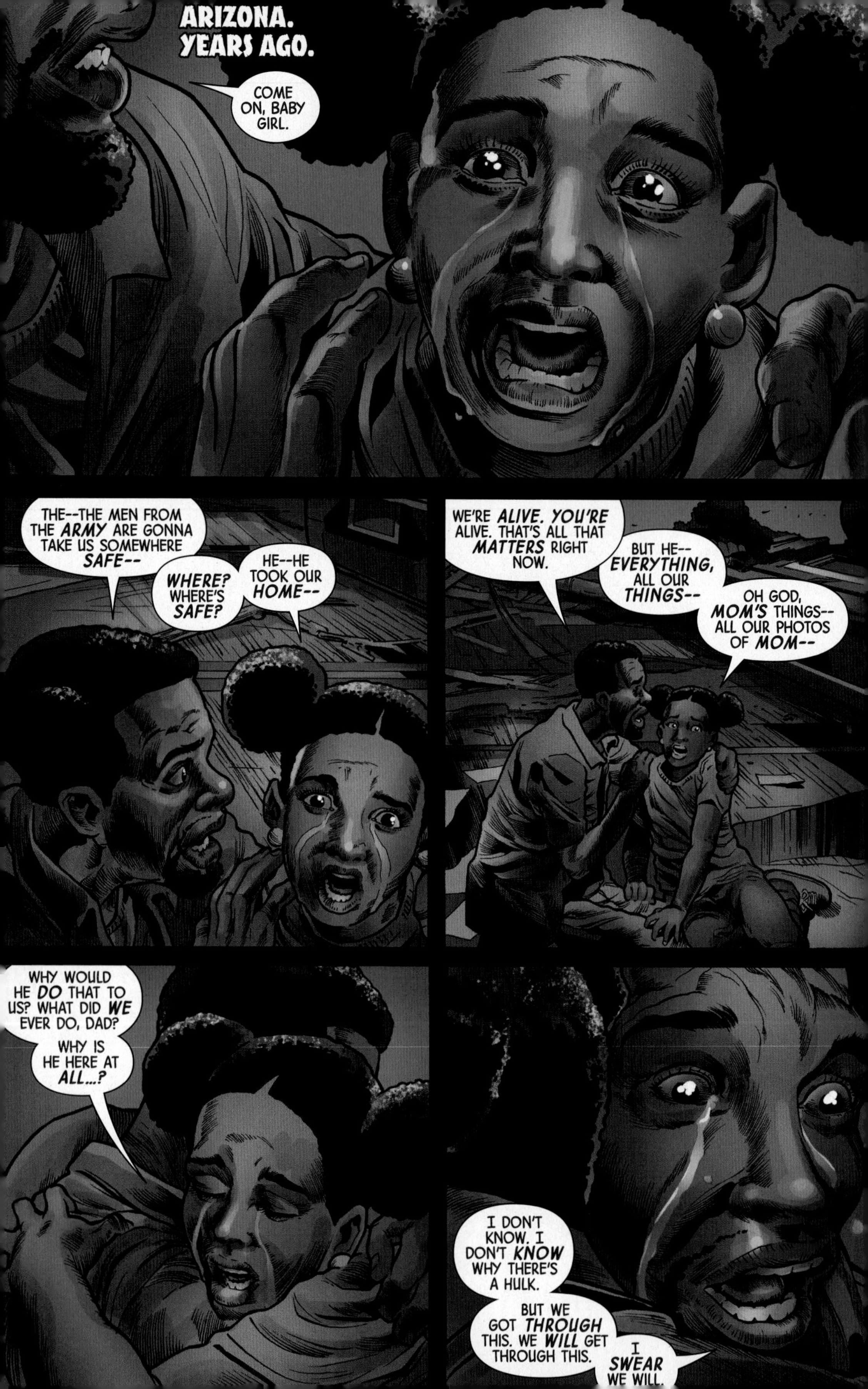
ARIZONA. YEARS AGO.
COME ON, BABY GIRL.
THE--THE MEN FROM THE ARMY ARE GONNA TAKE US SOMEWHERE SAFE--
WHERE? WHERE'S SAFE?
HE--HE TOOK OUR HOME--
WE'RE ALIVE. YOU'RE ALIVE. THAT'S ALL THAT MATTERS RIGHT NOW.
BUT HE-- EVERYTHING, ALL OUR THINGS--
OH GOD, MOM'S THINGS-- ALL OUR PHOTOS OF MOM--
WHY WOULD HE DO THAT TO US? WHAT DID WE EVER DO, DAD?
WHY IS HE HERE AT ALL...?
I DON'T KNOW. I DON'T KNOW WHY THERE'S A HULK.
BUT WE GOT THROUGH THIS. WE WILL GET THROUGH THIS.
I SWEAR WE WILL.

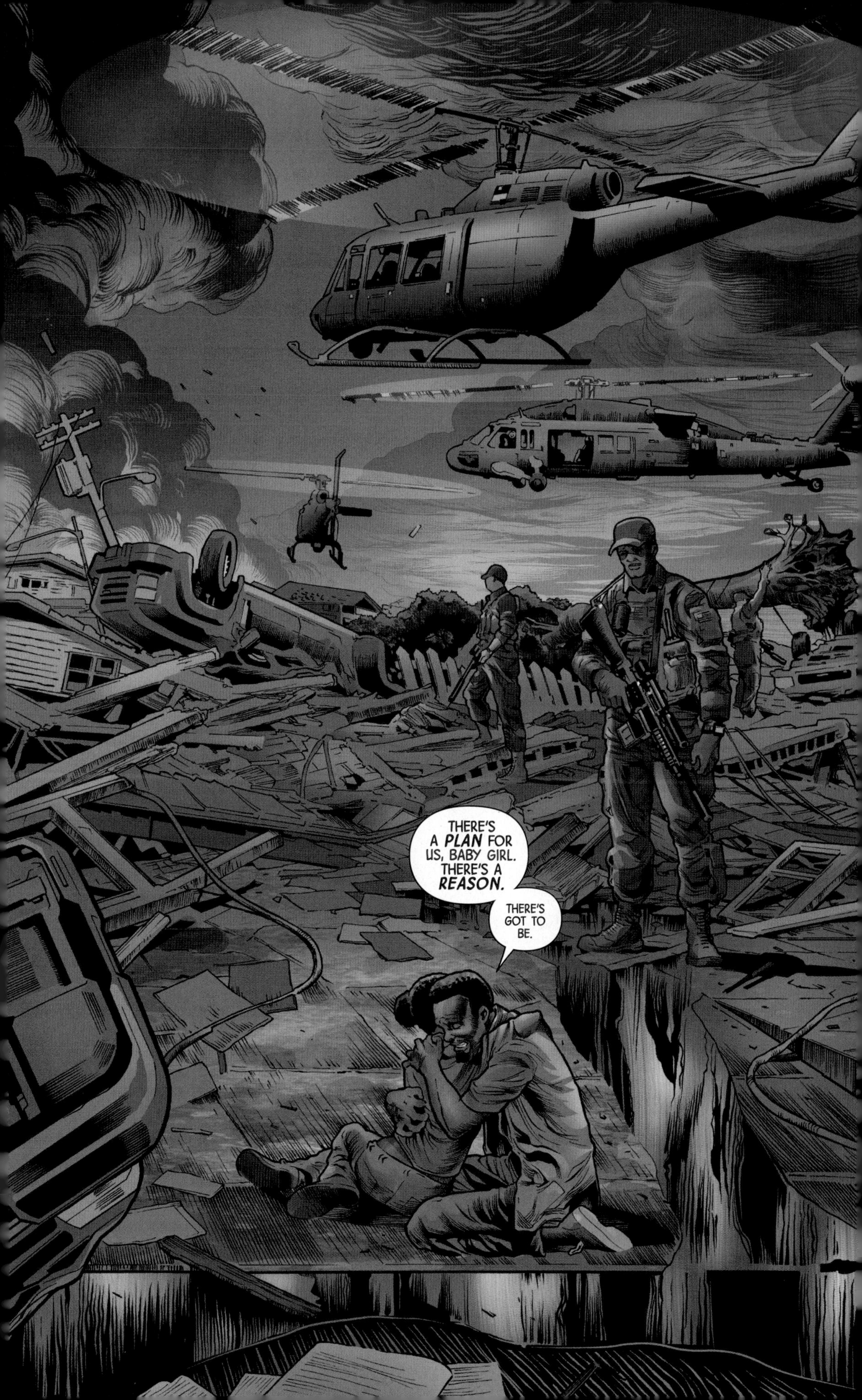
THERE'S A PLAN FOR US, BABY GIRL. THERE'S A REASON.
THERE'S GOT TO BE.

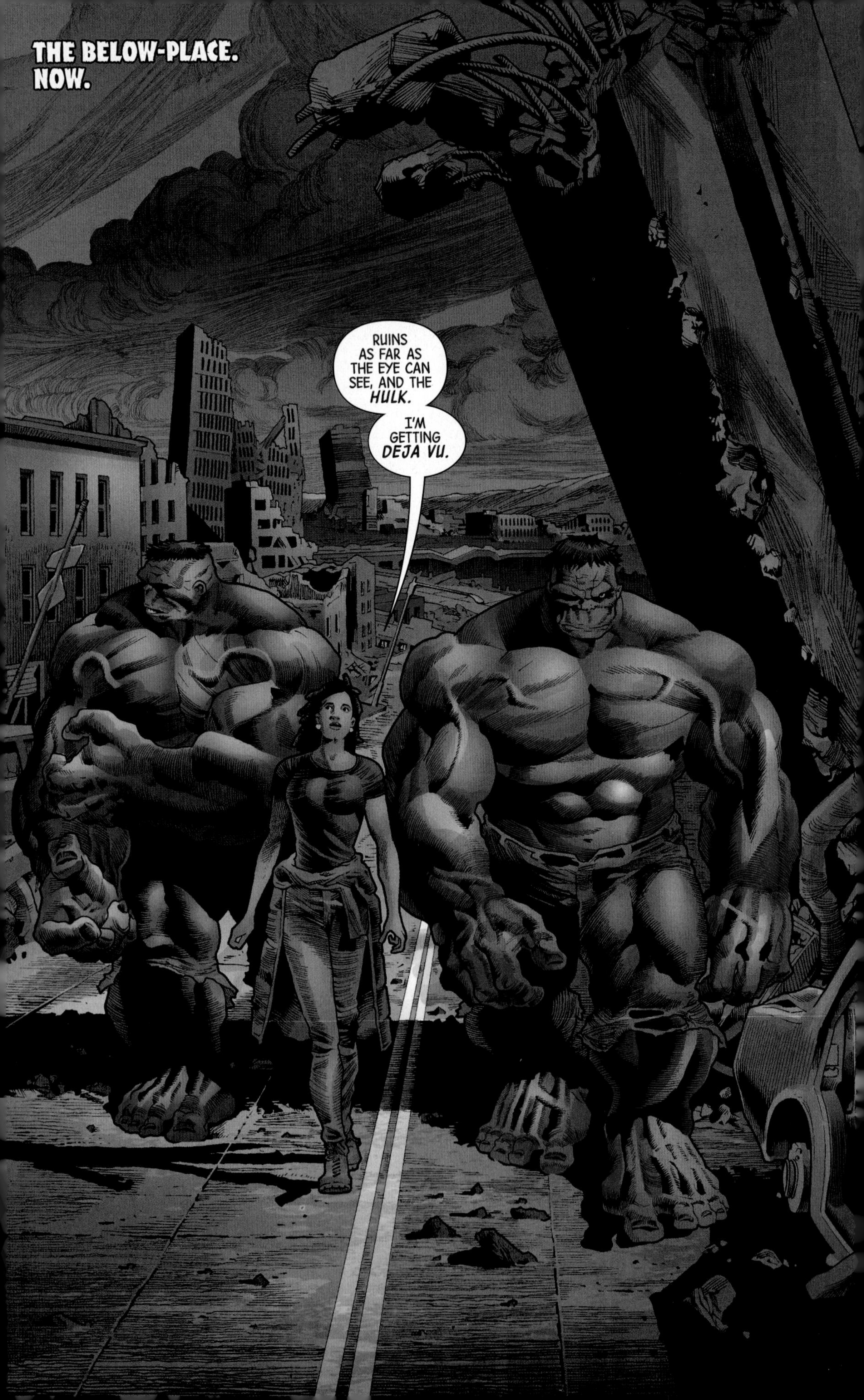

THE BELOW-PLACE. NOW.
RUINS AS FAR AS THE EYE CAN SEE, AND THE *HULK*.
I'M GETTING *DEJA VU*.

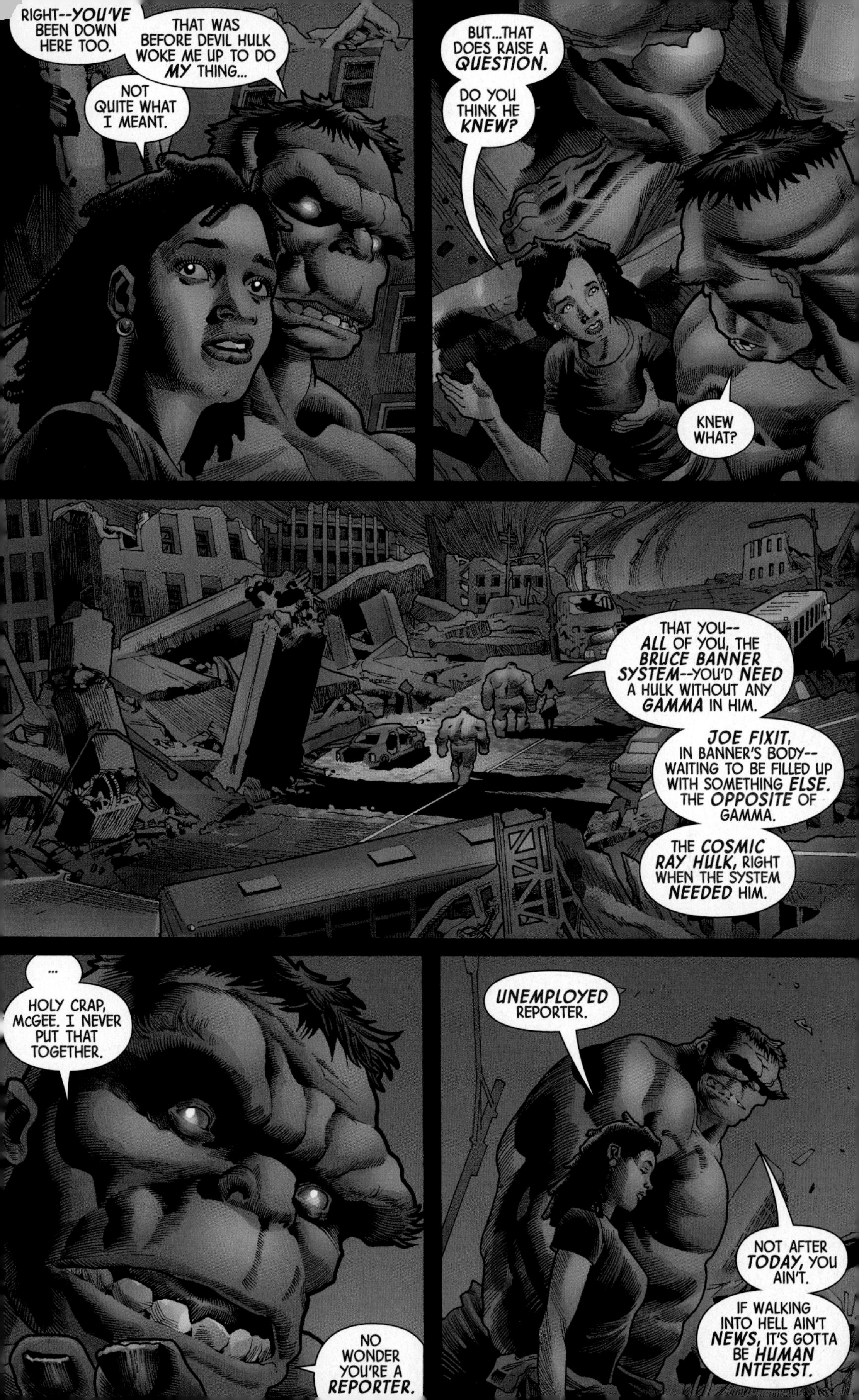
RIGHT--YOU'VE BEEN DOWN HERE TOO.
THAT WAS BEFORE DEVIL HULK WOKE ME UP TO DO MY THING...
NOT QUITE WHAT I MEANT.
BUT...THAT DOES RAISE A QUESTION.
DO YOU THINK HE KNEW?
KNEW WHAT?
THAT YOU-- ALL OF YOU, THE BRUCE BANNER SYSTEM--YOU'D NEED A HULK WITHOUT ANY GAMMA IN HIM.
JOE FIXIT, IN BANNER'S BODY-- WAITING TO BE FILLED UP WITH SOMETHING ELSE. THE OPPOSITE OF GAMMA.
THE COSMIC RAY HULK, RIGHT WHEN THE SYSTEM NEEDED HIM.
...
HOLY CRAP, McGEE. I NEVER PUT THAT TOGETHER.
NO WONDER YOU'RE A REPORTER.
UNEMPLOYED REPORTER.
NOT AFTER TODAY, YOU AIN'T.
IF WALKING INTO HELL AIN'T NEWS, IT'S GOTTA BE HUMAN INTEREST.

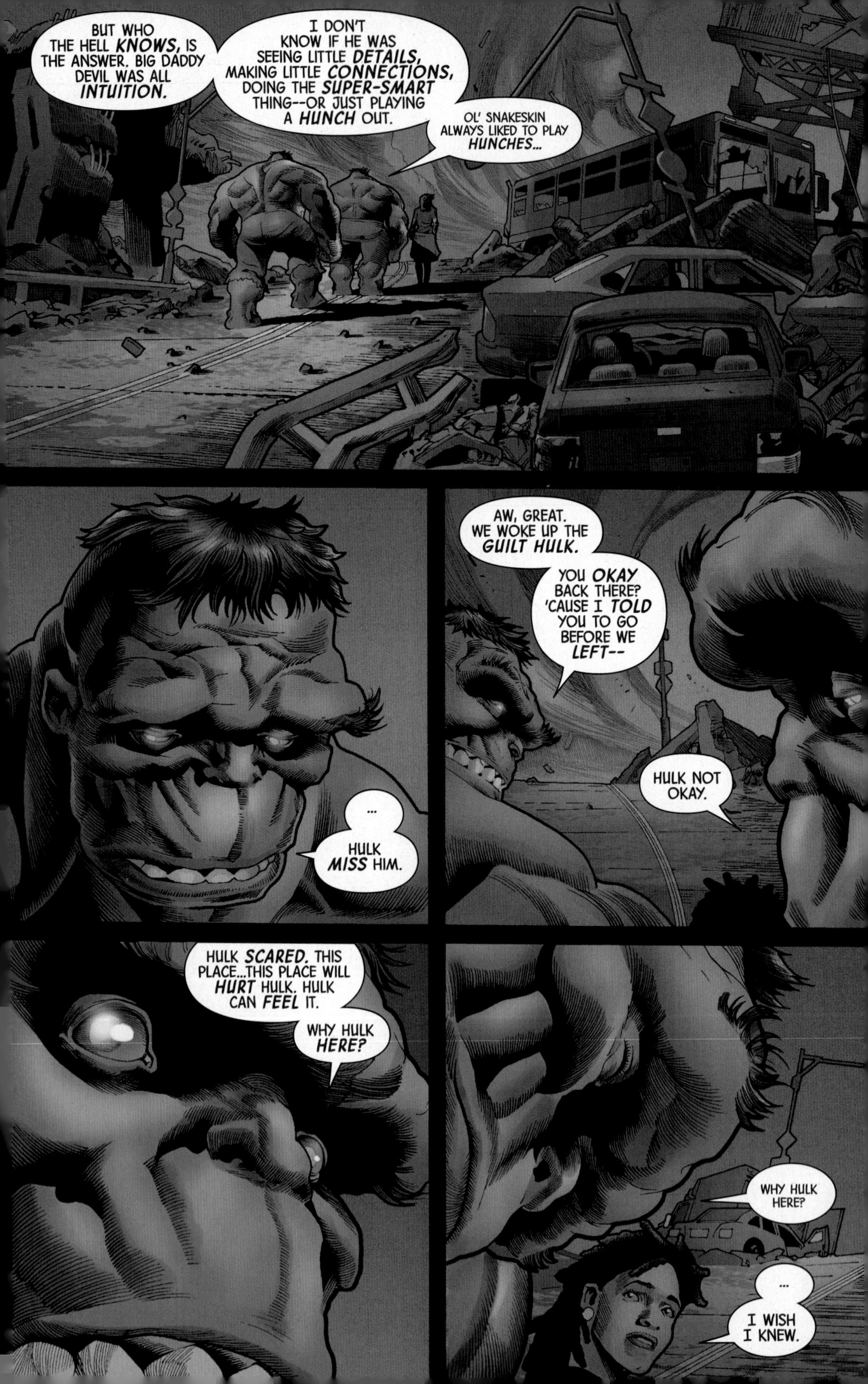
BUT WHO THE HELL KNOWS, IS THE ANSWER. BIG DADDY DEVIL WAS ALL INTUITION.
I DON'T KNOW IF HE WAS SEEING LITTLE DETAILS, MAKING LITTLE CONNECTIONS, DOING THE SUPER-SMART THING--OR JUST PLAYING A HUNCH OUT.
OL' SNAKESKIN ALWAYS LIKED TO PLAY HUNCHES...
...
HULK MISS HIM.
AW, GREAT. WE WOKE UP THE GUILT HULK.
YOU OKAY BACK THERE? 'CAUSE I TOLD YOU TO GO BEFORE WE LEFT--
HULK NOT OKAY.
HULK SCARED. THIS PLACE...THIS PLACE WILL HURT HULK. HULK CAN FEEL IT.
WHY HULK HERE?
WHY HULK HERE?
...
I WISH I KNEW.

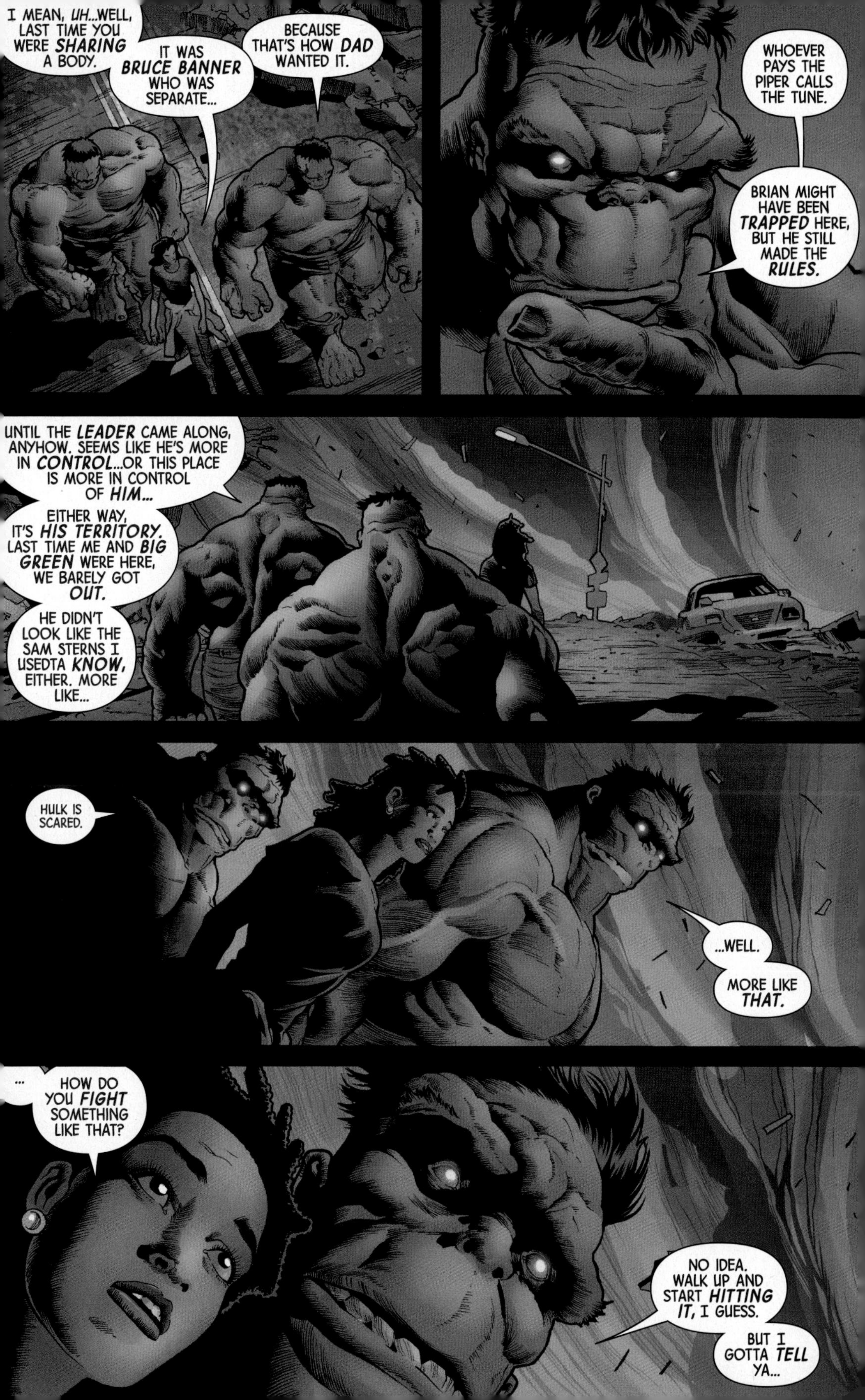
I MEAN, UH...WELL, LAST TIME YOU WERE SHARING A BODY.
IT WAS BRUCE BANNER WHO WAS SEPARATE...
BECAUSE THAT'S HOW DAD WANTED IT.
WHOEVER PAYS THE PIPER CALLS THE TUNE.
BRIAN MIGHT HAVE BEEN TRAPPED HERE, BUT HE STILL MADE THE RULES.
UNTIL THE LEADER CAME ALONG, ANYHOW. SEEMS LIKE HE'S MORE IN CONTROL...OR THIS PLACE IS MORE IN CONTROL OF HIM...
EITHER WAY, IT'S HIS TERRITORY. LAST TIME ME AND BIG GREEN WERE HERE, WE BARELY GOT OUT.
HE DIDN'T LOOK LIKE THE SAM STERNS I USEDTA KNOW, EITHER. MORE LIKE...
HULK IS SCARED.
...WELL.
MORE LIKE THAT.
...
HOW DO YOU FIGHT SOMETHING LIKE THAT?
NO IDEA. WALK UP AND START HITTING IT, I GUESS.
BUT I GOTTA TELL YA...

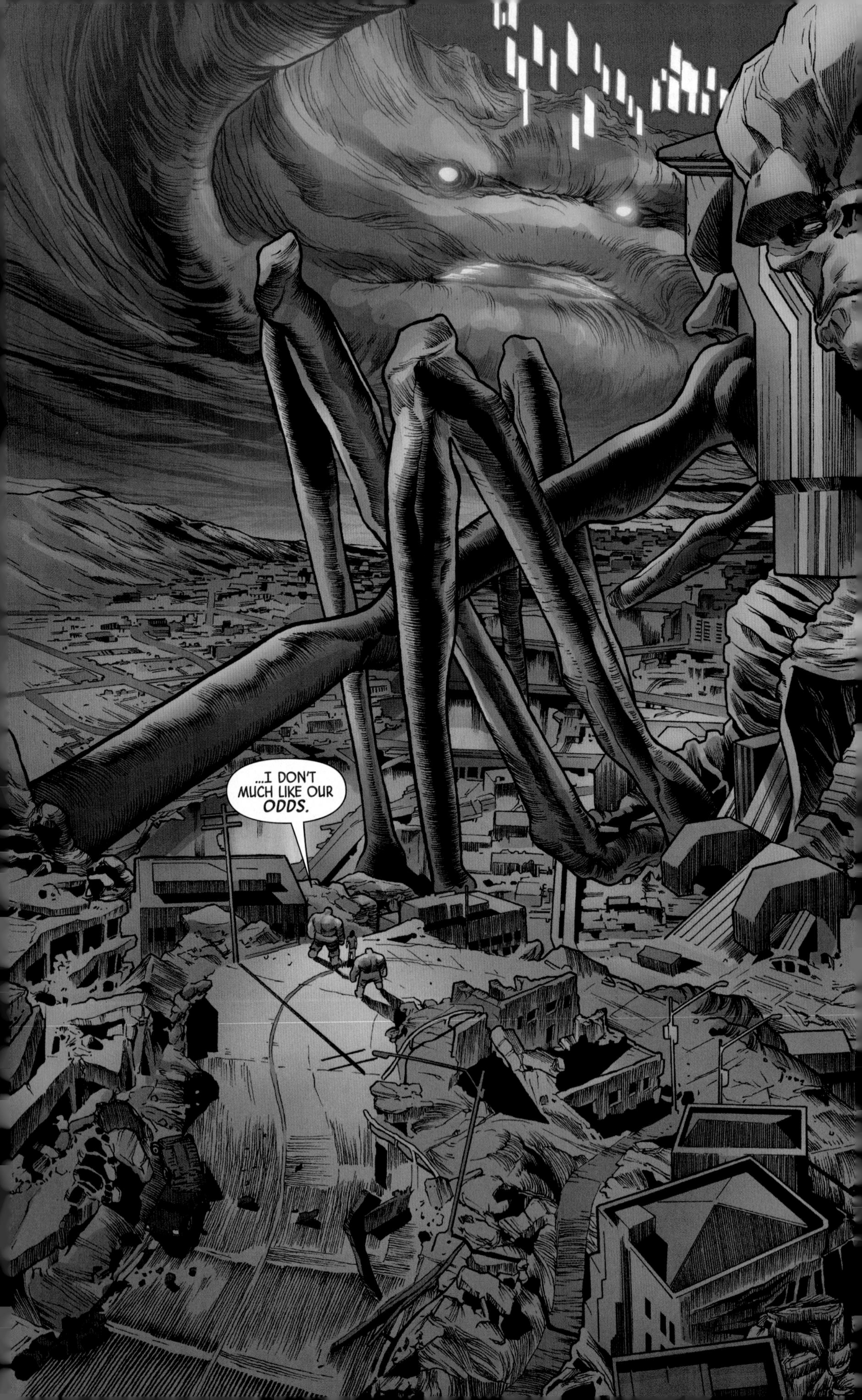
...I DON'T MUCH LIKE OUR ODDS.

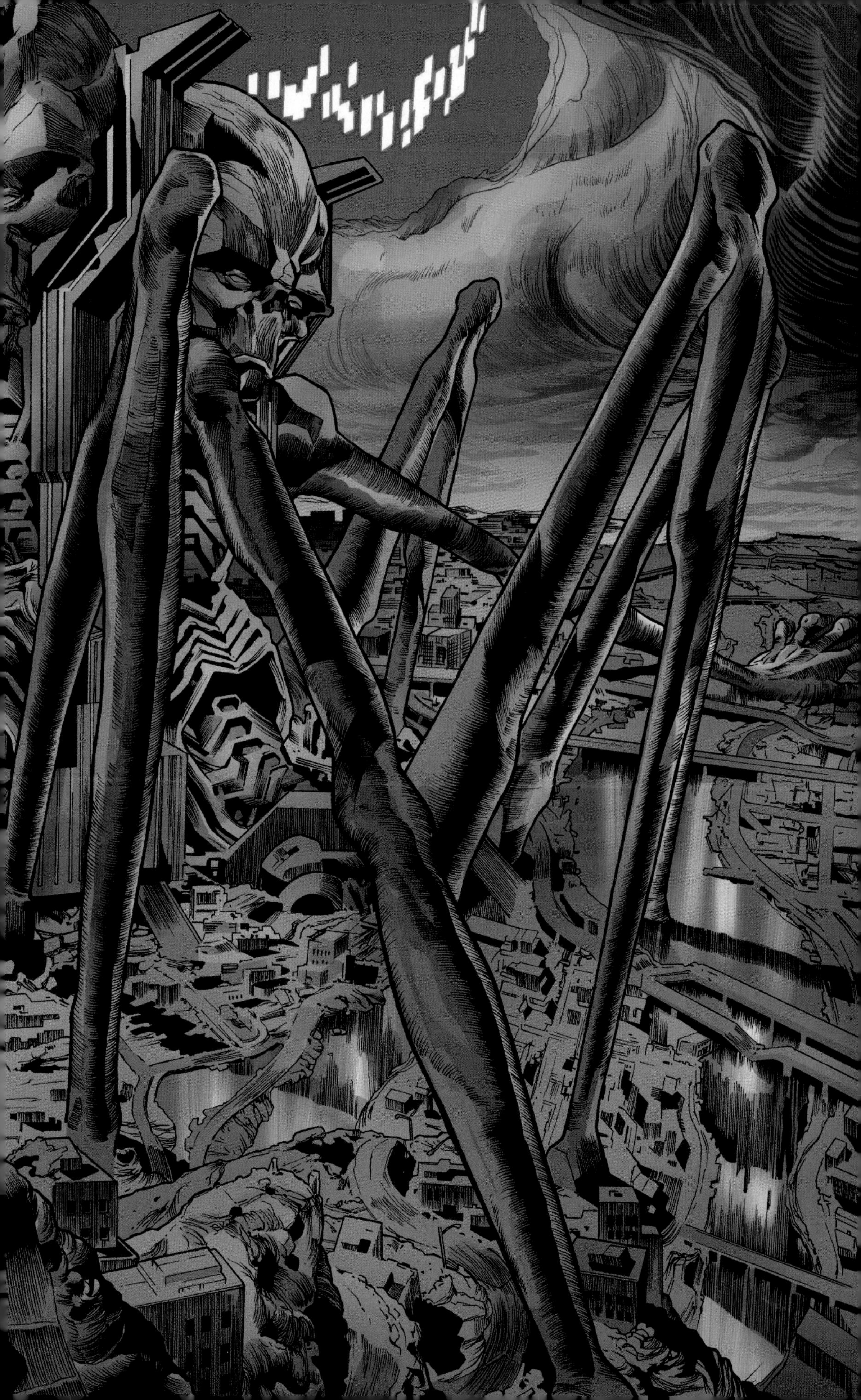

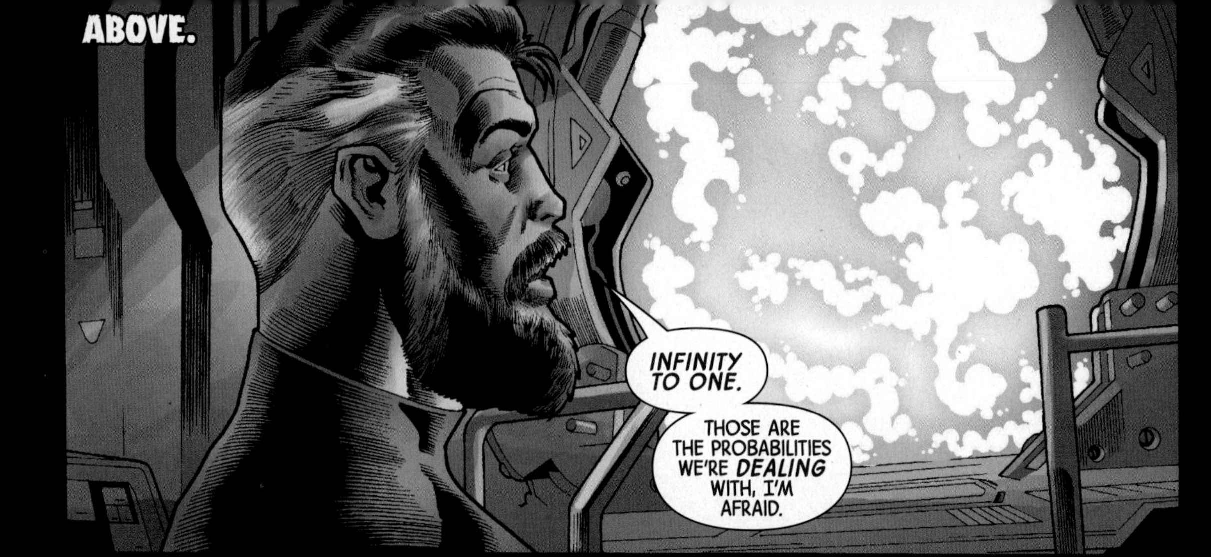
ABOVE.
INFINITY TO ONE.
THOSE ARE THE PROBABILITIES WE'RE DEALING WITH, I'M AFRAID.

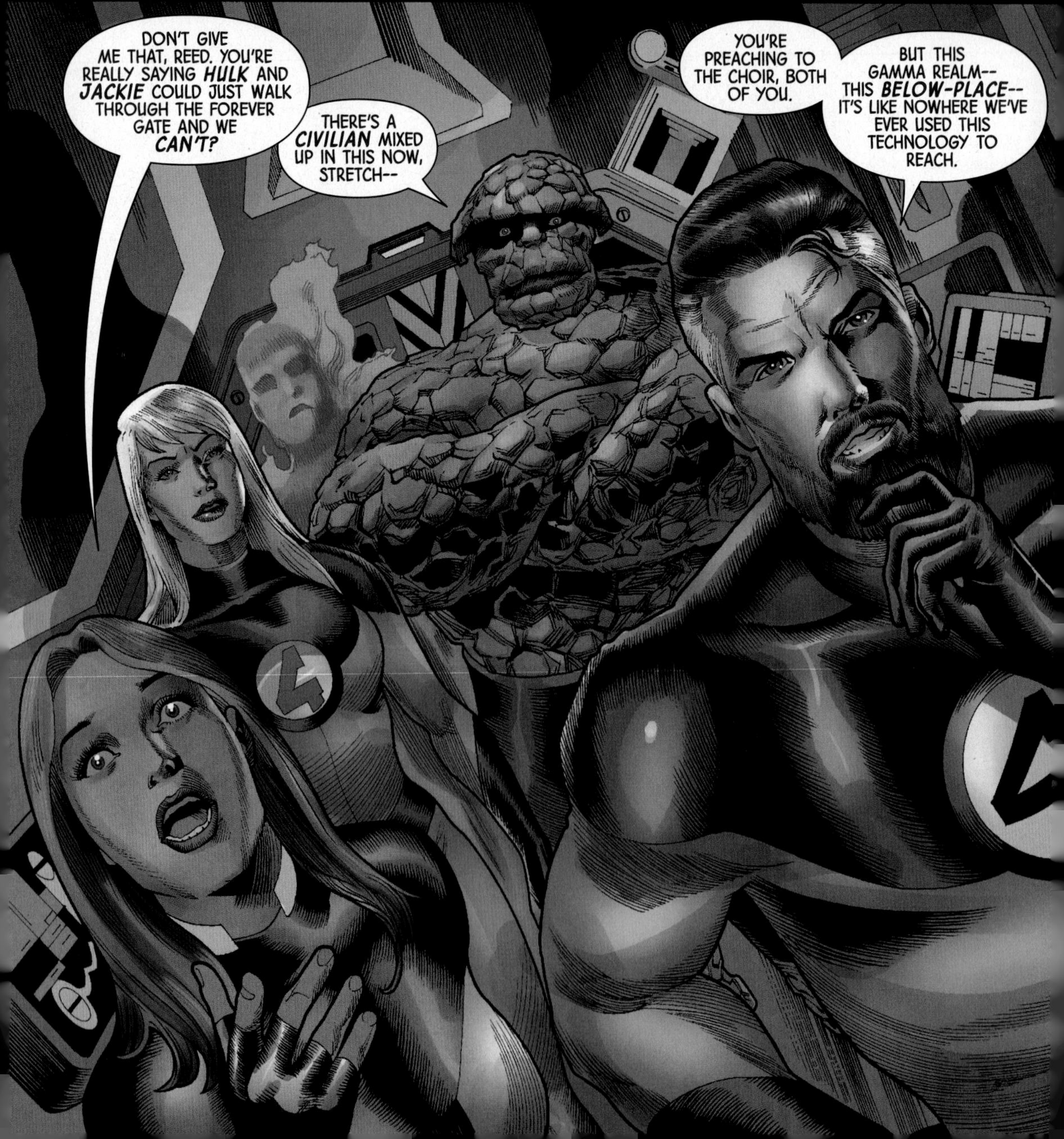
DON'T GIVE ME THAT, REED. YOU'RE REALLY SAYING HULK AND JACKIE COULD JUST WALK THROUGH THE FOREVER GATE AND WE CAN'T?
THERE'S A CIVILIAN MIXED UP IN THIS NOW, STRETCH--
YOU'RE PREACHING TO THE CHOIR, BOTH OF YOU.
BUT THIS GAMMA REALM-- THIS BELOW-PLACE-- IT'S LIKE NOWHERE WE'VE EVER USED THIS TECHNOLOGY TO REACH.

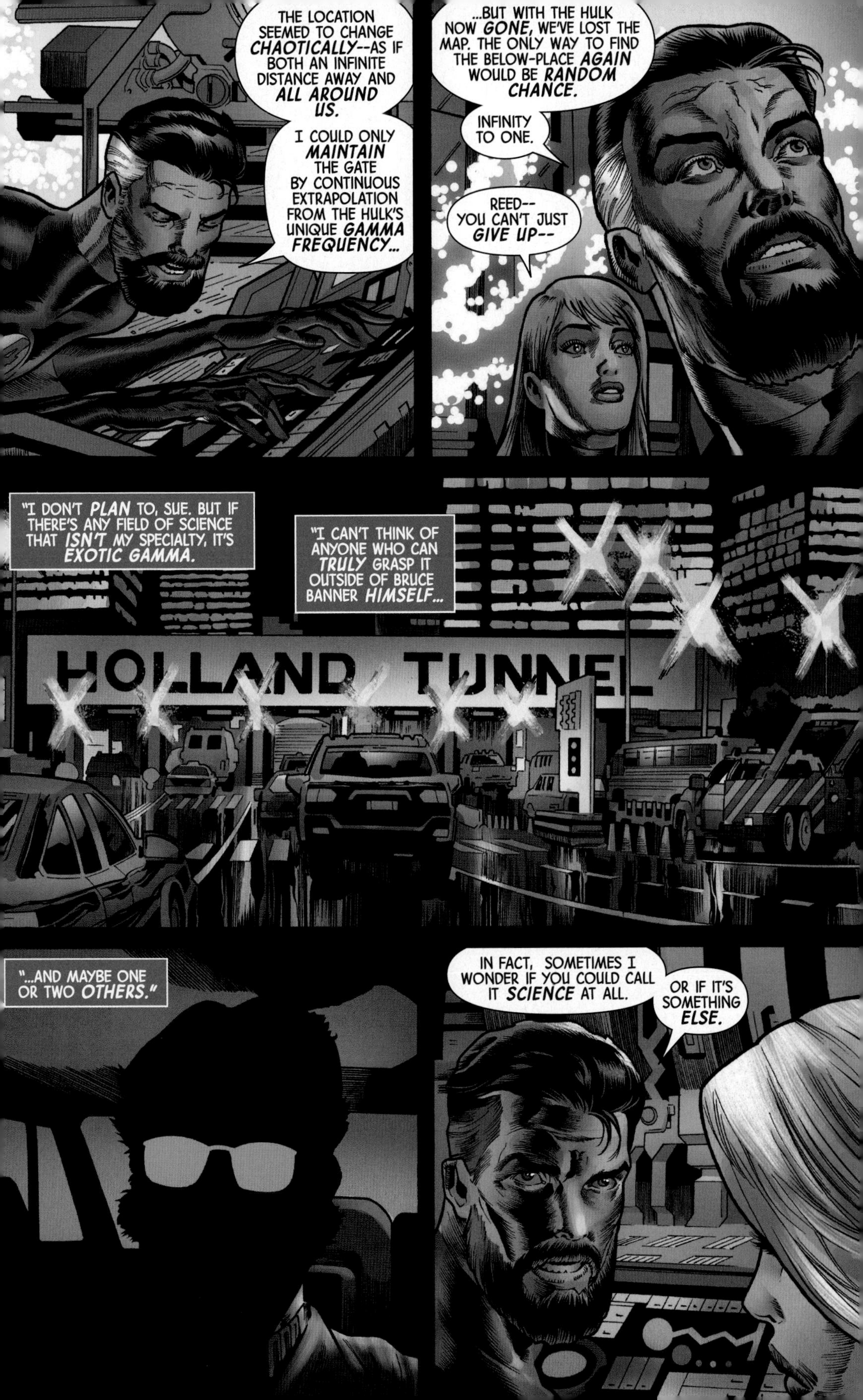
THE LOCATION SEEMED TO CHANGE CHAOTICALLY--AS IF BOTH AN INFINITE DISTANCE AWAY AND ALL AROUND US.
I COULD ONLY MAINTAIN THE GATE BY CONTINUOUS EXTRAPOLATION FROM THE HULK'S UNIQUE GAMMA FREQUENCY...
...BUT WITH THE HULK NOW GONE, WE'VE LOST THE MAP. THE ONLY WAY TO FIND THE BELOW-PLACE AGAIN WOULD BE RANDOM CHANCE.
INFINITY TO ONE.
REED-- YOU CAN'T JUST GIVE UP--
"I DON'T PLAN TO, SUE. BUT IF THERE'S ANY FIELD OF SCIENCE THAT ISN'T MY SPECIALTY, IT'S EXOTIC GAMMA.
"I CAN'T THINK OF ANYONE WHO CAN TRULY GRASP IT OUTSIDE OF BRUCE BANNER HIMSELF...
HOLLAND TUNNEL
"...AND MAYBE ONE OR TWO OTHERS."
IN FACT, SOMETIMES I WONDER IF YOU COULD CALL IT SCIENCE AT ALL.
OR IF IT'S SOMETHING ELSE.

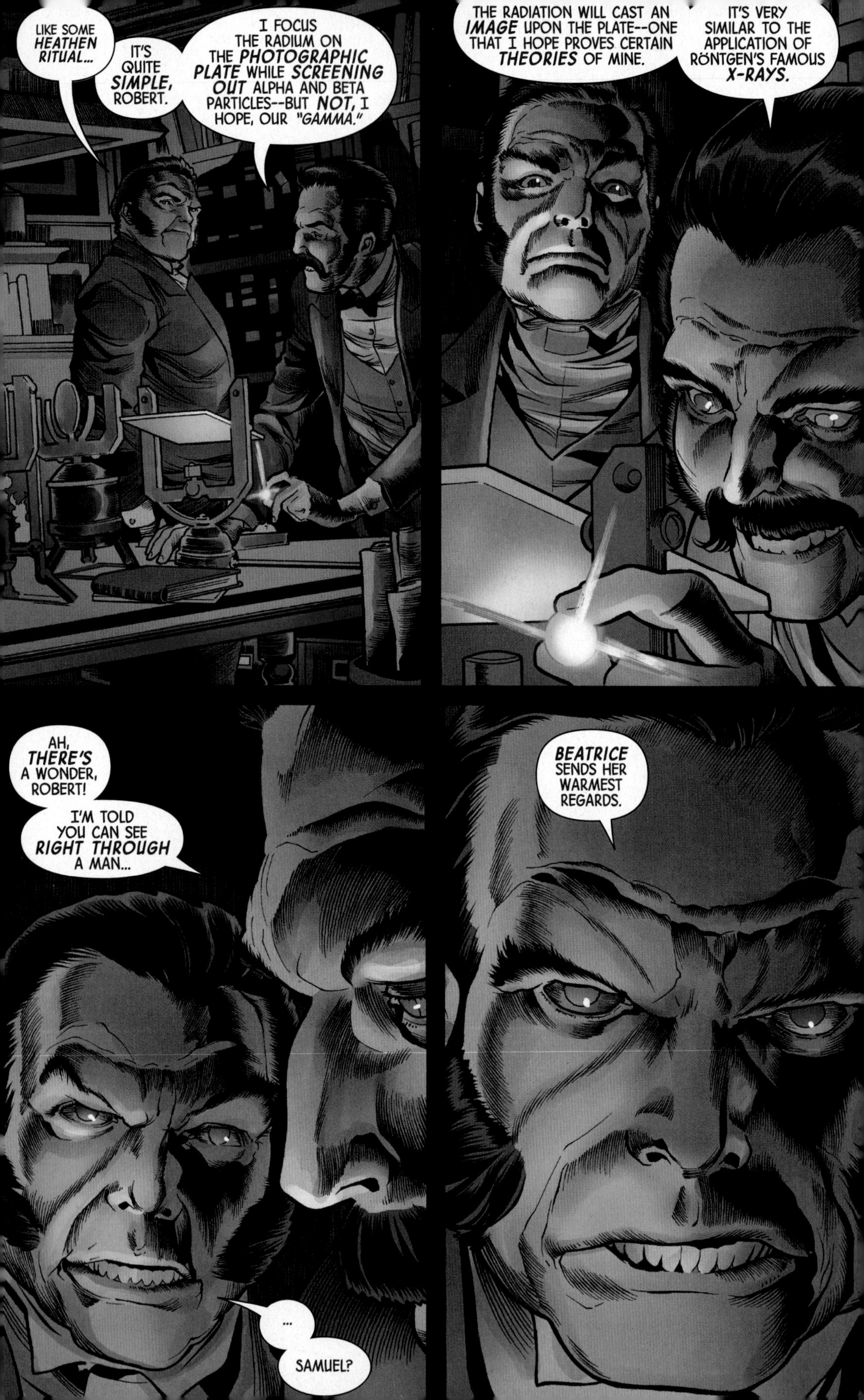
LIKE SOME HEATHEN RITUAL...
IT'S QUITE SIMPLE, ROBERT.
I FOCUS THE RADIUM ON THE PHOTOGRAPHIC PLATE WHILE SCREENING OUT ALPHA AND BETA PARTICLES--BUT NOT, I HOPE, OUR "GAMMA."
THE RADIATION WILL CAST AN IMAGE UPON THE PLATE--ONE THAT I HOPE PROVES CERTAIN THEORIES OF MINE.
IT'S VERY SIMILAR TO THE APPLICATION OF RÖNTGEN'S FAMOUS X-RAYS.
AH, THERE'S A WONDER, ROBERT!
I'M TOLD YOU CAN SEE RIGHT THROUGH A MAN...
...
SAMUEL?
BEATRICE SENDS HER WARMEST REGARDS.

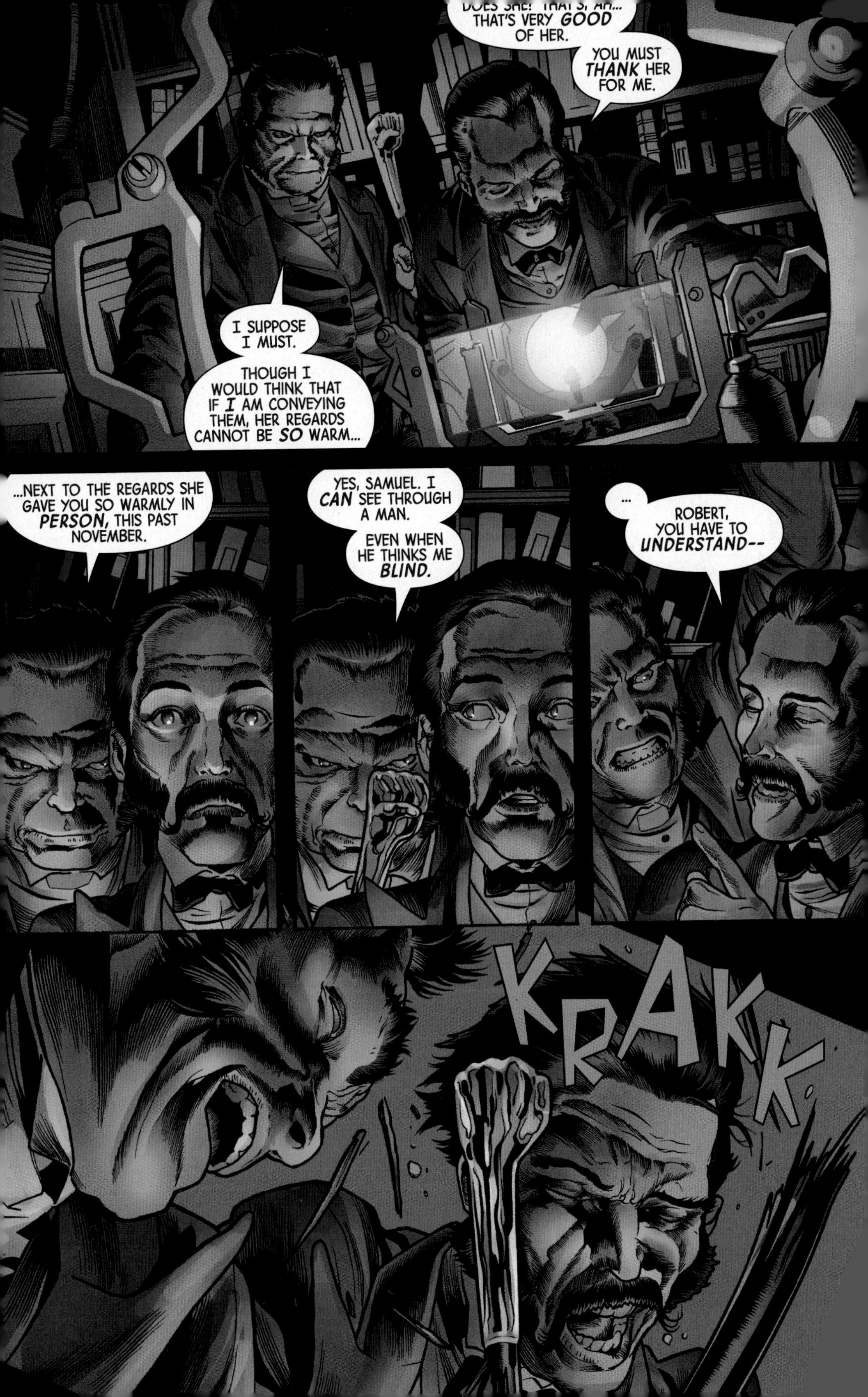

DOES SHE? THAT'S, AH... THAT'S VERY GOOD OF HER.
YOU MUST THANK HER FOR ME.
I SUPPOSE I MUST.
THOUGH I WOULD THINK THAT IF I AM CONVEYING THEM, HER REGARDS CANNOT BE SO WARM...
...NEXT TO THE REGARDS SHE GAVE YOU SO WARMLY IN PERSON, THIS PAST NOVEMBER.
YES, SAMUEL. I CAN SEE THROUGH A MAN.
EVEN WHEN HE THINKS ME BLIND.
...
ROBERT, YOU HAVE TO UNDERSTAND--
KRAKK

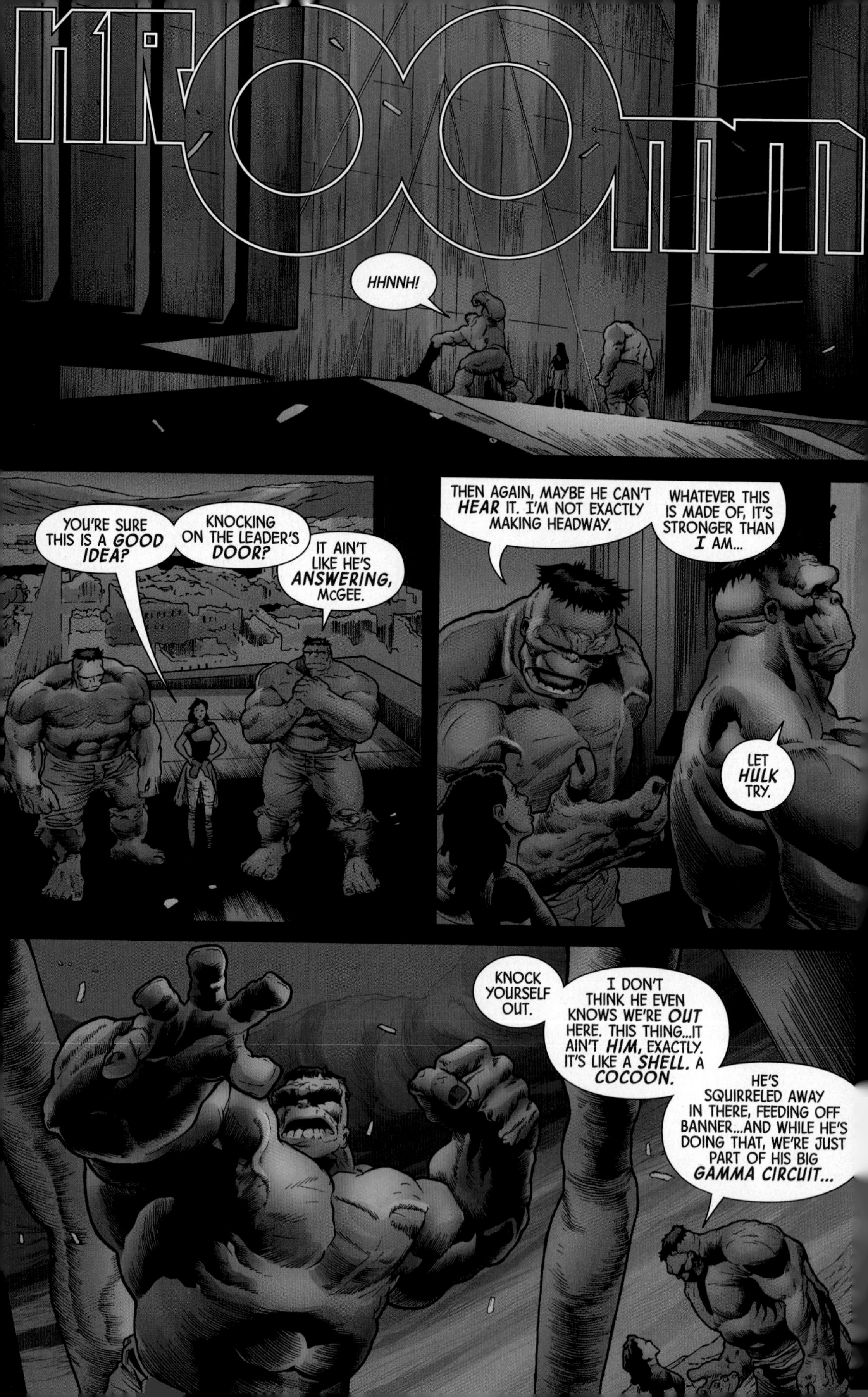
KROOOM
HHNNH!
YOU'RE SURE THIS IS A GOOD IDEA?
KNOCKING ON THE LEADER'S DOOR?
IT AIN'T LIKE HE'S ANSWERING, McGEE.
THEN AGAIN, MAYBE HE CAN'T HEAR IT. I'M NOT EXACTLY MAKING HEADWAY.
WHATEVER THIS IS MADE OF, IT'S STRONGER THAN I AM...
LET HULK TRY.
KNOCK YOURSELF OUT.
I DON'T THINK HE EVEN KNOWS WE'RE OUT HERE. THIS THING...IT AIN'T HIM, EXACTLY. IT'S LIKE A SHELL. A COCOON.
HE'S SQUIRRELED AWAY IN THERE, FEEDING OFF BANNER...AND WHILE HE'S DOING THAT, WE'RE JUST PART OF HIS BIG GAMMA CIRCUIT...

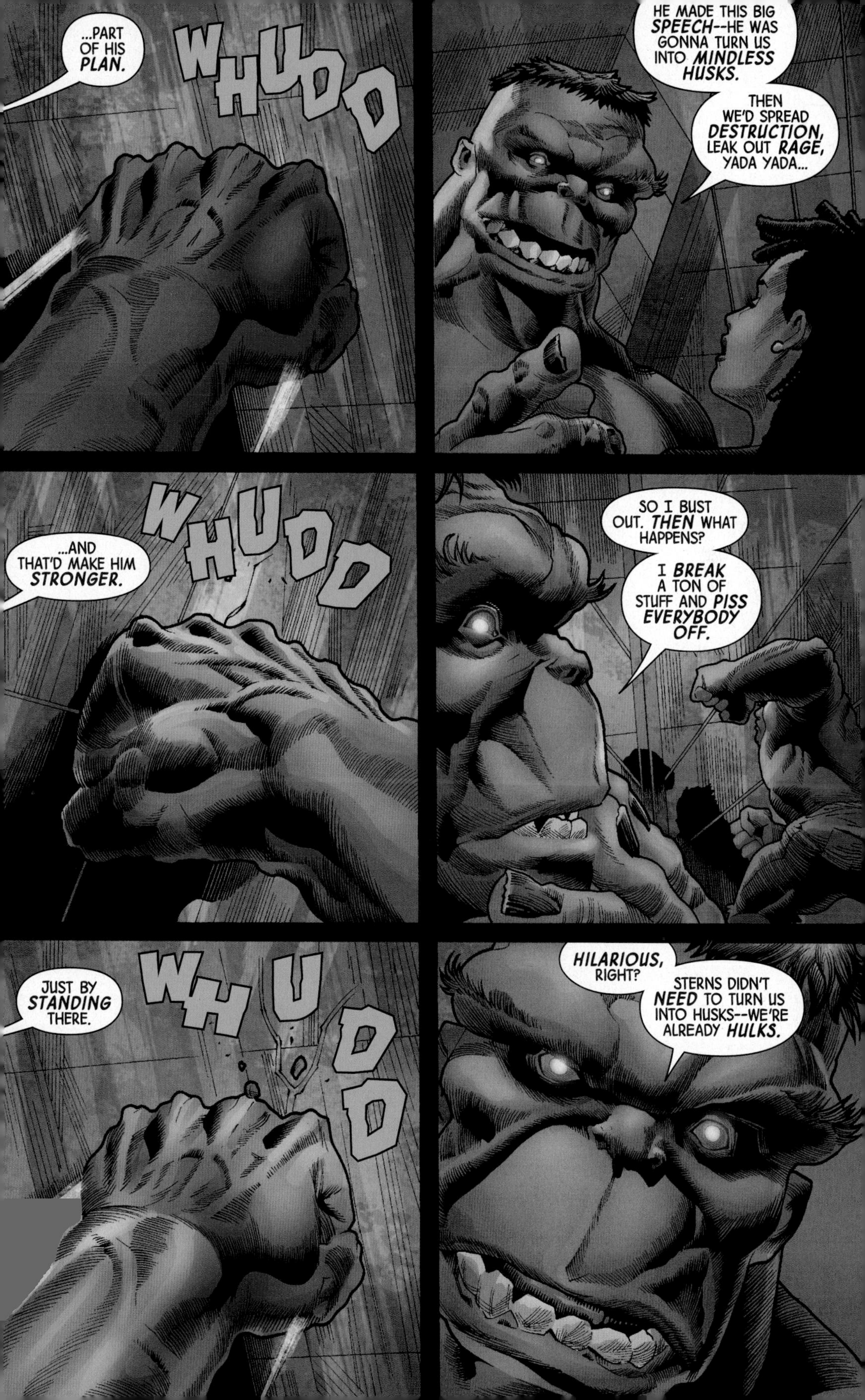
...PART OF HIS PLAN.
WHUDD
HE MADE THIS BIG SPEECH--HE WAS GONNA TURN US INTO MINDLESS HUSKS.
THEN WE'D SPREAD DESTRUCTION, LEAK OUT RAGE, YADA YADA...
...AND THAT'D MAKE HIM STRONGER.
WHUDD
SO I BUST OUT. THEN WHAT HAPPENS?
I BREAK A TON OF STUFF AND PISS EVERYBODY OFF.
JUST BY STANDING THERE.
WHUDD
HILARIOUS, RIGHT?
STERNS DIDN'T NEED TO TURN US INTO HUSKS--WE'RE ALREADY HULKS.

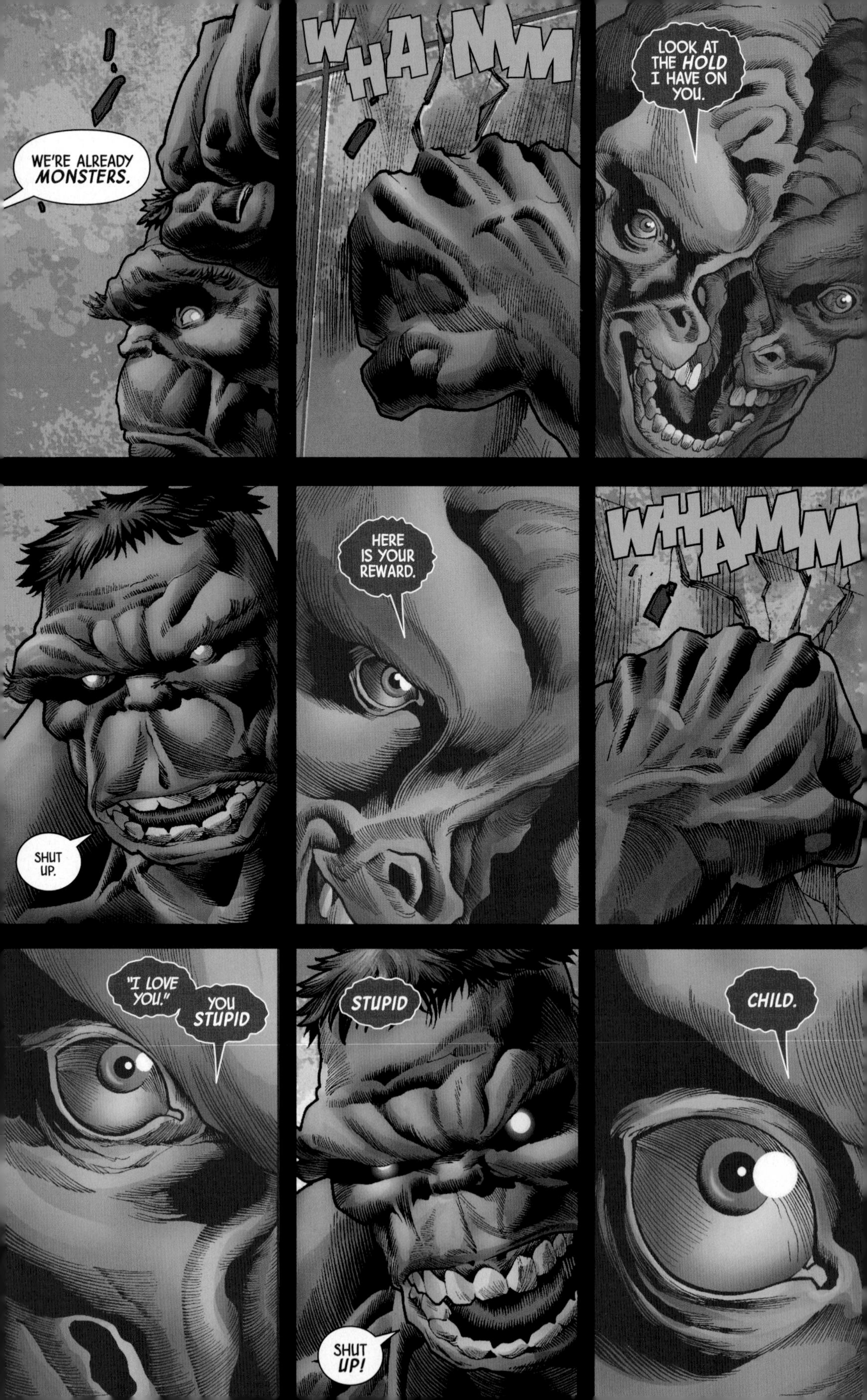
WE'RE ALREADY *MONSTERS.*
WHAMM
LOOK AT THE *HOLD* I HAVE ON YOU.
SHUT UP.
HERE IS YOUR REWARD.
WHAMM
"I LOVE YOU."
YOU *STUPID*
STUPID
SHUT *UP!*
CHILD.

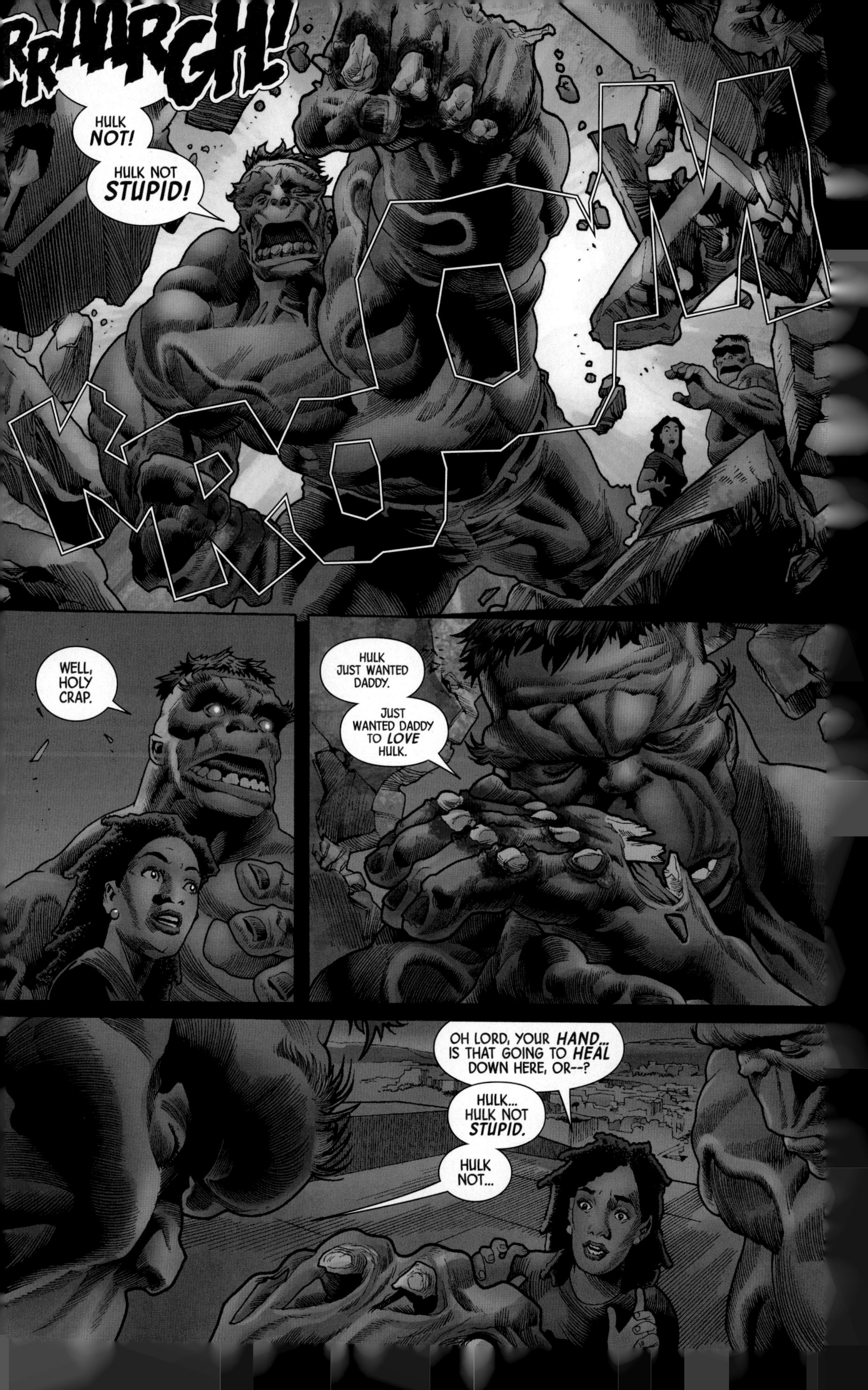
RRWARGH!
HULK NOT!
HULK NOT STUPID!
KRAKOOM
WELL, HOLY CRAP.
HULK JUST WANTED DADDY.
JUST WANTED DADDY TO LOVE HULK.
OH LORD, YOUR HAND... IS THAT GOING TO HEAL DOWN HERE, OR--?
HULK... HULK NOT STUPID.
HULK NOT...

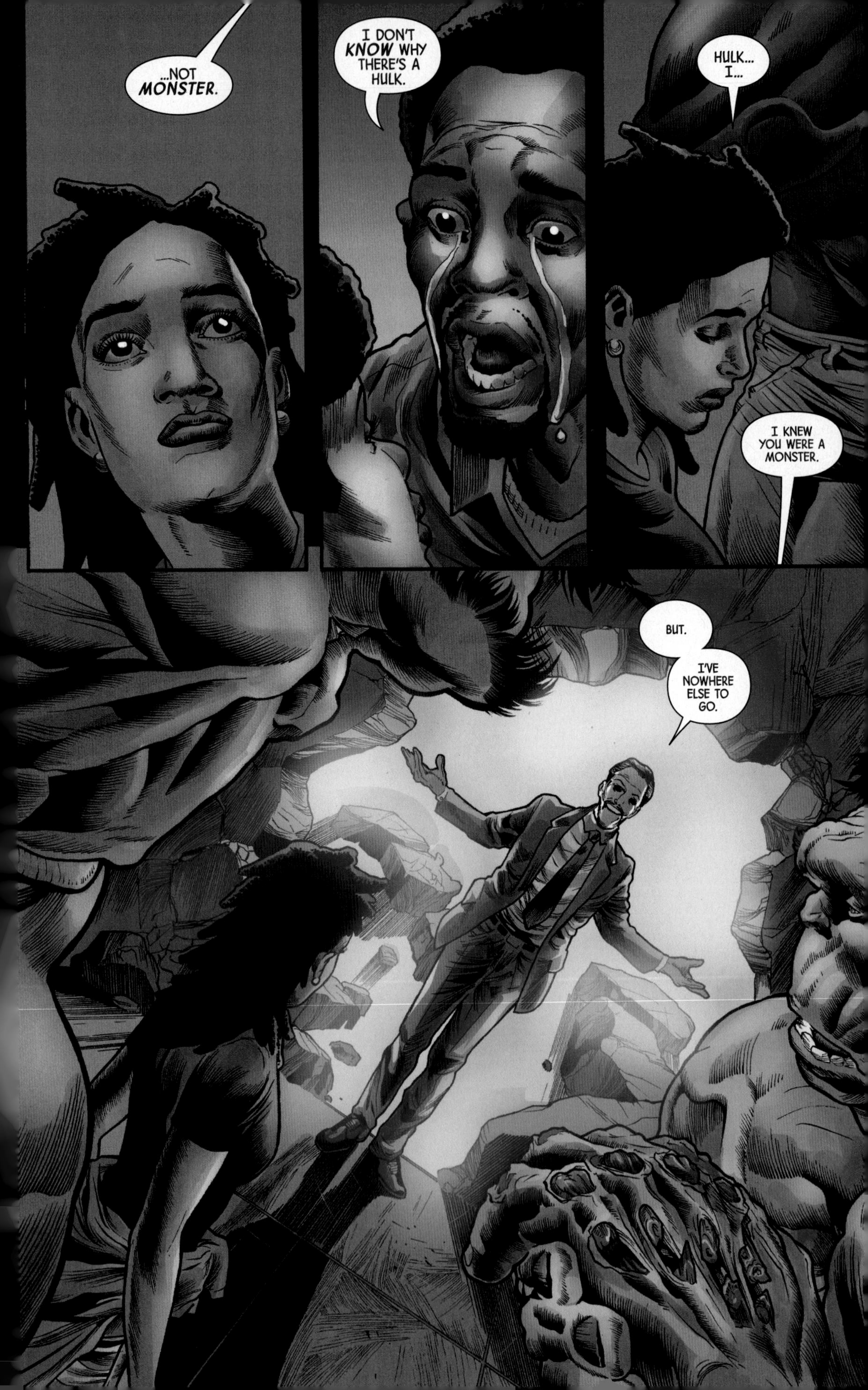
...NOT MONSTER.
I DON'T KNOW WHY THERE'S A HULK.
HULK... I...
I KNEW YOU WERE A MONSTER.
BUT.
I'VE NOWHERE ELSE TO GO.

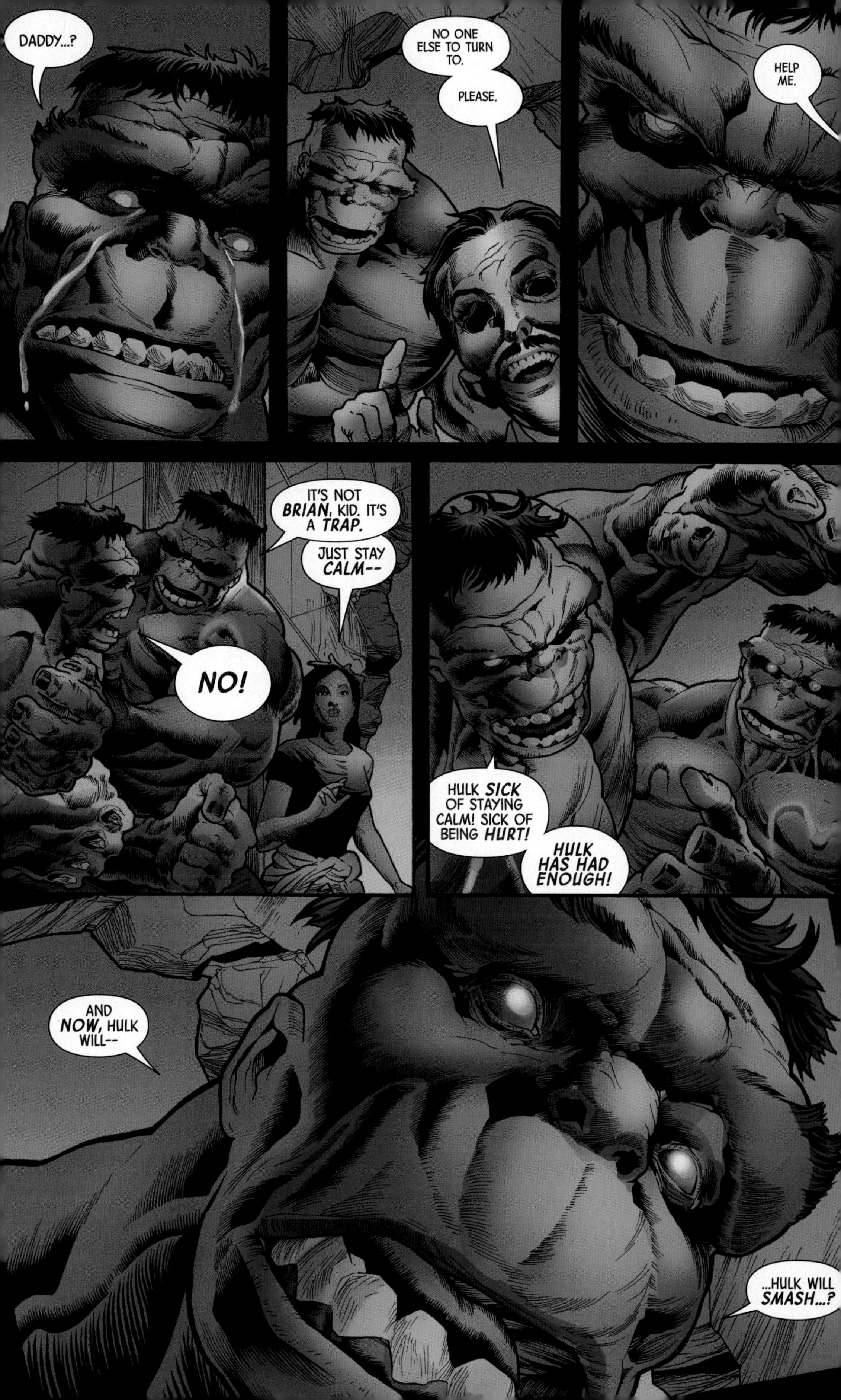
DADDY...?
NO ONE ELSE TO TURN TO.
PLEASE.
HELP ME.
IT'S NOT BRIAN, KID. IT'S A TRAP.
JUST STAY CALM--
NO!
HULK SICK OF STAYING CALM! SICK OF BEING HURT!
HULK HAS HAD ENOUGH!
AND NOW, HULK WILL--
...HULK WILL SMASH...?

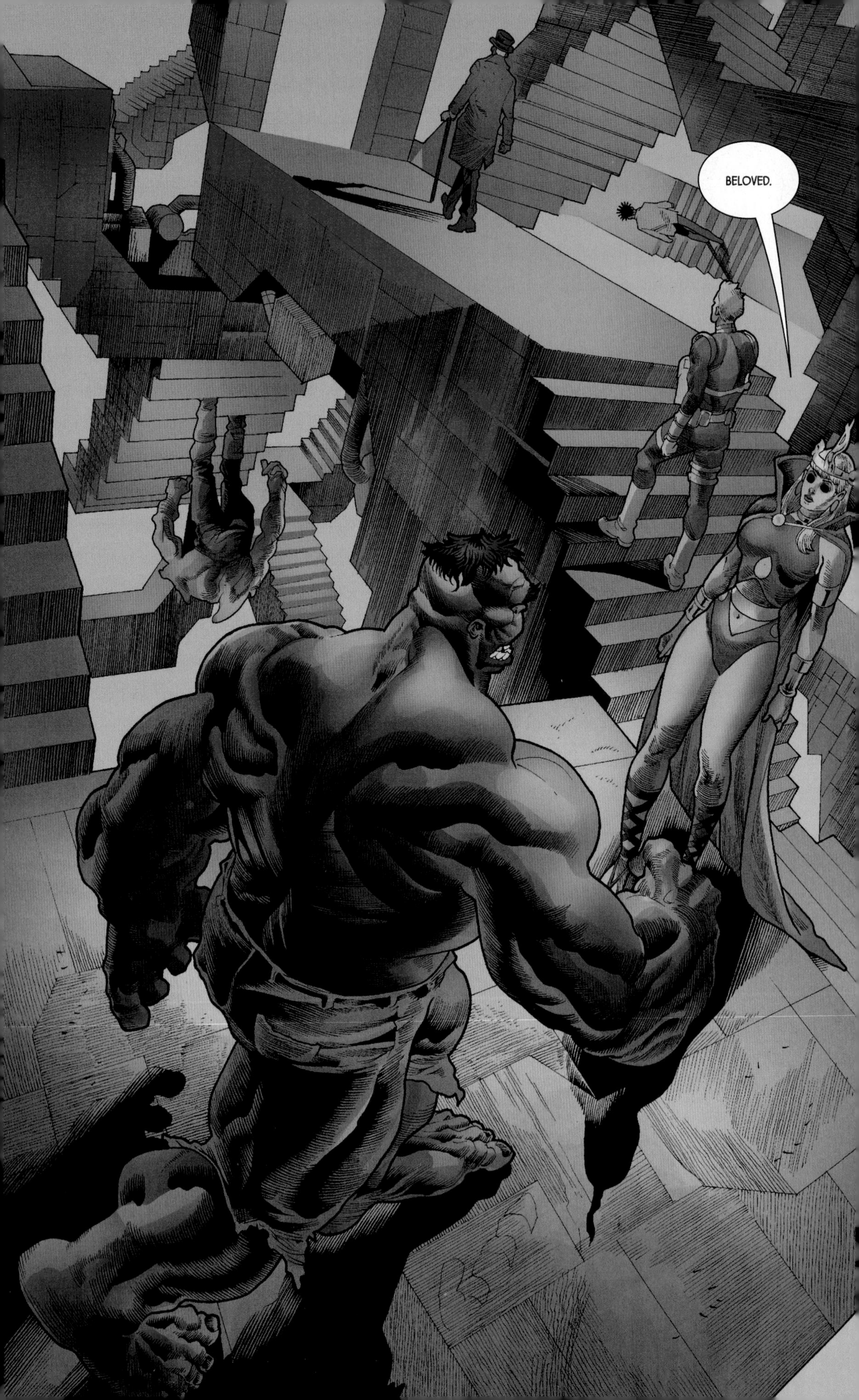
BELOVED.

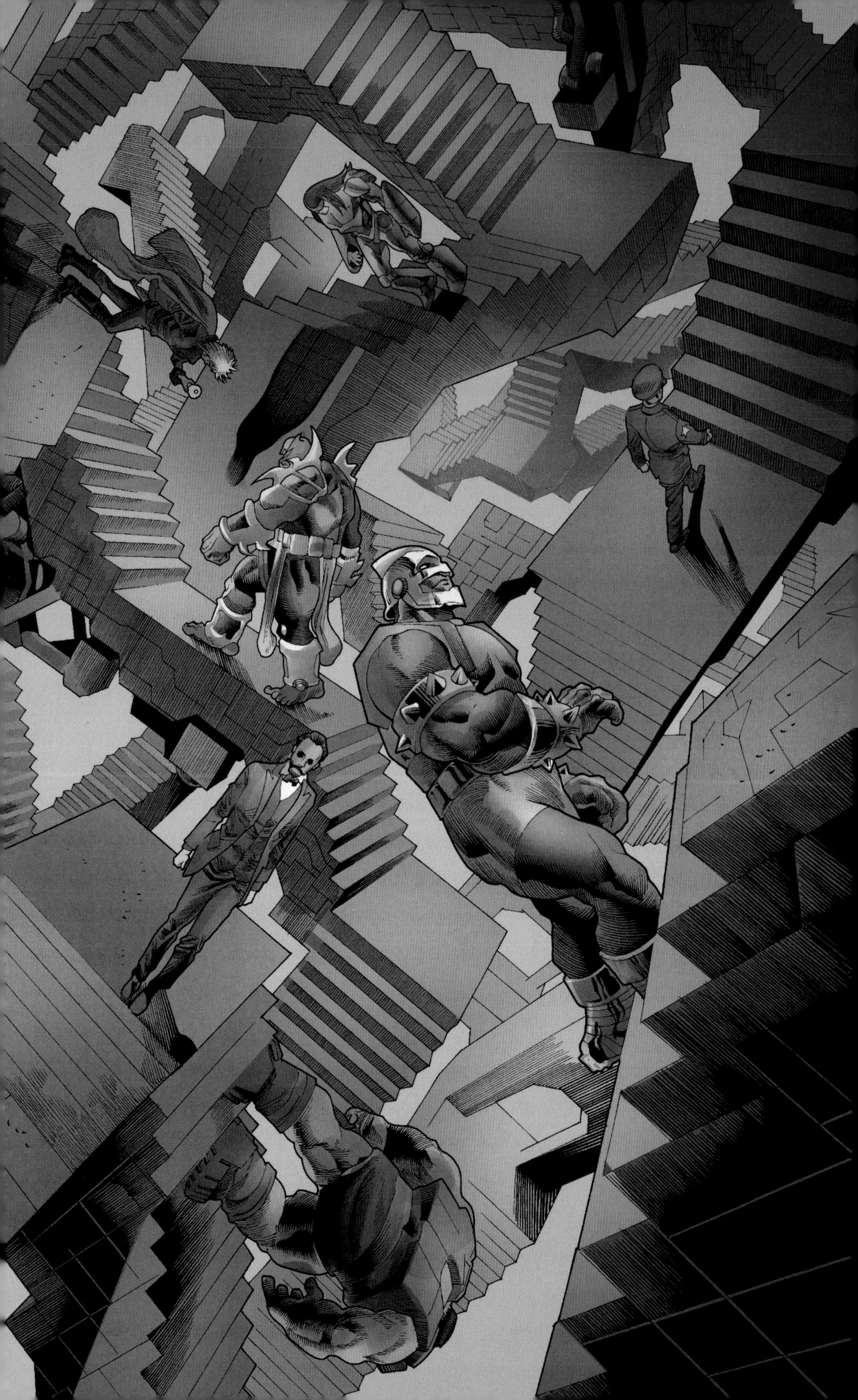

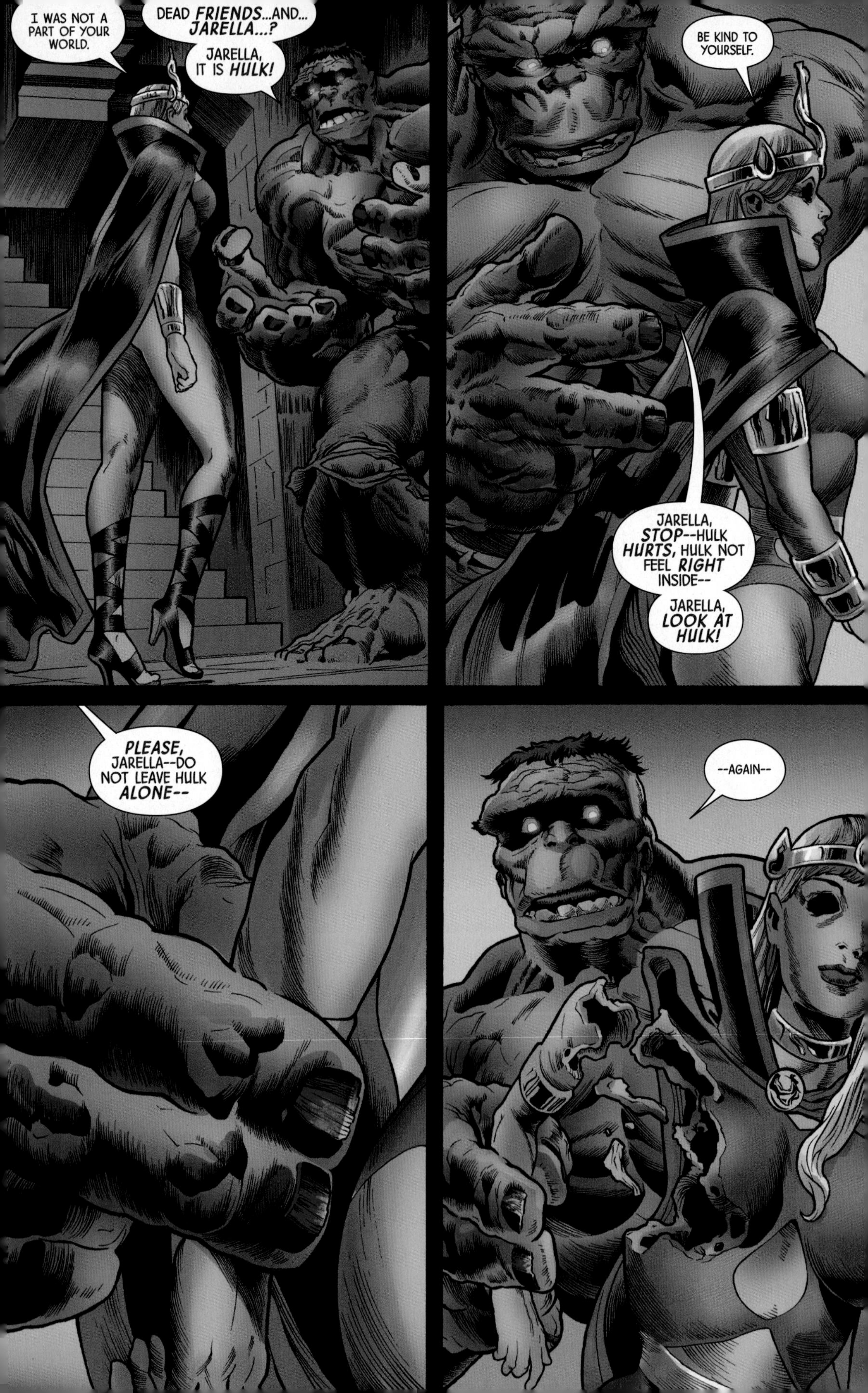
I WAS NOT A PART OF YOUR WORLD.
DEAD FRIENDS...AND... JARELLA...?
JARELLA, IT IS HULK!
BE KIND TO YOURSELF.
JARELLA, STOP--HULK HURTS, HULK NOT FEEL RIGHT INSIDE--
JARELLA, LOOK AT HULK!
PLEASE, JARELLA--DO NOT LEAVE HULK ALONE--
--AGAIN--

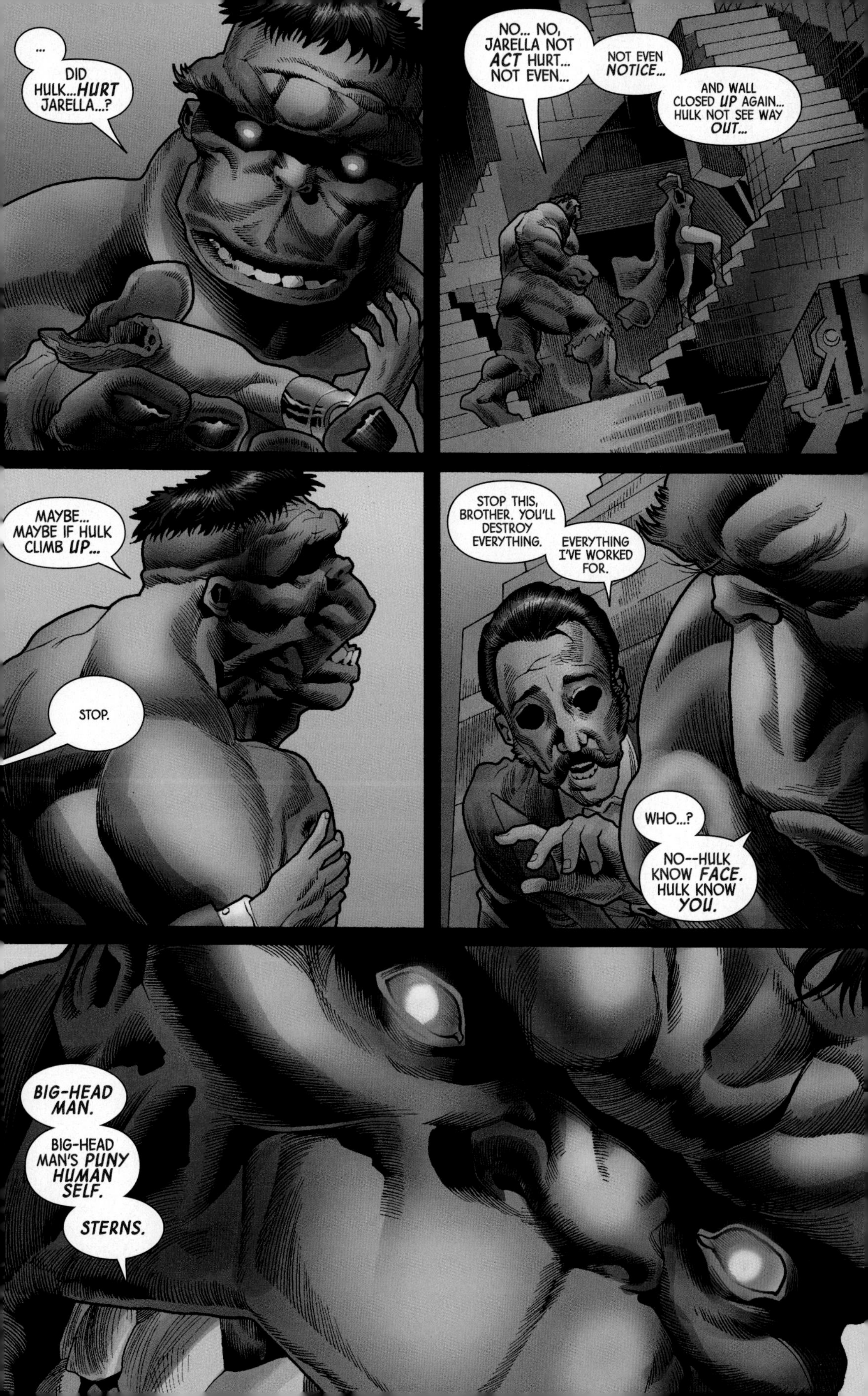
...
DID HULK...HURT JARELLA...?
NO... NO, JARELLA NOT ACT HURT... NOT EVEN...
NOT EVEN NOTICE...
AND WALL CLOSED UP AGAIN... HULK NOT SEE WAY OUT...
MAYBE... MAYBE IF HULK CLIMB UP...
STOP.
STOP THIS, BROTHER. YOU'LL DESTROY EVERYTHING.
EVERYTHING I'VE WORKED FOR.
WHO...?
NO--HULK KNOW FACE. HULK KNOW YOU.
BIG-HEAD MAN.
BIG-HEAD MAN'S PUNY HUMAN SELF.
STERNS.

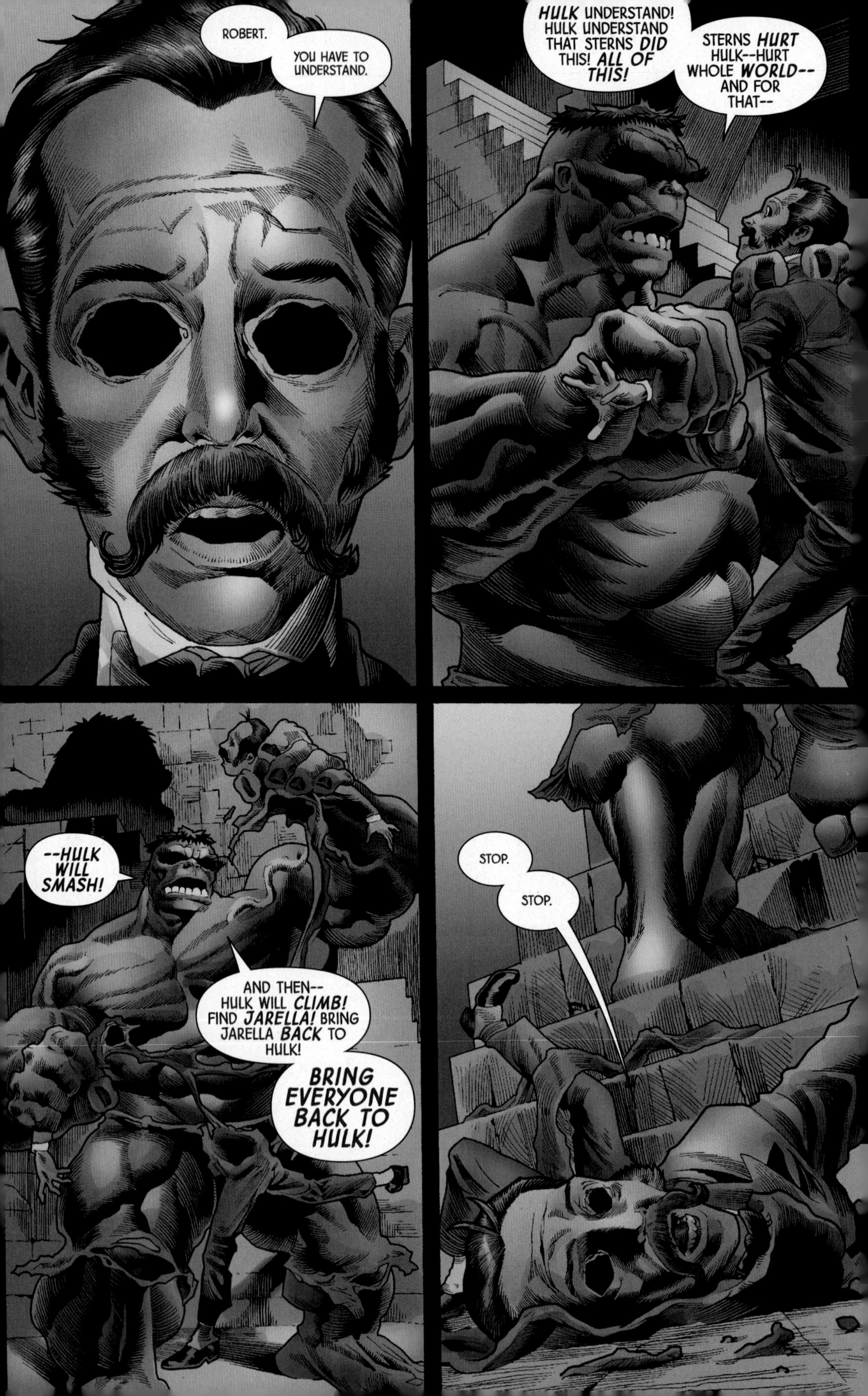
ROBERT.
YOU HAVE TO UNDERSTAND.
HULK UNDERSTAND! HULK UNDERSTAND THAT STERNS DID THIS! ALL OF THIS!
STERNS HURT HULK--HURT WHOLE WORLD-- AND FOR THAT--
--HULK WILL SMASH!
AND THEN-- HULK WILL CLIMB! FIND JARELLA! BRING JARELLA BACK TO HULK!
BRING EVERYONE BACK TO HULK!
STOP.
STOP.

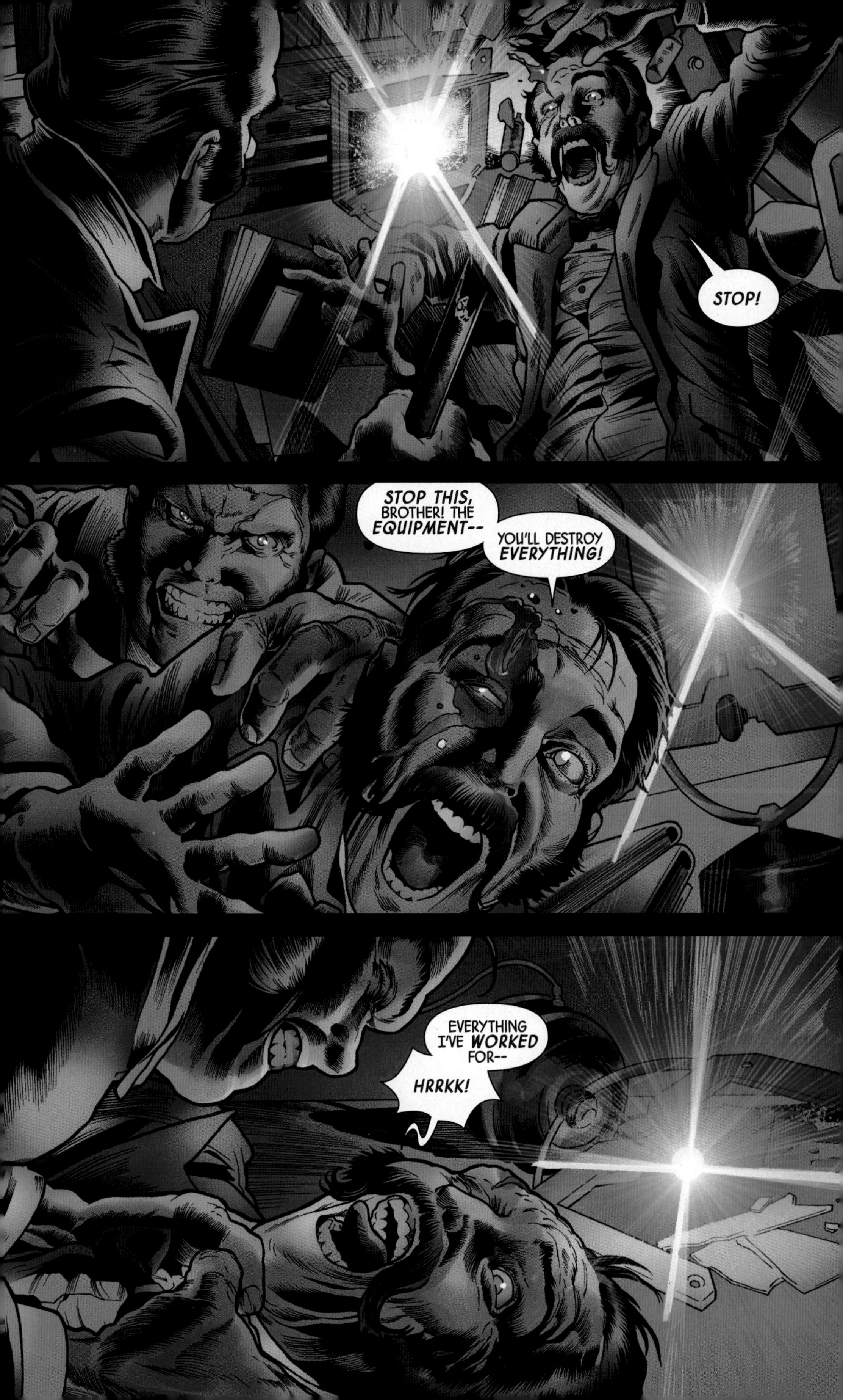
STOP!
STOP THIS, BROTHER! THE EQUIPMENT--
YOU'LL DESTROY EVERYTHING!
EVERYTHING I'VE WORKED FOR--
HRRKK!

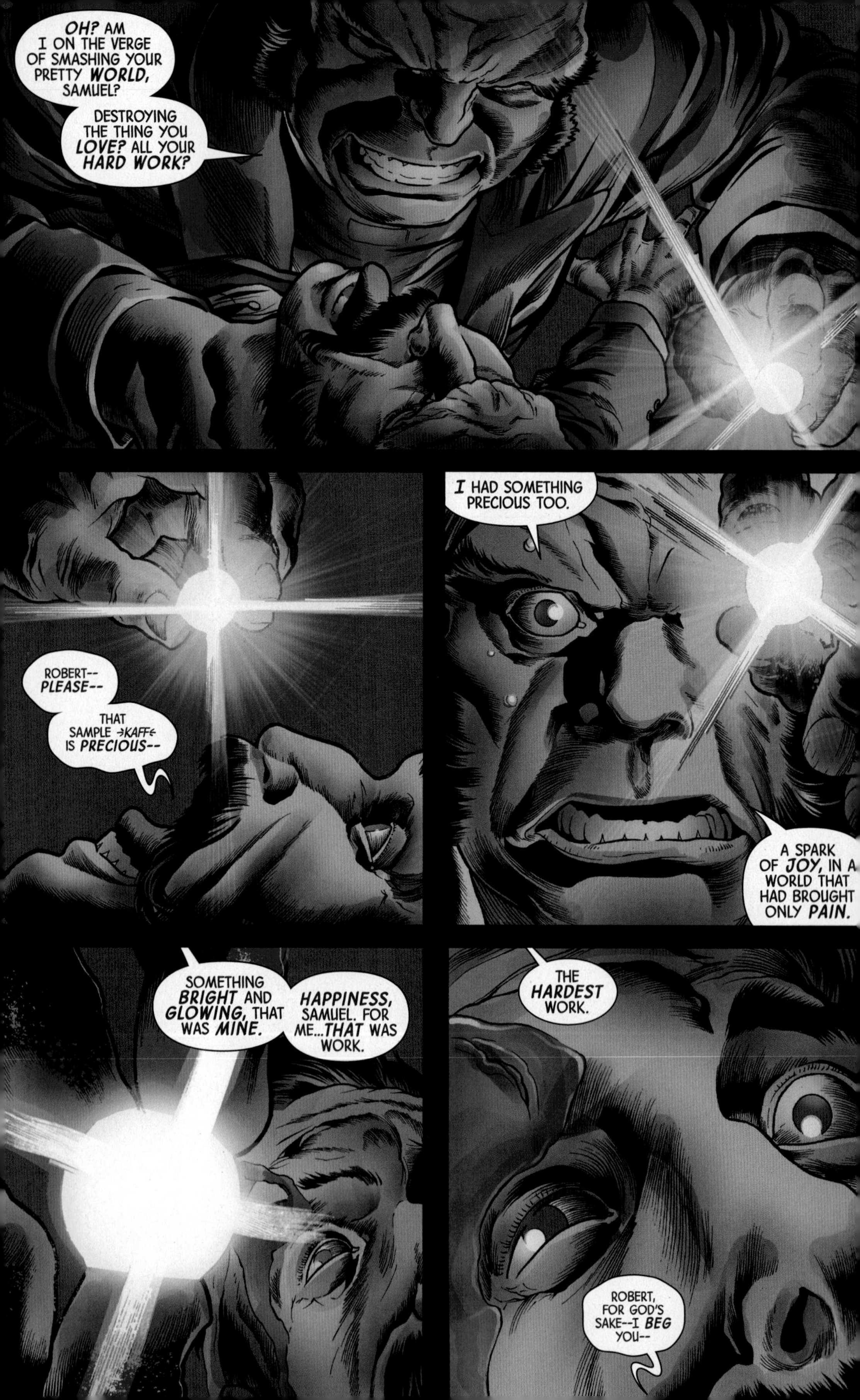
OH? AM I ON THE VERGE OF SMASHING YOUR PRETTY WORLD, SAMUEL?
DESTROYING THE THING YOU LOVE? ALL YOUR HARD WORK?
ROBERT-- PLEASE--
THAT SAMPLE ≯KAFF≮ IS PRECIOUS--
I HAD SOMETHING PRECIOUS TOO.
A SPARK OF JOY, IN A WORLD THAT HAD BROUGHT ONLY PAIN.
SOMETHING BRIGHT AND GLOWING, THAT WAS MINE.
HAPPINESS, SAMUEL. FOR ME...THAT WAS WORK.
THE HARDEST WORK.
ROBERT, FOR GOD'S SAKE--I BEG YOU--

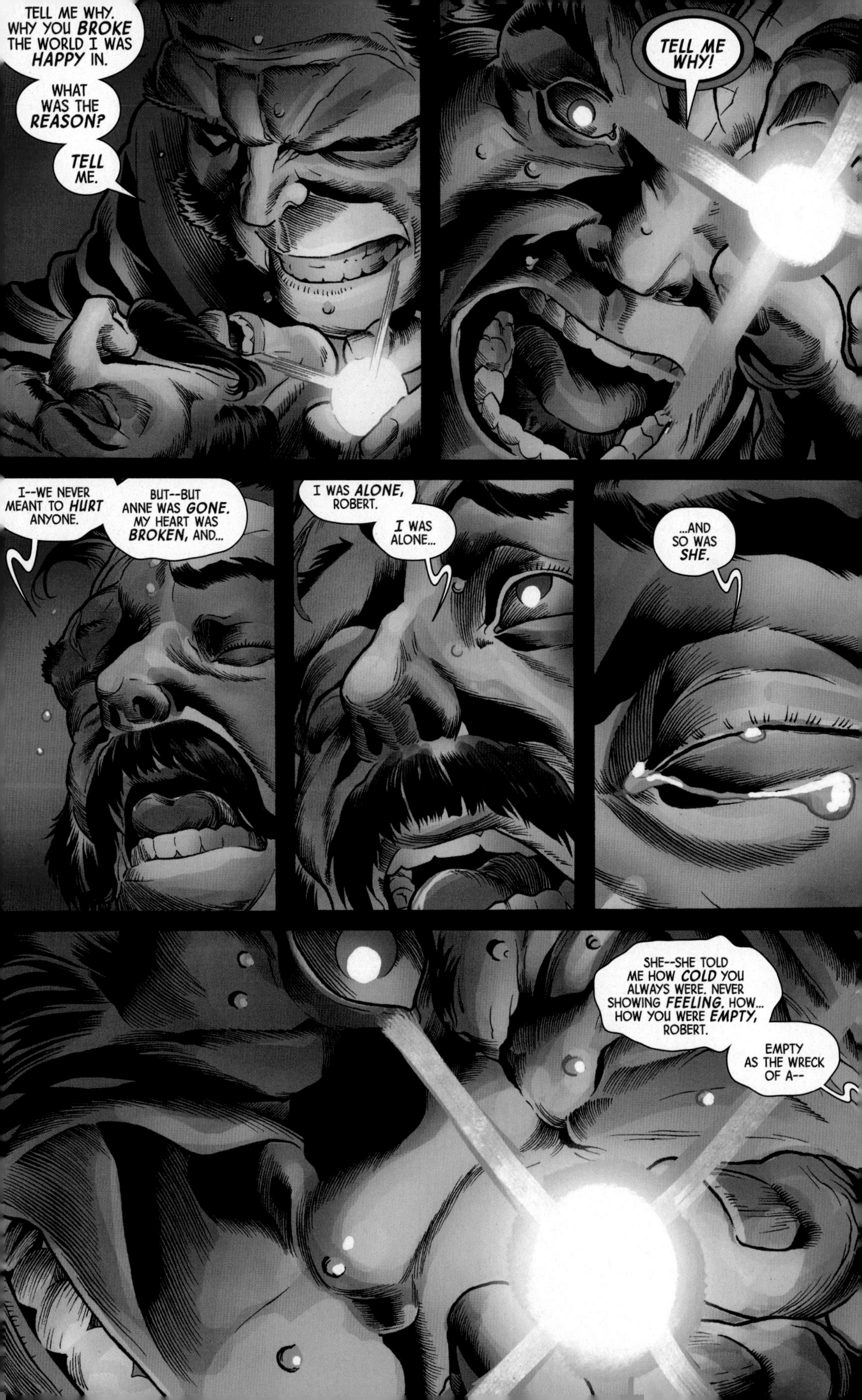
TELL ME WHY. WHY YOU BROKE THE WORLD I WAS HAPPY IN.
WHAT WAS THE REASON?
TELL ME.
TELL ME WHY!
I--WE NEVER MEANT TO HURT ANYONE.
BUT--BUT ANNE WAS GONE. MY HEART WAS BROKEN, AND...
I WAS ALONE, ROBERT.
I WAS ALONE...
...AND SO WAS SHE.
SHE--SHE TOLD ME HOW COLD YOU ALWAYS WERE. NEVER SHOWING FEELING. HOW... HOW YOU WERE EMPTY, ROBERT.
EMPTY AS THE WRECK OF A--

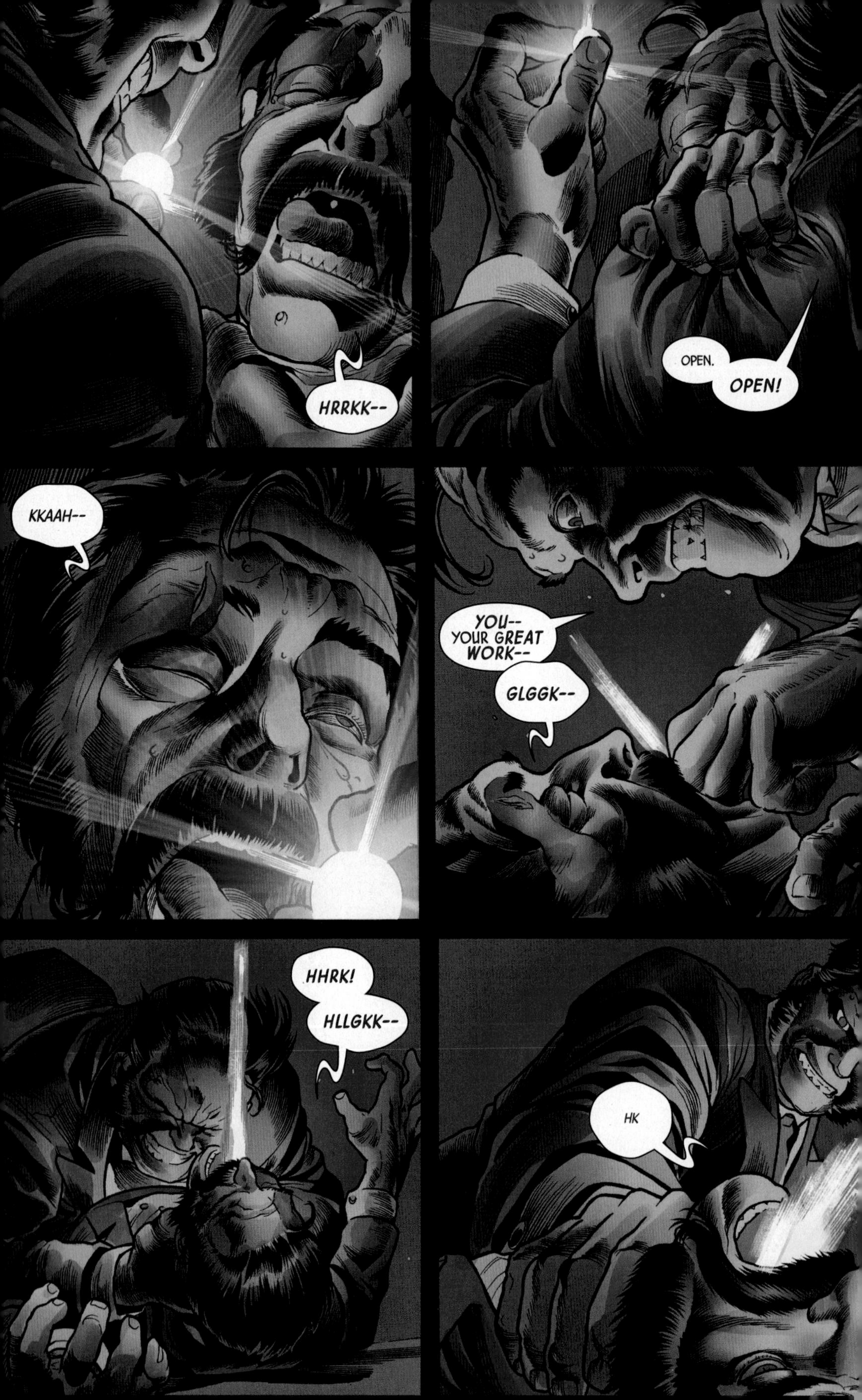
HRRKK--
OPEN.
OPEN!
KKAAH--
YOU--
YOUR GREAT
WORK--
GLGGK--
HHRK!
HLLGKK--
HK

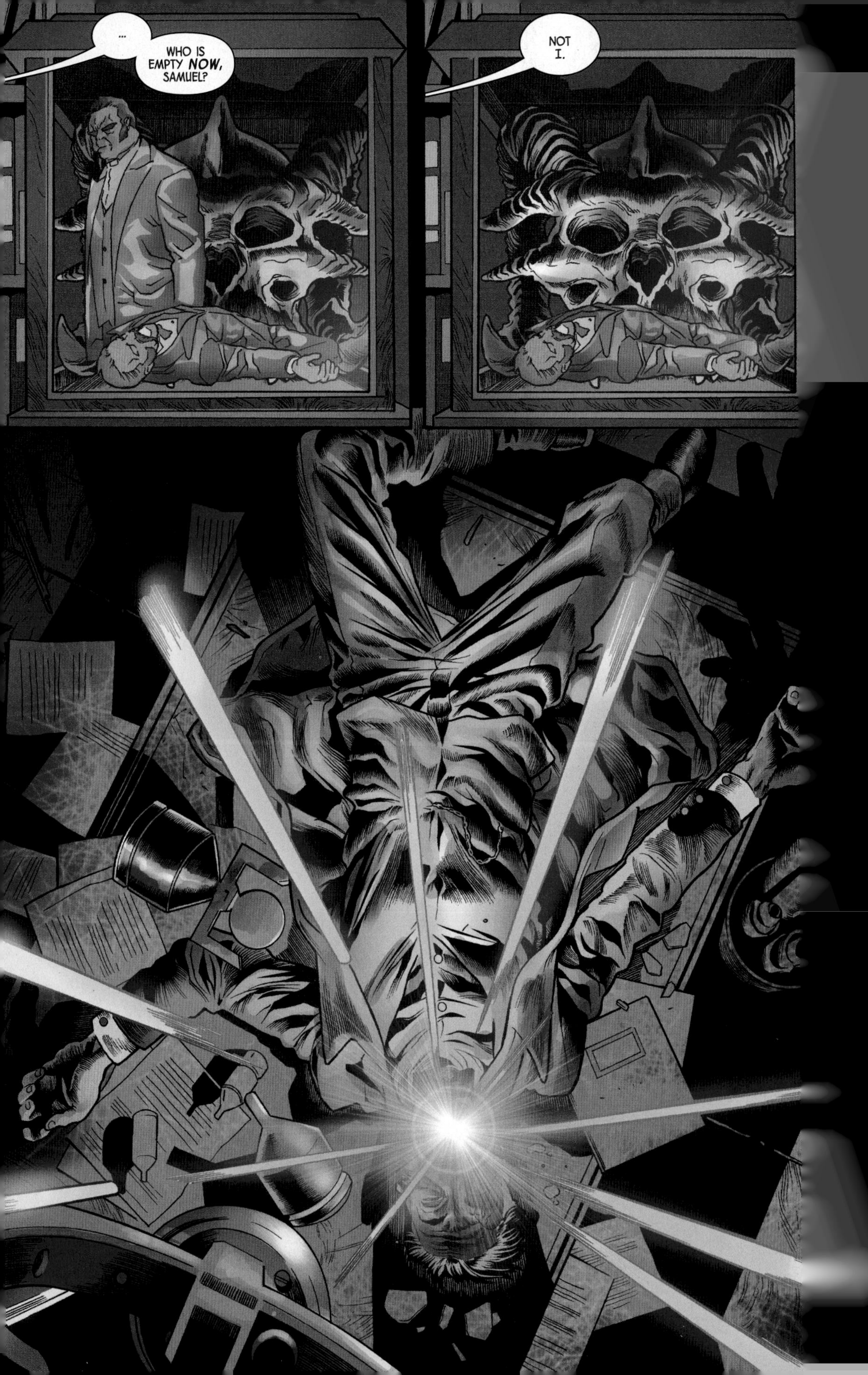
...
WHO IS EMPTY NOW, SAMUEL?
NOT I.

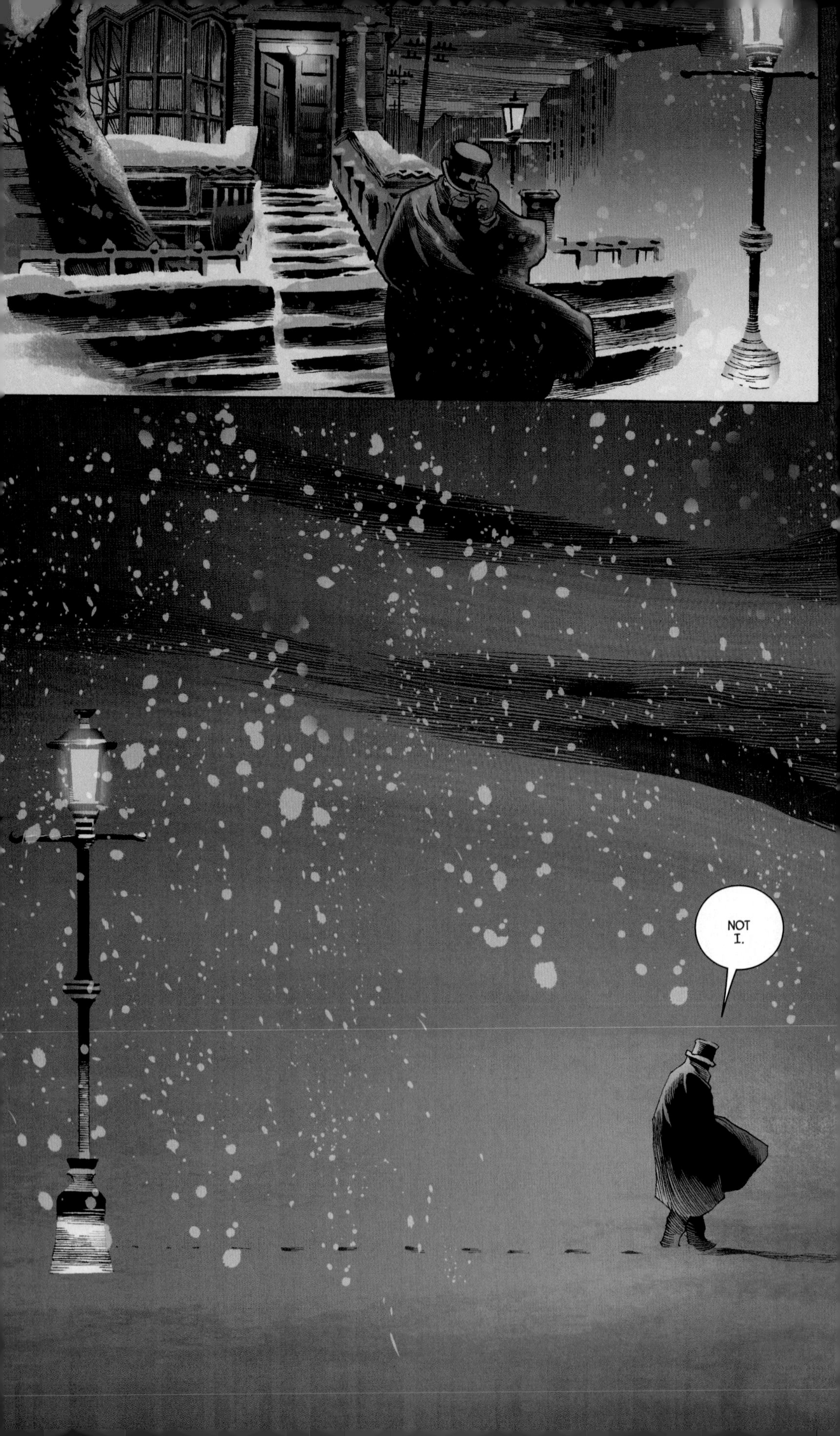
NOT I.

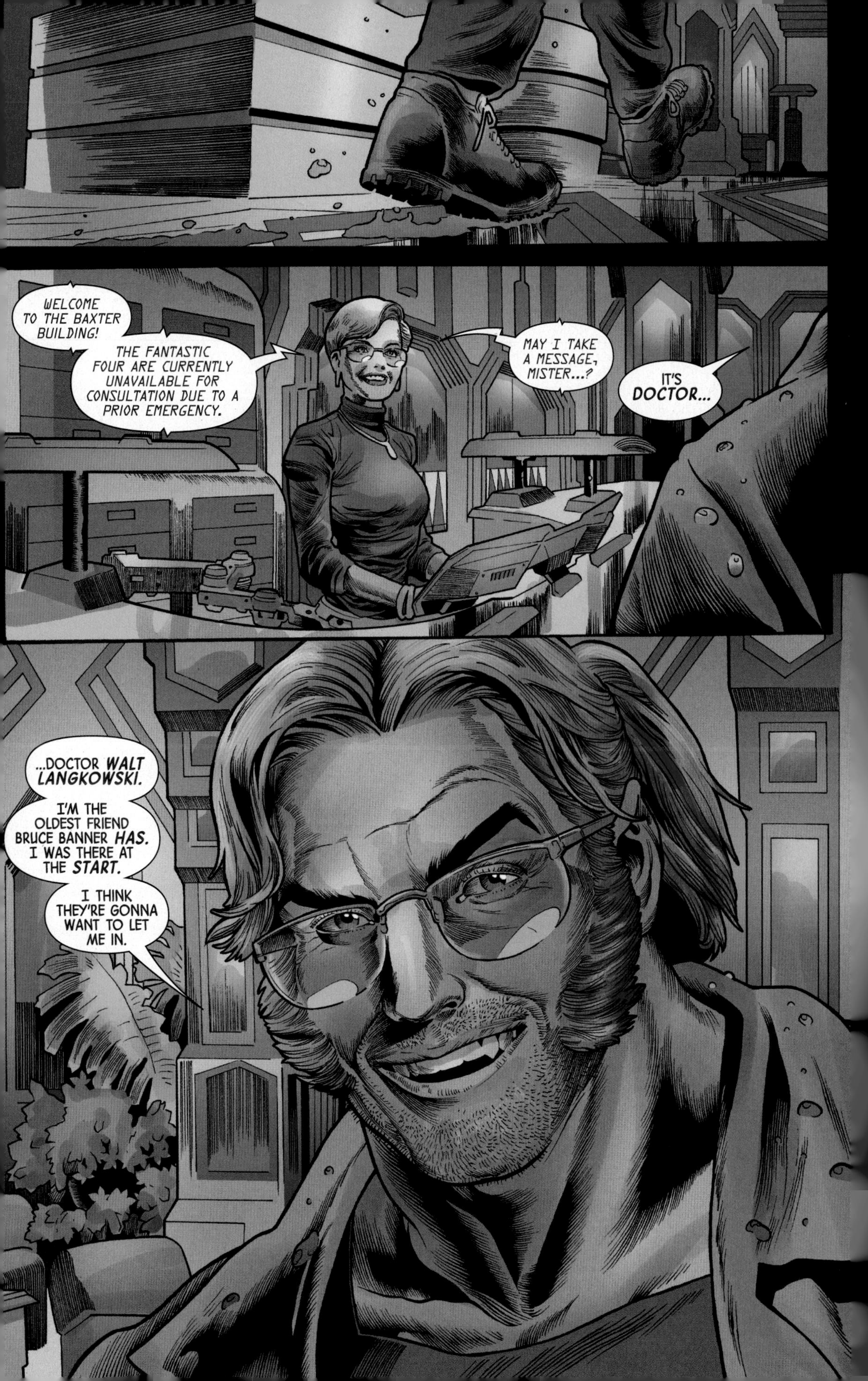
WELCOME TO THE BAXTER BUILDING!
THE FANTASTIC FOUR ARE CURRENTLY UNAVAILABLE FOR CONSULTATION DUE TO A PRIOR EMERGENCY.
MAY I TAKE A MESSAGE, MISTER...?
IT'S DOCTOR...
...DOCTOR WALT LANGKOWSKI.
I'M THE OLDEST FRIEND BRUCE BANNER HAS. I WAS THERE AT THE START.
I THINK THEY'RE GONNA WANT TO LET ME IN.

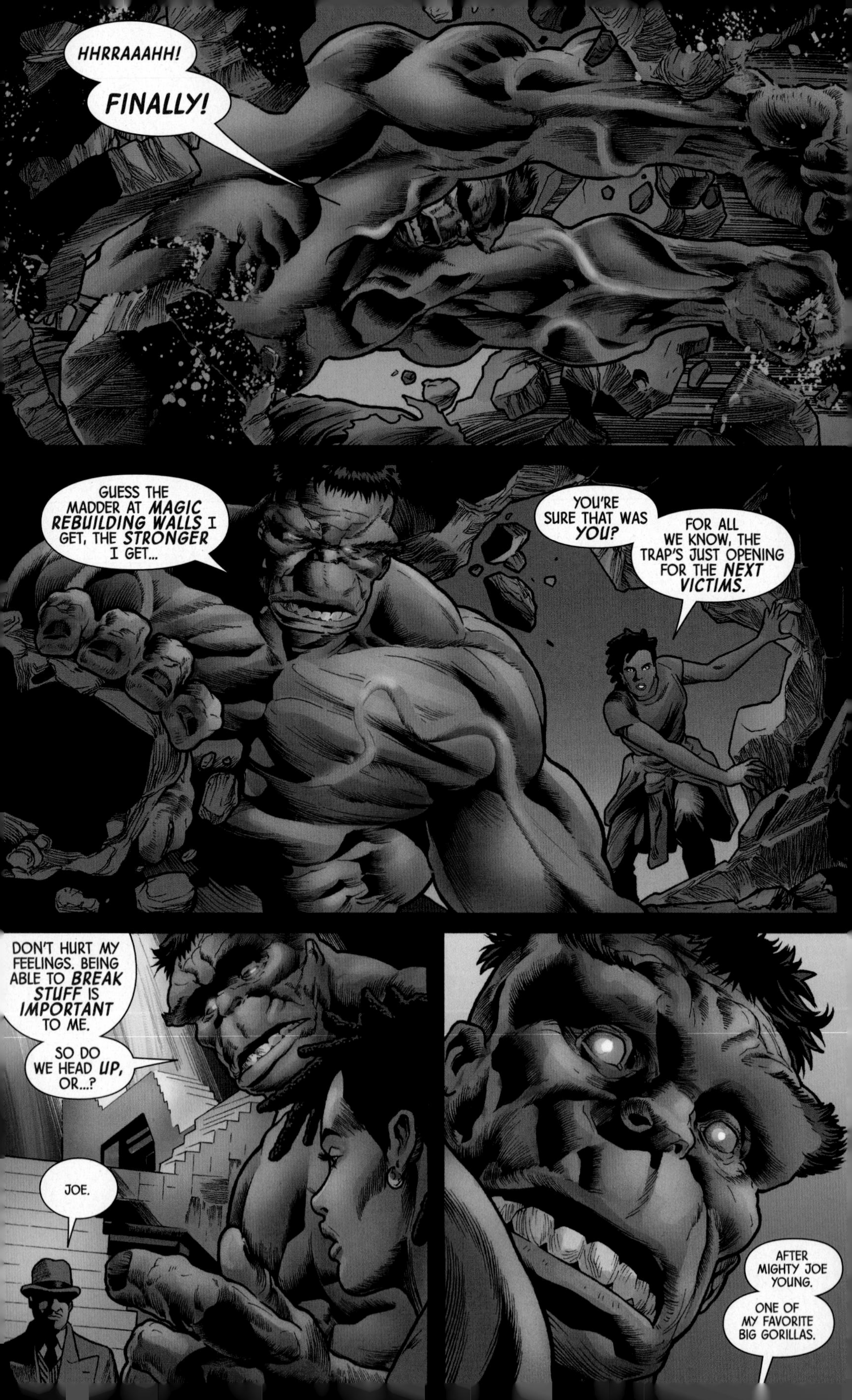
HHRRAAAHH!
FINALLY!
GUESS THE MADDER AT MAGIC REBUILDING WALLS I GET, THE STRONGER I GET...
YOU'RE SURE THAT WAS YOU?
FOR ALL WE KNOW, THE TRAP'S JUST OPENING FOR THE NEXT VICTIMS.
DON'T HURT MY FEELINGS. BEING ABLE TO BREAK STUFF IS IMPORTANT TO ME.
SO DO WE HEAD UP, OR...?
JOE.
AFTER MIGHTY JOE YOUNG.
ONE OF MY FAVORITE BIG GORILLAS.

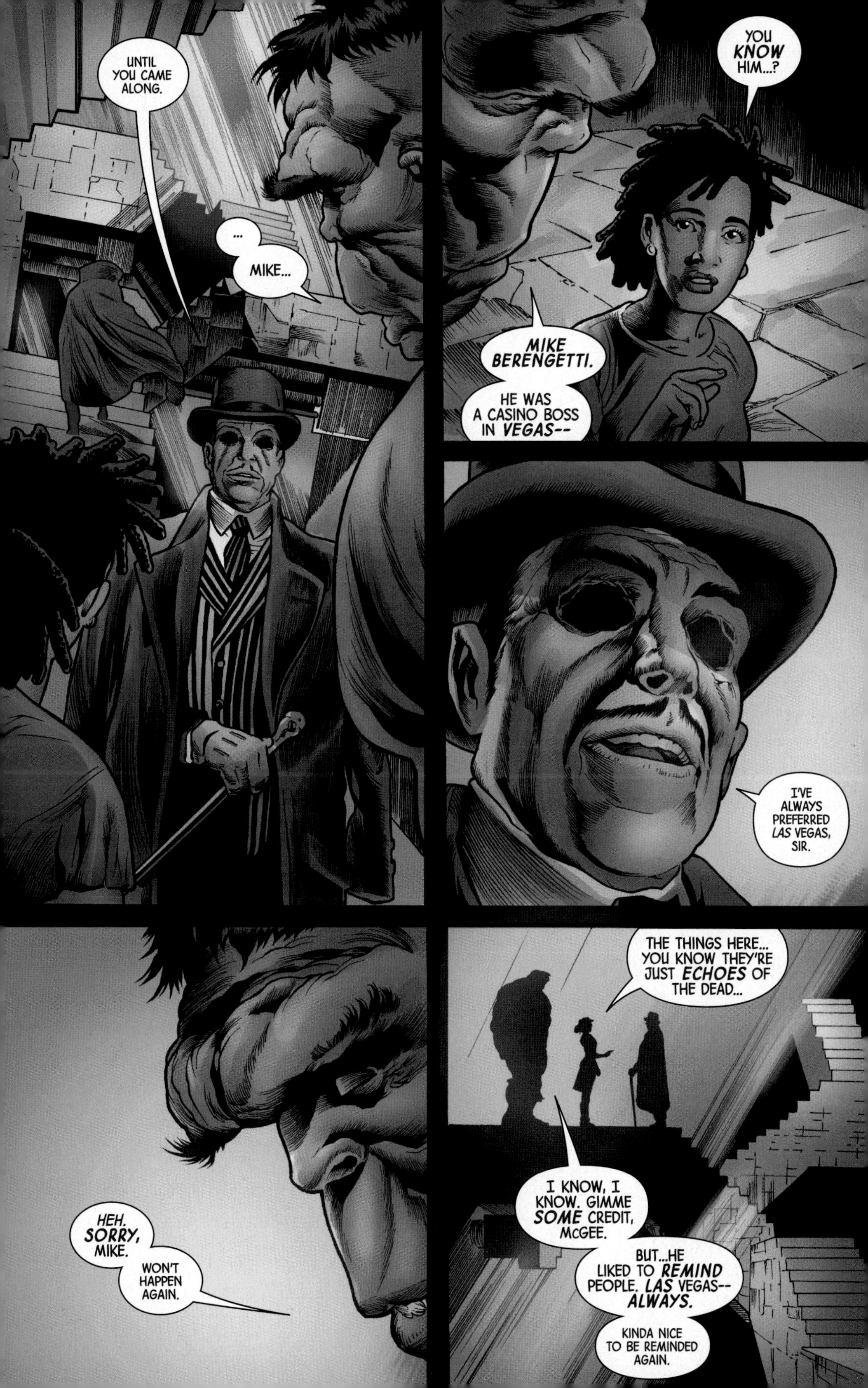
UNTIL YOU CAME ALONG.
...
MIKE...
YOU KNOW HIM...?
MIKE BERENGETTI.
HE WAS A CASINO BOSS IN VEGAS--
I'VE ALWAYS PREFERRED LAS VEGAS, SIR.
HEH. SORRY, MIKE.
WON'T HAPPEN AGAIN.
THE THINGS HERE... YOU KNOW THEY'RE JUST ECHOES OF THE DEAD...
I KNOW, I KNOW. GIMME SOME CREDIT, McGEE.
BUT...HE LIKED TO REMIND PEOPLE. LAS VEGAS-- ALWAYS.
KINDA NICE TO BE REMINDED AGAIN.

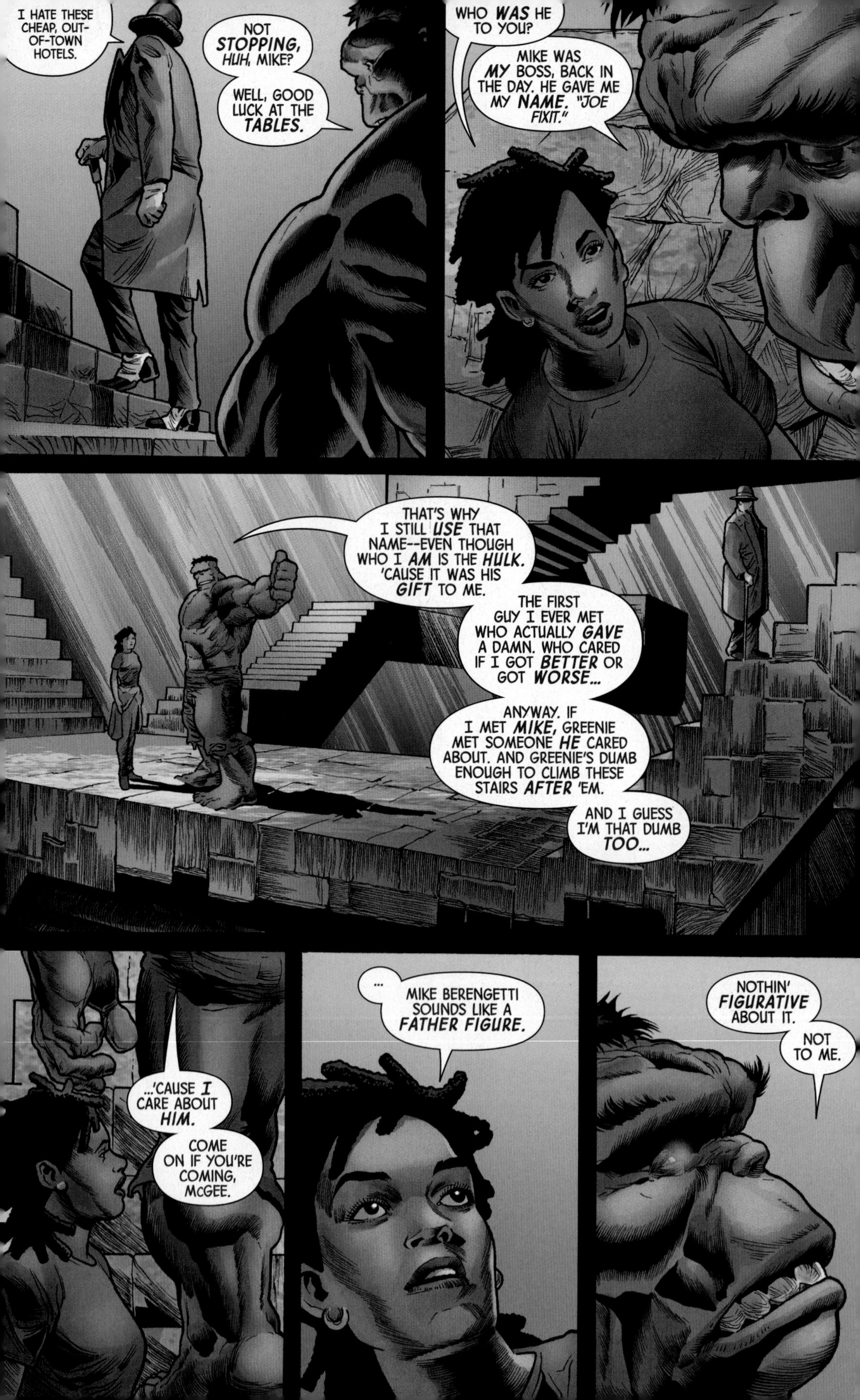

I HATE THESE CHEAP, OUT-OF-TOWN HOTELS.
NOT STOPPING, HUH, MIKE?
WELL, GOOD LUCK AT THE TABLES.
WHO WAS HE TO YOU?
MIKE WAS MY BOSS, BACK IN THE DAY. HE GAVE ME MY NAME. "JOE FIXIT."
THAT'S WHY I STILL USE THAT NAME--EVEN THOUGH WHO I AM IS THE HULK. 'CAUSE IT WAS HIS GIFT TO ME.
THE FIRST GUY I EVER MET WHO ACTUALLY GAVE A DAMN. WHO CARED IF I GOT BETTER OR GOT WORSE...
ANYWAY. IF I MET MIKE, GREENIE MET SOMEONE HE CARED ABOUT. AND GREENIE'S DUMB ENOUGH TO CLIMB THESE STAIRS AFTER 'EM.
AND I GUESS I'M THAT DUMB TOO...
...'CAUSE I CARE ABOUT HIM.
COME ON IF YOU'RE COMING, McGEE.
...
MIKE BERENGETTI SOUNDS LIKE A FATHER FIGURE.
NOTHIN' FIGURATIVE ABOUT IT.
NOT TO ME.

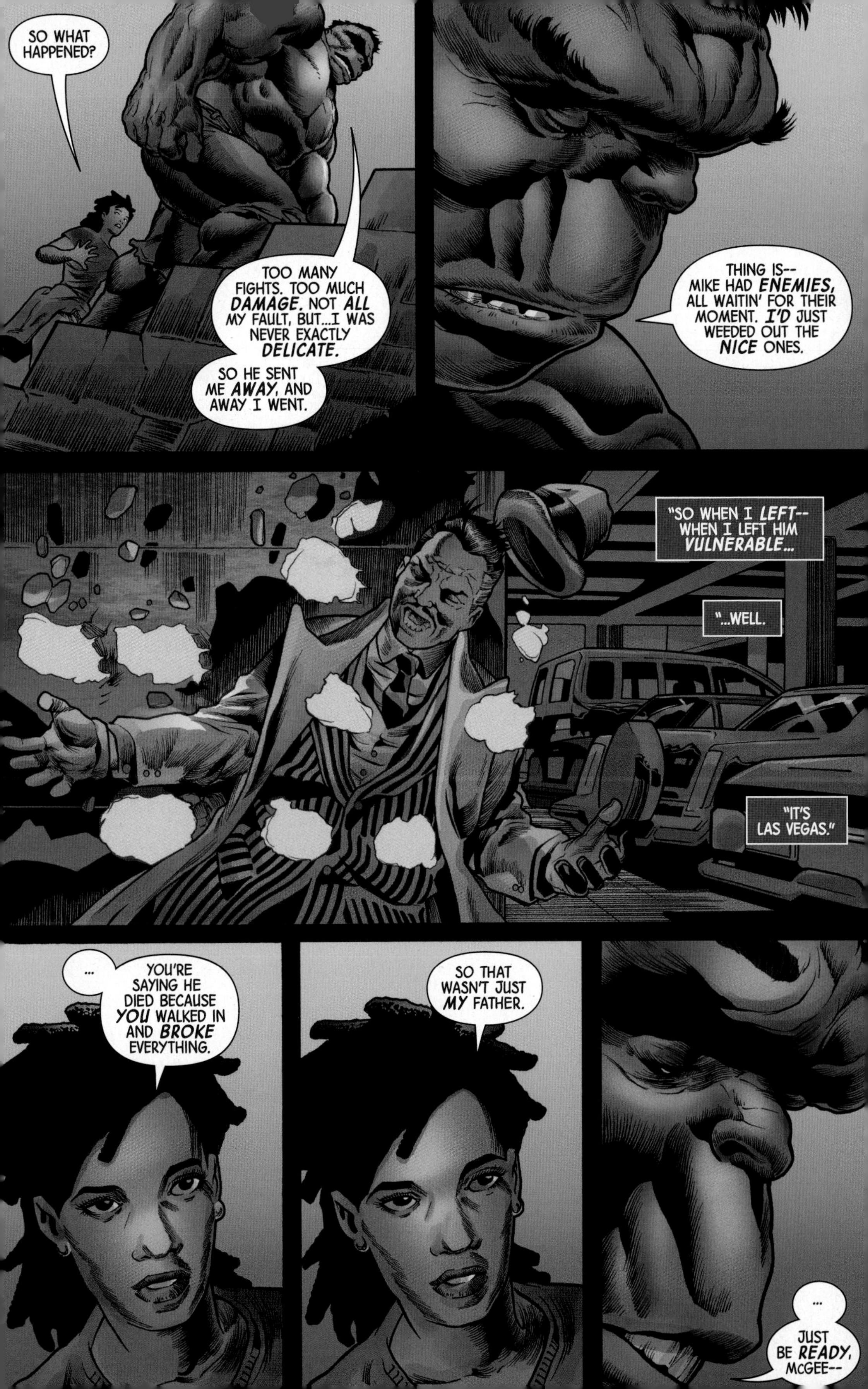
SO WHAT HAPPENED?
TOO MANY FIGHTS. TOO MUCH DAMAGE. NOT ALL MY FAULT, BUT...I WAS NEVER EXACTLY DELICATE.
SO HE SENT ME AWAY, AND AWAY I WENT.
THING IS-- MIKE HAD ENEMIES, ALL WAITIN' FOR THEIR MOMENT. I'D JUST WEEDED OUT THE NICE ONES.
"SO WHEN I LEFT-- WHEN I LEFT HIM VULNERABLE...
"...WELL.
"IT'S LAS VEGAS."
...
YOU'RE SAYING HE DIED BECAUSE YOU WALKED IN AND BROKE EVERYTHING.
SO THAT WASN'T JUST MY FATHER.
...
JUST BE READY, MCGEE--

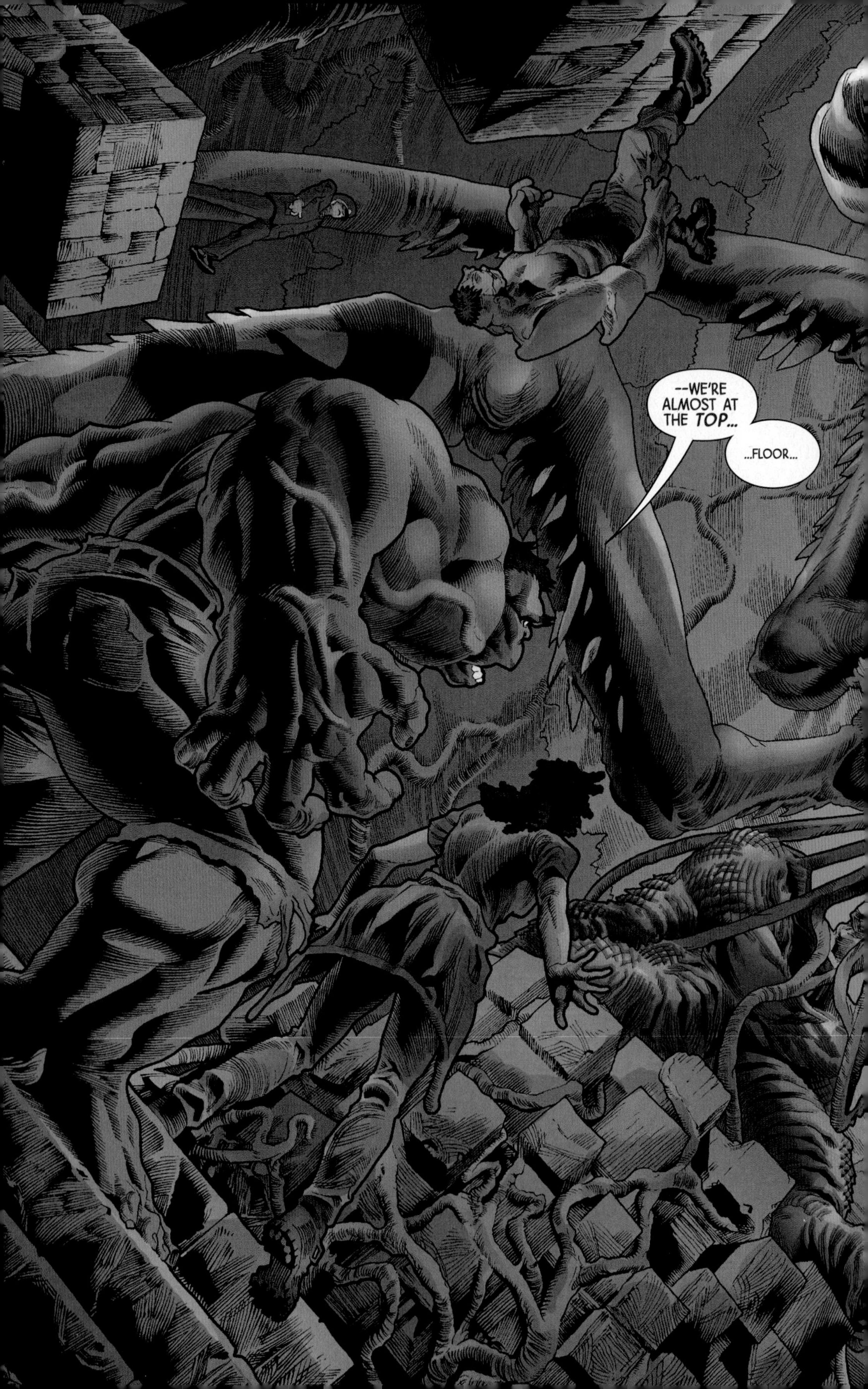
--WE'RE ALMOST AT THE *TOP*...
...FLOOR...

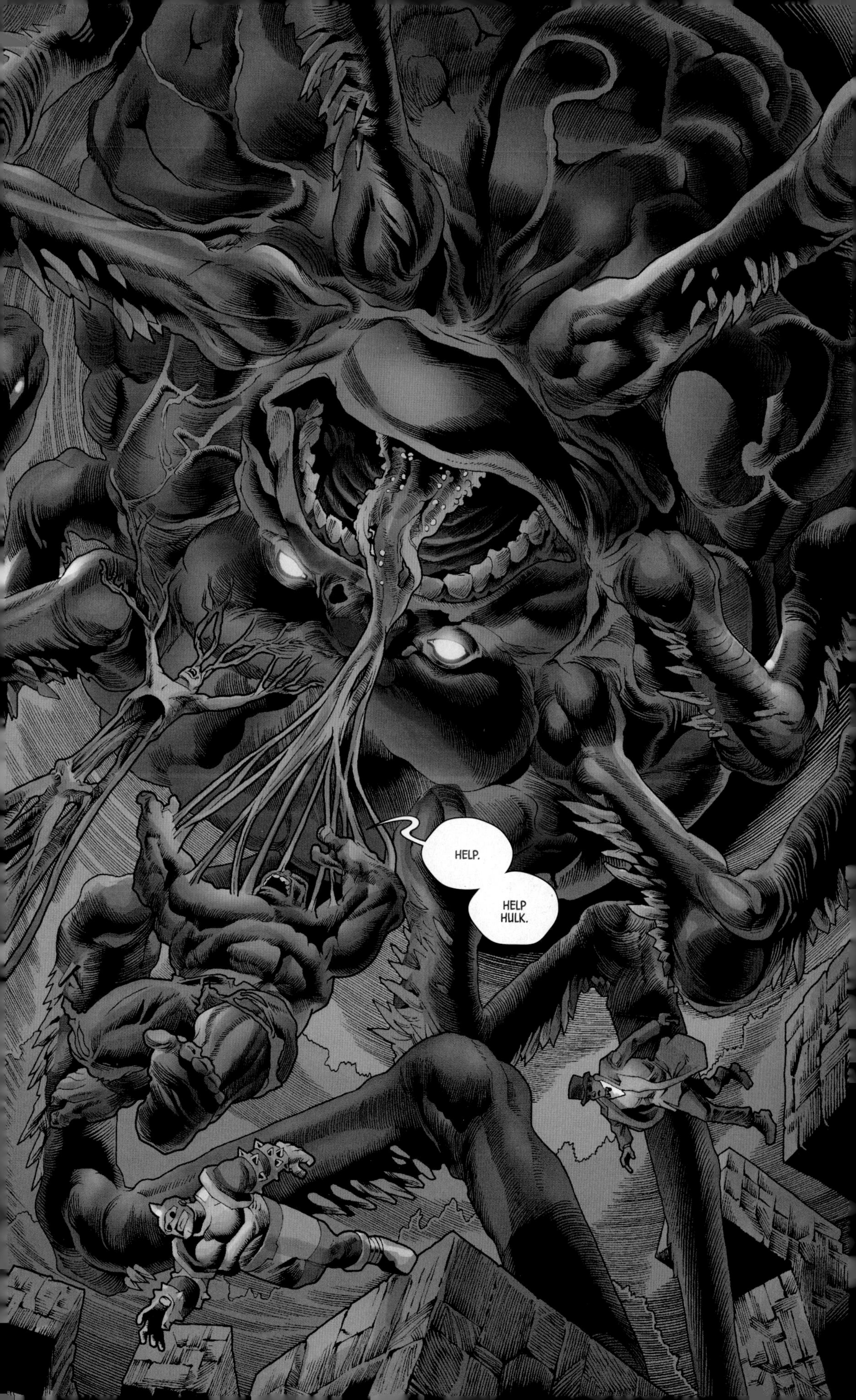
HELP.
HELP HULK.

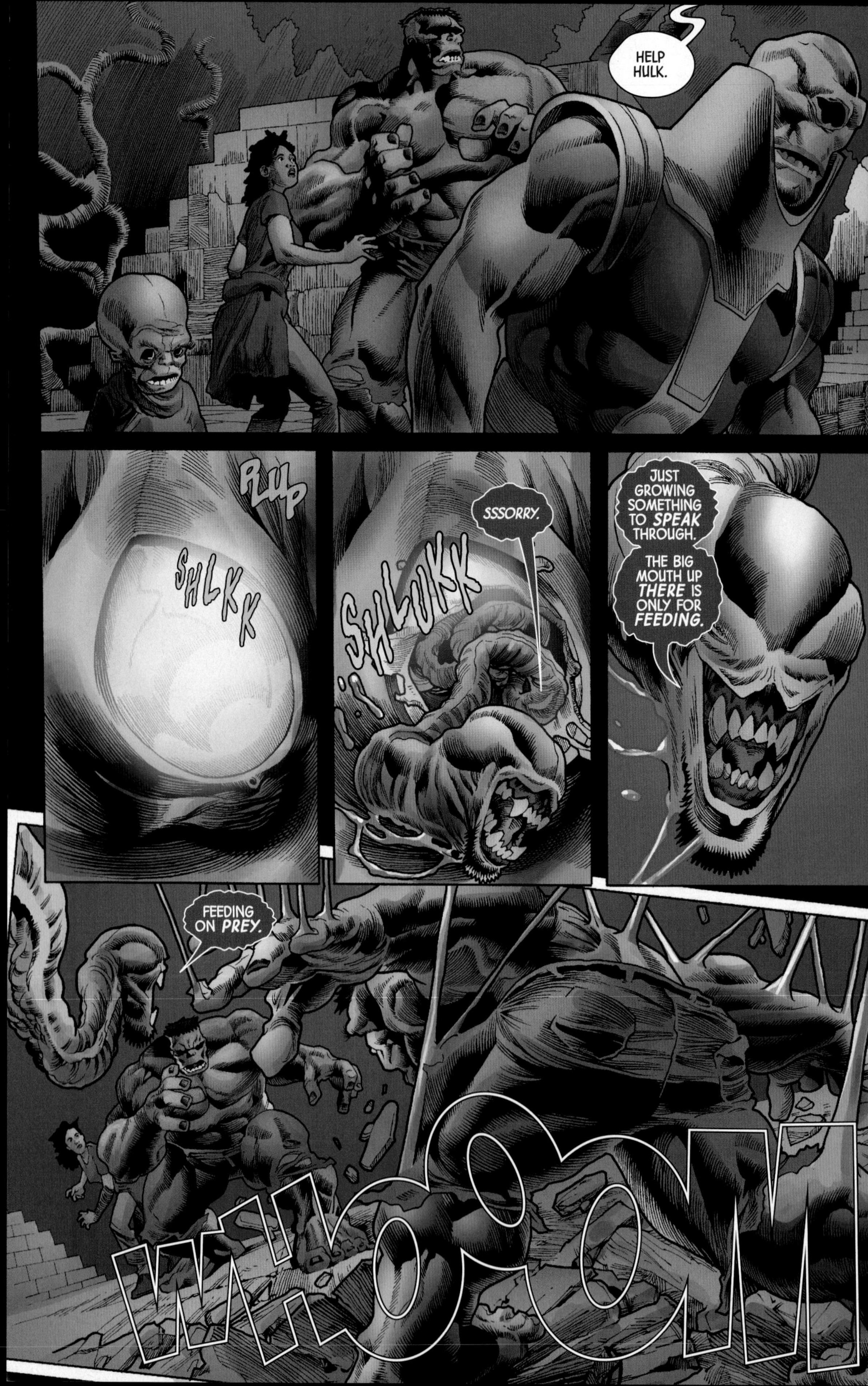
HELP HULK.
PLUP
SHLKK
SHLOKK
SSSORRY.
JUST GROWING SOMETHING TO *SPEAK* THROUGH.
THE BIG MOUTH UP *THERE* IS ONLY FOR *FEEDING*.
FEEDING ON *PREY*.
WHOOOOM

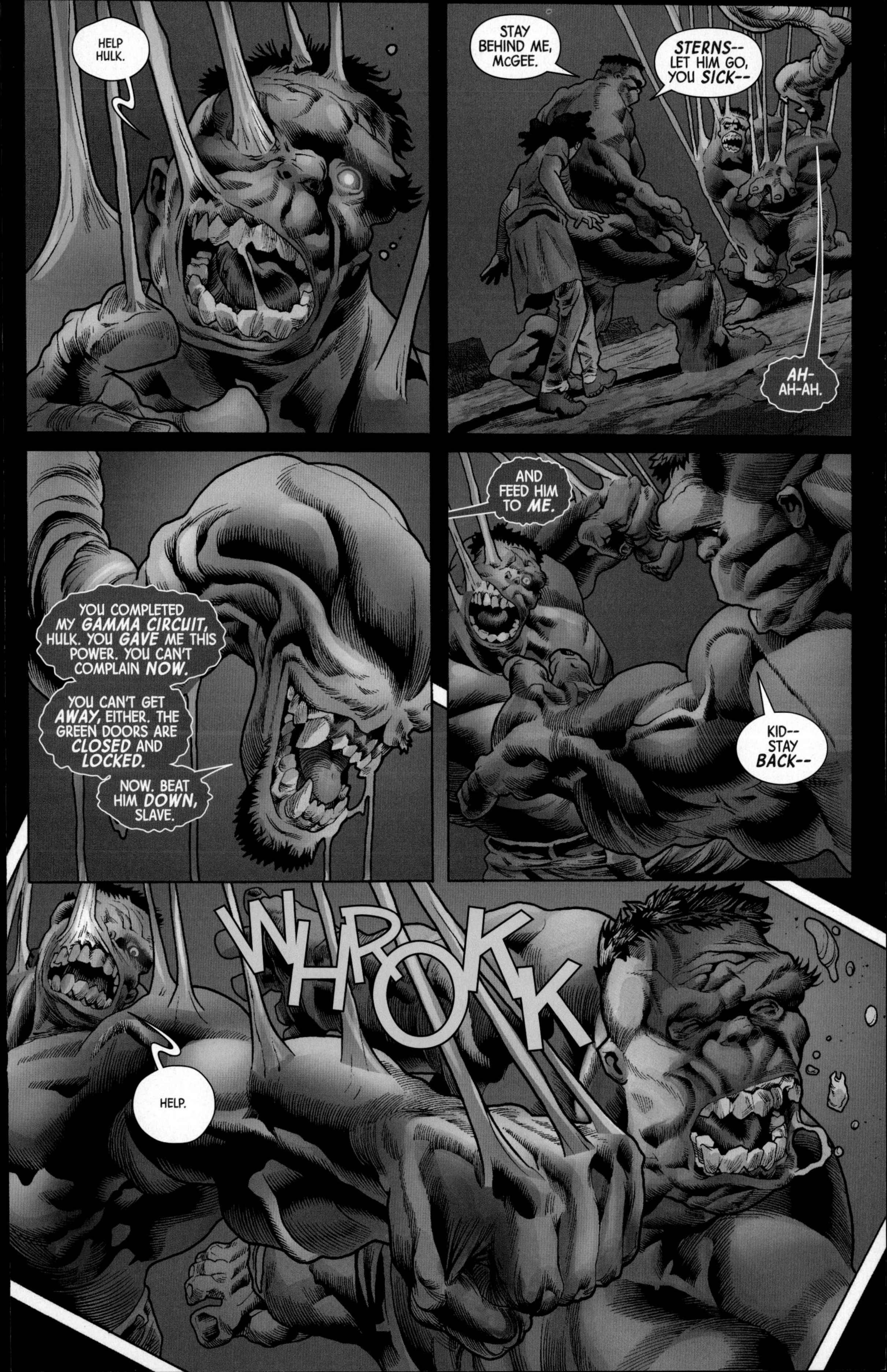
HELP HULK.
STAY BEHIND ME, McGEE.
STERNS-- LET HIM GO, YOU SICK--
AH- AH-AH.
YOU COMPLETED MY GAMMA CIRCUIT, HULK. YOU GAVE ME THIS POWER. YOU CAN'T COMPLAIN NOW.
YOU CAN'T GET AWAY, EITHER. THE GREEN DOORS ARE CLOSED AND LOCKED.
NOW. BEAT HIM DOWN, SLAVE.
AND FEED HIM TO ME.
KID-- STAY BACK--
WHROKK
HELP.

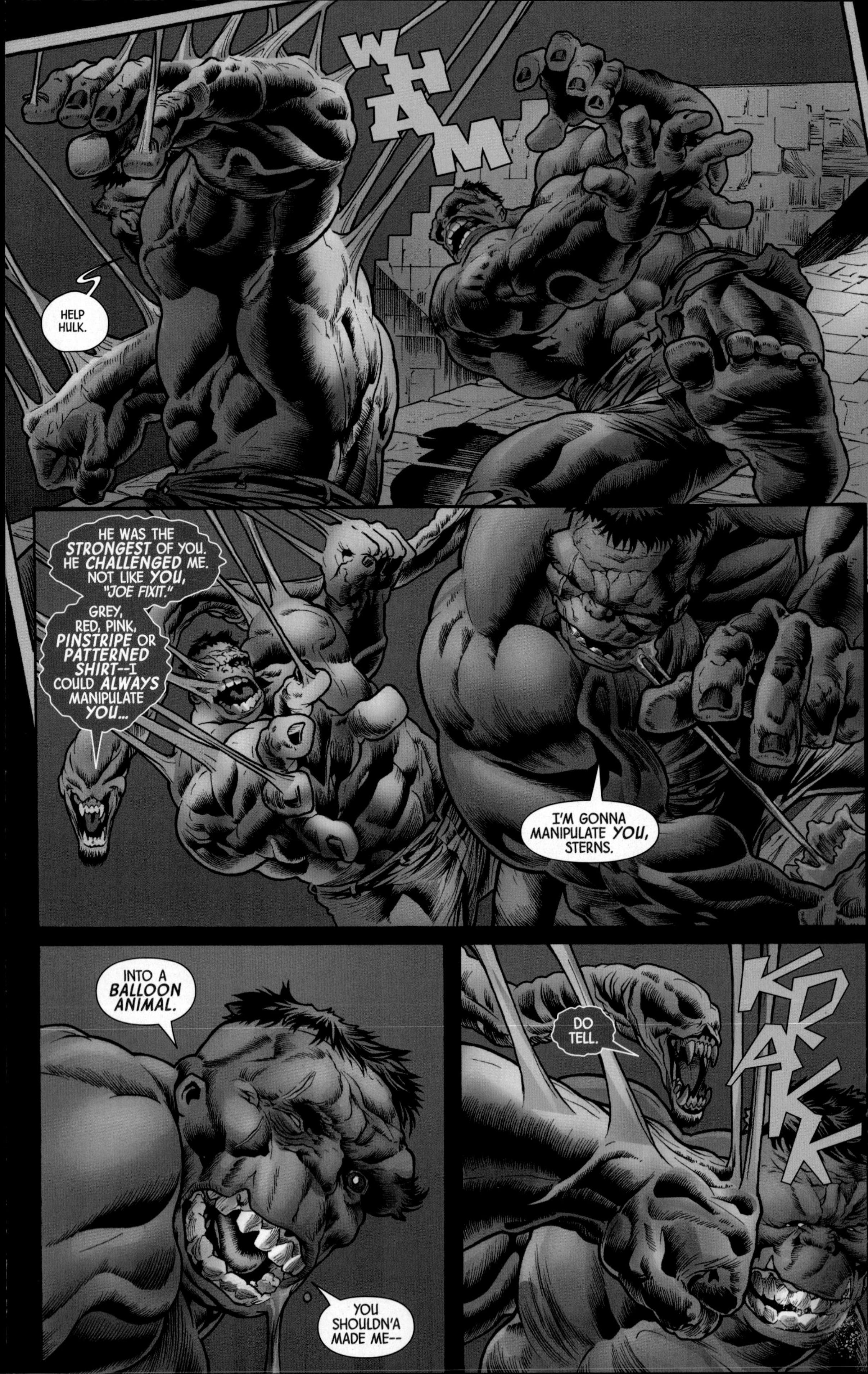
WHAM!
HELP HULK.
HE WAS THE *STRONGEST* OF YOU. HE *CHALLENGED* ME. NOT LIKE *YOU*, *"JOE FIXIT."*
GREY, RED, PINK, **PINSTRIPE** OR **PATTERNED SHIRT**--I COULD **ALWAYS** MANIPULATE **YOU**...
I'M GONNA MANIPULATE *YOU*, STERNS.
INTO A *BALLOON ANIMAL*.
YOU SHOULDN'A MADE ME--
DO TELL.
KRAKK

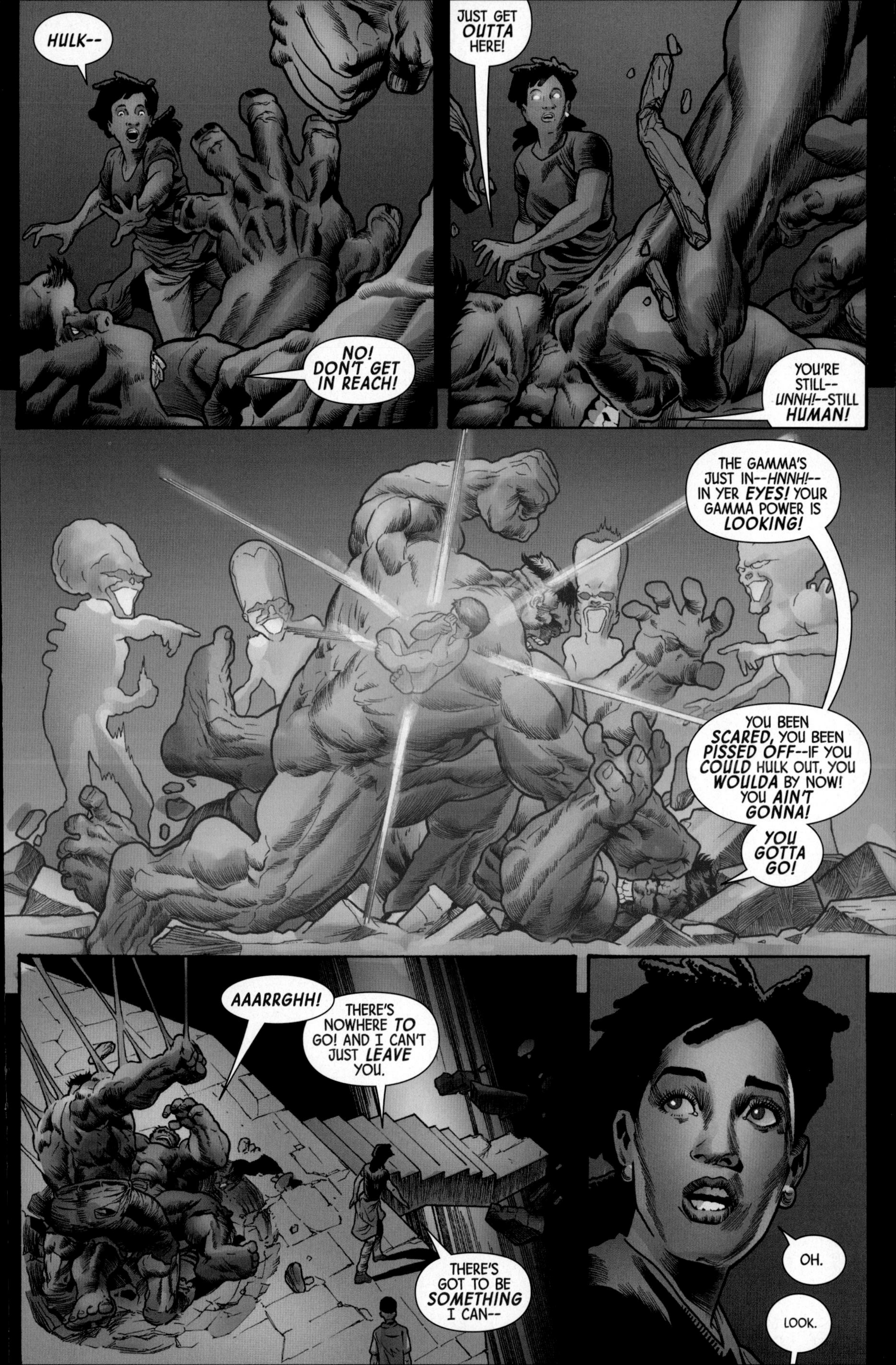
HULK--
NO! DON'T GET IN REACH!
JUST GET OUTTA HERE!
YOU'RE STILL-- UNNH!--STILL HUMAN!
THE GAMMA'S JUST IN--HNNH!-- IN YER EYES! YOUR GAMMA POWER IS LOOKING!
YOU BEEN SCARED, YOU BEEN PISSED OFF--IF YOU COULD HULK OUT, YOU WOULDA BY NOW! YOU AIN'T GONNA!
YOU GOTTA GO!
AAARRGHH!
THERE'S NOWHERE TO GO! AND I CAN'T JUST LEAVE YOU.
THERE'S GOT TO BE SOMETHING I CAN--
OH.
LOOK.

JUST LOOK.

"LOOK HIM IN THE EYE." I KNOW. I REMEMBER FROM THE LAST TIME.

DAD-- WHATEVER YOU ARE--I JUST...

...I JUST CAN'T, OKAY?

WE'RE GOING TO DIE HERE. I CAN'T.

I CAN'T DIE TALKING TO GHOSTS.

THERE'S A PLAN.

IS THERE?

REALLY?

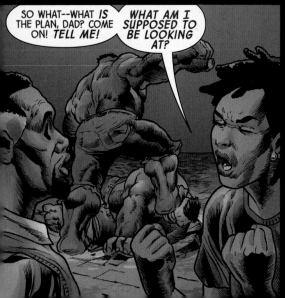

SO WHAT--WHAT IS THE PLAN, DAD? COME ON! TELL ME! WHAT AM I SUPPOSED TO BE LOOKING AT?

YOU.

LOOK AT YOU.

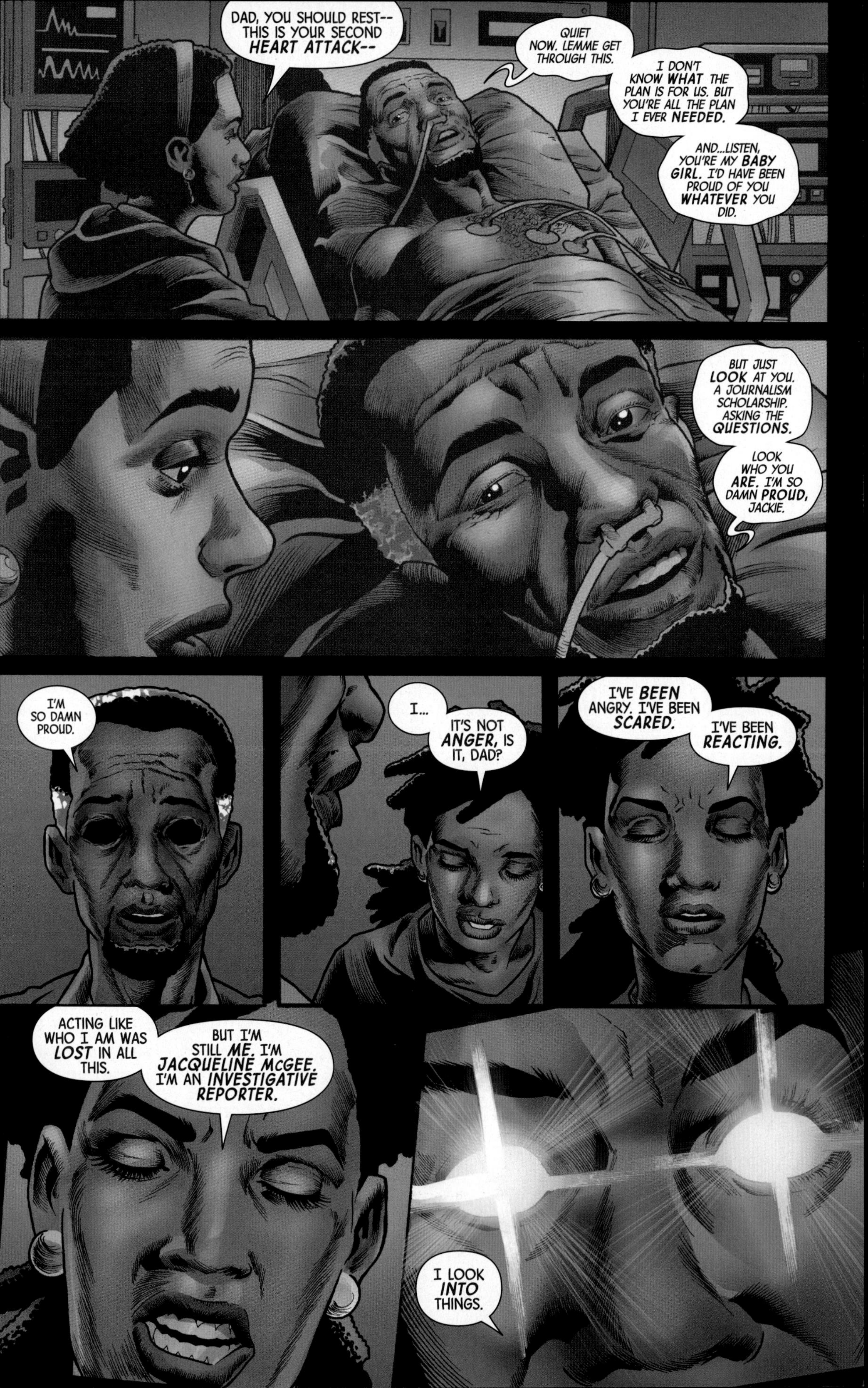
DAD, YOU SHOULD REST-- THIS IS YOUR SECOND HEART ATTACK--
QUIET NOW. LEMME GET THROUGH THIS.
I DON'T KNOW WHAT THE PLAN IS FOR US. BUT YOU'RE ALL THE PLAN I EVER NEEDED.
AND...LISTEN, YOU'RE MY BABY GIRL. I'D HAVE BEEN PROUD OF YOU WHATEVER YOU DID.
BUT JUST LOOK AT YOU. A JOURNALISM SCHOLARSHIP. ASKING THE QUESTIONS.
LOOK WHO YOU ARE. I'M SO DAMN PROUD, JACKIE.
I'M SO DAMN PROUD.
I...
IT'S NOT ANGER, IS IT, DAD?
I'VE BEEN ANGRY. I'VE BEEN SCARED.
I'VE BEEN REACTING.
ACTING LIKE WHO I AM WAS LOST IN ALL THIS.
BUT I'M STILL ME. I'M JACQUELINE McGEE. I'M AN INVESTIGATIVE REPORTER.
I LOOK INTO THINGS.

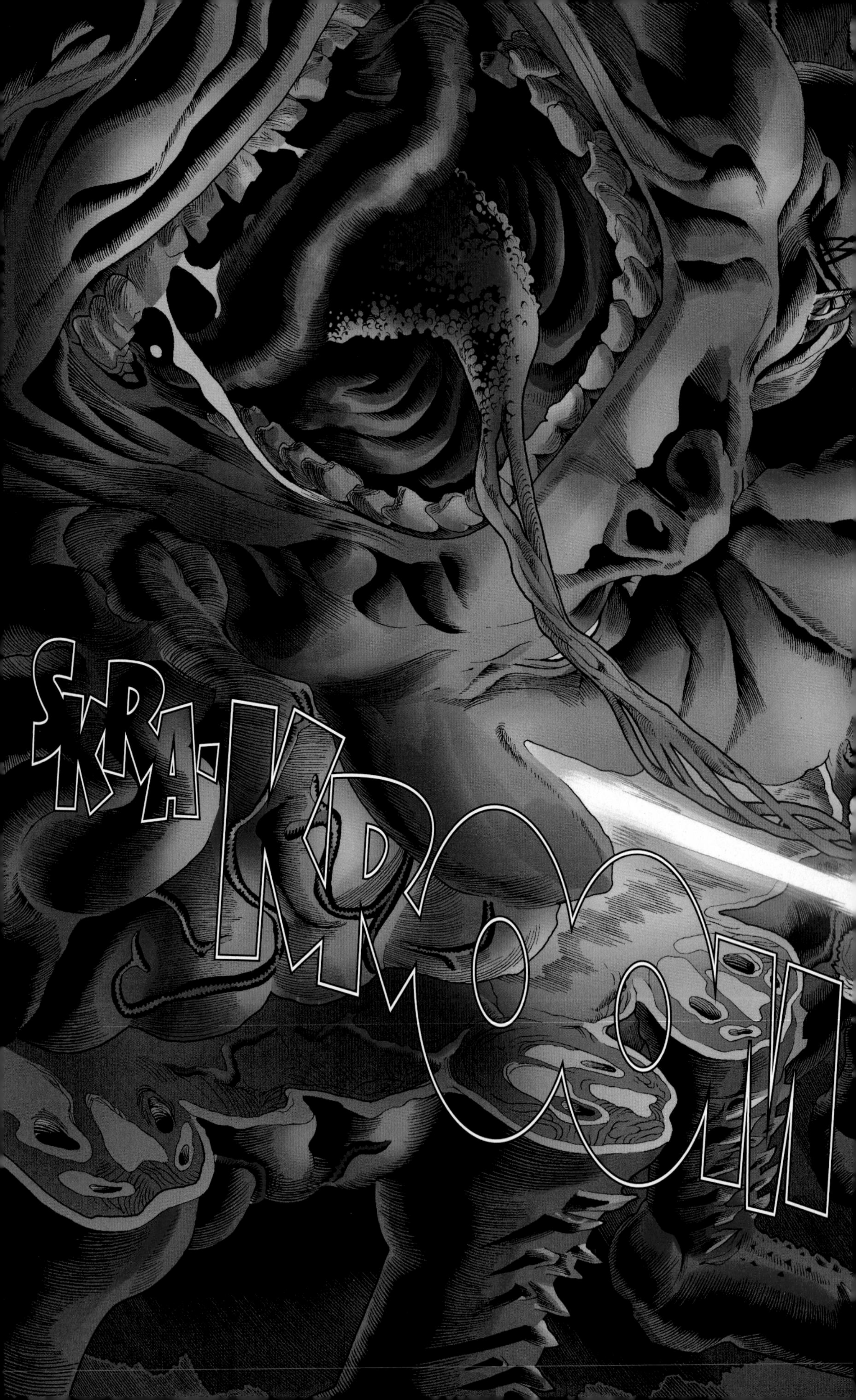
SKRA-KROOOM

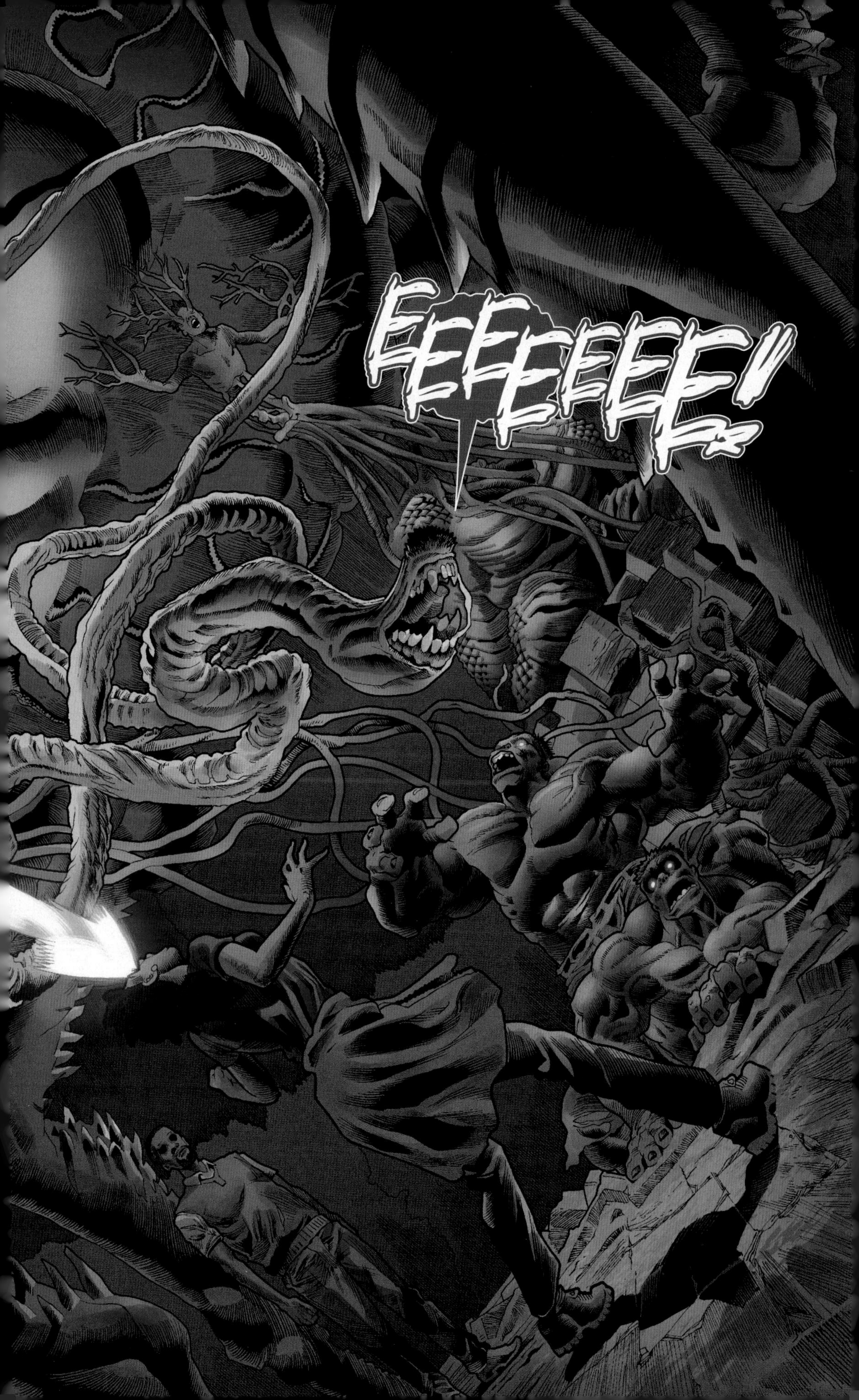
EEEEEEEEEE!

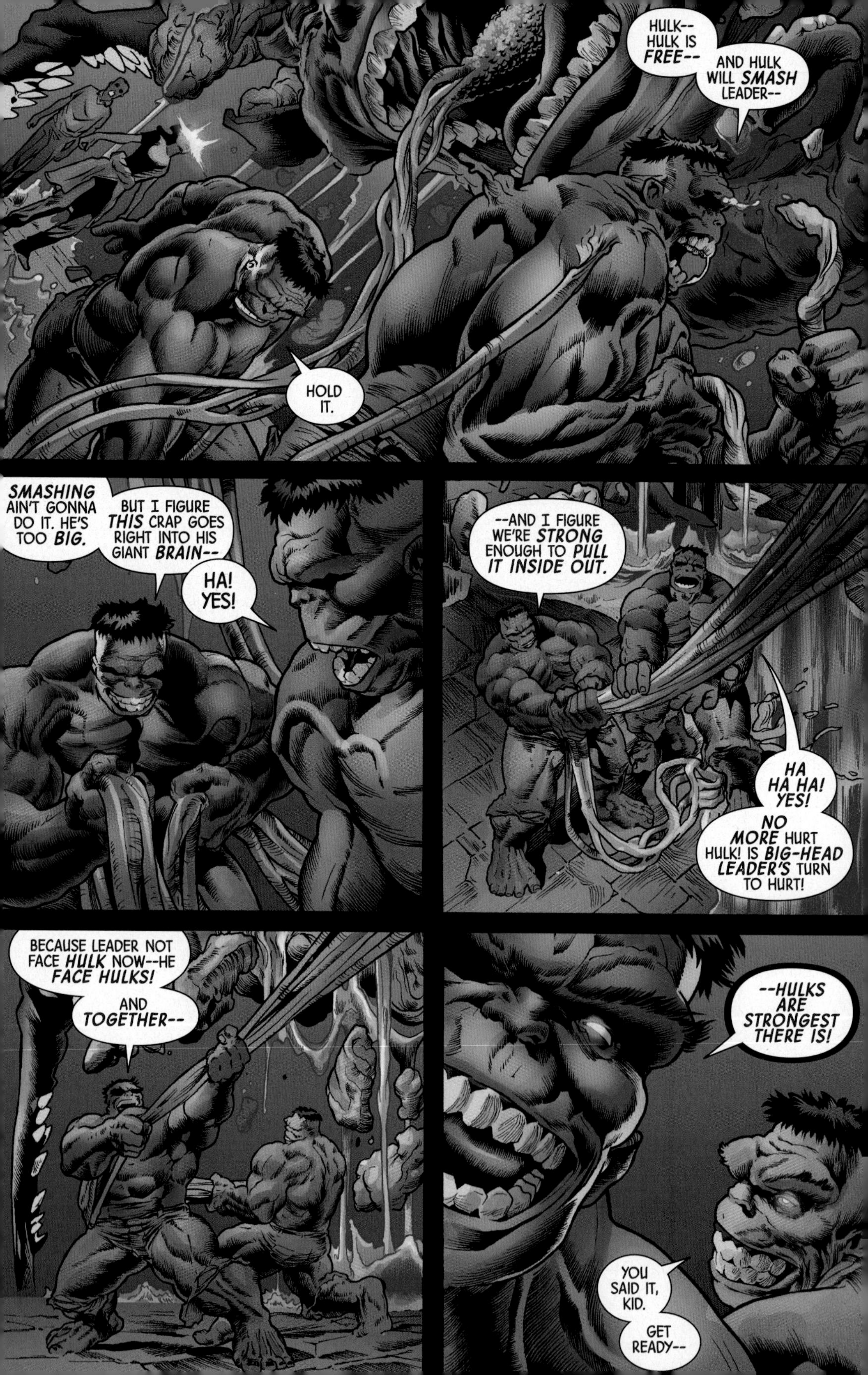
HULK-- HULK IS FREE--
AND HULK WILL SMASH LEADER--
HOLD IT.
SMASHING AIN'T GONNA DO IT. HE'S TOO BIG.
BUT I FIGURE THIS CRAP GOES RIGHT INTO HIS GIANT BRAIN--
HA! YES!
--AND I FIGURE WE'RE STRONG ENOUGH TO PULL IT INSIDE OUT.
HA HA HA! YES!
NO MORE HURT HULK! IS BIG-HEAD LEADER'S TURN TO HURT!
BECAUSE LEADER NOT FACE HULK NOW--HE FACE HULKS!
AND TOGETHER--
--HULKS ARE STRONGEST THERE IS!
YOU SAID IT, KID.
GET READY--

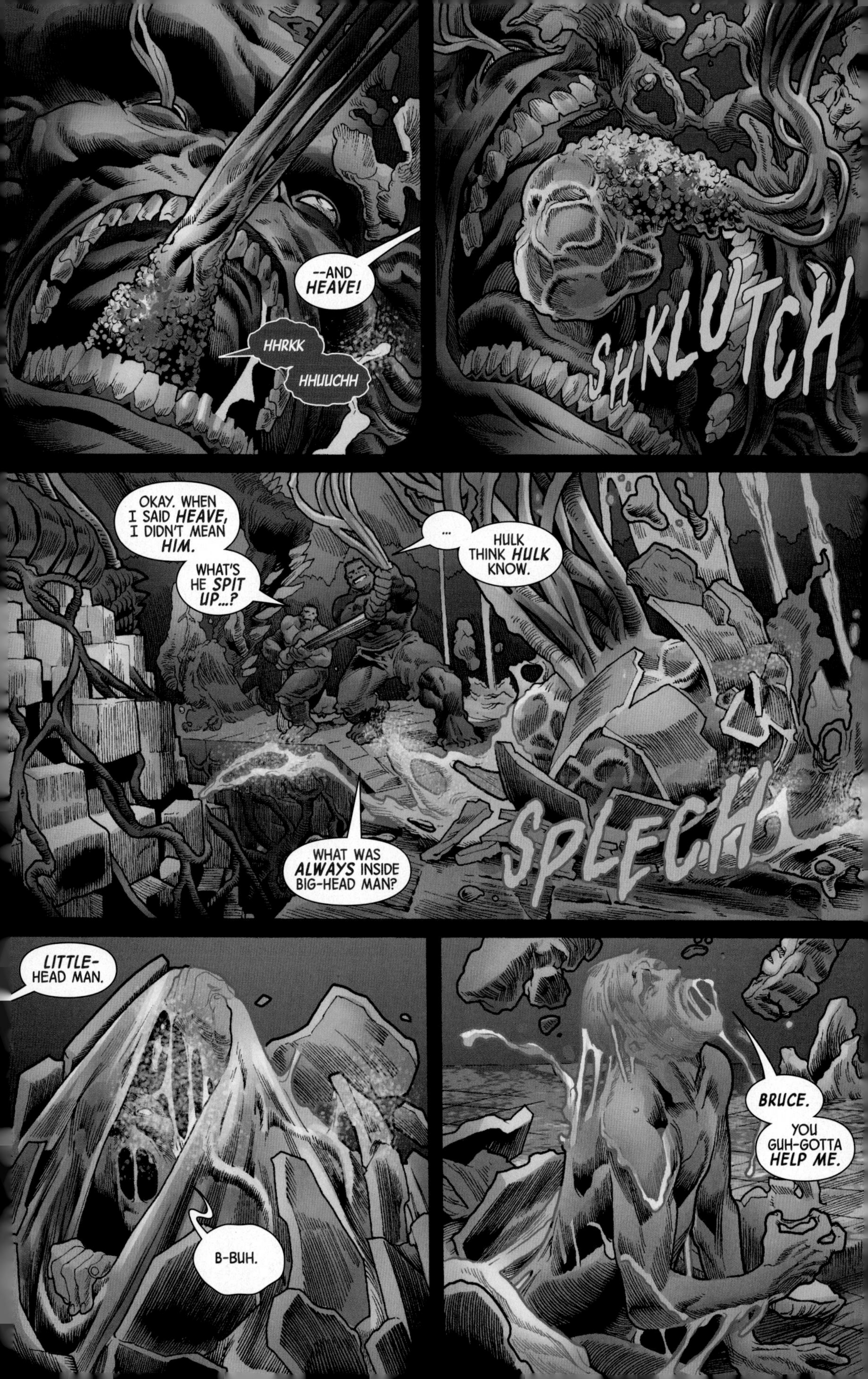
--AND HEAVE!
HHRKK
HHUUCHH
SHKLUTCH
OKAY. WHEN I SAID HEAVE, I DIDN'T MEAN HIM.
WHAT'S HE SPIT UP...?
...
HULK THINK HULK KNOW.
WHAT WAS ALWAYS INSIDE BIG-HEAD MAN?
SPLECH
LITTLE-HEAD MAN.
B-BUH.
BRUCE.
YOU GUH-GOTTA HELP ME.

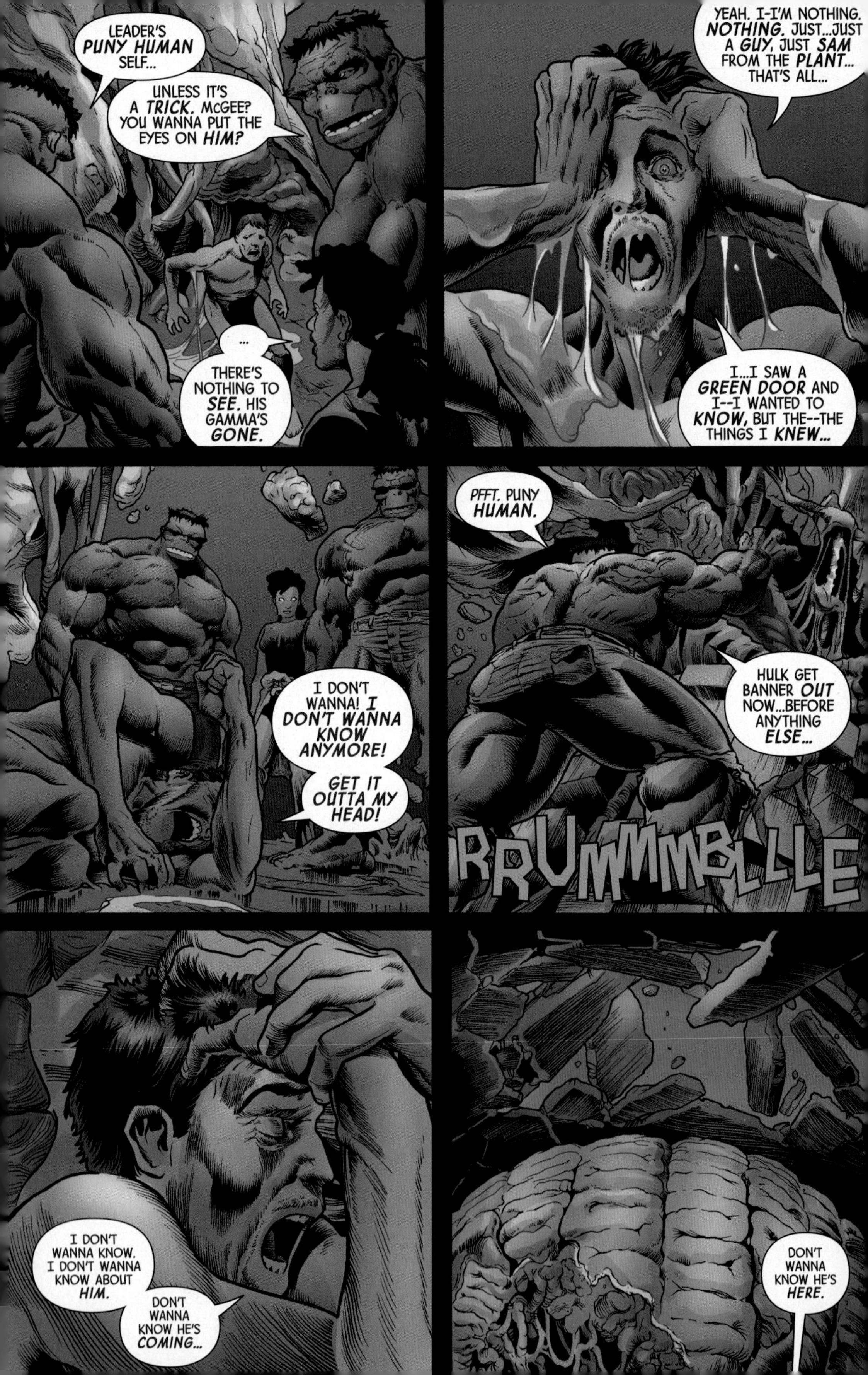
LEADER'S PUNY HUMAN SELF...
UNLESS IT'S A TRICK, McGEE? YOU WANNA PUT THE EYES ON HIM?
...
THERE'S NOTHING TO SEE. HIS GAMMA'S GONE.
YEAH. I-I'M NOTHING. NOTHING. JUST...JUST A GUY, JUST SAM FROM THE PLANT... THAT'S ALL...
I...I SAW A GREEN DOOR AND I--I WANTED TO KNOW, BUT THE--THE THINGS I KNEW...
I DON'T WANNA! I DON'T WANNA KNOW ANYMORE!
GET IT OUTTA MY HEAD!
PFFT. PUNY HUMAN.
HULK GET BANNER OUT NOW...BEFORE ANYTHING ELSE...
RRUMMMBLLE
I DON'T WANNA KNOW. I DON'T WANNA KNOW ABOUT HIM.
DON'T WANNA KNOW HE'S COMING...
DON'T WANNA KNOW HE'S HERE.

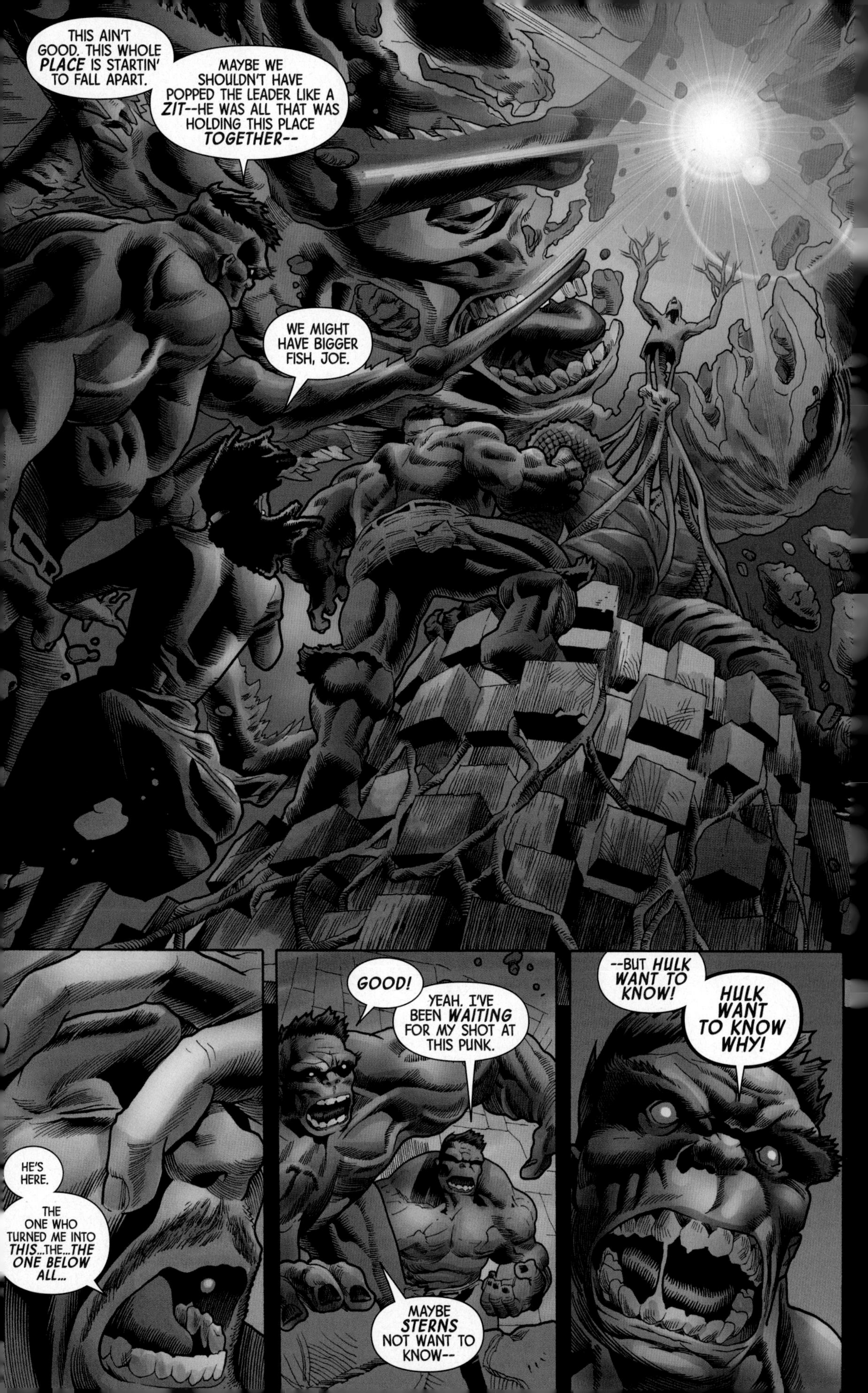
THIS AIN'T GOOD. THIS WHOLE PLACE IS STARTIN' TO FALL APART.
MAYBE WE SHOULDN'T HAVE POPPED THE LEADER LIKE A ZIT--HE WAS ALL THAT WAS HOLDING THIS PLACE TOGETHER--
WE MIGHT HAVE BIGGER FISH, JOE.
HE'S HERE.
THE ONE WHO TURNED ME INTO THIS...THE...THE ONE BELOW ALL...
GOOD!
YEAH. I'VE BEEN WAITING FOR MY SHOT AT THIS PUNK.
MAYBE STERNS NOT WANT TO KNOW--
--BUT HULK WANT TO KNOW!
HULK WANT TO KNOW WHY!

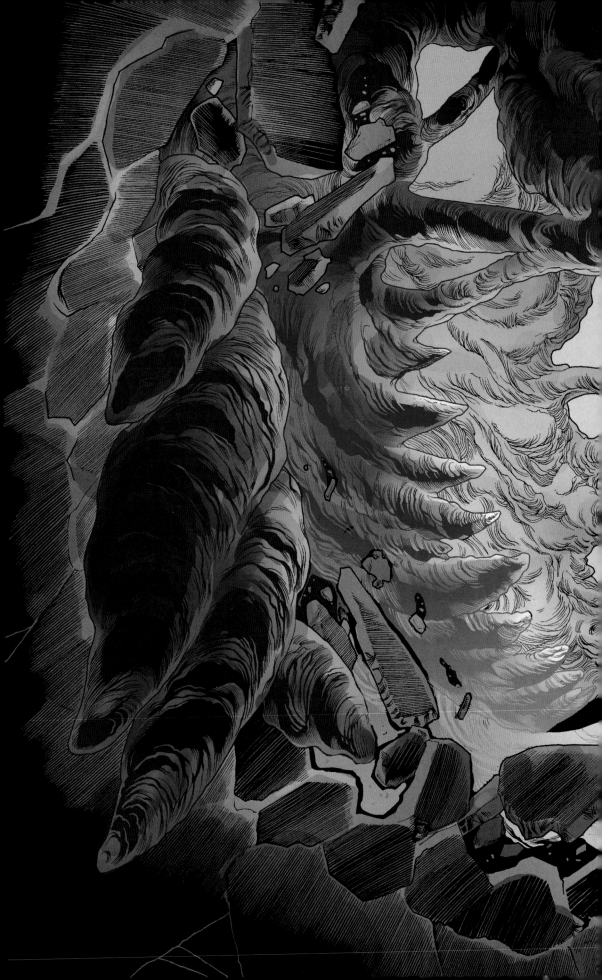

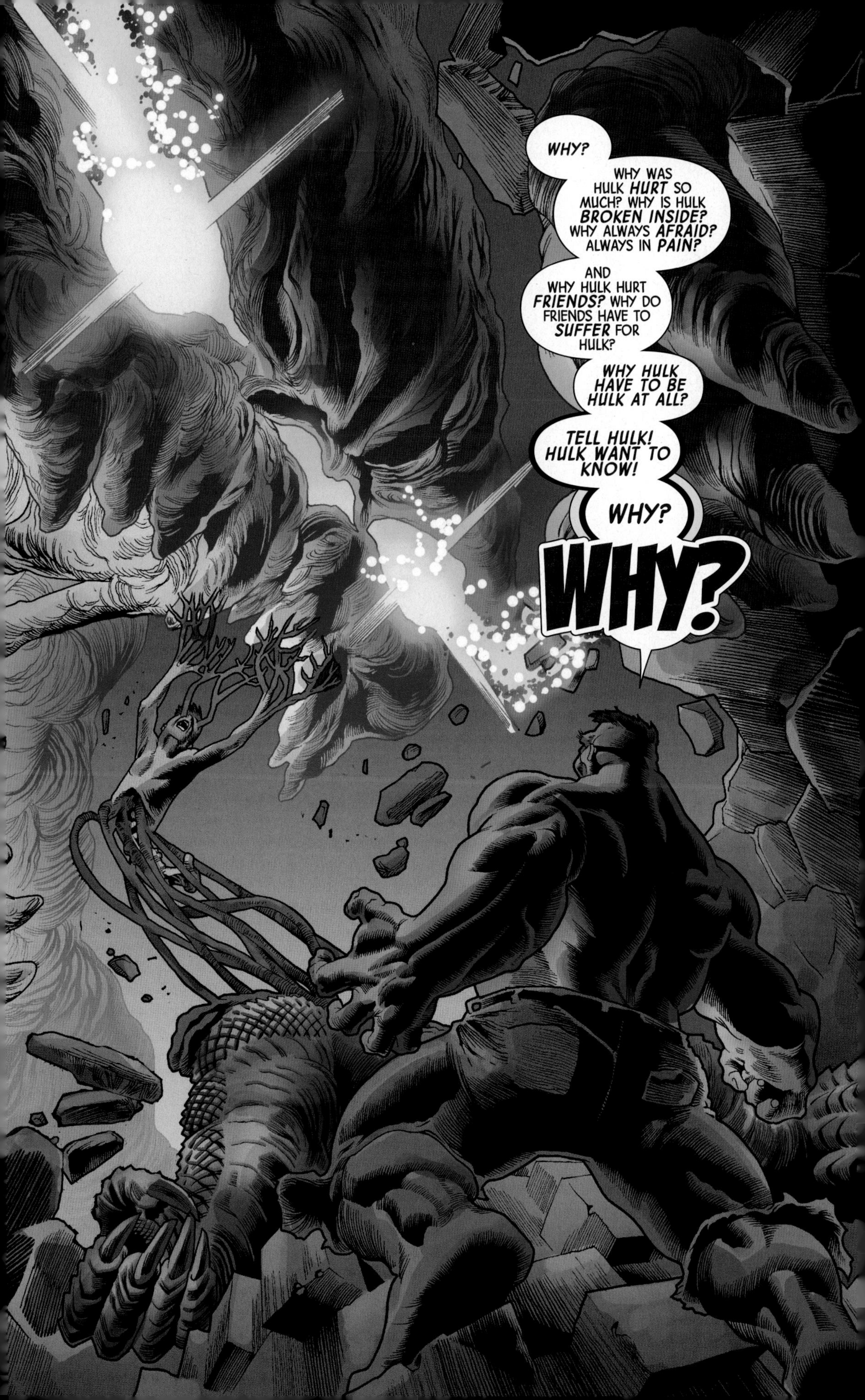
WHY?
WHY WAS HULK HURT SO MUCH? WHY IS HULK BROKEN INSIDE? WHY ALWAYS AFRAID? ALWAYS IN PAIN?
AND WHY HULK HURT FRIENDS? WHY DO FRIENDS HAVE TO SUFFER FOR HULK?
WHY HULK HAVE TO BE HULK AT ALL?
TELL HULK! HULK WANT TO KNOW!
WHY?
WHY?

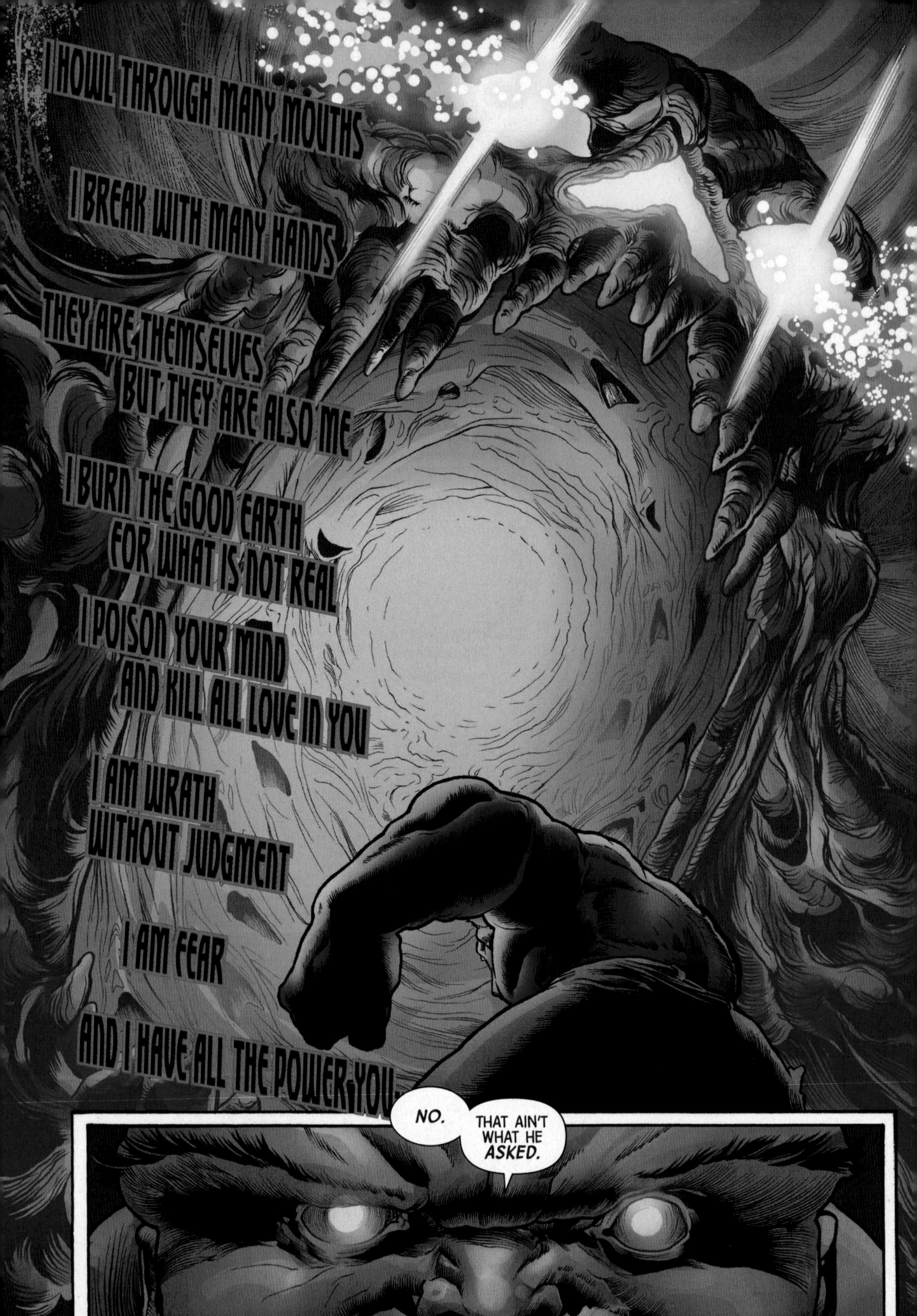
I HOWL THROUGH MANY MOUTHS
I BREAK WITH MANY HANDS
THEY ARE THEMSELVES BUT THEY ARE ALSO ME
I BURN THE GOOD EARTH FOR WHAT IS NOT REAL
I POISON YOUR MIND AND KILL ALL LOVE IN YOU
I AM WRATH WITHOUT JUDGMENT
I AM FEAR
AND I HAVE ALL THE POWER YOU...
NO.
THAT AIN'T WHAT HE ASKED.

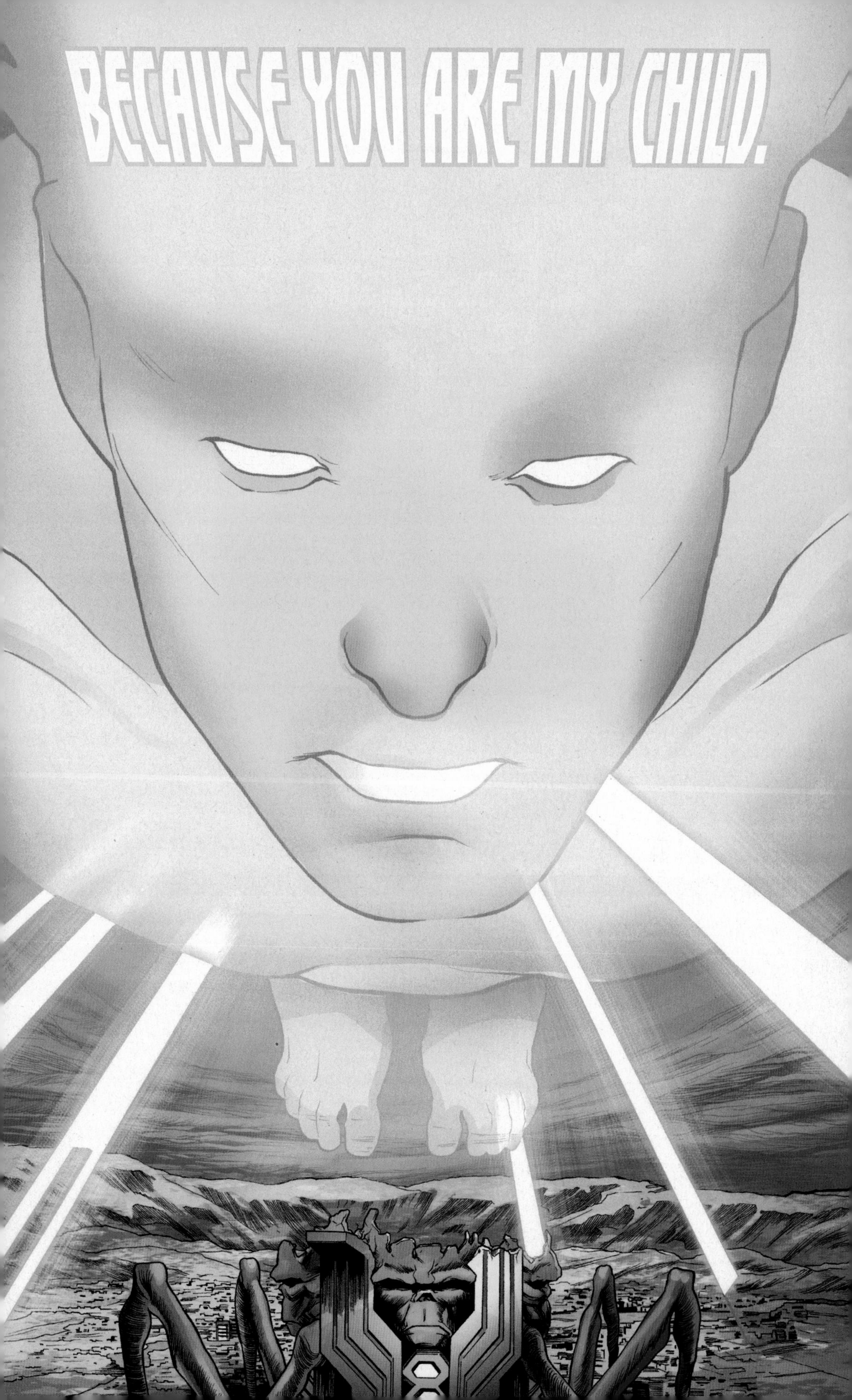
BECAUSE YOU ARE MY CHILD.

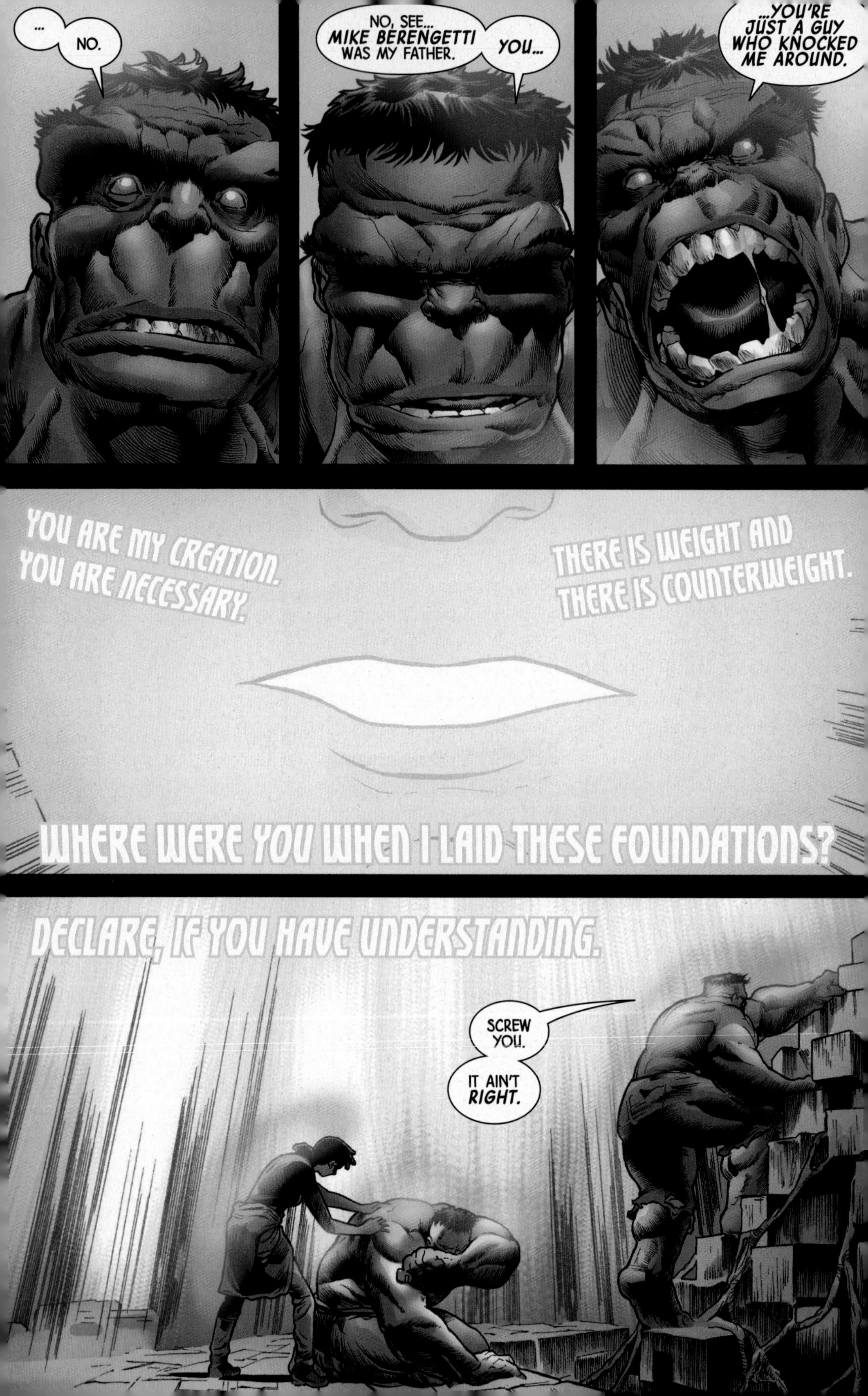
...
NO.
NO, SEE... MIKE BERENGETTI WAS MY FATHER.
YOU...
...YOU'RE JUST A GUY WHO KNOCKED ME AROUND.
YOU ARE MY CREATION. YOU ARE NECESSARY.
THERE IS WEIGHT AND THERE IS COUNTERWEIGHT.
WHERE WERE YOU WHEN I LAID THESE FOUNDATIONS?
DECLARE, IF YOU HAVE UNDERSTANDING.
SCREW YOU.
IT AIN'T RIGHT.

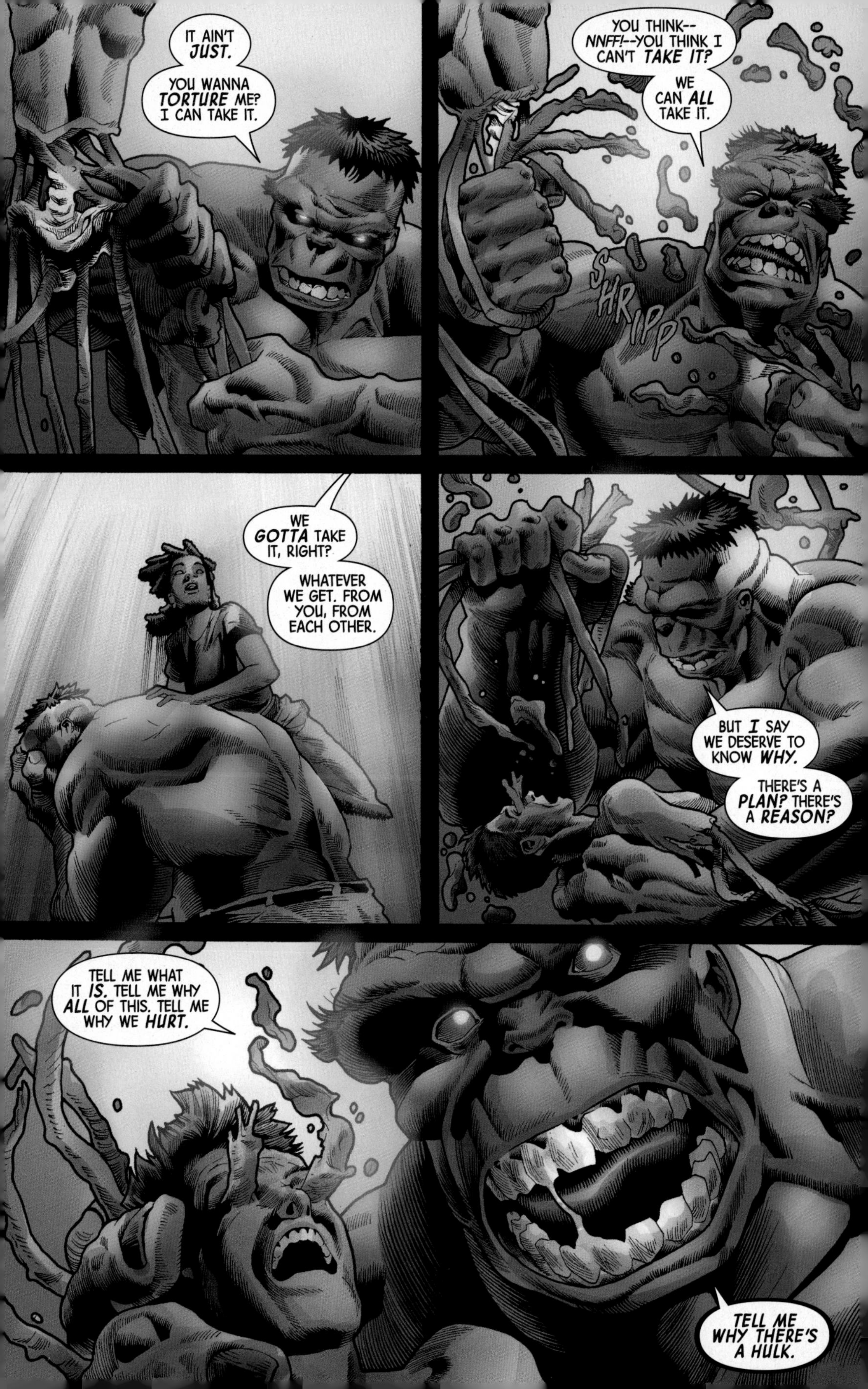
IT AIN'T JUST.
YOU WANNA TORTURE ME? I CAN TAKE IT.
YOU THINK-- NNFF!--YOU THINK I CAN'T TAKE IT?
WE CAN ALL TAKE IT.
SHRIPP
WE GOTTA TAKE IT, RIGHT?
WHATEVER WE GET. FROM YOU, FROM EACH OTHER.
BUT I SAY WE DESERVE TO KNOW WHY.
THERE'S A PLAN? THERE'S A REASON?
TELL ME WHAT IT IS. TELL ME WHY ALL OF THIS. TELL ME WHY WE HURT.
TELL ME WHY THERE'S A HULK.

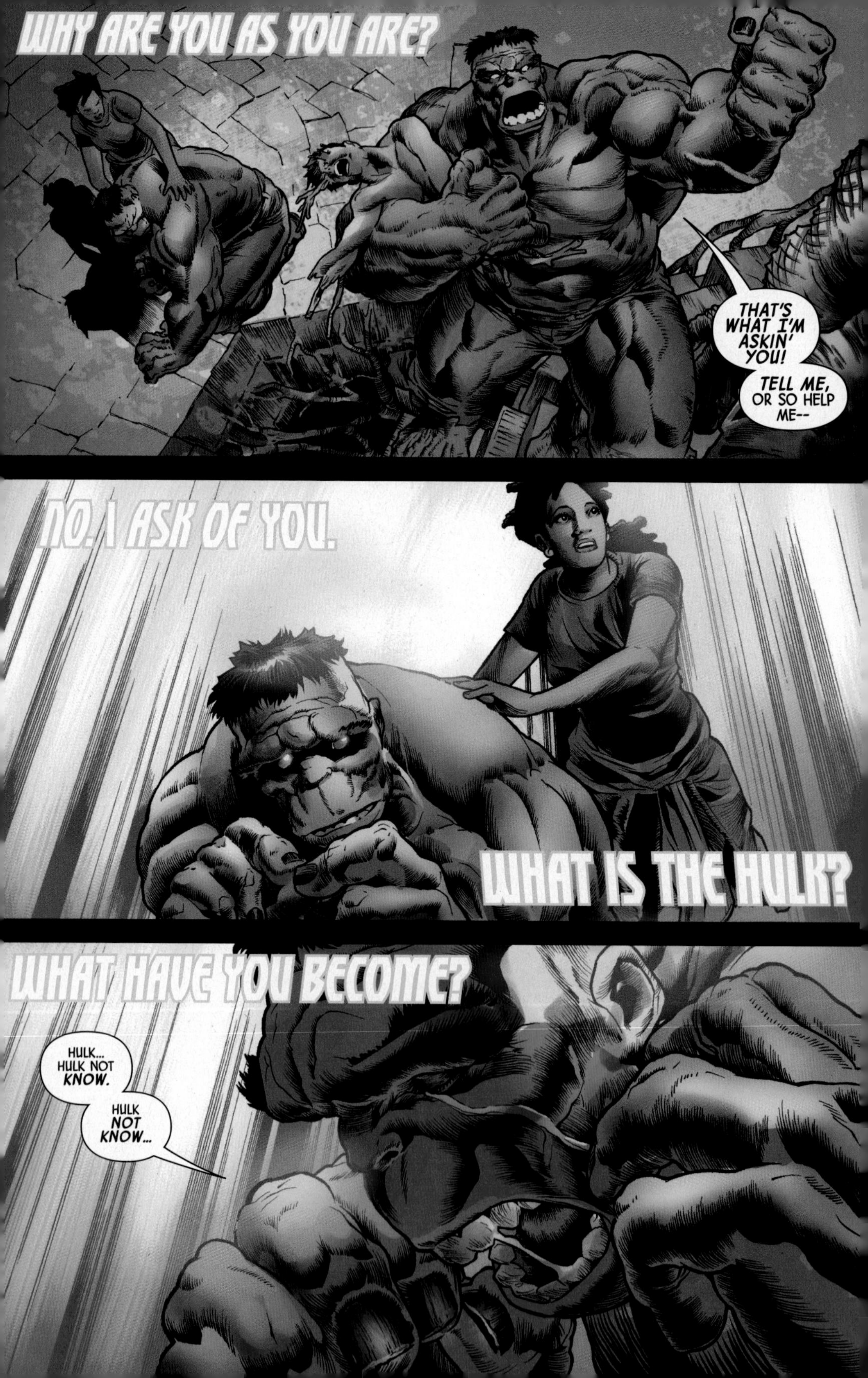
WHY ARE YOU AS YOU ARE?
THAT'S WHAT I'M ASKIN' YOU!
TELL ME, OR SO HELP ME--
NO. I ASK OF YOU.
WHAT IS THE HULK?
WHAT HAVE YOU BECOME?
HULK... HULK NOT KNOW.
HULK NOT KNOW...

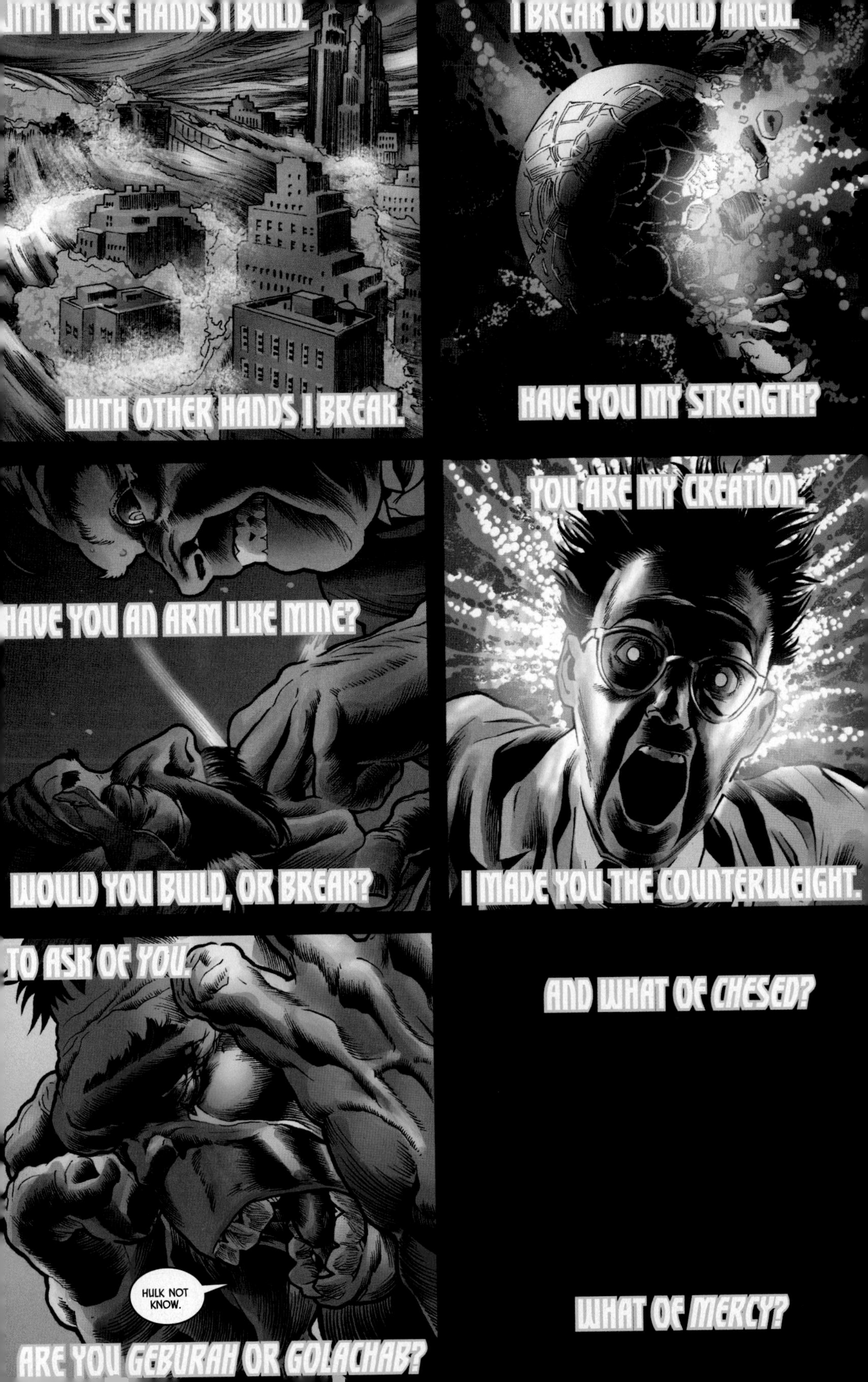
ITH THESE HANDS I BUILD.
WITH OTHER HANDS I BREAK.
I BREAK TO BUILD ANEW.
HAVE YOU MY STRENGTH?
HAVE YOU AN ARM LIKE MINE?
WOULD YOU BUILD, OR BREAK?
YOU ARE MY CREATION.
I MADE YOU THE COUNTERWEIGHT.
TO ASK OF *YOU.*
HULK NOT KNOW.
ARE YOU *GEBURAH* OR *GOLACHAB?*
AND WHAT OF *CHESED?*
WHAT OF *MERCY?*

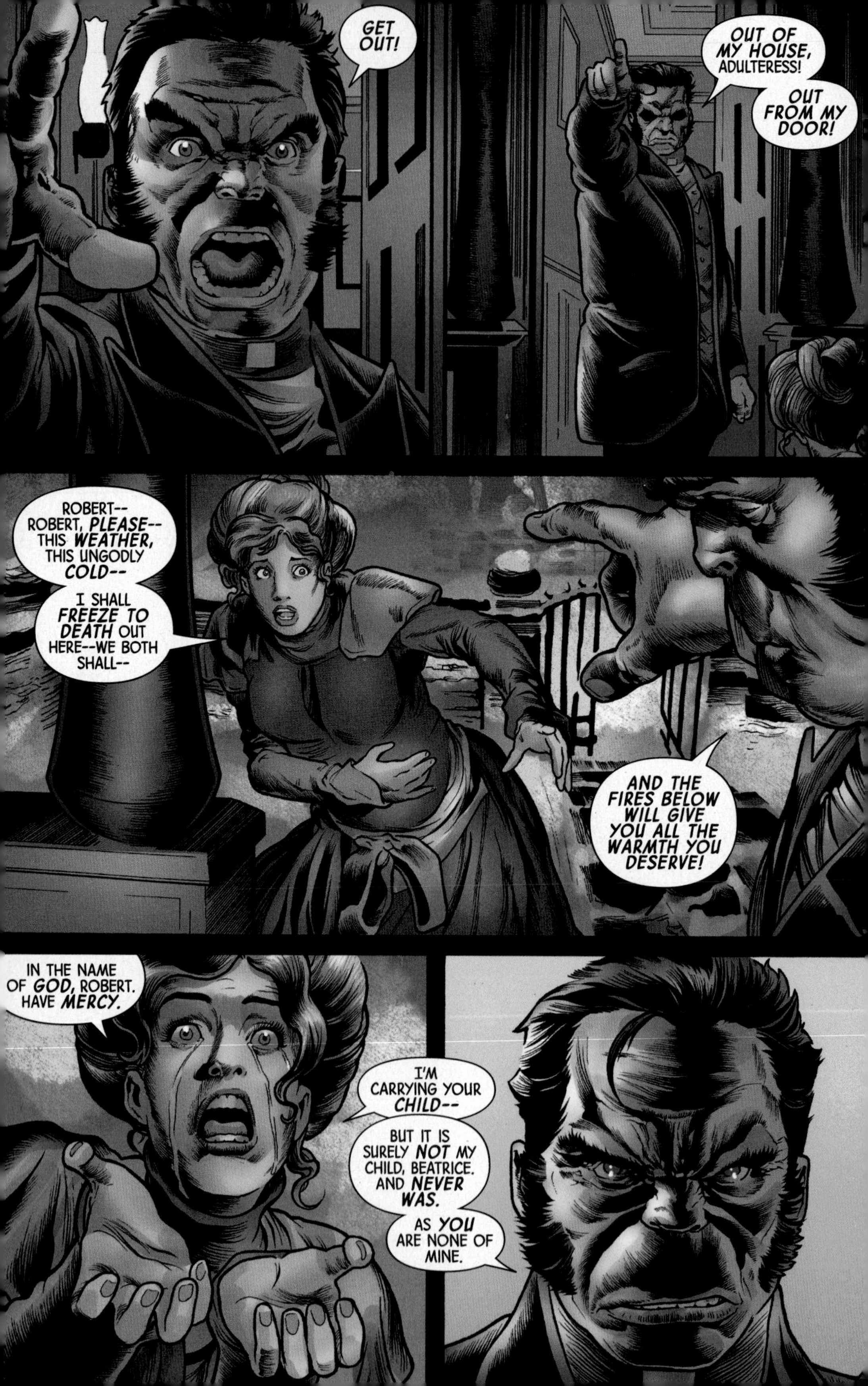
GET OUT!
OUT OF MY HOUSE, ADULTERESS!
OUT FROM MY DOOR!
ROBERT-- ROBERT, PLEASE-- THIS WEATHER, THIS UNGODLY COLD--
I SHALL FREEZE TO DEATH OUT HERE--WE BOTH SHALL--
AND THE FIRES BELOW WILL GIVE YOU ALL THE WARMTH YOU DESERVE!
IN THE NAME OF GOD, ROBERT. HAVE MERCY.
I'M CARRYING YOUR CHILD--
BUT IT IS SURELY NOT MY CHILD, BEATRICE. AND NEVER WAS.
AS YOU ARE NONE OF MINE.

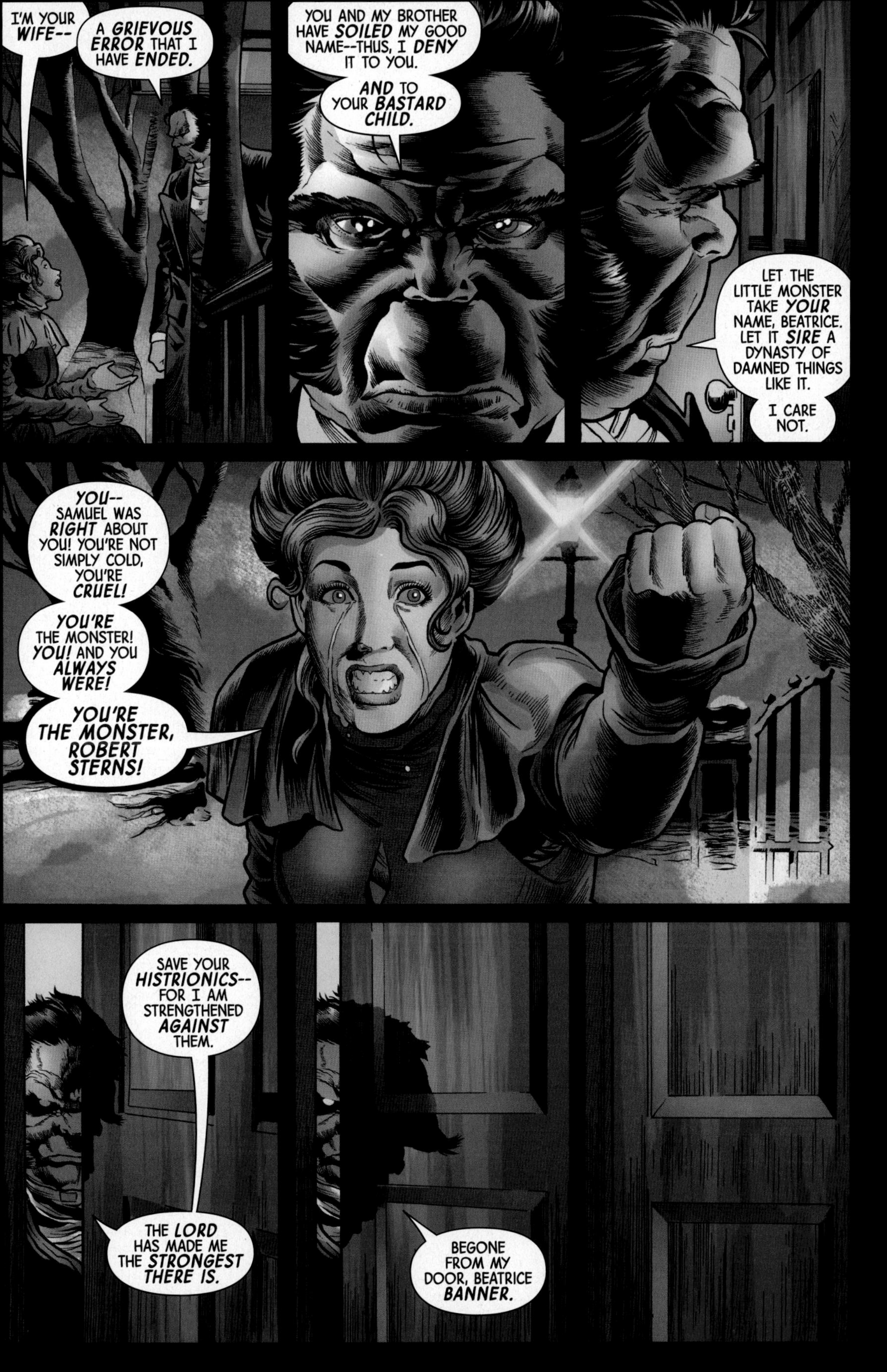
I'M YOUR WIFE--
A GRIEVOUS ERROR THAT I HAVE ENDED.
YOU AND MY BROTHER HAVE SOILED MY GOOD NAME--THUS, I DENY IT TO YOU.
AND TO YOUR BASTARD CHILD.
LET THE LITTLE MONSTER TAKE YOUR NAME, BEATRICE. LET IT SIRE A DYNASTY OF DAMNED THINGS LIKE IT.
I CARE NOT.
YOU-- SAMUEL WAS RIGHT ABOUT YOU! YOU'RE NOT SIMPLY COLD, YOU'RE CRUEL!
YOU'RE THE MONSTER! YOU! AND YOU ALWAYS WERE!
YOU'RE THE MONSTER, ROBERT STERNS!
SAVE YOUR HISTRIONICS-- FOR I AM STRENGTHENED AGAINST THEM.
THE LORD HAS MADE ME THE STRONGEST THERE IS.
BEGONE FROM MY DOOR, BEATRICE BANNER.

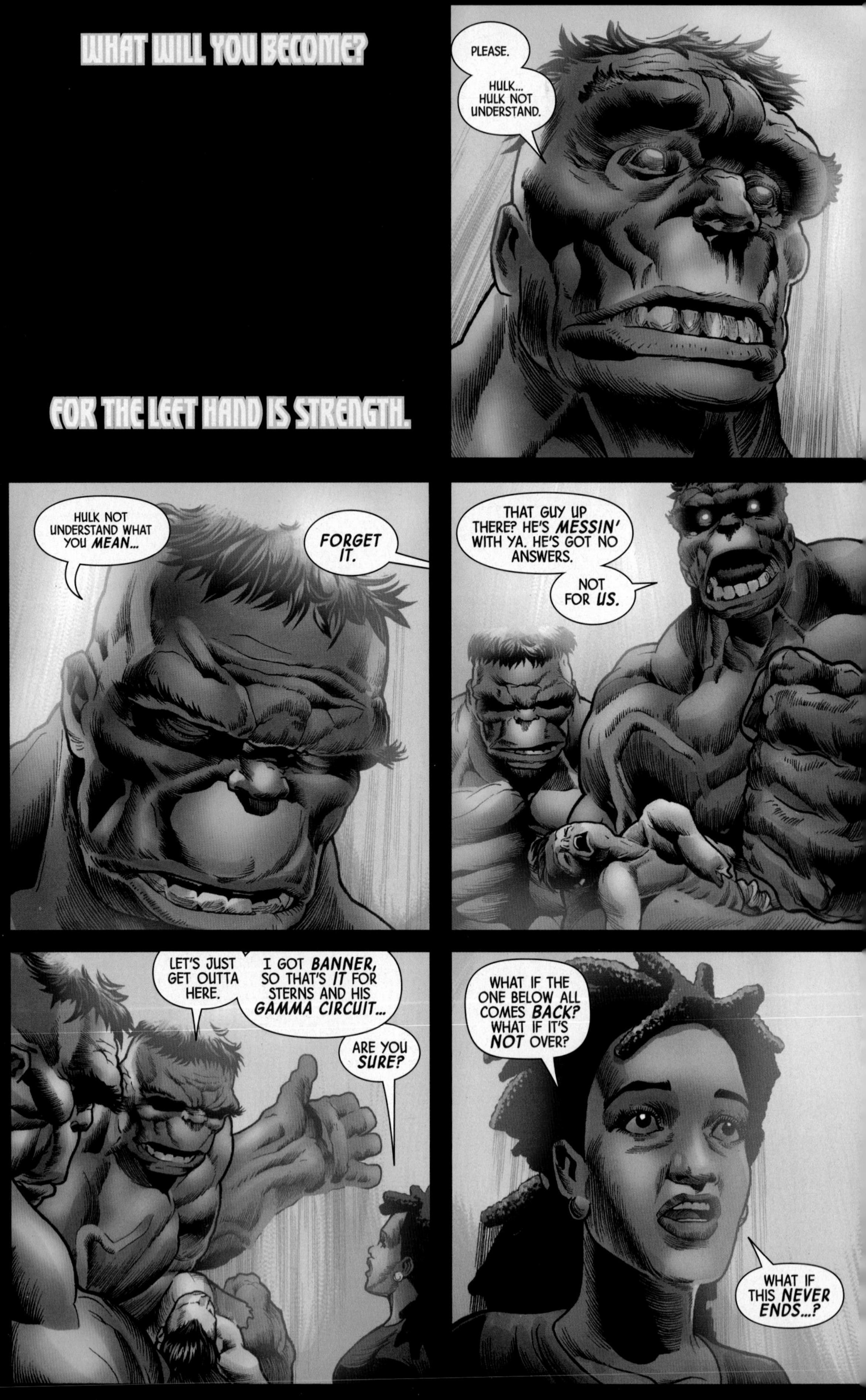
WHAT WILL YOU BECOME?
FOR THE LEFT HAND IS STRENGTH.
PLEASE.
HULK... HULK NOT UNDERSTAND.
HULK NOT UNDERSTAND WHAT YOU MEAN...
FORGET IT.
THAT GUY UP THERE? HE'S MESSIN' WITH YA. HE'S GOT NO ANSWERS.
NOT FOR US.
LET'S JUST GET OUTTA HERE.
I GOT BANNER, SO THAT'S IT FOR STERNS AND HIS GAMMA CIRCUIT...
ARE YOU SURE?
WHAT IF THE ONE BELOW ALL COMES BACK? WHAT IF IT'S NOT OVER?
WHAT IF THIS NEVER ENDS...?

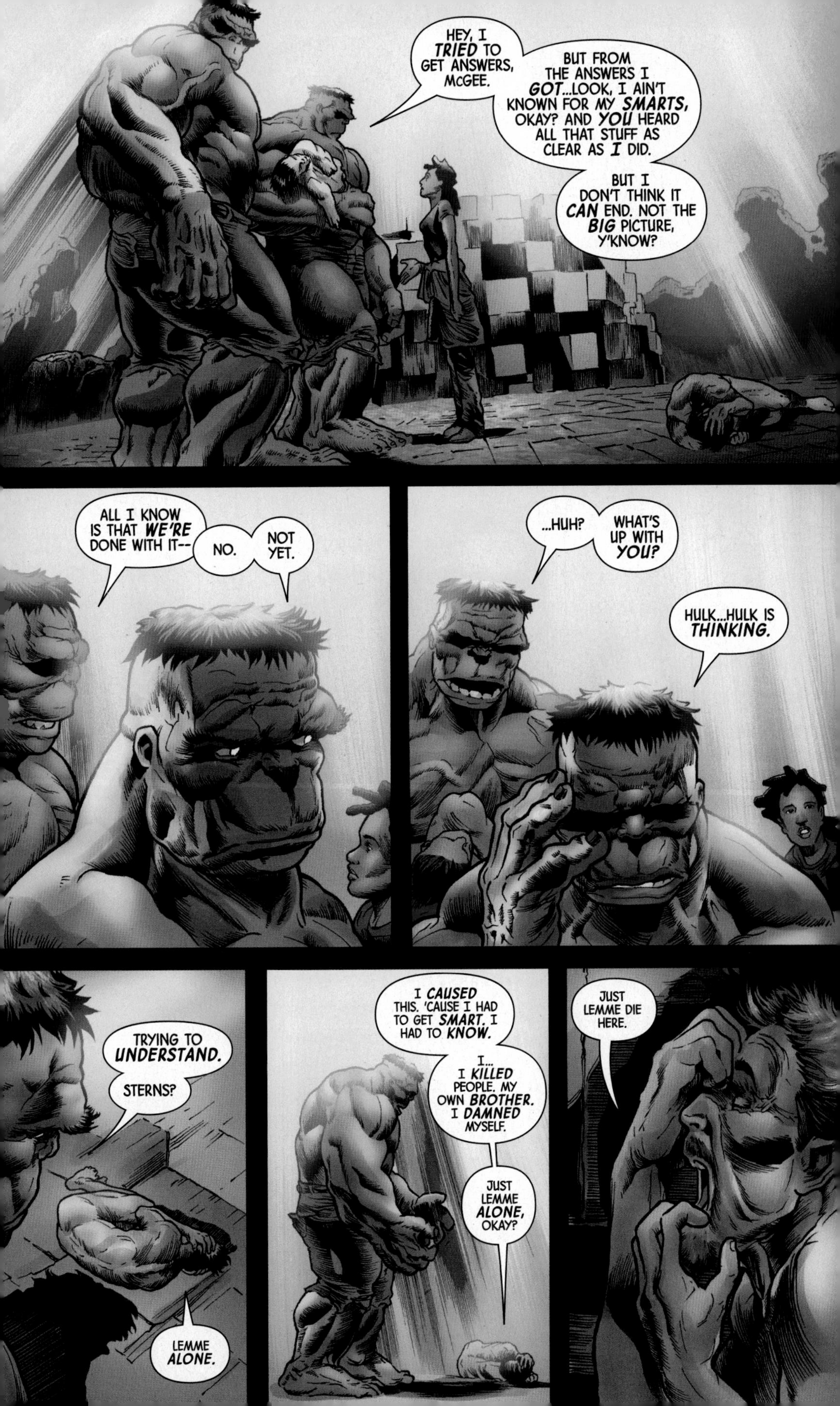
HEY, I TRIED TO GET ANSWERS, McGEE.
BUT FROM THE ANSWERS I GOT...LOOK, I AIN'T KNOWN FOR MY SMARTS, OKAY? AND YOU HEARD ALL THAT STUFF AS CLEAR AS I DID.
BUT I DON'T THINK IT CAN END. NOT THE BIG PICTURE, Y'KNOW?
ALL I KNOW IS THAT WE'RE DONE WITH IT--
NO.
NOT YET.
...HUH?
WHAT'S UP WITH YOU?
HULK...HULK IS THINKING.
TRYING TO UNDERSTAND.
STERNS?
LEMME ALONE.
I CAUSED THIS. 'CAUSE I HAD TO GET SMART. I HAD TO KNOW.
I... I KILLED PEOPLE. MY OWN BROTHER. I DAMNED MYSELF.
JUST LEMME ALONE, OKAY?
JUST LEMME DIE HERE.

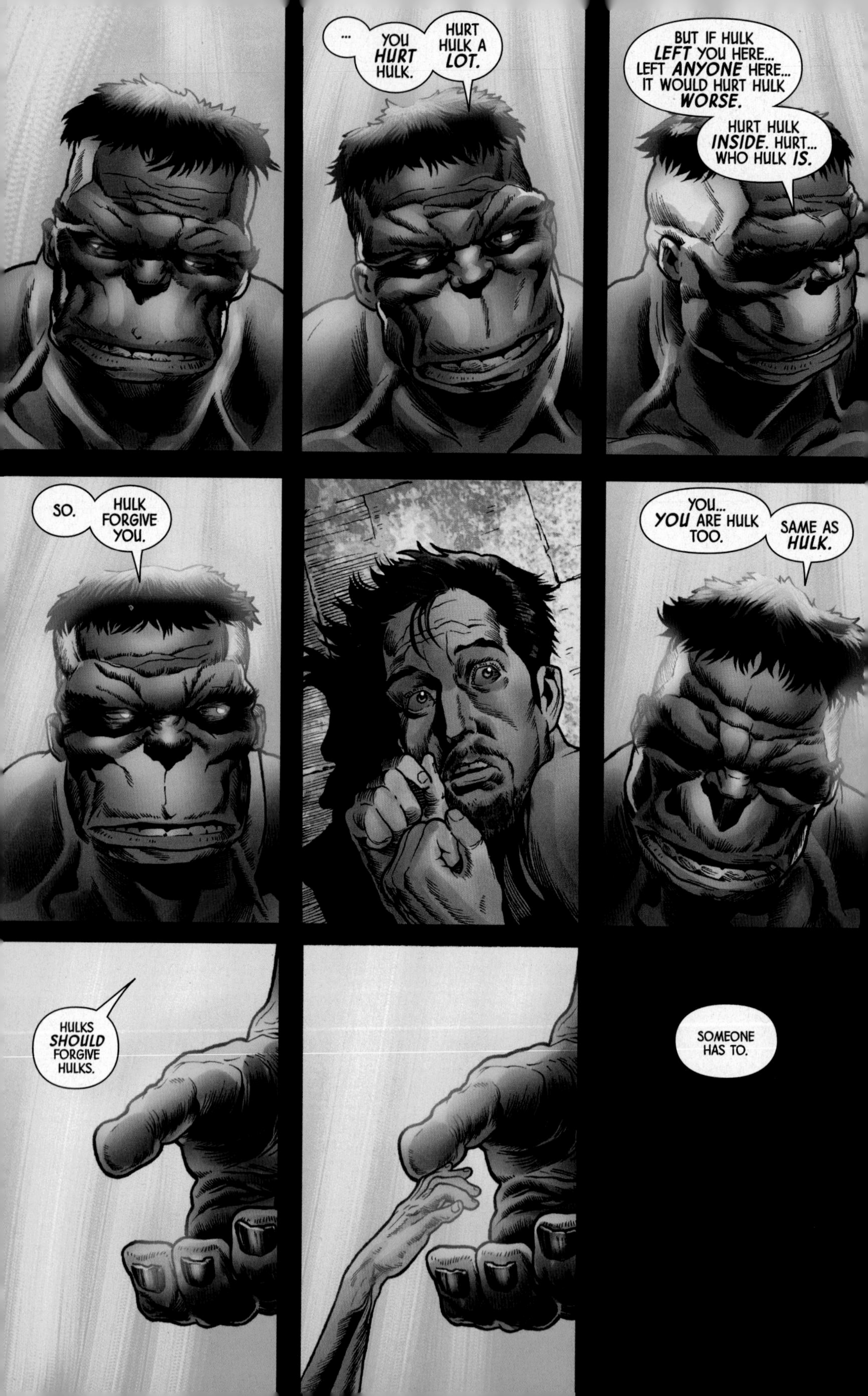
...
YOU HURT HULK.
HURT HULK A LOT.
BUT IF HULK LEFT YOU HERE... LEFT ANYONE HERE... IT WOULD HURT HULK WORSE.
HURT HULK INSIDE. HURT... WHO HULK IS.
SO.
HULK FORGIVE YOU.
YOU... YOU ARE HULK TOO.
SAME AS HULK.
HULKS SHOULD FORGIVE HULKS.
SOMEONE HAS TO.

BUT THE RIGHT HAND IS MERCY.

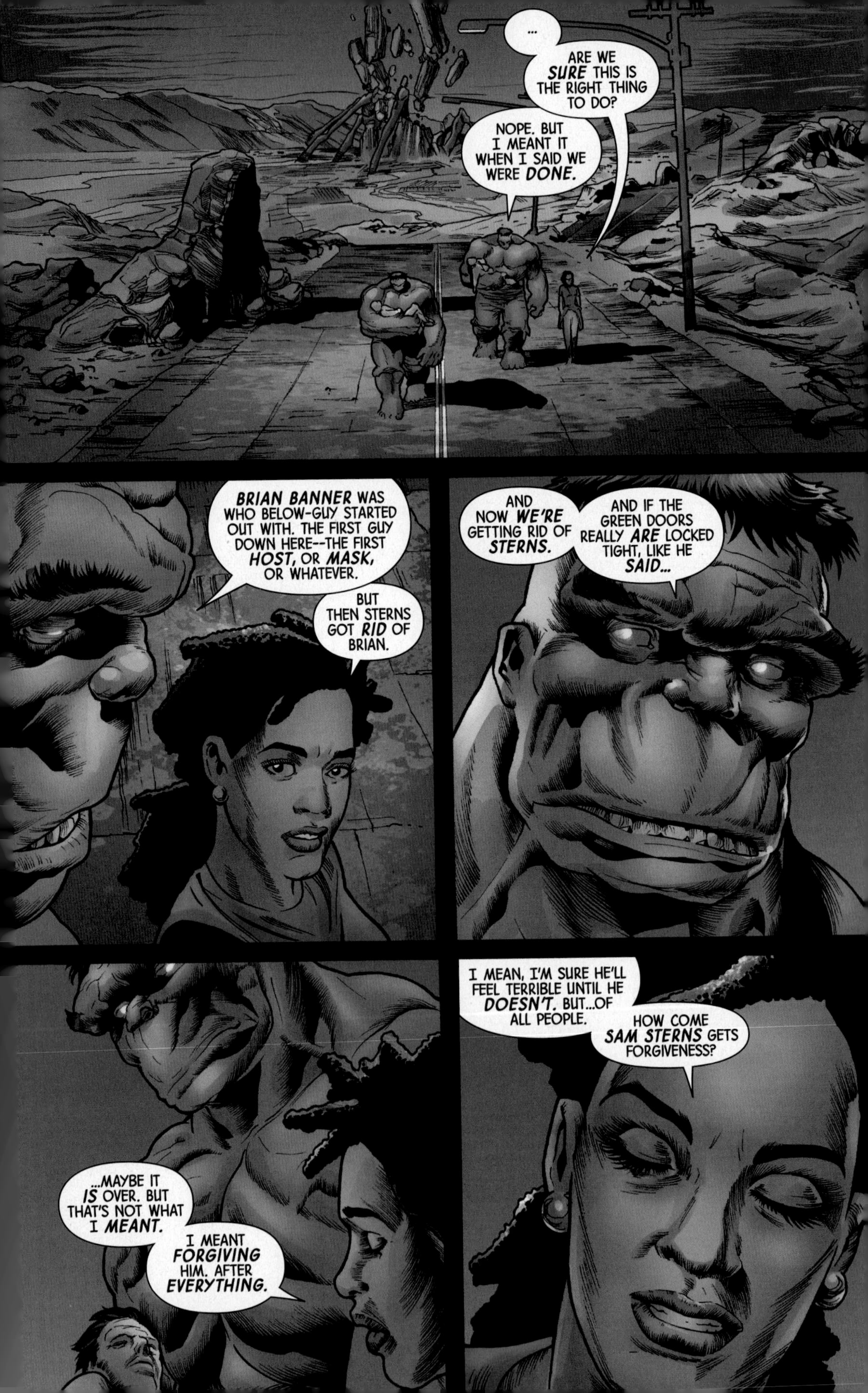
...
ARE WE SURE THIS IS THE RIGHT THING TO DO?
NOPE. BUT I MEANT IT WHEN I SAID WE WERE DONE.
BRIAN BANNER WAS WHO BELOW-GUY STARTED OUT WITH. THE FIRST GUY DOWN HERE--THE FIRST HOST, OR MASK, OR WHATEVER.
BUT THEN STERNS GOT RID OF BRIAN.
AND NOW WE'RE GETTING RID OF STERNS.
AND IF THE GREEN DOORS REALLY ARE LOCKED TIGHT, LIKE HE SAID...
...MAYBE IT IS OVER. BUT THAT'S NOT WHAT I MEANT.
I MEANT FORGIVING HIM. AFTER EVERYTHING.
I MEAN, I'M SURE HE'LL FEEL TERRIBLE UNTIL HE DOESN'T. BUT...OF ALL PEOPLE.
HOW COME SAM STERNS GETS FORGIVENESS?

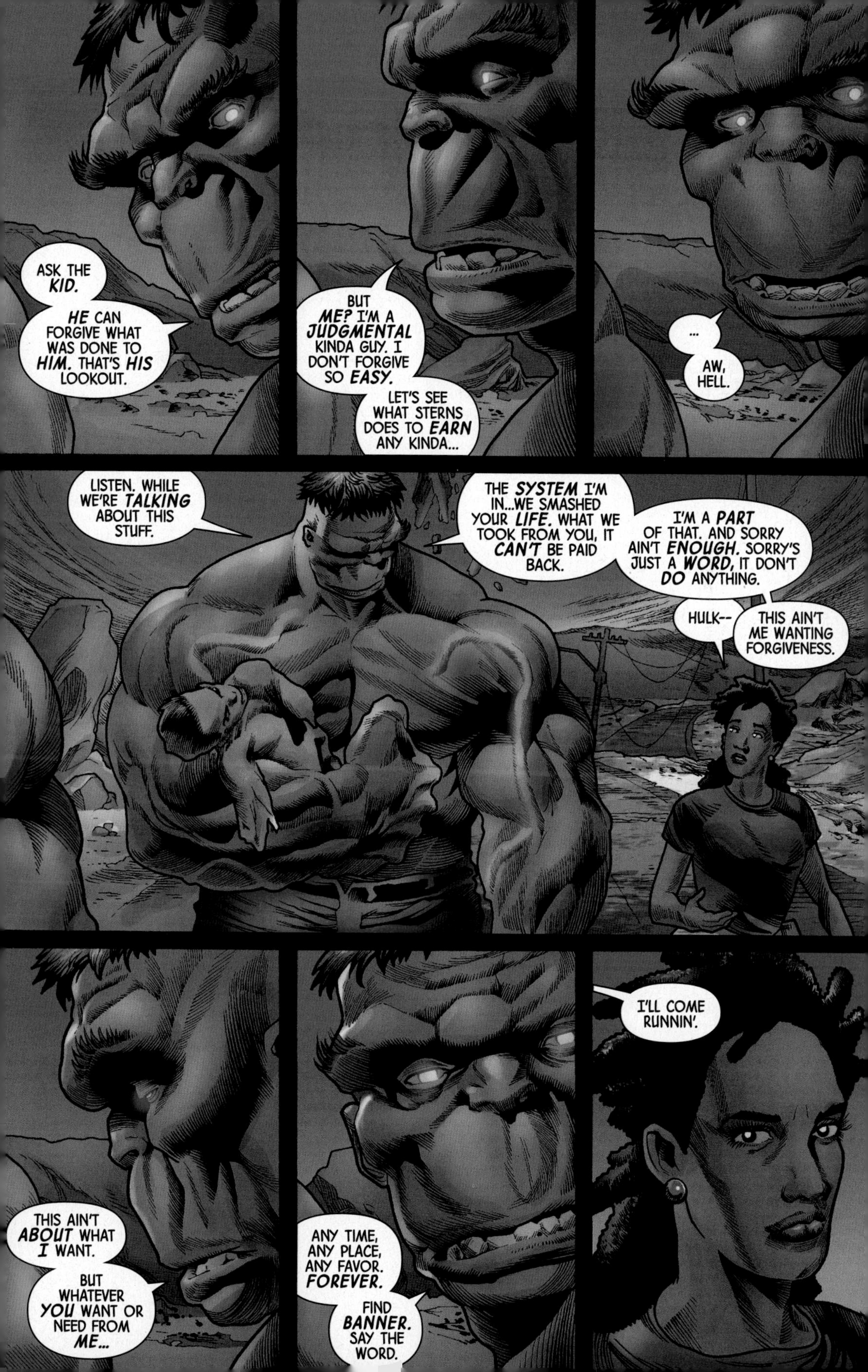
ASK THE KID.
HE CAN FORGIVE WHAT WAS DONE TO HIM. THAT'S HIS LOOKOUT.
BUT ME? I'M A JUDGMENTAL KINDA GUY. I DON'T FORGIVE SO EASY.
LET'S SEE WHAT STERNS DOES TO EARN ANY KINDA...
...
AW, HELL.
LISTEN. WHILE WE'RE TALKING ABOUT THIS STUFF.
THE SYSTEM I'M IN...WE SMASHED YOUR LIFE. WHAT WE TOOK FROM YOU, IT CAN'T BE PAID BACK.
I'M A PART OF THAT. AND SORRY AIN'T ENOUGH. SORRY'S JUST A WORD, IT DON'T DO ANYTHING.
HULK--
THIS AIN'T ME WANTING FORGIVENESS.
THIS AIN'T ABOUT WHAT I WANT.
BUT WHATEVER YOU WANT OR NEED FROM ME...
ANY TIME, ANY PLACE, ANY FAVOR. FOREVER.
FIND BANNER. SAY THE WORD.
I'LL COME RUNNIN'.

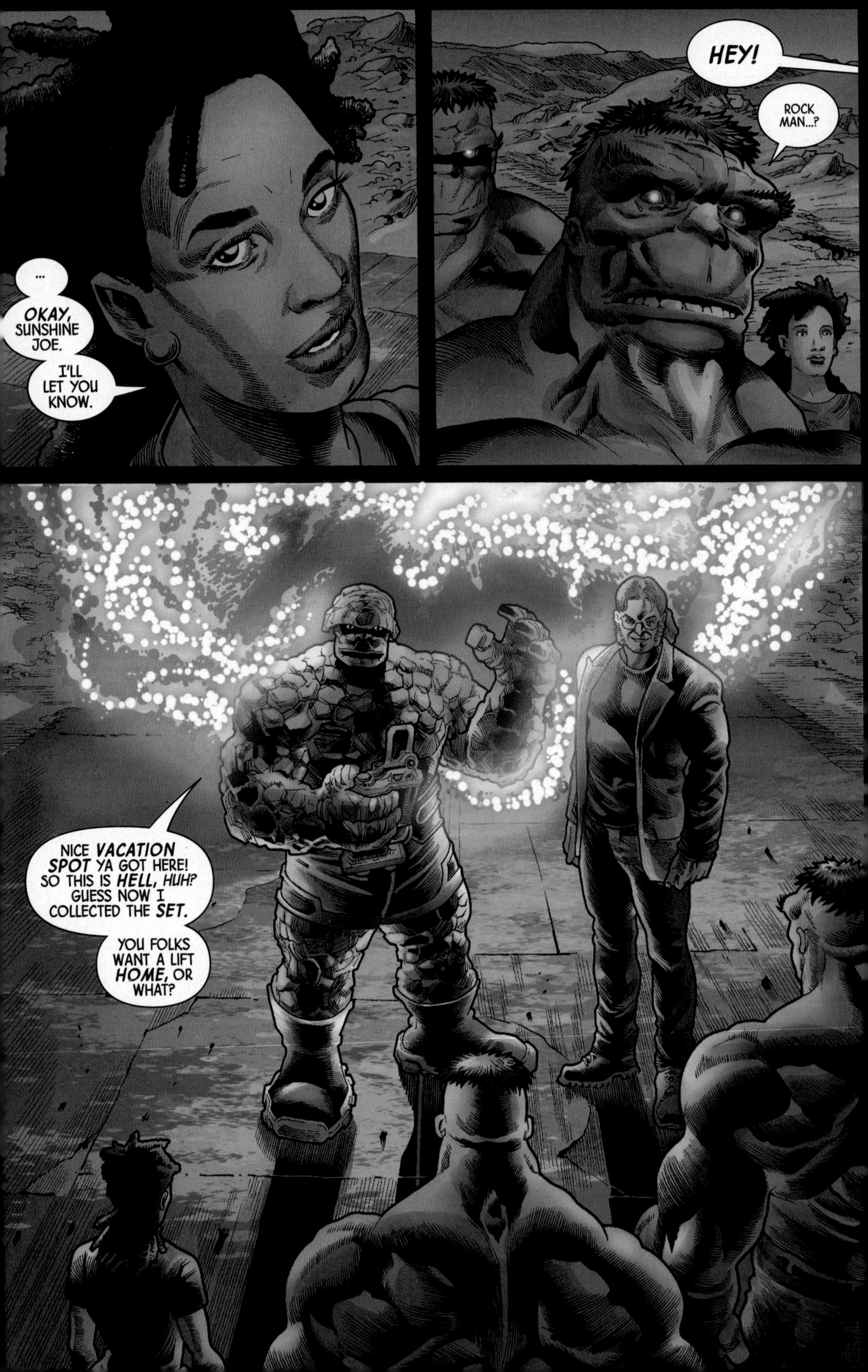
...
OKAY, SUNSHINE JOE.
I'LL LET YOU KNOW.
HEY!
ROCK MAN...?
NICE VACATION SPOT YA GOT HERE! SO THIS IS HELL, HUH? GUESS NOW I COLLECTED THE SET.
YOU FOLKS WANT A LIFT HOME, OR WHAT?

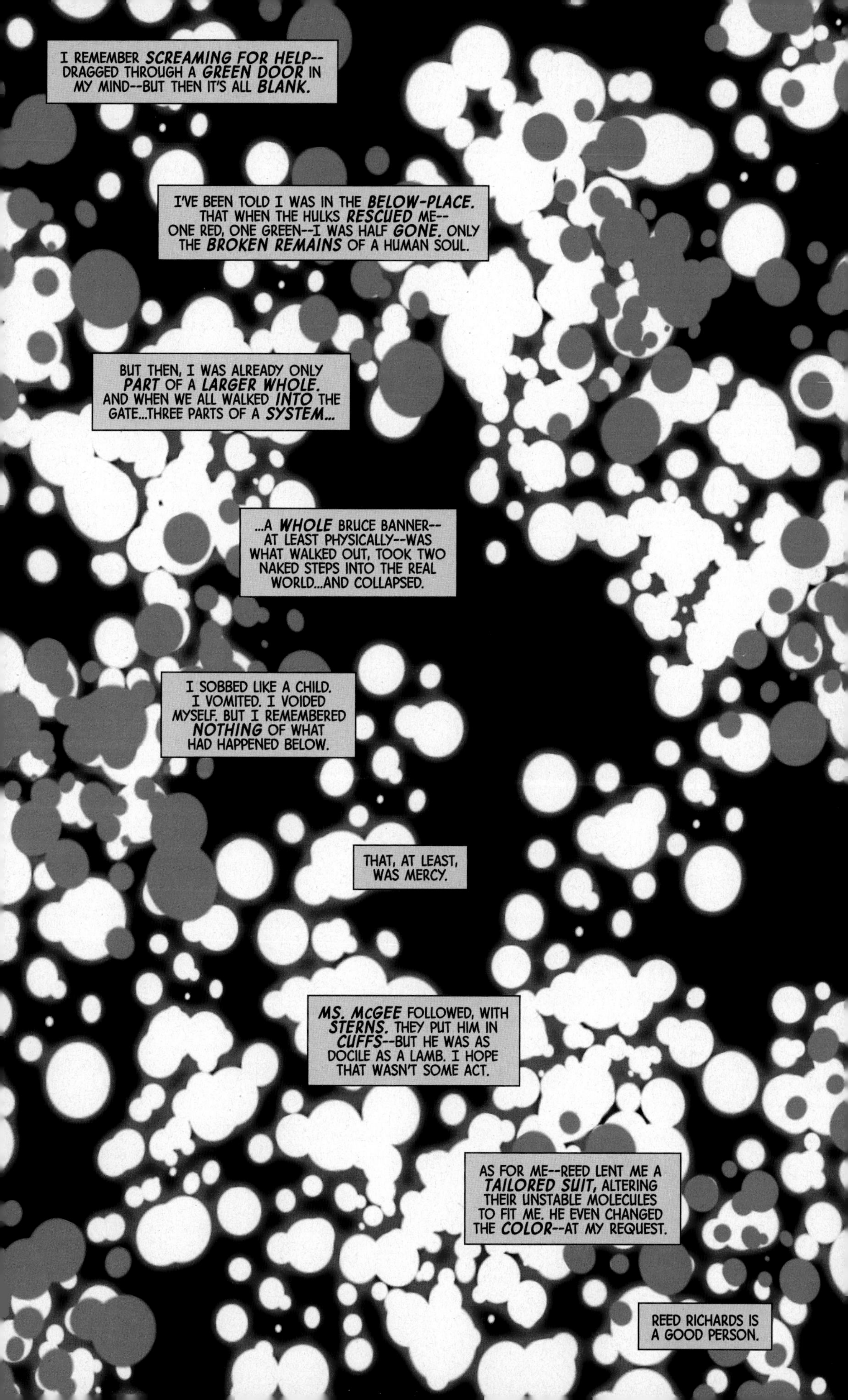
I REMEMBER SCREAMING FOR HELP--DRAGGED THROUGH A GREEN DOOR IN MY MIND--BUT THEN IT'S ALL BLANK.
I'VE BEEN TOLD I WAS IN THE BELOW-PLACE. THAT WHEN THE HULKS RESCUED ME--ONE RED, ONE GREEN--I WAS HALF GONE. ONLY THE BROKEN REMAINS OF A HUMAN SOUL.
BUT THEN, I WAS ALREADY ONLY PART OF A LARGER WHOLE. AND WHEN WE ALL WALKED INTO THE GATE...THREE PARTS OF A SYSTEM...
...A WHOLE BRUCE BANNER--AT LEAST PHYSICALLY--WAS WHAT WALKED OUT, TOOK TWO NAKED STEPS INTO THE REAL WORLD...AND COLLAPSED.
I SOBBED LIKE A CHILD. I VOMITED. I VOIDED MYSELF. BUT I REMEMBERED NOTHING OF WHAT HAD HAPPENED BELOW.
THAT, AT LEAST, WAS MERCY.
MS. McGEE FOLLOWED, WITH STERNS. THEY PUT HIM IN CUFFS--BUT HE WAS AS DOCILE AS A LAMB. I HOPE THAT WASN'T SOME ACT.
AS FOR ME--REED LENT ME A TAILORED SUIT, ALTERING THEIR UNSTABLE MOLECULES TO FIT ME. HE EVEN CHANGED THE COLOR--AT MY REQUEST.
REED RICHARDS IS A GOOD PERSON.

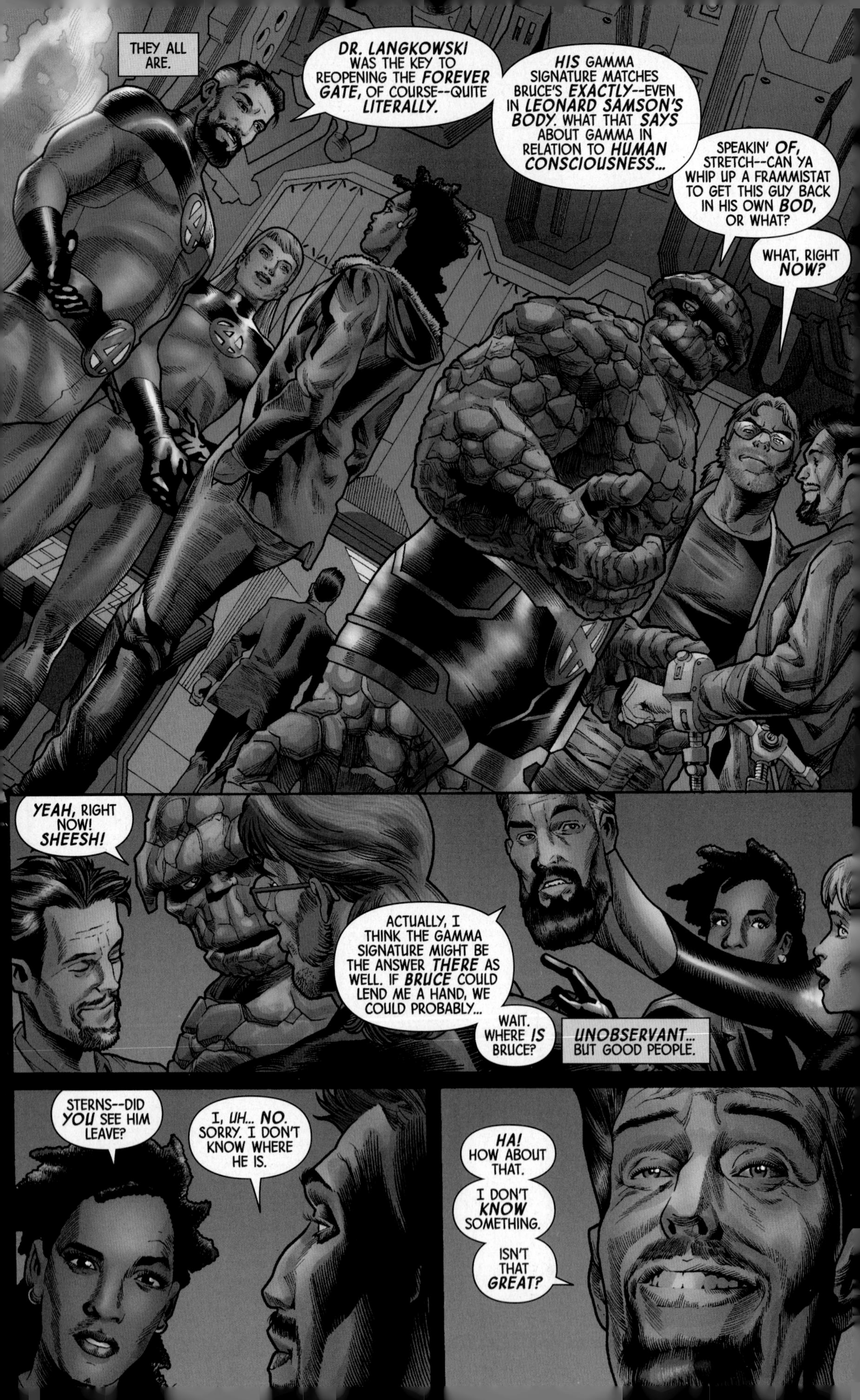
THEY ALL ARE.
DR. LANGKOWSKI WAS THE KEY TO REOPENING THE FOREVER GATE, OF COURSE--QUITE LITERALLY.
HIS GAMMA SIGNATURE MATCHES BRUCE'S EXACTLY--EVEN IN LEONARD SAMSON'S BODY. WHAT THAT SAYS ABOUT GAMMA IN RELATION TO HUMAN CONSCIOUSNESS...
SPEAKIN' OF, STRETCH--CAN YA WHIP UP A FRAMMISTAT TO GET THIS GUY BACK IN HIS OWN BOD, OR WHAT?
WHAT, RIGHT NOW?
YEAH, RIGHT NOW! SHEESH!
ACTUALLY, I THINK THE GAMMA SIGNATURE MIGHT BE THE ANSWER THERE AS WELL. IF BRUCE COULD LEND ME A HAND, WE COULD PROBABLY...
WAIT. WHERE IS BRUCE?
UNOBSERVANT... BUT GOOD PEOPLE.
STERNS--DID YOU SEE HIM LEAVE?
I, UH... NO. SORRY. I DON'T KNOW WHERE HE IS.
HA! HOW ABOUT THAT.
I DON'T KNOW SOMETHING.
ISN'T THAT GREAT?

YES! HULK HAS HEARD THIS! BIG TALK FROM BIG BAD THING--BUT NO WHY!
AND WE ALL WANNA KNOW WHY. WHY, YOU GET IT?
BECAUSE WE DON'T NEED TO KNOW WHO.
WE ALREADY KNOW WHO. WHAT, YOU THINK YOU'RE HIDING IT?
YOU THINK WE DON'T KNOW WHOSE HULK YOU ARE?
COME ON! SHOW ME YOUR OTHER FACE, YOU PIECE OF CRAP!
SHOW ME YOUR REAL FACE!

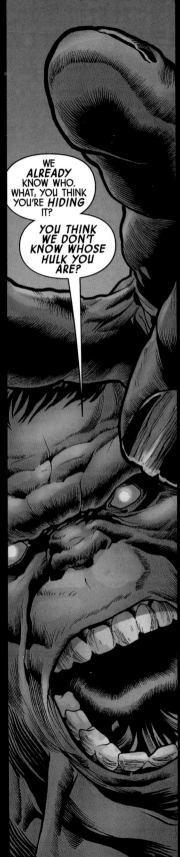

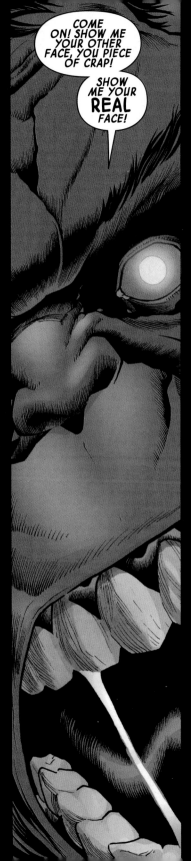

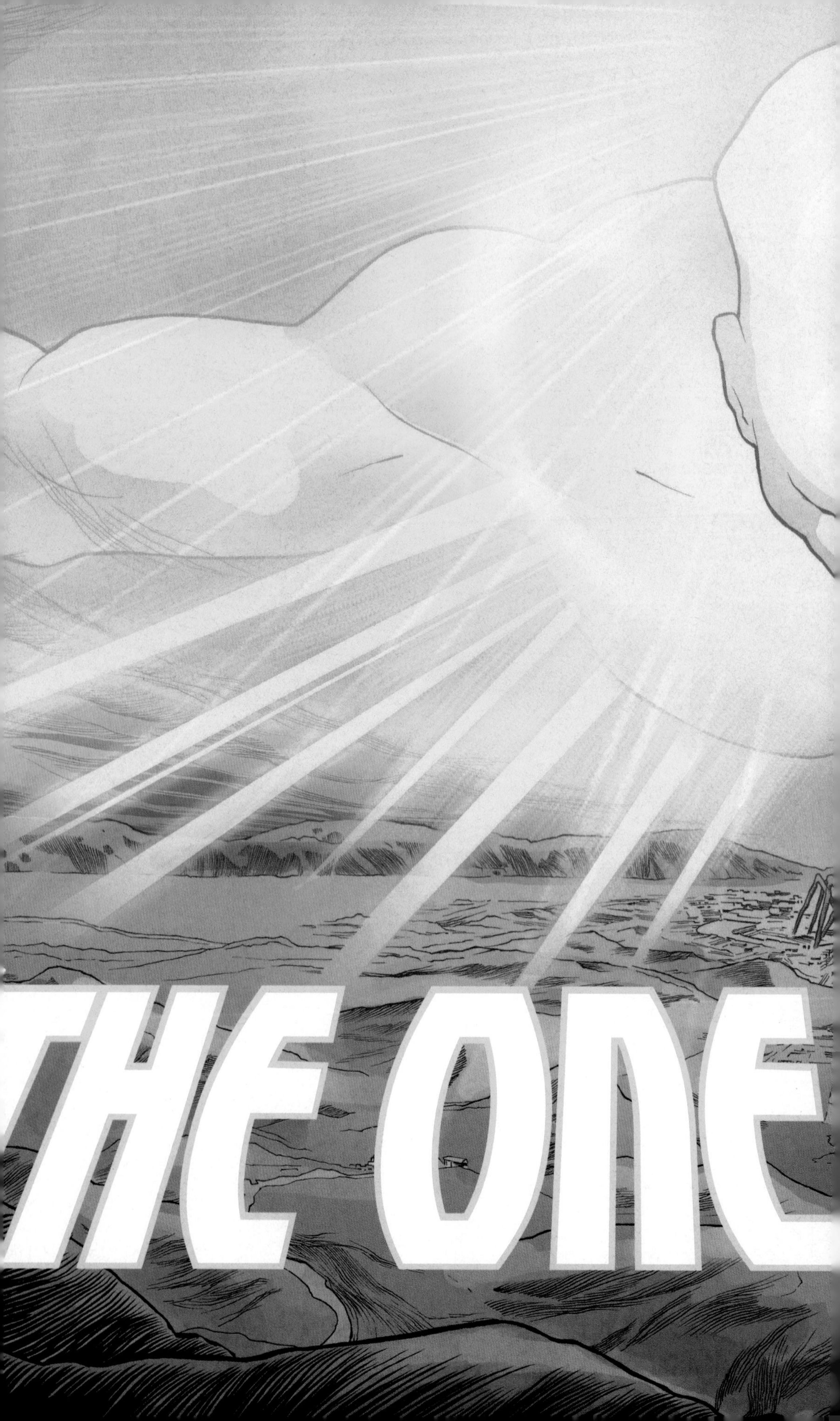
THE ONE

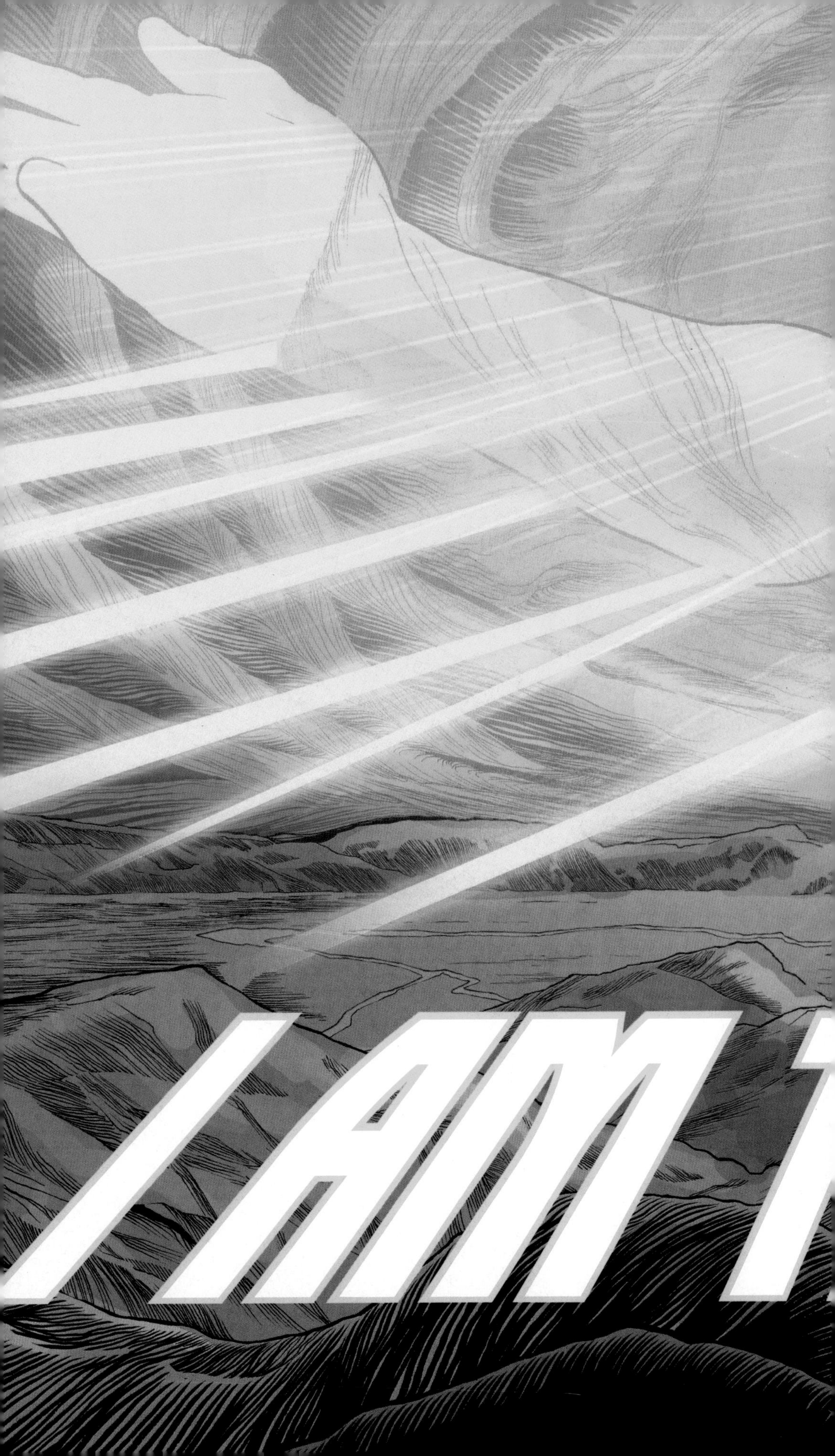
I AM

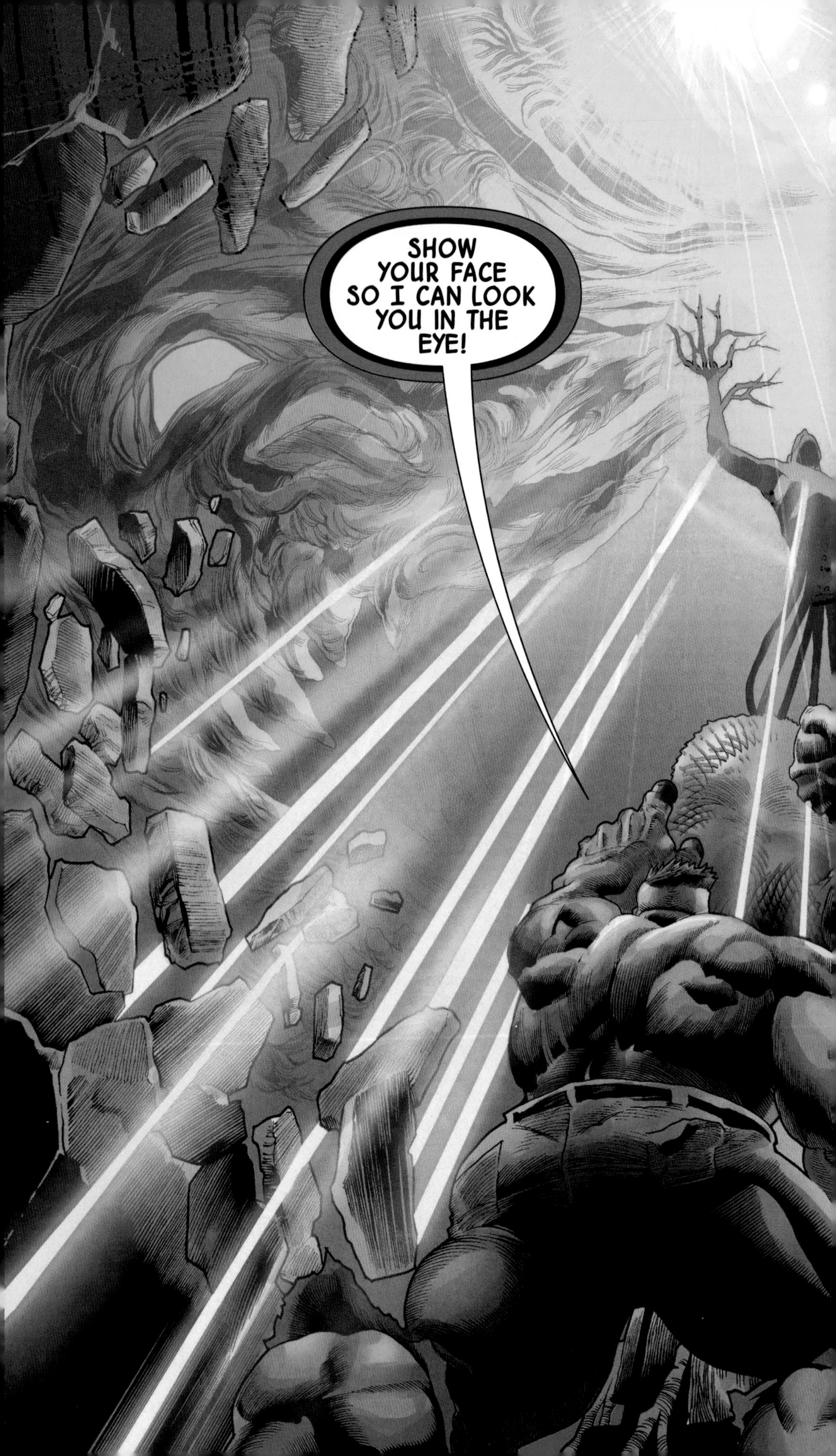
SHOW YOUR FACE SO I CAN LOOK YOU IN THE EYE!

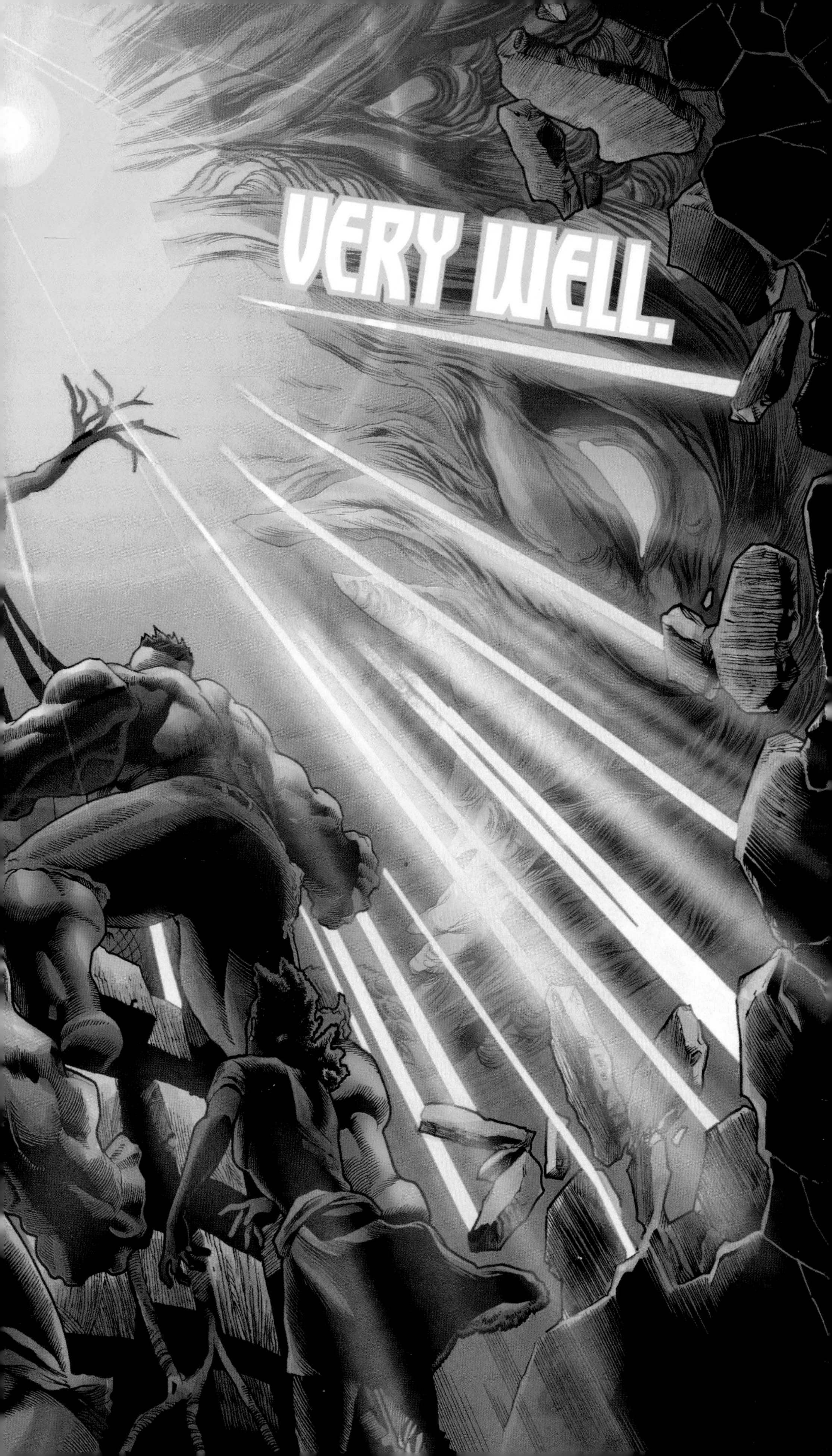
VERY WELL.

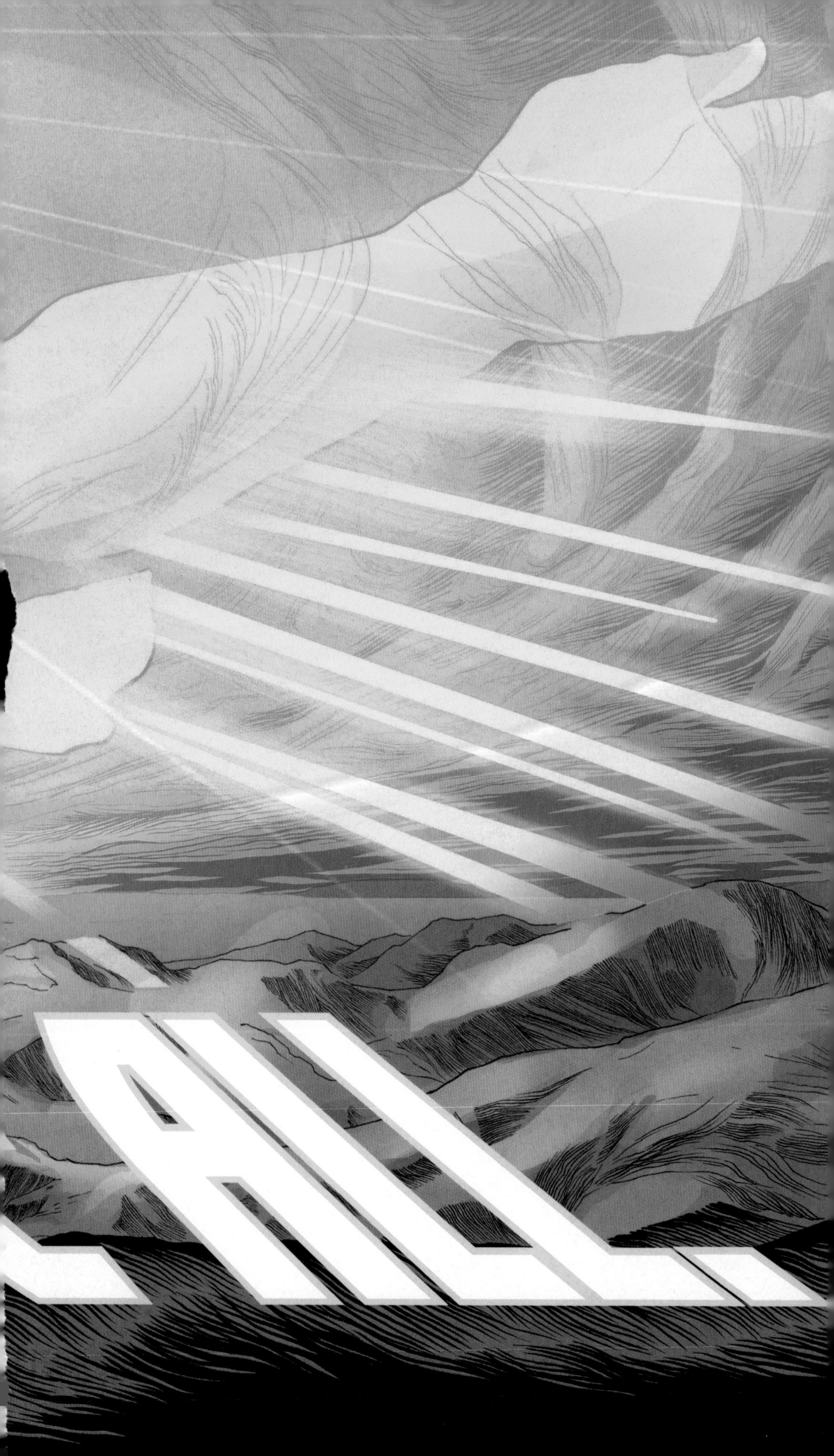
..ALL...

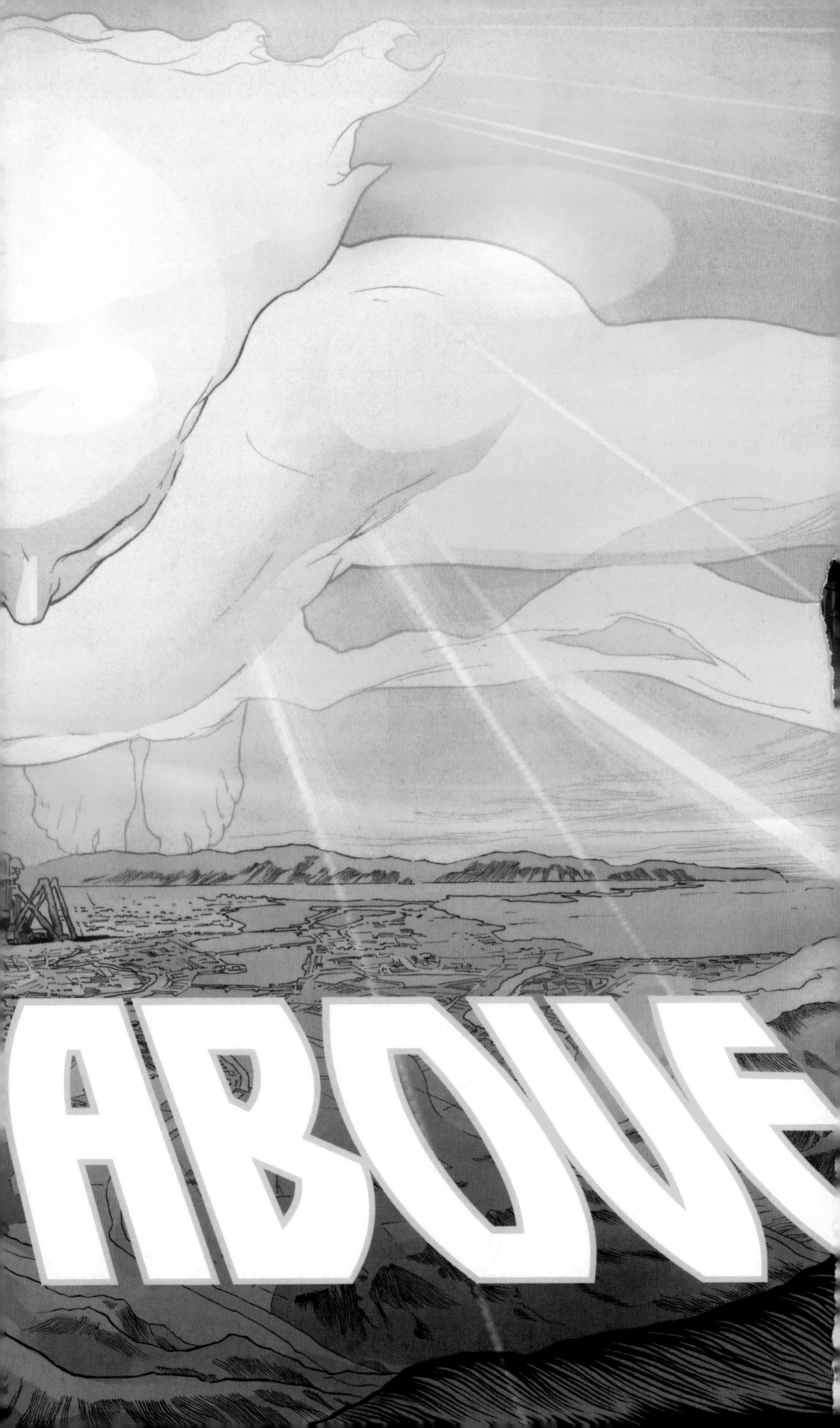
ABOVE

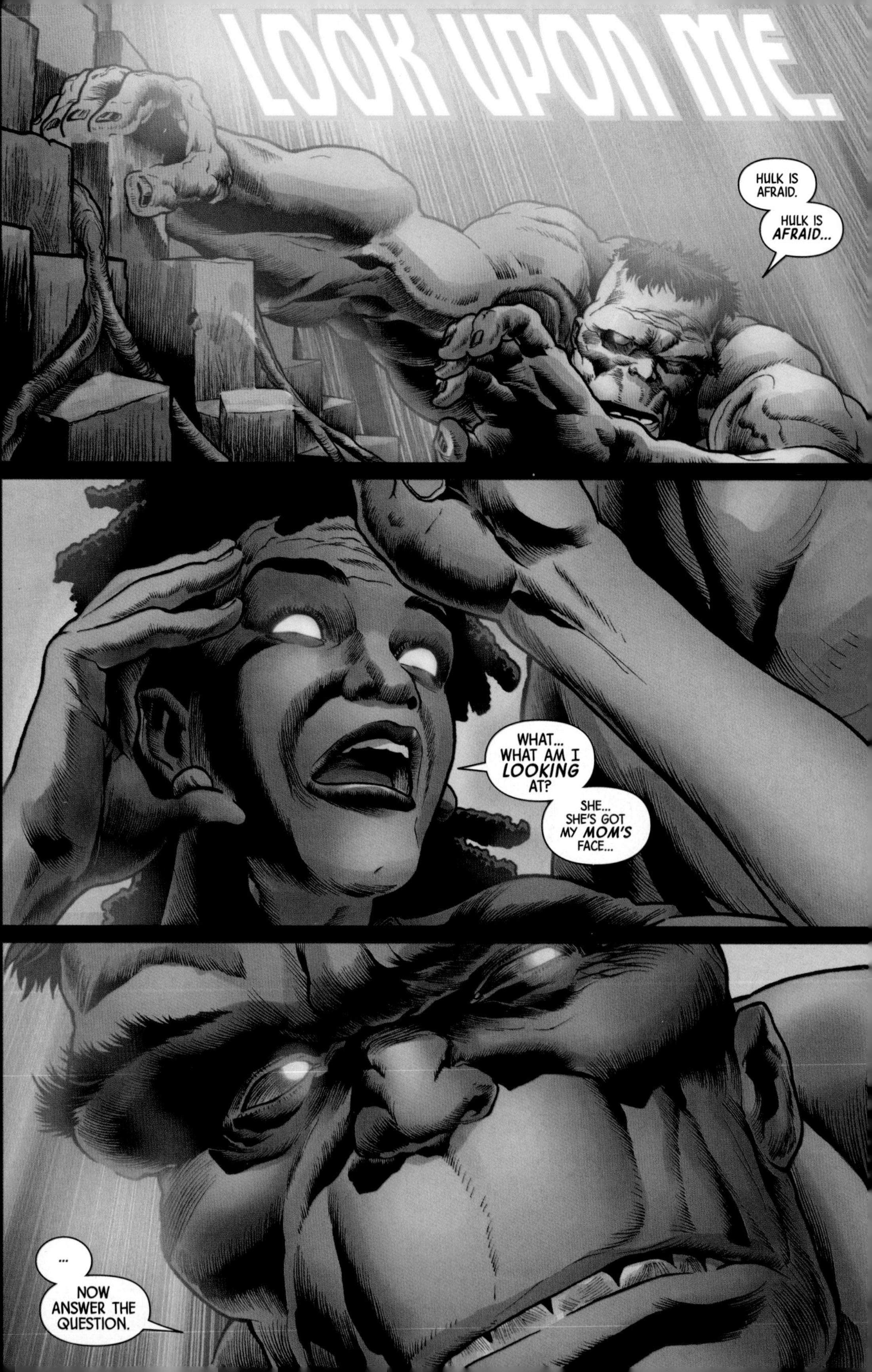
LOOK UPON ME.
HULK IS AFRAID.
HULK IS *AFRAID...*
WHAT... WHAT AM I *LOOKING* AT?
SHE... SHE'S GOT MY *MOM'S* FACE...
...
NOW ANSWER THE QUESTION.

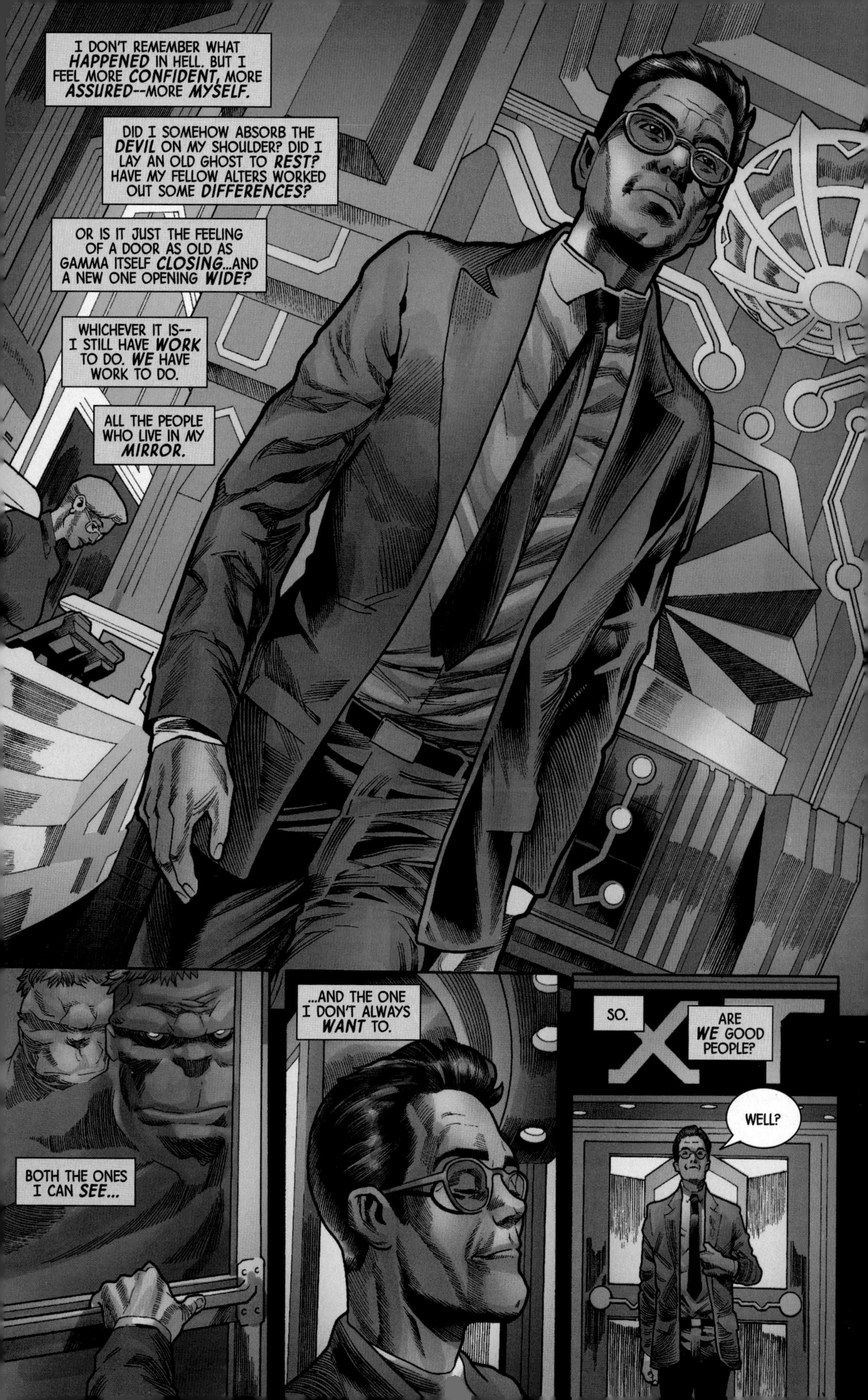
I DON'T REMEMBER WHAT HAPPENED IN HELL. BUT I FEEL MORE CONFIDENT, MORE ASSURED--MORE MYSELF.
DID I SOMEHOW ABSORB THE DEVIL ON MY SHOULDER? DID I LAY AN OLD GHOST TO REST? HAVE MY FELLOW ALTERS WORKED OUT SOME DIFFERENCES?
OR IS IT JUST THE FEELING OF A DOOR AS OLD AS GAMMA ITSELF CLOSING...AND A NEW ONE OPENING WIDE?
WHICHEVER IT IS-- I STILL HAVE WORK TO DO. WE HAVE WORK TO DO.
ALL THE PEOPLE WHO LIVE IN MY MIRROR.
BOTH THE ONES I CAN SEE...
...AND THE ONE I DON'T ALWAYS WANT TO.
SO.
ARE WE GOOD PEOPLE?
WELL?

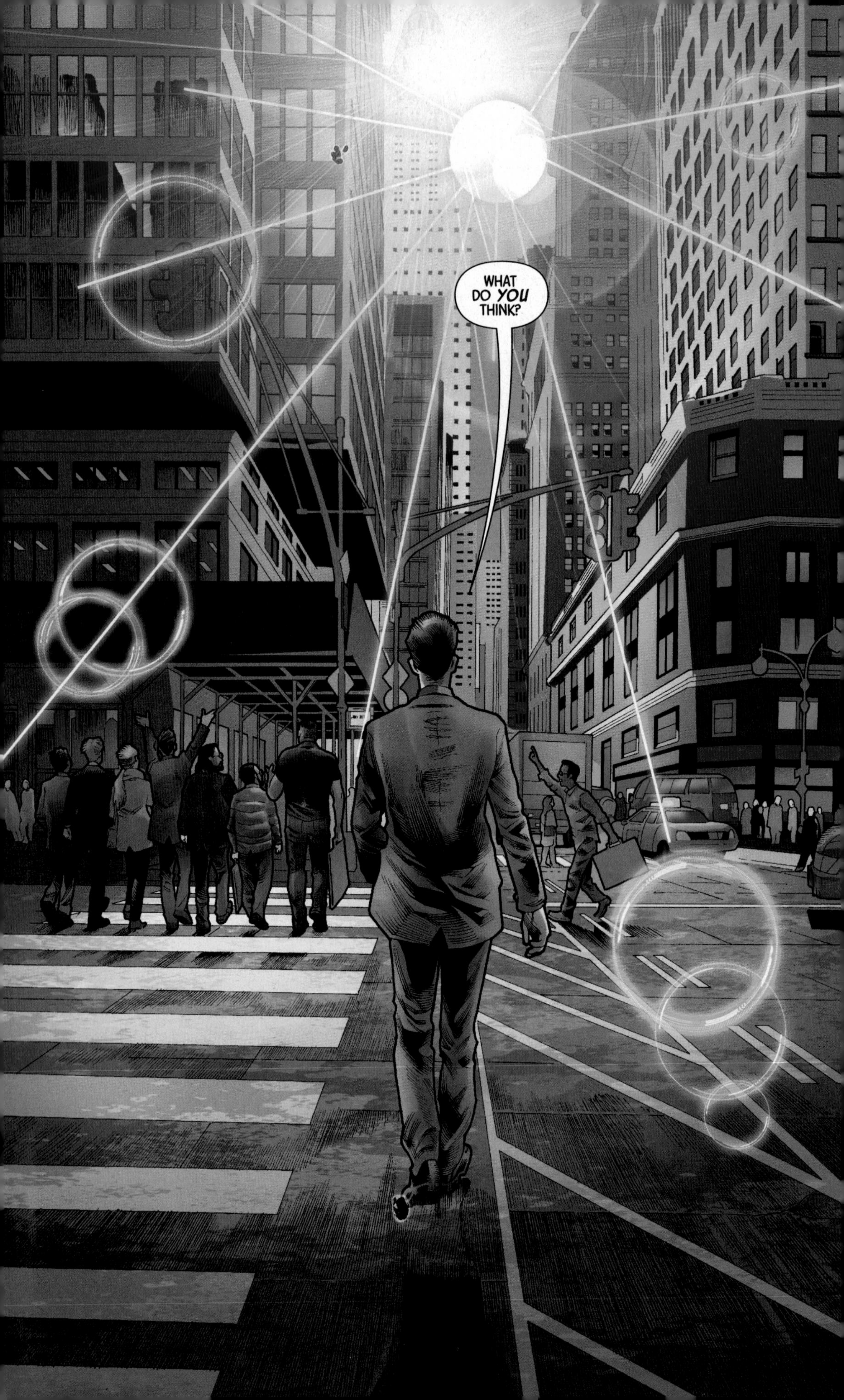
WHAT DO YOU THINK?

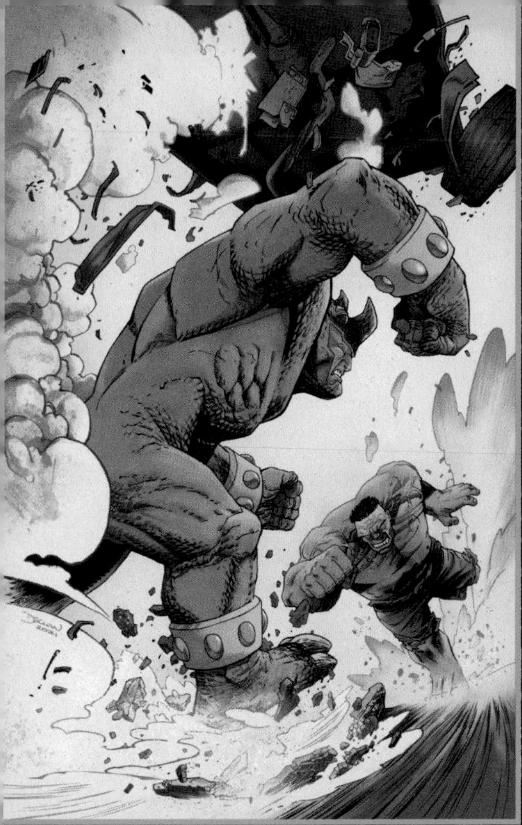

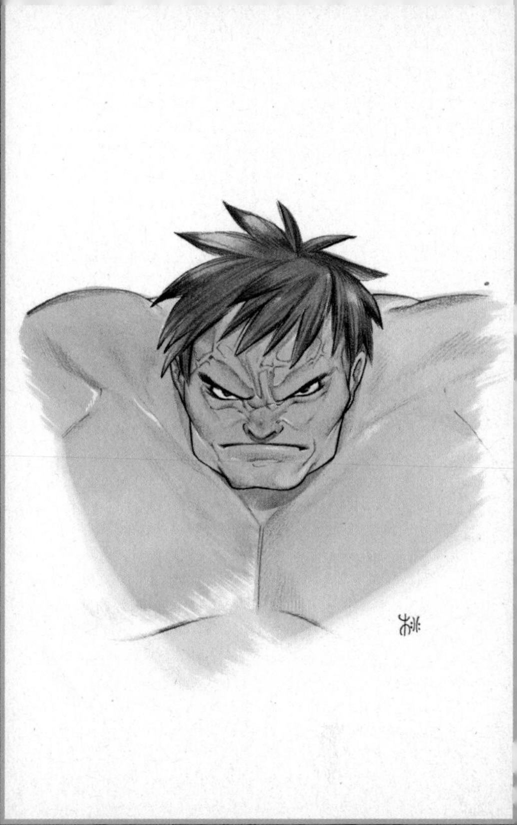

DECLAN SHALVEY
#47 SPIDER-MAN VILLIANS VARIANT

PEACH MOMOKO
#48 MARVEL ANIME VARIANT

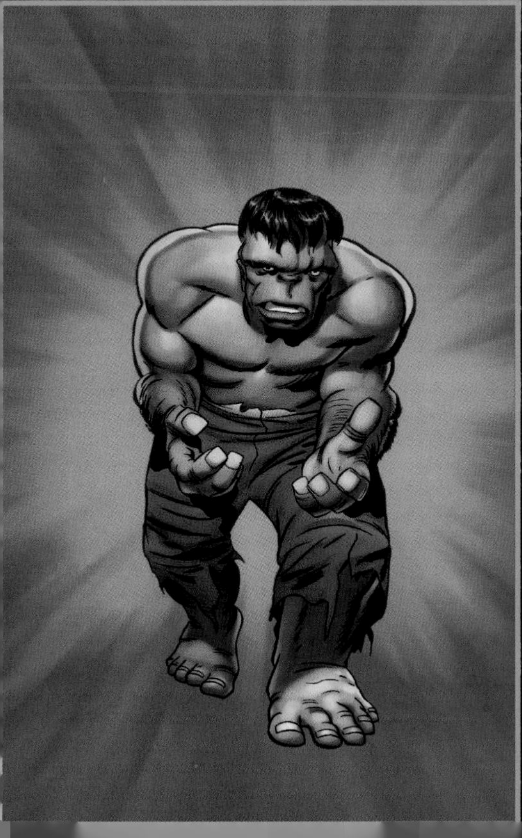

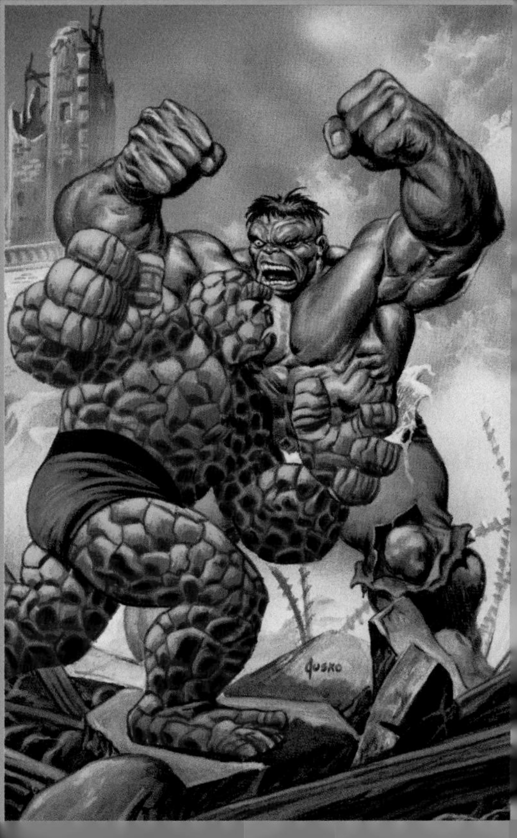

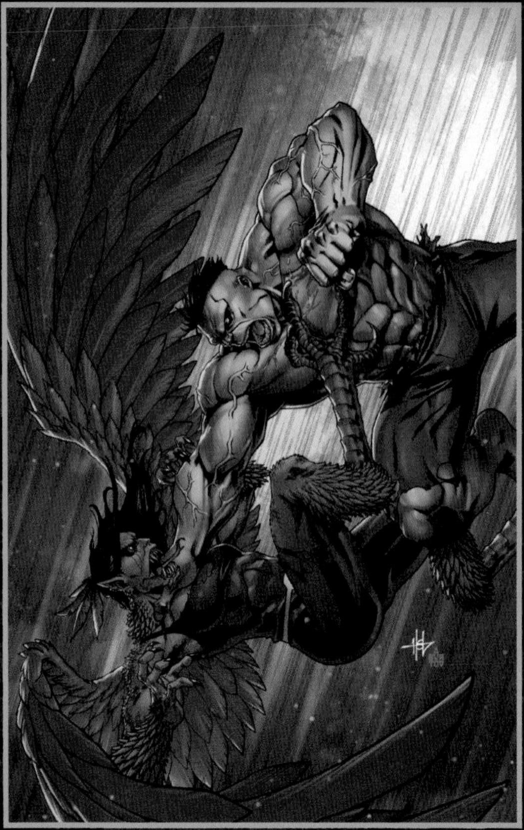

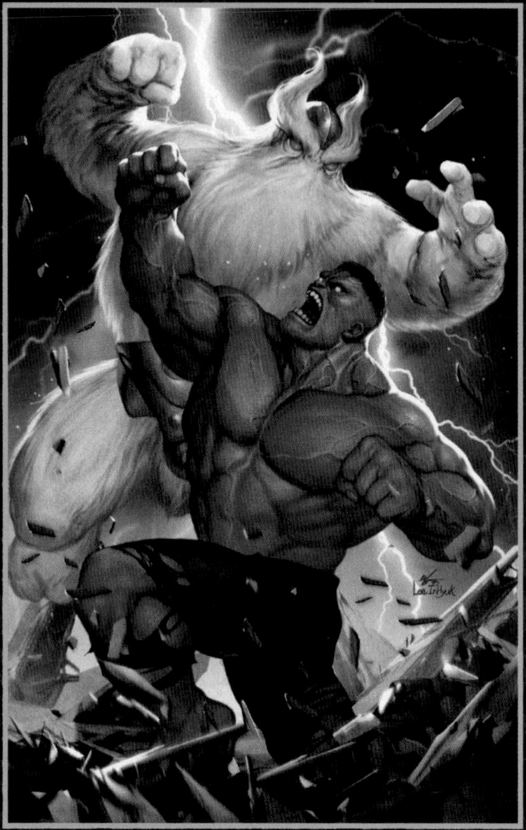

CREEES LEE & JESUS ABURTOV
#50 VARIANT

INHYUK LEE
#50 VARIANT

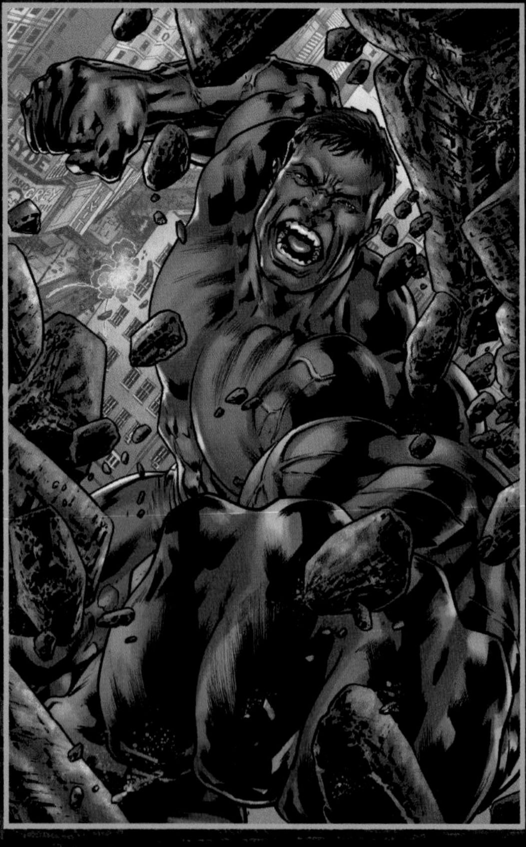

BRYAN HITCH & ALEX SINCLAIR

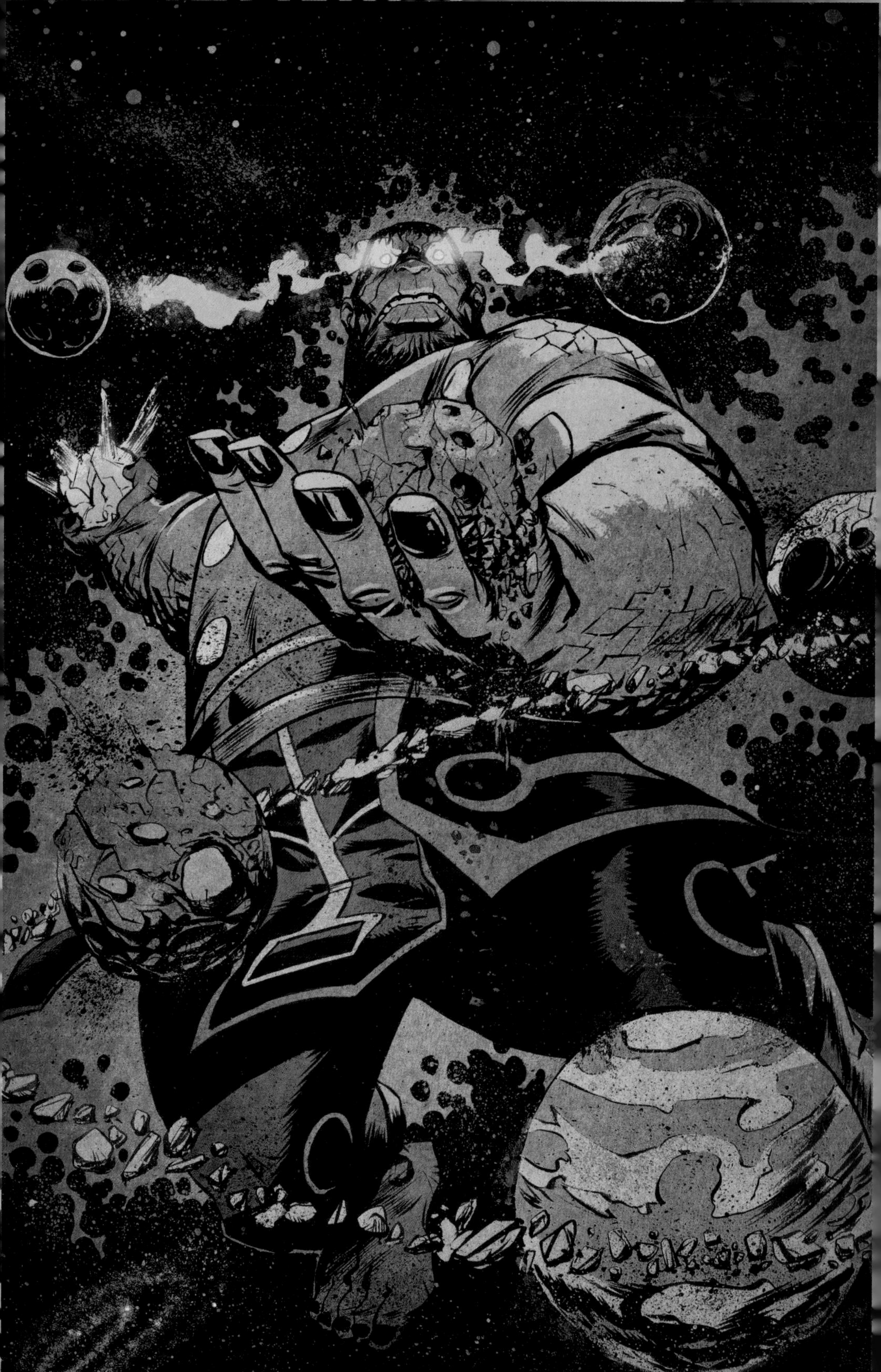

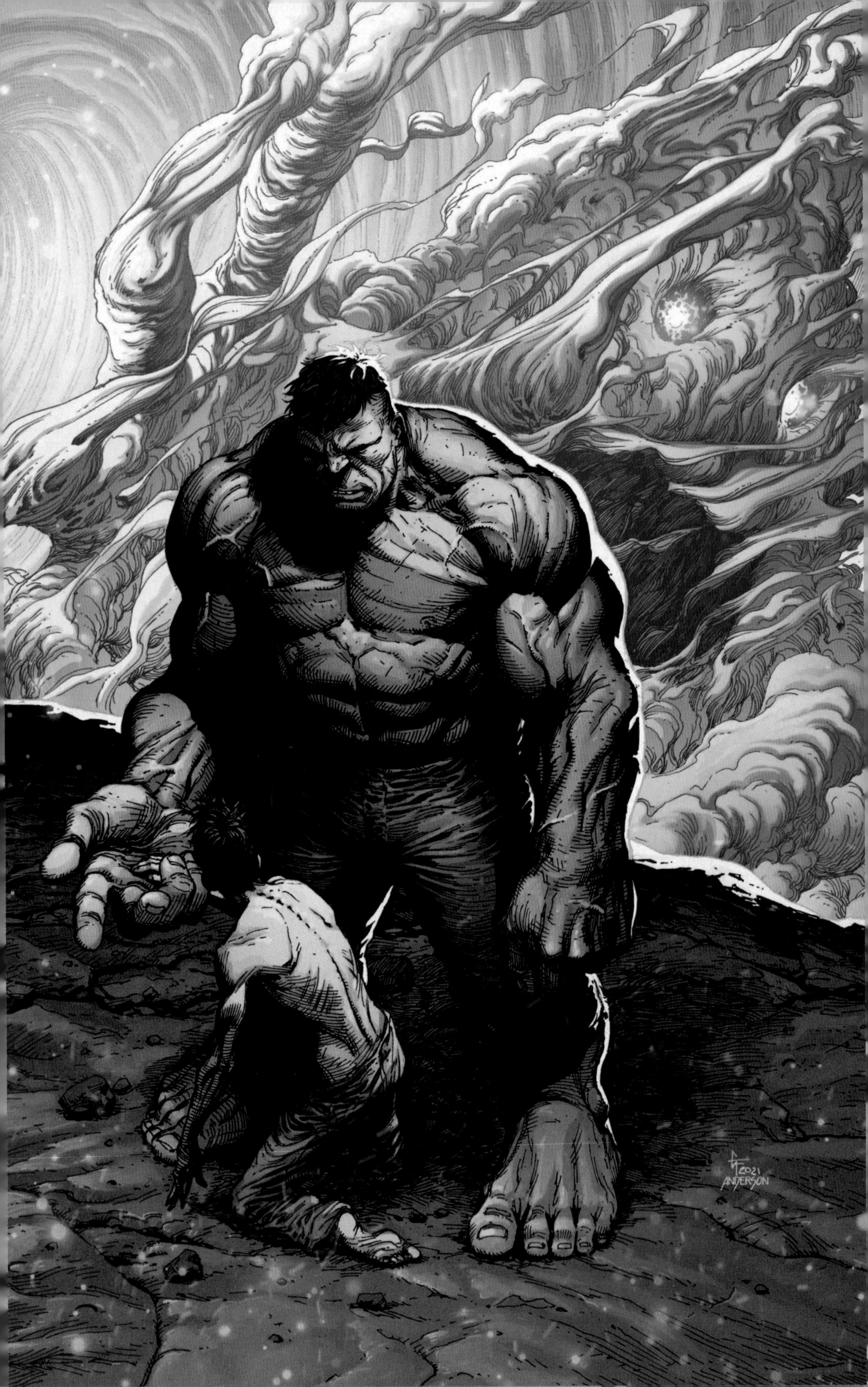
2021
ANDERSON